SMALL BUSINESS COMPUTERS

A GUIDE TO EVALUATION AND SELECTION

Prentice-Hall Series in Data Processing Management

Leonard I. Krauss, Editor

SMALL BUSINESS COMPUTERS

A GUIDE TO EVALUATION AND SELECTION

KOICHIRO R. ISSHIKI, Ph.D.

California State Polytechnic University, Pomona

Prentice-Hall, Inc., Englewood Cliffs, NJ 07632

Library of Congress Cataloging in Publication Data

Isshiki, Koichiro R.
　　Small business computers, a guide to evaluation and
selection.

　　(Prentice-Hall series in data processing management)
　　Bibliography: p.
　　Includes index.
　　1. Electronic digital computers.　　2. Small business—
Data Processing.　I. Title.　II. Series.
QA76.5.I834　　　658'.054　　　81-11836
ISBN 0-13-814152-5　　　　　AACR2

Editorial/production supervision
　and interior design by *Mary Carnis*
Cover design by *Frederick Charles, Ltd.*
Cover photo courtesy of Intel Corporation
Manufacturing Buyer: *Gordon Osbourne*

Printed in the United States of America

10　9　8　7　6　5　4　3　2

ISBN　0-13-814152-5

Prentice-Hall International, Inc., *London*
Prentice-Hall of Austrialia Pty. Limited, *Sydney*
Prentice-Hall of Canada, Ltd., *Toronto*
Prentice-Hall of India Private Limited, *New Delhi*
Prentice-Hall of Japan, Inc., *Tokyo*
Prentice-Hall of Southeast Asia Pte. Ltd., *Singapore*
Whitehall Books Limited, *Wellington, New Zealand*

To Taka, My Son

CONTENTS

5 PROS AND CONS OF COMPUTER SYSTEMS AND OUTSIDE SERVICES   **116**

6 HOW TO SELECT AND INSTALL A COMPUTER   **128**

PREFACE

This is a book about the evaluation and selection of small computers. It has been written for readers who know little or nothing about computers or the mathematics, accounting, finance, and legal contracts involving computers, and also for those who are knowledgeable but have a need to expand or better their knowledge in this area. This book is intended to appeal to four groups of readers:

1. Most important are those who now manage or set policy for a business and are considering or selecting a first computer for that business. Managers who are replacing or thinking about replacing an existing system will also find the methods introduced in this text beneficial.
2. Students in programs leading to degrees in the fields of information science, business, and data processing.
3. Those who wish to acquire a small computer (perhaps a personal computer at home) for their own interest.
4. Anyone who has authority or responsibility to purchase equipment for an organization. The methods and steps introduced in this book should prove helpful in the selection of most capital investments where competing sources of equipment are concerned.

This book is not a primer concerning what a computer is and how it is programmed. Rather, it focuses on management considerations in determining the feasibility, economics, evaluation, selection, contracts, and practicability of installing a computer.

The computer plays an important role in today's society. These machines keep getting smaller, less expensive, faster, and easier to use. With the advent of technology, better-performing computers at lower cost will lead to more computer use. The computer will become an even more integral part of our daily lives in the near future. Small business is no exception to the effects of this fast-changing technology. However, the technological advances that have been made are not yet being fully utilized in solving real business problems for small business people.

The increasing complexity of today's world, with governmental regulations, labor unions, stronger competition, and inflation, has caused greater demands than ever on small business to gather more information. For example, in the governmental area, business now has more complex tax reports. In the customer service area, customers are demanding more rapid response and better information on the status of their orders. Moreover, inflation has caused tremendous pressures to keep inventory down and turn over receivables faster. What it really boils down to is a need for faster, less expensive, and accurate information. By and large, this is the need that many small business computer manufacturers are addressing, by providing various types and sizes of micro-, mini-, and small business computers. The focus of this book is to help the reader make pragmatic business decisions: What kind of system is needed? How do we go about getting it? What kind of things can be done to assure successful installation?

Most books reflect the background and interests of the author, and this one is no exception. My experience derives from many years in the computer and higher-education fields. The treatment in this book is a combination of my perspective as business consultant, computer expert, and university professor. Many computer-related books have been written from a rather limited point of view, which usually involves either a computer expert looking at business or a business manager looking at computers. In this book I have utilized my experience in three important areas in order to, hopefully, present a more balanced perspective. The criteria therefore are how a computer can be made to work for a business manager in improving performance and profitability and how a manager can obtain assistance in evaluating and selecting a small computer.

This book has been divided into 12 chapters. Chapter 1 covers key considerations regarding deciding whether to computerize. The principal considerations include what should be done before selecting a computer, criteria for deciding to computerize, and whether or not a firm actually needs a computer. It lists sources of information for computers and services. Chapter 2 deals with components and configurations of small business computers and their capabilities and limitations. Typical components of small business computers, such as floppy disk, keyboard display, and serial printers, are described. Chapter 3 discusses various small computers, such as micro-computers, minicomputers, and small business computers. Their unique features, vendors, and system configurations are presented. Chapter 4 discusses economic factors involved in computerization—a departure from most computer texts. Questions and answers this chapter provides include: What are the values of computer utilization? What are the alternative methods for evaluating computer economic benefits? What are the payback-period method, the average-rate-of-return method, the time-adjusted rate-of-return (discounted-cash-flow) method, and the present-value method? Chapter 5 discusses the various computer services and selection criteria. What type of computer service is best for your organization: an in-house computer, a service bureau, a time-sharing service, or possibly a combination? What are the advantages and disadvantages of the in-house computer, time-sharing and remote-computing service, and computer service bureau? Chapter 6 discusses how to acquire a computer. It includes 10 practical steps for installing your first computer, steps involved in preparing a request for proposal (RFP), and a sample RFP. Chapter 7 covers various methods for the selection of a computer or EDP service, from no-cost-and-less-time to large-amount-of-cost-and-time methods. Some of the methods discussed are subjective judgment, application bench mark, the weighted-score technique, the cost-value technique, the cost/performance ratio method, and the simulation method. Chapter 8 describes the selection of system software, including operating systems and computer languages. It defines software, language, operating system, file management, utilities, data-base management, and application software. An approach to choosing among BASIC, FORTRAN, RPG, COBOL, and other languages for use with a small computer is presented. Chapter 9 discusses the choice between developing or selecting application software. What are the advantages and disadvantages of package programs and custom programs? How can one evaluate and select package software? This chapter answers these questions, describes steps for the selection of package programs, and provides checklists for comparing common business application programs. Chapter 10 discusses computer rental, lease, and purchase options. It begins with a description of basic concepts of computer acquisition and evaluation methods, including present-value concept, economic life, salvage value, and depreciation. Next, rental, lease, and purchase contracts are discussed, including their various advantages and disadvantages. Finally, it illustrates sample computer acquisition and evaluation using the present-value method—rent, lease, or purchase option. Chapter 11 explains the computer contract and how to avoid computer contracting pitfalls, including disputable areas and questions, timing of contracts, and legal analysis of standard commercial computer purchase and lease contracts. The legal analysis of provisions includes those of price, transportation, risk of loss, taxes, maintenance, supplies, warranty, configuration changes, and more. Chapter 12 describes additional assistance that is avaliable to small businesses, and answers the questions: What is a small business? What services can small businesses get from the government, universities, and other institutions? Management assistance, financial assistance, contract assistance, and technical assistance are also discussed.

The appendix presents six small business cases based on actual experience. Described are choices to be made among alternative systems: in-house computer, interactive time-sharing, leased minicomputer, enhanced manual, and distributed.

The author is indebted to the many persons who have contributed either directly or indirectly, prior to and during the development of this book.

Much of the experience reflected in the book has been gained through assisting various small businesses as a consultant for the Small Business Development Center (SBDC) and teaching courses on small business computers and small business application programming at California State Polytechnic University, Pomona.

I am grateful to the faculty members and students of the Computer Information Systems Department of the university for their support, suggestions, and contributions throughout the development of the book. In particular, I wish to thank Thomas H. Athey for granting permission for the use of the MECCA Approach Concept in Cases A and B. I also want to thank Roger Manfield for contributing Case B and Section 9-2.

Last, but certainly not least, I acknowledge Ms. Karen Harvey and Ms. Kay Stockwell for their excellent editing and the editors at Prentice-Hall for their editorial suggestions and encouragement.

It is hoped by this author that small business people will find the book to be a helpful tool to use during the process of assessing and acquiring a small computer for their business needs.

Koichiro R. Isshiki

SMALL BUSINESS COMPUTERS

A GUIDE TO EVALUATION AND SELECTION

1

KEY CONSIDERATIONS
IN DECIDING TO COMPUTERIZE

Computers are becoming increasingly popular with small businesses, being used for applications such as payroll, accounts receivable, accounts payable, inventory control, general ledger, order processing, and others. However, before deciding to computerize, there are many factors that small businesses must consider.

1-1 COMPUTERS FOR SMALL BUSINESS

As computer equipment continues to decrease in size and price, demand for computers in small business continues to increase. Most people in the computer industry believe that compact, low-cost business data-processing computers will soon be nearly as commonplace and indispensable in most offices as telephones and typewriters.

Small companies are turning to EDP (electronic data processing) for the same reasons that larger companies did in the past. The volume of paperwork and related processing is increasing to a point where new procedures are needed for information gathering and decision making. As with large companies, the ever-increasing costs and complexities of doing business are forcing the owners of small businesses to find new ways to cut labor cost, in-

1

stitute production efficiencies, conserve inventories, control critical inventory items, and improve service. A wisely chosen computer can help immeasurably in these important areas.

What kind of computer is best for small businesses? Are microcomputers (Figure 1-1), small business computers, minicomputers, or large computers most suitable? Should you buy, lease, or rent a computer? How can you determine whether your firm would really benefit from installing a computer? Instead of installing a computer, should you use time-sharing services or service bureaus? How should you select the best data-processing service for your company's needs? These are key questions to which solutions will be offered or suggested in this book.

1-2   BEFORE SELECTING A COMPUTER

A computer is simply a tool. It is not, inherently, a solution. Before the appropriate tool for a given job can be selected, both the problem and the objectives to be attained must be clearly defined. Failure to understand this concept is the quickest way to get lost in the computer selection maze. Comparing different vendors' hardware (computers) before defining the company's reporting requirements, determining data flow and volume, and identifying application areas is a common error. *Top management must set the objectives of computer use.* Studies indicate that where management involvement and support are high, computer installations are usually successful.

Use the same criteria as for another piece of equipment. A mystique has grown up around computer hardware. It creates a great problem for small businesspeople who are trying to learn about and compare computers. If a small business owner wished to buy a lathe, he or she would probably exercise much more caution than when buying a computer system. A computer system should be a labor-saving device, and it should provide some increase in productivity and/or better information to the business.

Do not be carried away with computer hardware that has bells and whistles. Measure the computer by how useful it is. A small computer system may be slow in operation. However, as long as it is useful (i.e., it produces what it is supposed to produce in the time allotted), that computer system is acceptable. Some people argue about computer speed, saying, for example: "My machine can run faster than your machine by 10 nanoseconds." They are out of touch with reality in the practical world of small business.

1-3   SOME CRITERIA FOR DECIDING TO COMPUTERIZE

Computerization criteria are not immediately obvious. The rules of thumb that are applicable to large systems are not always practical for small systems. Among other factors, one must consider factors such as sales revenue,

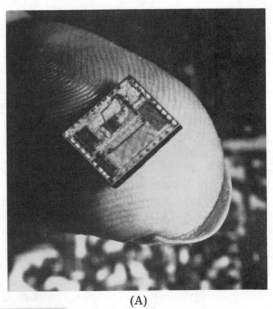

(A)

(B)

Figure 1-1. Intel's 8748 one-chip
microcomputer. (A) Intel's 8748
chip, illustrated on a finger, contains the electronic circuitry to perform the calculations required of a
computer, and it can store the data
on which it will operate. (B) Intel's
8080A wafer with package and
chips—industry standard microprocessor. (Courtesy of Intel Corp.)

3

the frequency and number of transactions, and the alternative cost of hiring more staff.

1-3.1   Company Sales Revenue

Finance is an important factor to consider. Can your firm afford a computer system? One rule of thumb is that a company can afford to spend approximately 1 to 2% of gross sales for data-processing use (see Table 1-1). This is the figure that keeps computer firms in business with banks and insurance companies. In larger operations, this is one of the common budget guidelines. In a small operation, let's see what it produces. If, for example, a firm's sales are $3,000,000 per year, the approximate expenditure for EDP could be $60,000 per year or $5,000 per month. With this budget it appears that this firm can afford a minicomputer system. If annual sales total approximately $500,000, the approximate expenditure for EDP can be $10,000 per year or $833 per month. Theoretically, this firm can afford a microcomputer system. A distributor may be receiving $3,000,000 in business a year, but if most of the income is paid out to replenish stock, may really be a very small distributor. In such a case, volume does not mean much. On the other hand, $3,000,000 is a moderate figure for a small manufacturer. Sales alone may therefore be a poor criterion on which to make the decision to computerize.

TABLE 1-1
Who Can Afford What?

Company Gross (Sales)	Annual (Monthly) Amount You Can Spend			Size of Computer Affordable
	0.5% of Gross Sales	1% of Gross Sales	2% of Gross Sales	
$20,000,000	$100,000 ($8,333)	$200,000 ($16,667)	$400,000 ($33,333)	Large mini/midi
$10,000,000	$50,000 ($4,167)	$100,000 ($8,333)	$200,000 ($16,667)	Large mini
$5,000,000	$25,000 ($2,083)	$50,000 ($4,167)	$100,000 ($8,333)	Mini/large mini
$2,500,000	$12,500 ($1,042)	$25,000 ($2,083)	$50,000 ($4,167)	Micro/mini
$1,000,000	$5,000 ($417)	$10,000 ($833)	$20,000 ($1,667)	Micro
$500,000	$2,500 ($208)	$5,000 ($416)	$10,000 ($833)	Small micro/micro
$250,000	$1,250 ($104)	$2,500 ($208)	$5,000 ($416)	Small micro
$100,000	$500 ($42)	$1,000 ($83)	$2,000 ($166)	Personal computers

1-3.2 Number of Transactions

For a small business facing the computerization decision, the number of transactions may be a better criterion than sales (Figure 1-2). Many small businesses could use a small computer in a specific area of activity. If a firm is processing 100 invoices or orders per day, it could conceivably use a mi-

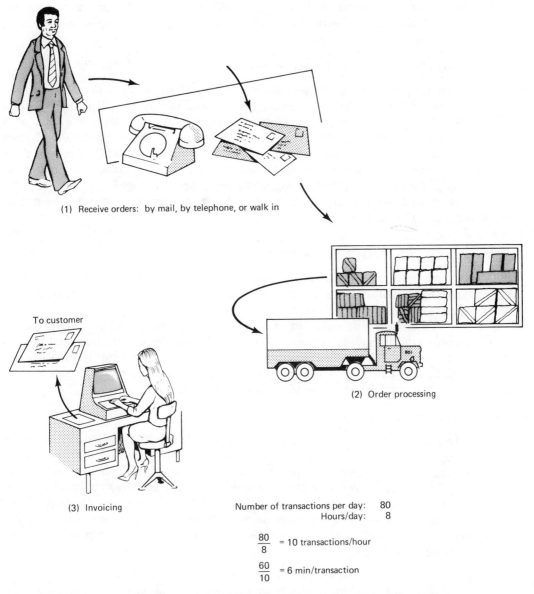

(1) Receive orders: by mail, by telephone, or walk in

To customer

(3) Invoicing

(2) Order processing

Number of transactions per day: 80
Hours/day: 8

$$\frac{80}{8} = 10 \text{ transactions/hour}$$

$$\frac{60}{10} = 6 \text{ min/transaction}$$

Figure 1-2. A computerization criterion: number of transactions.

crocomputer system. To manually process 100 invoices, one person has to process 12.5 invoices per hour or one invoice each 4.8 minutes. This person's time would be better utilized in a computerized operation, particularly if invoices have to be sorted or distributed in more than one sequence. For example, if invoices have to be sorted numerically to maintain records by invoice numbers and alphabetically by customer name to maintain records by customer account, or if a study reveals that a small business is spending considerable time distributing information, then a computer can be very effective.

1-3.3   Alternative Cost of Hiring Another Person

Typically, the cost of a small business computer system is about equivalent to the cost of a clerk. Therefore, one could use as a justification the fact that the annual cost of employing a person approximates the cost of a proposed small computer system. Usually, small businesspeople will start to consider the purchase of a computer not when they wish to reduce their staff but when they consider increasing their staff. Thus, if a firm could buy a computer without hiring additional personnel, and use the computer for more than 1 year, it has a good basis for deciding whether or not to computerize.

1-4   DOES YOUR FIRM NEED A COMPUTER?

One of the most crucial and yet most difficult questions to answer is: Does your firm really need a computer to solve problems, increase profits, and/or improve service (Figure 1-3)?

   To answer this question, both a *feasibility study* and a *EDP economic benefit study* should be conducted. The feasibility study (discussed below) will assist in determining whether installation of a computer is a feasible solution, and the EDP economic benefit study (discussed in Chapter 4) will provide a basis for anticipated economic benefit.

1-4.1   A Feasibility Study

What is a feasibility study, and what does it involve? The feasibility study attempts to measure the anticipated costs and the potential savings in order to make an informed decision as to the most beneficial course of action for the firm. It involves a careful analysis of current business practices and operations. It depends on key questions asked, how various aspects of the business are involved, and to what degree. There are, of course, various ways to approach each individual situation, but the following types of questions may be appropriate:

> Would it be beneficial to install a computer?
>
> Would a computerized system reduce inventory cost compared with the current manual or mechanical system?

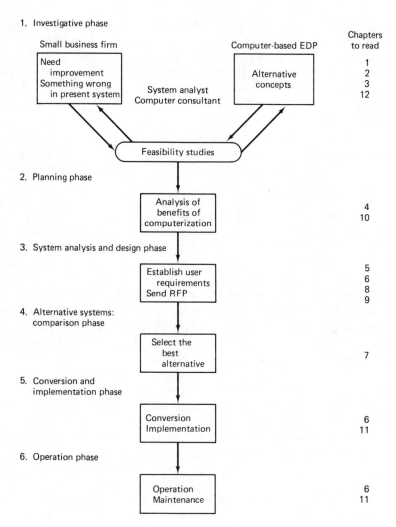

1. Investigative phase

Small business firm   Computer-based EDP   Chapters to read

| Need improvement Something wrong in present system | System analyst Computer consultant | Alternative concepts | 1 2 3 12 |

Feasibility studies

2. Planning phase

| Analysis of benefits of computerization | 4 10 |

3. System analysis and design phase

| Establish user requirements Send RFP | 5 6 8 9 |

4. Alternative systems: comparison phase

| Select the best alternative | 7 |

5. Conversion and implementation phase

| Conversion Implementation | 6 11 |

6. Operation phase

| Operation Maintenance | 6 11 |

Figure 1-3. Systematic EDP system development cycle for small business.

Would a computerized system increase productivity?
Would a computerized system reduce labor cost?
Would a computerized system improve customer service?
Would a computerized system increase profits?
Would a computerized system provide an edge over the competition?

For instance, if an inventory stock is quite large and the business commonly experiences situations such as out-of-stock items, unknown quantities on hand, unknown reorder quantities, or excessive amounts of certain items,

7

the business might consider computerizing their inventory and control of inventory. This can reduce hidden costs, such as loss of sales (and customers), excessive use of storage by slow-moving items, loss of discounts on purchase prices, and the ability to analyze inventory instead of just trying to keep up with physical count and control. On the other hand, if a business carries a small amount of inventory and has good control of it, a computerized system is probably not necessary.

Productivity can be increased by a computerized system if timely and accurate information is provided. This will give workers and management the necessary reports with which to efficiently and effectively increase productive decisions and output for the company. Productivity can also be increased by preparing budgets of future resource use and scheduling resources to be used so as to provide maximum effort for the company. Improved processes have been developed by computer simulations that would allow greater productivity overall for the benefit of the company.

A business should consider a computer system if it will reduce labor (management and line personnel) costs. Reduced labor costs might include less time spent on decisions, less idle wait time of employees because of timely and accurate schedules and reports, and less employee time spent seeking inventory or quantities on hand for customers and management, thus raising the number of customer contacts by each employee. This will lead to increasing sales and customer goodwill.

A computerized system can increase customer service by giving employees more time to assist customers, by supplying customers with accurate and up-to-date information, and also possibly allow employees time to create solutions to customer complaints.

Faster turnaround time and increased accuracy of information, together with improved customer relations, should increase profits and create an edge over any competitors who fall below these new levels of operation or customer satisfaction.

It is also important to recognize and concentrate on problem areas or areas where there is opportunity for growth. One can then focus the feasibility study on specific areas and, consequently, minimize its cost. The following are prime targets for a feasibility study:

Where operational delays occur

Where inventory is excessive or inadequate

Where work is highly repetitive

Where work is highly quantitative

Where clerical costs are high

Where a high volume of information or data is processed or required

Where reporting is inadequate or unreliable

Where accuracy of information is vital

Where timeliness of information is vital

Where an information explosion has developed because of rapid company expansion or growth, a contractual requirement, or similar factor

Any areas where work flow or information become slowed down or piled up are good places to initialize a feasibility study. A well-done feasibility study should show up any specific problem areas that would need closer inspection to help define the problems associated with the overall operation.

All work that is highly repetitive, such as filling orders by hand or processing customer statements, should be considered in the study. Part or all of such jobs could possibly become computerized.

The feasibility study should also focus on areas of a business that have a high volume of sales. Since information and reports dealing with high-volume sales require many quantitative entries and calculations, this area should be analyzed carefully.

If a business is considering hiring one or more specialized personnel such as accounting clerks, this area should be included in the study. Usually, the cost of one specialized clerk would support a small computer system.

The study should also determine whether any part of the business process requires unusual amounts of information. For example, an insurance company processes many customer policies, accident reports, claims, and renewal notices that agents spend a great deal of time filling out. If the company is fairly active, some of the general routine paper processing could be computerized.

Another area to study is the reports "produced" by different departments. If the present methods of compiling reports easily provide managers with information they need to make decisions, this area of study would not be required. However, if the report information aids little in management decisions or provides the wrong information, a detailed study should be considered. This area is even more significant if personnel cannot presently keep up with current reporting schedules.

If a business is required to keep accurate and timely records, this area must be covered thoroughly. For example, businesses are required by law to keep accurate and up-to-date information on employee payroll, government tax reporting, or reports. If the volume of information becomes too large for present personnel to handle in a timely manner, the study should investigate this problem area for possible solutions.

After an initial period of development, a business starts to achieve a positive return on investment and thus creates an ongoing concern. When this point is reached, production or services, number of employees, and/or market share can increase. When this happens, most of information and reports developed previously become outdated and a greater need for more timely information is created. This area of the study should be covered in depth.

Having focused attention on specific areas of concern, an informal feasibility study can now be conducted. The steps to take are:

1. Analyze the flow of information from beginning to end as precisely as possible.
2. Analyze the current business operations, methods, and procedures in each department.
3. Collect and study all forms. Are they necessary? Could any be combined or redesigned for greater efficiency?
4. Collect and determine the actual use of all reports.
5. Estimate and compare the costs and benefits of the current and proposed systems (refer to Chapter 4).

After this initial, informal feasibility study, if a computer seems called for, computer systems information should be solicited from vendors and a system analyst hired to make a detailed feasibility study (see Chapter 6). Without such a preliminary needs study, the system analyst would waste considerable effort and time determining needs instead of reviewing, analyzing, and recommending hardware specifications, file organization, and system specifications.

In summary, *it is vital that you, as a user, be able to tell a vendor or system analyst what your needs are and what you want a computer to do for you.*

1-5   FINDING INFORMATION ON COMPUTER AND SERVICES

In today's business environment, managers are coming to depend more and more on computers to aid them in combating ever-increasing paperwork and to assist them with inventory control and accounting.

Many managers, especially in the small business category, lack the expertise needed to select a computer tailored for their needs. Some purchase a computer that is too small for their needs and thus totally inadequate to perform the functions for which they plan to use it. Others face the dilemma of not being able to get the proper software for the system they have chosen, and end up paying more than they can afford or have budgeted for.

To make an intelligent decision, a systematic EDP analysis is strongly advised. This will aid in avoiding costly mistakes and save time and money in the long run.

Before initiating a EDP analysis, it may be desirable to locate information on which to base forthcoming decisions. Sources for this information are listed in the following sections.

1-5.1   Acquisition of Computer and Services

In addition to this book, the following materials may be useful to a company that is about to begin the lengthy computer-acquisition process.

1. *A Guide to Successful Computer System Selection* (D.P.M.A., 505 Busse Highway, Park Ridge, IL 60068). This guide covers systems and evaluation. It discusses financial and legal considerations, and compares single- versus multivendor systems.

2. *Personal Computers for the Businessman* (Management Information Corp., 140 Barclay Center, Cherry Hill, NJ 08034). This booklet is for the first-time user. It describes differences between micro- and minicomputers and shows the potential user a strategy to follow when buying a computer.

3. Vendors and distributors.
   Almost any vendor or distributor has free booklets available. Many of them present criteria for evaluating computers and then relate their equipment to these criteria. Although these evaluations are often biased, when used to make comparisons they can help the user to develop a sound overall perspective.

1-5.2   Hardware

Selecting a computer and its peripheral equipment is very difficult. There are many brands on the market, each with varing capabilities. For this consideration, the following publications are a good source of information:

1. *Auerbach Information Management Services* (Auerbach Publishers, Inc., 6560 North Park Drive, Pennsauken, NJ 08109). This is a survey of computer manuufacturers. The companies are listed in alphabetical order with each of their available models. Included are general configurations such as size, standard equipment, optional equipment if available, protocol, computer languages, standard price, and the year each model was introduced.

2. *Datapro Reports on Minicomputers* (Datapro Research Corp., Delran, NJ 80875). These are reports on specific commercially available systems, including surveys of micro-, mini-, and small business computers. The computers in each category are listed alphabetically, with specifications such as data formats, storage, CPU, I/O control, software, and pricing. Also included is a survey report that rates both the systems and the performance and support of vendors, based on user feedback.

3. *Minicomputer Review* (GML Information Services, 594 Marrett Road, Lexington, MA 02173).

4. *PCC's Reference Book* (People's Computer Co., 1263 El Camino Real, Menlo Park, CA 94025).

1-5.3   Software

Software is what supports hardware; therefore, great care should be taken in its acquisition. You can either develop your own software or buy it in package form from the vendor or an outside agency.

1. *ICP Software Directory* (International Computer Programs, Inc., 1119 Keystone Way, Carmel, IN 46032).

2. *Minicomputer Software Quarterly* (IMS, Inc., 215 Oak Street, Natick, MA 01760).

3. *Packaged Software Buyer's Guide* (Management Information Corp., 140 Barclay Center, Cherry Hill, NJ 08034).

4. "How to Buy Software Packages" (Datapro Feature Report 70E-010-2a, Datapro 70, Datapro Research Corp., Delran, NJ 08075).

1-5.4   Periodicals

A wealth of information can be obtained from periodicals. Many articles are written about particular systems when they first come out and many vendors advertise in these periodicals. Some periodicals have a subscription fee but many are free.

1. *Periodical Guide for Computerist* (E. Berg Publications, 1360 S.W. 199th Street, Aloha, OR 97005). This periodical has an index of over 1,000 computing articles from many different magazines. It is free of charge.

2. *Computerworld* (797 Washington Street, Newton, MA 02160). This is a weekly newspaper that contains articles about the computer world, from computer crime to computer benefits. It is structured very much like a newspaper. It costs $1 a copy or, by subscription, $25 a year.

3. *Datamation* (1801 South La Cienega Blvd., Los Angeles, CA 90035). Reviews all aspects of the computer world and has the widest circulation among publications of this type. It is a monthly magazine and is free with qualification.

4. *Minicomputer News* (1050 Commonwealth Avenue, Boston, MA 02215). This magazine contains news about both mini- and microcomputers. It is a biweekly magazine with a subscription fee of $6 per year.

5. *Mini-Micro Systems* (221 Columbus Avenue, Boston, MA 02116). Covers mini- and microcomputers and peripherals. An informative and useful magazine for those seeking mini-/microcomputer knowledge. Qualified U.S. subscriptions are free; others cost $30 per year.

6. *Interface Age* (16704 Marquardt Avenue, Cerritos, CA 90701). The use of microcomputers in the office and home. Subscriptions are $14 per year.

7. *Personal Computing* (1050 Commonwealth Avenue, Boston, MA 02215). A monthly magazine that contains programs and informative articles about computers. Subscriptions are $14 per year.

8. *Byte* (70 Main Street, Peterborough, NH 03458). A small-systems journal for personal and microcomputers. Subscriptions are $18 per year.

9. *SBC Magazine* (Box 1176 Brookdale Station, Bloomfield, NJ 07003). SBC (Small Business Computer) is a magazine geared for first-time and about-to-become data processing user. SBC is a monthly publication with an annual subscription rate of $9.

10. *Small Systems World* (5336 San Fernando Road, Glendale, CA 91202). This monthly publication is oriented toward small businesses and minicomputers. It is free to qualified subscribers; otherwise $15 per year.

11. *Computer Decisions* (Hayden Publishing, Inc., 50 Essex Street, Rochelle Park, NJ 07662). This publication has recently begun to cover small computers. Qualified U.S. subscriptions are free; others cost $24 per year.

In addition to those listed here, many other periodicals contain useful information.

1-5.5   Associations

Associations can also be useful to potential users in their selection of a system.

1. Association of Small Computer Users (75 Manhattan Drive, Boulder, CO 80308). This association provides bench-mark test comparisons of competing systems, a users' information exchange, and selected publications to help users assess the market.
2. Data Processing Management Association (505 Busse Highway, Park Ridge, IL 60068). Commonly referred to as DPMA, this is a professional association of data-processing managers, systems analysts, and computer programmers.

1-5.6   Consultants

A systems consultant is a person who has the knowledge and experience necessary to advise you in this area. Seeking the assistance of a qualified consultant is a good investment if you don't know much about computers.

1. *An Introduction to Software and Consultants* (Hewlett-Packard, Loveland, CO 80537). This free brochure [Form 5952-8992(09)] discusses locating and using independent consultants.
2. Association of Management Consultants, Inc. (AMC) (811 E. Wisconsin Avenue, Milwaukee, WI 53202). A directory of members is available.
3. Independent Computer Consultants Association (ICCA) (P.O. Box 27412, St. Louis, MO 63141). These consultants are experts in the mini- and microcomputer fields.

1-5.7   Computer Conferences and Exhibitions

Computer conferences and exhibitions are another good way to gather information. The attendance fees for most conferences are free or nominal. Some of them conduct seminars; this is yet another way to gain knowledge about computer systems. Conferences are usually advertised weeks ahead over radio, television, and in computer magazines. The following is a list of computer conferences.

1. NCC (National Computer Conference). The NCC has a vast display of computers and services that are available to end users.
2. Interface West. This conference displays small business computer systems and conducts seminars about various phases of data processing.
3. Mini-Micro Computer Conference.
4. Small Business Computer Conference.

In the Yellow Pages of your local telephone directory, under "Data Processing Services and Data Systems—Consultants and Designers," you will find services and consultants available in your local area.

1-6   TEN COMMANDMENTS FOR BUYERS OF SMALL COMPUTERS

1. Do not get your computer education from a salesperson.
2. Check each vendor's experience and reputation.
3. Do not underconfigure the system.
4. Weigh risk factors as well as cost factors.
5. Visit other installations.
6. Keep in mind that *caveat emptor* (let the buyer beware) is especially applicable with regard to the quality of package softwares.
7. Do not endlessly modify package software. Resolve to limit the number of modifications.
8. Select as many widely available basic system features as possible, to enhance the availability and longevity of both the programs and the system. [For example, if you are looking for a microcomputer system, consider the following basic features; (a) 8080, Z80, 6800, 9900 family; (b) BASIC language; (c) S100 bus; (d) RS232; and (e) CPM.
9. Check the expansion capabilities of the system in terms of the probable direction of your firm's future growth.
10. Obtain a written warranty that contains all agreements arrived at verbally.

2

BASIC CONFIGURATION
AND COMPONENTS OF A
SMALL COMPUTER SYSTEM

2-1 CONFIGURATION OF A SMALL COMPUTER SYSTEM

A computer is a machine that is able to take in information (data), process that information, and produce answers, reports, and so on, through the medium of data processing. Basically, a computer is organized as shown in Figure 2-1, and performs five distinct functions:

1. *The control unit* directs the operations within the computer; it is the traffic cop for information and instructions. It retrieves instructions from memory, decodes them, and uses them to execute the required operations.

2. *The arithmetic and logical unit* (ALU) performs all the arithmetic calculations (addition, subtraction, multiplication, and division). The logical unit has the ability to recognize and make decisions depending on variables being greater than, equal to, or less than constants or other variables.

3. *Memory* is the storage element of the central processing unit (CPU). Data and instructions reside in the memory and are available when called upon by a storage or memory address. The size of the memory will vary with the size of the CPU and the system. Part of the memory within the CPU is used for control storage, that is, the storage of the operating (system) instructions that control the flow of data and program instructions.

15

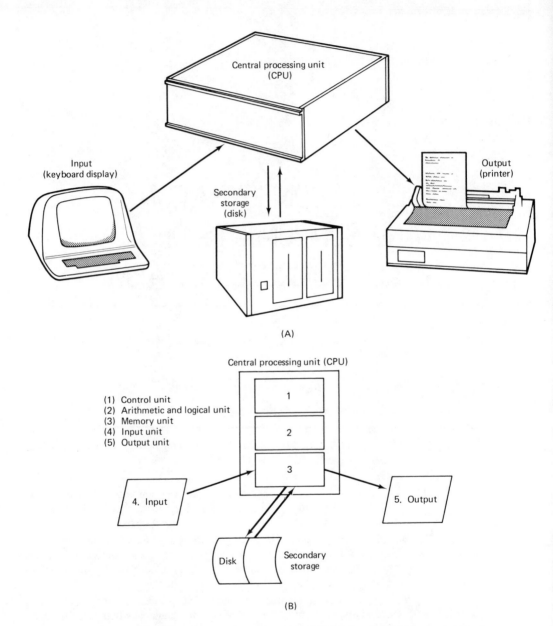

Figure 2-1. A small computer system. (A) Configuration. (B) Schematic diagram.

4, 5. *Input/output (I/O) functions* are used to feed information into the computer and to obtain answers from it. Input and output devices are generally separate from, and operate much more slowly than, the central processing unit.

Basically, there are two types of processing approaches, on-line interactive and batch processing. Data are presented at the input function, where they should be ready for processing. In Figure 2-2 an employee's time card is used as example input. In on-line interactive processing, the information on time cards is directly keyed into the computer, through the terminals or keyboards, for further processing. Most small computers use the on-line interactive processing approach illustrated in the figure. In batch processing, the time cards are keypunched and verified and then read into the computer via the card reader for immediate processing or spooled (stored) on magnetic disks or magnetic tapes for processing later.

Most large main-frame computers utilize batch processing, as illustrated in Figure 2-3.

Information read into a computer is stored in memory. When the reading (or storage) operation is complete, the control section of the CPU issues instructions to process the information. The ALU will then calculate, for example, the amount earned by each employee by multiplying the hours

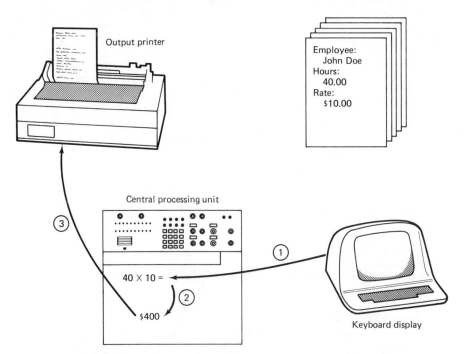

Figure 2-2. Interactive processing in the small computer system.

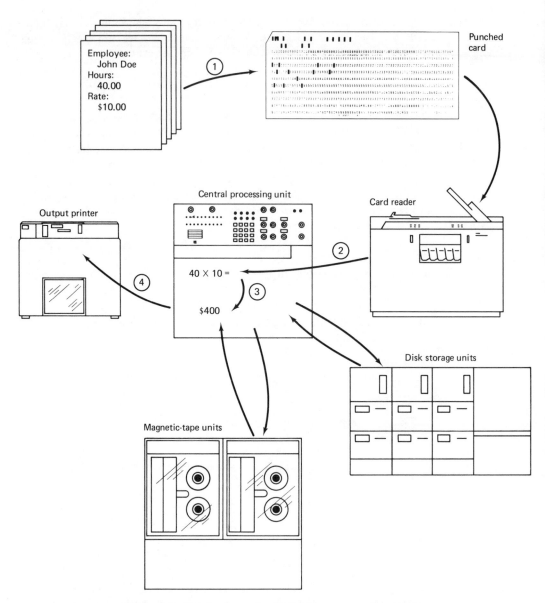

Figure 2-3. Batch processing in the large computer system.

worked by the hourly rate for each employee. The processing is complete when all the information has been processed. The computer is then capable of producing a report of the information processed (the output), as well as retaining it in another area of memory.

The function of memory or storage is to "remember" or store the information presented, such as an employee's name, hours worked, rate, gross pay, net pay, and so on. Memory consists of:

1. The main storage, which is part of the control storage of the CPU.
2. The auxiliary storage, which is separate from main storage and may consist of core or other storage devices (such as magnetic tapes and disks).

The arithmetic unit performs any addition, subtraction, multiplication, and division operation that a program calls for. The logic unit is used for comparison, as in the case of two employee numbers.

The control section of the computer is the computer's "supervisor." It controls the traffic of instructions and of information (data) that is to be manipulated and stored. It has circuitry to decode instructions and issue commands to the remaining functions in the system. When all processing has been completed, the control section issues a command to print and, in our example, it prints employees' payroll checks.

We now have a general knowledge of the operation of the five components that together make up what we call a computer system.

2-2   COMPONENTS OF A SMALL COMPUTER SYSTEM

In the small business system, the collection of computer components and peripherals are logically connected to enable interactive data manipulation. A typical collection of such equipment includes (see Figure 2-4):

The central processing unit (CPU)
Mass storage devices
Input devices
Output devices

The main component of a small business computer system is the computer (CPU) itself, with a given amount of memory. Next, a mass storage device or devices should be attached for file storage, working storage, system software storage, compilers or language storage, and application program storage. Typical mass storage devices for small business systems are floppy disk drives, rigid disk drives, and magnetic tape drives. One or more input terminals for direct data entry constitute the typical input devices. A serial printer and a line printer are typical output devices for hard-copy records in the small business systems. Most systems will also contain some communications facilities to provide for remote data entry. When an entire collection of these hardware components is combined with system software (operating system, computer languages, etc.) and application software (accounts receivable program, inventory control program, etc.), a complete small business computer system emerges.

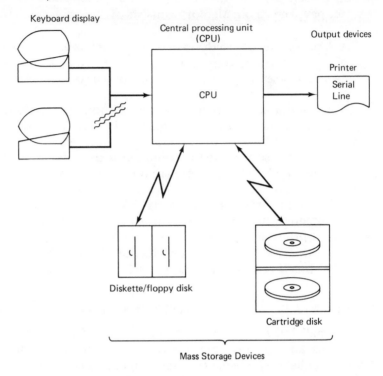

Input devices

Keyboard display

Central processing unit
(CPU)

Output devices

CPU

Printer

Serial
Line

Diskette/floppy disk

Cartridge disk

Mass Storage Devices

Figure 2-4. Typical small business computer system.

2-2.1 Central Processing Unit

The central processing unit (CPU) is the heart of the computer system. As we discussed in Section 2-1, the basic functions of a computer are (1) the control function; (2) the arithmetic and logical function; and (3) the storage function. These basic functions are performed by computers regardless of their size, which could be as large as the IBM 370-168 or as small as the PET (personal computer) by Commandor. A main-frame processor as typically found in the large system, however, is not usually practical in a small business system because of its size, complexity, required special environment, and cost. Therefore, main-frame computers are excluded from this discussion. In a minicomputer design, the five basic functions are usually implemented by means of transistor–transistor logic, often called T^2L ("T squared L"). It is the most common bipolar technology, offering the high-speed logic found in larger computers. In a microcomputer design, the same functions are generally contained on a single chip about $\frac{1}{4}$ inch in size.

In terms of comparison between a minicomputer and a microcomputer, a minicomputer offers the advantages of speed, flexibility, and capacity in terms of system throughput and instruction sets. A microcomputer system offers the advantages of small size, lower cost, and increased reliability (because of fewer components). Comparative data will not be discussed further in this section as a more detailed discussion of various small computers is included in Chapter 3.

Core and metal–oxide–semiconductor (MOS) are the two most commonly used types of CPU memory in small computer systems (see Figure 2-5). The MOS memory type tends to be used in microcomputers, and core

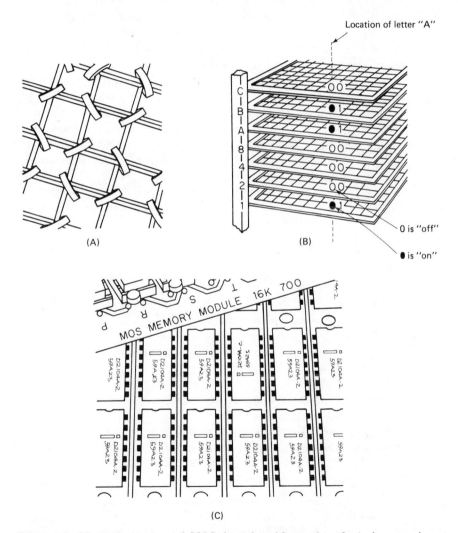

Figure 2-5. Magnetic cores and MOS (metal–oxide–semiconductor) memories. (A) Plane of magnetic cores. (B) Character "A" represented in core memory. (C) A MOS memory board.

memory tends to be used in minicomputers or larger minicomputer systems. Generally, core memory is more expensive than MOS memory. A computer with core memory does not lose data in the event of a power failure or power loss to the system. On the other hand, a computer with MOS memory will lose data unless there is power protection, such as a battery pack. Some systems have automatic restart logic in the event of a power failure.

Computer people are very often asked by businesspeople: "What is the size of this computer?" The answer will usually be given in terms of CPU memory size, such as "It's 128K." The 128K indicates a CPU memory capacity of 128,000 given characters. The more memory available, the more flexible and expensive the system will be. The manner in which the operating system handles memory may make a big difference in the processing speed and/or flexibility of memory.

Many systems require a partition of memory when keyboard display stations are added to the existing system. The amount of memory necessary may vary from 6K to 12K. An individual memory board (e.g., 8K) is usually very easy to add to an existing CPU. In a small computer system, rarely would the entire CPU have to be replaced in order to add 8K memory to the system. Nonetheless, the cost of adding memory should be considered as part of the cost of adding the keyboard station.

Following is a list of questions to ask when considering the purchase of a CPU.

Checklist for CPU

1. Can the main memory accommodate the largest application program and operating system simultaneously? YES _____ NO _____

2. How much memory is available in the CPU? _____K
   Minimum _____K Maximum _____K _____

3. Can the present computer system be incorporated into a larger system without modifying or changing the existing software? YES _____ NO _____

4. What type of memory does the CPU have?
   _____Core _____MOS

5. Does the CPU have automatic restart logic in the event of a power failure? YES _____ NO _____

6. Can a segment of memory be added without replacing the entire existing CPU? YES _____ NO _____

7. If the CPU has MOS memory, is there a power battery-pack protection feature in the system? YES _____ NO _____

8. Does the CPU have self-diagnostic logic built in to warn a maintenance person when the system is beginning to fail? YES _____ NO _____

9. Does the system require a dedicated line for the computer?   YES _____   NO _____

10. Does the system require a static-electricity-free room?   YES _____   NO _____

11. Does the system require temperature-controlled room?   YES _____   NO _____

12. Does the system require a special dust-free room?   YES _____   NO _____

13. Does the system require a room with a raised floor to house the computer's air-conditioning and water-cooling system?   YES _____   NO _____

14. Which types of electrical power service is required to operate the computer system, 110 V or 220 V?   _____

2-2.2   Mass Storage Devices

A mass storage device is used primarily as an extension of primary storage in a computer. It is often called secondary storage, and is used to store system software, compilers (computer languages), application programs, object programs, and data files. Data files for application programs may consist of the inventory file, customer file, accounts receivable file, accounts payable file, and general ledger file. Obviously, the mass storage device plays an essential role in a small business system. Mass storage in small systems usually consists of magnetic disk or magnetic tape. The magnetic-disk unit is primarily used for on-line interactive secondary storage in the small computer system. The mass storage magnetic-tape unit is generally used as backup for the disk unit.

Magnetic Disk

In a magnetic-disk storage system, data are stored on tracks of a flat circular platter. Each disk read/write head moves across the tracks until the proper track is found and waits until the desired information is rotated to a position underneath the head. Then the read/write head reads or writes specific information. The disk platter spins at a constant speed at all times and data are either read or written while the platter continues to spin. The majority of disk systems can be subdivided into three groups (see Figure 2-6):

Floppy disks (flexible disks)
Disk cartridges (top- or front-loading)
Disk packs (hard disks)

Floppy disks have a lower capacity than disk packs, generally 80,000 to 4,000,000 bytes (characters). Disk packs, on the other hand, are of higher capacity. Their typical storage capacity can range from 50 to more than 1,000 megabytes (1 megabyte represents 1,000,000 characters). The storage

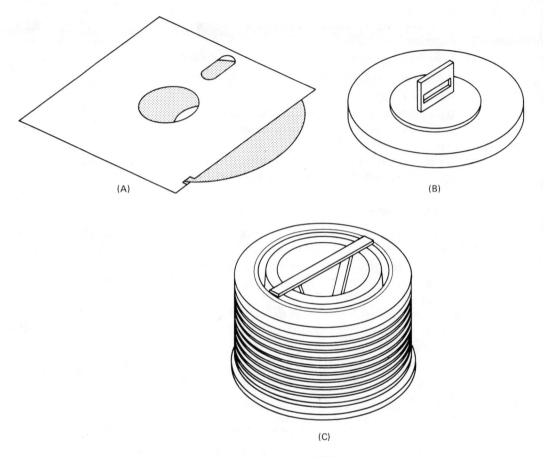

Figure 2-6. Three categories of disks for small business computers. (A) Floppy disk (diskette). (B) Cartridge disk. (C) Disk pack (hard disk).

capacity of disk cartridges is somewhere between that of floppy disks and disk packs.

The floppy disk is housed in a plastic cartridge which resembles the cardboard jackets in which 45-rpm audio records are sold (Figure 2-7). The cartridge is slid into the disk drive, and the disk is rotated inside the cartridge. The read/write head is brought inside the cartridge and moved from track to track. The read/write head of most floppy disks contacts the surface in order to read and write the information. Many floppy disks are presently available, with the most recent systems having both faster access capability and increased storage capacity. Today, the two most typical physical sizes of floppy disks are $5\frac{1}{4}$ and 8 inches. Some companies have introduced a dual-density $3\frac{1}{2}$-inch floppy disk. A typical middle-of-the-range floppy disk system has about 600K characters of storage and an average access time of 500 milliseconds.

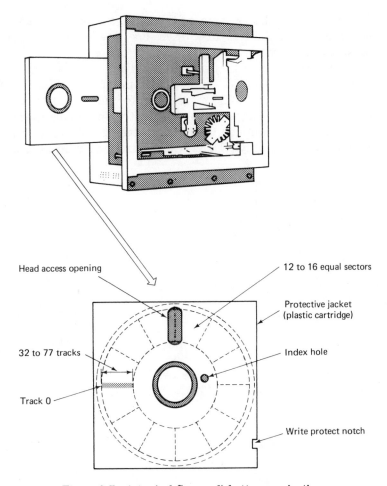

Figure 2-7. A typical floppy diskette organization.

Users who wish to acquire a floppy disk system are faced with bewildering options. Some examples are the following:

A *single-density* recording diskette on a *single-sided* drive
A *double-density* recording diskette on a *single-sided* drive
A *single-density* recording diskette on a *dual-sided* drive
A *double-density* recording diskette on a *dual-sided* drive

The double-density recording diskette has twice the data capacity of its single-density counterpart. Similarly, the dual-sided disk drive has twice the data capacity of a single-sided drive. Each side of a dual-sided disk drive has its own read/write head, so that two completely different sets of information can be written on the two sides of a diskette.

25

Figure 2-8 shows some of the storage capacities of various disks. It is worth checking the new disk drives and new storage media, which may better suit your needs.

Traditionally, disk packs (hard disk) have been used as direct-access storage devices (DASD) for large computer systems. The requirement for small data bases (10 to 20 megabytes) for small computer systems prompted the advent of the cartridge disk. Recently, the Winchester disk-pack technology has been introduced to the cartridge-size disk. In disks of this type the head-to-disk assembly (HDA) is sealed from outside air and is nonremovable.

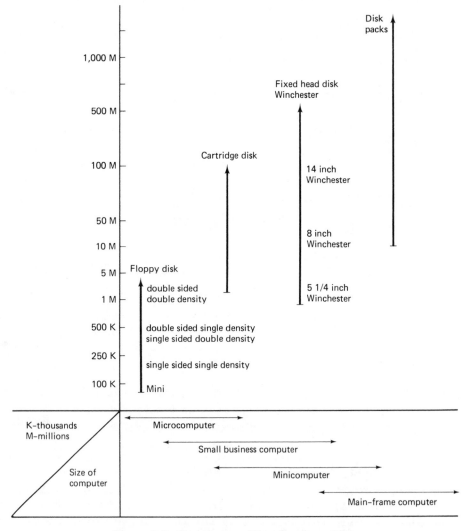

Figure 2-8. Storage capacities of various disks.

Since the Winchester disk drive is free of contaminants in the external air, head crashes caused by dust and dirt particles are virtually eliminated. Users of standard disk packs and cartridge disks still have this problem to contend with. In the sealed environment of a Winchester disk drive, the read/write head can rotate at high-speed 20 microinches above the high-density magnetic surface. Thus, this type of disk drive provides high-speed, low-cost storage per character. Other benefits of the Winchester disk drives are extremely high reliability and no preventive maintenance, such as changing the air filter or cleaning and aligning the disk heads. Eight- and 14-inch Winchester disk drives are currently available (Figures 2-9 and 2-10). The 8-inch Winchester drive can accommodate a 40-megabyte capacity or less for smaller computer systems, while the 14-inch Winchester disk drive can provide less than 100 megabytes to over 500 megabytes storage capacity for minicomputer or large-minicomputer systems. The major drawback of the Winchester disk drive is its nonremovability (fixed disk), due to the nature of Winchester disk-drive construction. The user cannot take the disk cartridge out and put it in the vault or take it home. For this reason, information on the Winchester disk must be backed up by some a removable storage medium. On the larger Winchester disk drive, industry standard $\frac{1}{2}$-inch magnetic tape is a primary backup device. Half-inch magnetic tape can provide high-speed storage capacity, and low-cost storage per character. This type of backup is not cost-effective for the 8-inch Winchester drives, however, because a $\frac{1}{2}$-inch magnetic tape drive costs much more than the 8-inch Winchester disk drive. Floppy-disk backup offers a solution for the smaller 8-inch Winchester disk, which ranges from 2 megabytes, capacity to less than 10 megabytes.

Figure 2-9. Eight-inch Winchester disk drive. The device at the left is a typical 8-inch floppy disk drive with 1 million characters of storage. The Micropolis Microdisk at the right (8-inch Winchester disk drive) has the same overall dimensions, but can store up to 45 million characters (unformatted). (Courtesy of Micropolis Corp.)

Figure 2-10. Fourteen-inch Winchester disk drive. Left: Shugart SA4000 14-inch Winchester disk drive can store up to 29 million characters (unformatted) or 24.8 million characters (formatted). Right: Shugart SA800 floppy disk drive can store up to 800,000 characters (double density) or 400,000 characters (single density). (Courtesy of Shugart Associates.)

If the user wishes to back up a 5-megabyte Winchester disk drive, he or she can copy the information it contains by using five 1-megabyte floppy diskettes. Floppy-disk backup is not cost-effective for an 8-inch Winchester disk drive of greater than 10-megabyte capacity because too much time will be wasted daily on backup procedures. As far as storage capacity is concerned, tape-cartridge backup is a better solution than floppy diskettes for the 8-inch Winchester disk. Most tape cartridges can provide enough capacity for transfer of the data from one entire 8-inch Winchester disk, providing cost-effective storage and ease of use. Cassette drives are also used to back up the smaller-capacity Winchester disk, providing low cost, small physical size, and ease of use. But the disadvantages of cassette tape drives are low reliability, low storage capacity, low data-transfer rate, and lack of industry standardization. The backup question for the Winchester disk drive will remain with us for at least the near future.

The technology in the disk field is constantly changing. Alternatives to the standard disk drives include bubble memory devices (BMD), charge-coupled devices (CCD), and optical disk memories. Some of these devices can provide much higher capacities and faster access, but currently none can compete effectively on a cost/performance basis with hard-disk drives. However, bubble memory devices could ultimately replace hard-disk storage media. A BMD could be used in place of a hard disk to store the operating system, utilities, file management, and data-base system. Bubble memories will probably not supplant the floppy disk because the BMD off-line cost per byte (character), or per storage medium, will be much higher than that of any diskette.

The bubble memory cost is projected to be about 100 millicents per bit in the next year or two and 20 millicents per bit by 1985, and the floppy diskette will cost less than 0.1 millicent per bit [1].*

Charge-coupled devices (CCD) could be used ultimately to replace large hard disk drives, but currently the CCD has a much higher cost per character than the Winchester disk drive. Optical disk memories are another candidate for large hard-disk replacement in the future. The Philips optical disk memory, made under the Magnavox brand, is claimed to have a 6,000-megabyte capacity on one side of a 12-inch disk [2]. Data stored on optical disks are not yet alterable; once written on optical disk, they cannot be changed or erased.

The technology in the disk field is changing every day, and the user is advised to check new disk drives and new storage media available before a specific disk drive or mass storage medium is selected for the small computer system.

Checklist for Mass Storage Units (Disk Storage)

1. Can the mass storage unit store all the programs and data necessary to operate the system? YES _____ NO _____

2. What is the disk-drive capacity?
   _____K   Minimum _____K
   Maximum _____K   _____

3. Can the disk storage be removed from the disk drive? YES _____ NO _____

4. Can the information stored on the mass storage be backed up or copied easily? YES _____ NO _____

5. How long does it take to back up a disk to other storage media? _____minutes   Minimum _____ minutes
   Maximum _____ minutes

6. What types of mass storage media can be used for backup? Diskette _____   Cartridge disk _____
   Other _____   _____

7. Can a disk drive be added to the existing system? If yes, how many? _____ YES _____ NO _____

8. What types of mass storage disks can be added?
   Diskette _____   Cartridge disk _____
   Disk pack _____   _____

9. Can the system accommodate a Winchester disk drive? If yes, is it an 8-inch disk drive or a 14-inch disk drive? _____ inch   YES _____ NO _____

*Numbers in brackets refer to end-of-chapter reference lists.

With magnetic tape, data are stored sequentially on a tape strip. To find a specific record, the computer must search the tape sequentially. Each record must be checked until the appropriate information is found. During this process, the tape drive has to start, come to full speed, read the tape, read the record, and then stop. This is done for each record. It is a slow process. On the other hand, to find a specific record on a magnetic disk, the computer can skip to a specific track which contains a specific record, then search only that track sequentially until the specific record is located. This direct searching method increases the speed of processing substantially.

In a small business computer system, the following three categories of magnetic tape are used:

> Standard tape drives
>
> Cartridge recorders
>
> Cassette tape recorders

Figures 2-11 to 2-13 show these three typical categories of magnetic tapes. Standard tape drives (Figure 2-11) can read and write at tape speeds varying between 12.5 and 75 ips (inches per second). The speed based on an 800-bpi (bytes per inch) density becomes equivalent to a transfer rate between 10,000 and 60,000 bps (bytes per second). A byte represents a character or a number. The tape length is typically 2,400 ft and the width is $\frac{1}{2}$ inch. If we use 800 bpi, the standard tape (2,400 ft) can contain 23,040,000 characters. The recording tape is usually either seven-track or nine-track, which means that seven or nine separate read/write heads can simultaneously read or write one digital character. The recording density of the seven-track tape drive will usually be either 200, 556, or 800 bpi and the recording density of the nine-track unit will usually be either 800 or 1,600 bpi.

The second category of magnetic tape is a cartridge-type recorder (Figure 2-12). It combines the ease of handling and compactness of the small cassette tape with the more reliable performance of the standard magnetic tape drive. Most cartridge recorders have been designed for digital recording. Therefore, they provide a faster transfer rate and greater recording capacity than do the small cassette tape recorders. The 3M cartridge recorder has been designed specifically for high transfer rates. It reads and writes at 90 ips and searches at 180 ips. The tape width is $\frac{1}{4}$ inch. The recording density is 1,600 bpi. The speed of reading and writing based on an 1,600-bpi density is equivalent to 144,000 bps (bytes per second).

The third category of magnetic tape is a digital cassette recorder (Figure 2-13). The main advantages of cassette tape over other magnetic tapes are its low cost, compact size, and ease of loading into a reader. The major disad-

Figure 2-11. (A) Standard magnetic tape drive. (Courtesy of Sperry Univac.) (B) Standard magnetic tape. Since the beginning of the computer era, the standard removable storage medium has been magnetic tape. Its most popular configuration is the 2400-ft reel in $\frac{1}{2}$-inch width. Each frame of data (transverse to the direction of tape motion) usually contains 7 or 9 data bits plus a parity bit. Recording densities range up to 6,250 such frames per inch (normally specified as "bits per inch"). Tape is generally the most cost-effective removable storage medium; its disadvantages are longer access time and susceptibility to damage through improper operator care and handling. (Courtesy of 3M.)

(A)

(B)

(A)

(B)

Figure 2-12. (A) Cartridge drive. New generation 3M HCD-75 High Capacity Cartridge Drive, the size of a standard floppy disk drive, can record 67 megabytes of user data—48 times the capacity of current 4-by 6-inch cartridges—to serve as backup for fixed-disk systems. (Courtesy of 3M.) (B) Cartridge tape. (Courtesy of American National Supply Corp., Gardena, Calif.)

vantage of the cassette tape is the relatively low data reliability, because it was originally designed for audio applications. The cassette tape length is typically 300 ft and the width is 0.15 inch. Cassette tape drives are based on either continuous or incremental recording methods. Both types of recording are performed bit-serially on one or two tracks.

The continuous recording method of cassette tapes writes serially on the tape in groups of 8 bits or 1 byte, which represents a character. Characters are recorded in a synchronous manner. Continuous-recording cassette tapes can store up to 700,000 characters per tape. The incremental recording method of cassette tape recorders writes data by starting and stopping

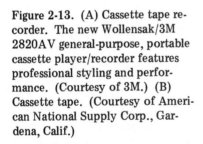

(A)

(B)

Figure 2-13. (A) Cassette tape recorder. The new Wollensak/3M 2820AV general-purpose, portable cassette player/recorder features professional styling and performance. (Courtesy of 3M.) (B) Cassette tape. (Courtesy of American National Supply Corp., Gardena, Calif.)

the tape for each character. Therefore, it eliminates the need for interrecord gaps, which represent typically 0.5 to 1 inch between records.

The continuous-recording method requires interrecord gaps. The incremental-recording method of cassette tape, which does not require interrecord gaps, utilizes lower density, thus limiting the cassette storage capacity to the range 50,000 to 100,000 characters per cassette. The cassette recording is bit serial in form rather than parallel interface. The bit-serial interface may be either a 20-mA current loop or EIA RS-232C-compatible. These low-transfer-rate devices are designed to operate under or at a slow speed of 10 to 120 cps (characters per second). Therefore, the cassette tapes are used primarily as secondary or backup storage in personal computer systems or small microcomputer systems.

2-2.3   Input Devices

Virtually all input terminals on today's interactive computer systems use a keyboard. Keyboard input by a human operator is still the principal means of entering data, program information, and commands. A keyboard terminal can generally be used for both the input and output of a small computer. Relatively few devices are either strictly for input or strictly for output. Examples of input-only devices are card readers, badge readers, and the like. On the other hand, examples of output-only devices are printers and plotters. These output devices are discussed in more detail in the next section.

A large group of combined input/output (I/O) devices are termed interactive. An interactive terminal falls into one of two categories: (1) keyboard/display—a keyboard attached to a cathode ray tube (CRT), and (2) keyboard/printer—a keyboard attached to a hard-copy printer. One can visualize that a keyboard printer is very similar to a typewriter. A keyboard display is a keyboard with a CRT. In fact, quite often a keyboard and a TV monitor are utilized as I/O devices in small microcomputer systems.

When considering the keyboard terminal, whether attached to a CRT or a hard-copy printer, one should closely examine the keyboard makeup for such features as full standard typewriter alphanumeric format, 10-key pad, and the arrangement and number of special function keys. These features are important to simplify learning and to speed up the data process itself.

Keyboard Display Terminals

Keyboard display terminals (see Figures 2-14 to 2-17) differ from keyboard printers mainly in not having the capacity to produce hard copy. Distinguishing features of display terminals include the size of the display area, the number of characters per line and lines per display, the number of different characters that can be displayed, and the character-generation techniques. The number of characters that can be displayed at one time varys from 240 to 1,980 or more. The larger the number of characters a display terminal can display at one time, the better it is. For example, can the operator see an entire invoice at once on the display terminal rather than only a portion of it at a time? Most low-cost display terminals measure between 10 and 14 inches diagonally and display a maximum of approximately 2,000 characters. The user should also be concerned about the transfer speed of the input unit. How fast can the keyboard display terminal transfer input data to the central processing unit (CPU)? The transfer rate ranges from fewer than 120 characters per second to over 960 characters per second. A slow input terminal slows down the operator entering data to the computer.

Figure 2-14. Keyboard display terminals: ADM-3A+ dumb terminal. An expanded version of the original ADM-3A dumb terminal, the ADM-3A+ features a 12-inch monitor, upper/lowercase display, built-in numeric keypad, RS-232C/20-mA current loop interface, program mode, and individual cursor control keys. (Courtesy of Lear Siegler/ Data Products Division), Anaheim, Calif.)

The characters are usually formed by a 5×7 or 7×9 dot matrix. A 7×9 dot matrix display offers higher-resolution character, but a 5×7 dot matrix is usually adequate for most small computer applications. The display itself is generally based on the CRT, but the relatively new plasma dis-

Figure 2-15. Keyboard display terminal: ADM-42 smart terminal. Featuring up to eight pages of memory, the microprocessor-based ADM-42 smart terminal responds to the demand for a low-cost modular product that permits the separation of keyboard, video display, and central circuitry. Functionally compatible with the earlier ADM-2 model, it offers 16 function keys and total flexibility of format, security, editing, interface, and transmission. (Courtesy of Lear Siegler/ Data Products Division, Anaheim, Calif.)

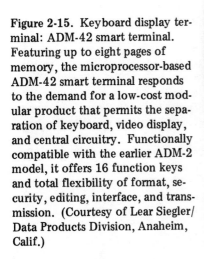

Figure 2-16. Keyboard display terminal: The Graphic 7. California Computer Products, Inc. (CalComp) markets the Graphic 7 line of intelligent interactive display systems. The Graphic 7, manufactured by CalComp's parent company, Sanders Associates, Inc., incorporates stroke/refresh technology which provides dynamic line-drawing capabilities. A basic Graphic 7 system consists of a 21-inch CRT display, terminal controller, interface, and keyboard. Both four-color and monochromatic displays are available. The system shown includes an optional track ball unit. [Courtesy of CalComp (California Computer Products, Inc.).]

play device, which uses a gas-discharge technique, may become a low-cost display for small computer systems.

Keyboard display terminals have gained much popularity among almost all competitive small business systems suppliers as the standard for the input terminal. Some of the reasons for this are:

1. It is easy to use. One only has to interact with the keyboard, not with paper and ribbon.

Figure 2-17. Keyboard display terminal: full-page display unit and keyboard of Xerox 860. The Xerox 860 information processing system enables users to handle a variety of office tasks and combine processing of text, business records, and data. The Basic 860 system includes full-page display unit, keyboard, printer, and controller, together with the operating system and text-processing software and a set of generic applications programs providing additional features. Optional peripheral modules and software applications packages are available. (Courtesy of Xerox Corp.)

2. There is practically no noise in the use of a keyboard display terminal compared with a keyboard printer.

3. It has an instantaneous response.

4. A keyboard display terminal has higher reliability levels than a keyboard printer does because there are fewer mechanical parts in the CRT.

5. Selective blink allows portions of the message to flash to attract the attention of the operator.

6. Most intelligent keyboard terminals have editing capabilities and the option of a block mode or teletype mode.

Many keyboard display terminals can be operated in either a teletype mode or a block mode. In a teletype mode, each character, when entered from the keyboard onto the screen, is transmitted simultaneously to the small computer. In a block mode, the entire message can be typed and edited off-line on the screen before it is transmitted in full to the computer. Today, most keyboard display terminals have incorporated a high degree of intelligence in the terminal that permits some preprocessing functions to be included in the display. This intelligence allows some editing capabilities in the display and speeds up the data-entry operation. These terminals are sometimes called intelligent terminals, in contrast to simple (dummy) terminals, which do not have these capabilities. The innovation of intelligent terminals also frees more computer time to serve other uses, as these terminals can perform some of the functions that were formerly carried out by a central computer.

A limitation of keyboard display terminals is that no permanent copy of the display remains. If a permanent copy is necessary, the operator must manually copy the information on the display, or use the display in conjunction with a hard-copy output device such as a serial printer or keyboard printer. Nevertheless, the keyboard display terminals are widely used on small business computers because they are fast, economical, and convenient I/O devices.

Checklist for Input Units (Keyboard Display Terminals)

1. Can the operating system accommodate more than one terminal? YES _____   NO _____

2. How many keyboard display terminals can be added to the existing system? _____ terminals
Minimum _____ units   Maximum _____ units

3. If more than one terminal is operating at a time, can each terminal be processing a different task? YES _____   NO _____

4. Does the input terminal have the intelligence to edit the input data so the CPU can be released for more important tasks? YES _____   NO _____

5. Does the input terminal have special functions such as a moving cursor, a flashing light on screen, and other easy-to-use functions? _____   YES ____   NO ____

6. Does the input terminal have numeric 10-pad keys?   YES ____   NO ____

7. How many characters can be displayed at one time on a keyboard display terminal? _____ characters
   Fewer than 1,000 _____ 1,920 _____ 1,980 or more _____

8. Does the system provide input terminal key control features?   YES ____   NO ____

9. Does the system provide foreground/background capability? (For example, can the system print reports while the user is inquiring information from keyboard display terminal?)   YES ____   NO ____

10. How fast can the keyboard display terminal transfer data to and from the central processing unit?
    _____ cps
    Fewer than 120 cps _____
    Between 120 and 480 cps _____
    960 or more cps _____

11. Can the system support a keyboard printer?   YES ____   NO ____

12. How far can the keyboard display terminal be away from the central processing unit?
    Different room _____ less than 100 ft
    Different building _____ less than 250 ft
    Different city _____ more than 500 ft

Keyboard Printers

Keyboard printers (Figures 2-18 to 2-21) are also used as interactive data-entry terminals. However, they are more widely used when hard-copy records are required at remote sites and lower station costs are important. These units typically have built-in communications facilities that allow them to function much like a keyboard display terminal with the computer. Therefore, they are relatively easy to interface to the machine. Some manufacturers have even incorporated very costly but effective small portable keyboard printer terminals that have essentially the same features as their stationary keyboard printer terminals.

Some keyboard printers, such as the ASR 33 and ASR 35 Teletypes, are also equipped with paper-tape facilities. This enables input data to be sent to the CPU from either the keyboard or punched paper tape, and output data to be printed out or punched into paper tape. Other keyboard printer devices, such as the Texas Instrument Silent 700 terminal, provide magnetic-tape facilities. Generally, keyboard printers are equipped with a

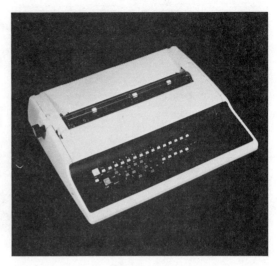

Figure 2-18. Keyboard/printer: TermiNet 2030. TermiNet 2030 is a keyboard/printer that contains a dual 8085 microprocessor. Its features include the following: (1) fully programmable, vertical and horizontal formatting—top and bottom of form, left and right margins; (2) 30 cps printing speed with 60-cps bidirectional catch-up capability; (3) adjustable for 2, 3, 4, 6, 8, or 12 lines per inch; (4) 20-character nonvolatile answer-back capability; and (5) digital display for print position and status indication. (Courtesy of General Electric Company.)

switch that enables the device to be operated on-line or off-line. It can be placed in the line mode (on-line) and be connected directly to the CPU in order to transmit or receive data on-line. It can also be placed in the local mode (off-line) and operated as an ordinary electrical typewriter or as an off-line data storage device with a magnetic- or paper-tape facility. These ma-

Figure 2-19. Keyboard and terminal: Comm Center 1 and Terminal Systems, Model 43. The Comm Center 1 from Henriksen Data Systems offers both wire services (Telex and TWX) and telephone hookup (DDD). It receives and transmits messages via Telex, TWX, or DDD through Terminal Systems, Model 43. Standard features include nonvolatile keyboard programmable answer-back, keyboard dialing, 4K bytes of memory, and compatibility with high-speed printers. Expanding Comm Center 1 memory from its standard 4K-byte capacity to 8K, 12K, or 16K bytes can allow a user to pack more or longer messages into the machine for transmitting or receiving. (Courtesy of Heriksen Data Systems and Terminal Systems, Inc.)

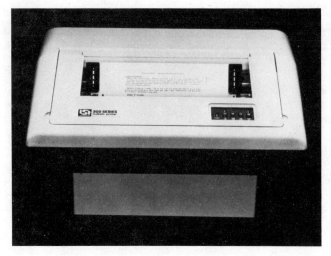

Figure 2-20. Printers: 300 Series Matrix Printers. The patented Ballistic print head on Lear Siegler's matrix printers is designed to significantly increase head life and operate at a 100% duty cycle. The 300 Series Ballistic printers are 180-cps bidirectional printers and are available with both serial and parallel interfaces. The 300 Series provides 14 switch-selectable form lengths, 14 perforation skip-over formats, and full horizontal and vertical tabulation control, plus character-compression buffers. (Courtesy of Lear Siegler/Data Products Division, Anaheim, Calif.)

chines can transmit data at rates of 10 to 30 characters per second. They cost from less than $1,000 to over $10,000.

Small Computer Card Readers

Several types of card readers (Figure 2-22) are designed specifically for use on small computer systems. They are smaller than units designed for larger computers, often small enough to fit on a tabletop. The principal use

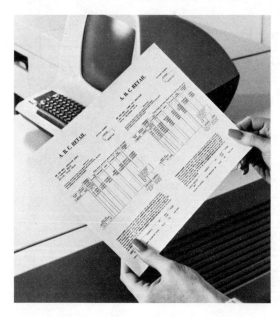

Figure 2-21. Printers: laser scanner in Xerox 9700 Electronic Printing System. Laser scanner in the Xerox 9700 electronic printing system projects images of both the form and all the information on it for simultaneous printing—in this case, two at a time. All images are created electronically, so choices of forms design and type styles are virtually unlimited. The system uses standard- size plain paper and prints at a rate of two pages a second. (Courtesy of Xerox Corp.)

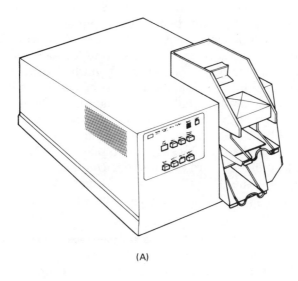

(A)

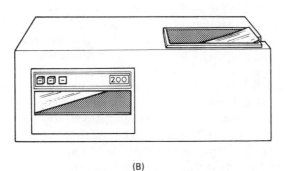

(B)

Figure 2-22. Small computer card readers. (A) Hewlett-Packard 7260A card reader. (B) The Model 200 from True Data Corporation reads at a speed of up to 200 80-column cards per minute. Capable of interfacing with most of the popular minicomputers, the 200 is one of the lower-priced members of True Data's line of punched-card readers, which includes manual-feed units as well as units rated at up to 1,000 cards per minute.

of the card reader is to transmit the information contained on the punched card directly into the memory or storage unit of the computer. This function can be accomplished at speeds ranging from 100 cards per minute to over 300 cards per minute in the small computer system. In comparison, a card reader for large computers can process as many as 2,000 cards per minute.

There are basically two kinds of punched-card readers: the wire-brush type and the photoelectric type. In the wire-brush type, the card is read row by row by a series of wire brushes, one for each card column. A punched hole is detected when a wire brush is pushed through a punched hole in the card and contacts the metal roller just below the card. In photoelectric card readers, cards are read column by column. A light source passes a beam of light through each card as it moves. If one or more holes is present in a column, the light beam falls upon a sensing device, emitting a pulse. If no hole is present, the light is blocked and no pulse is emitted.

The punched card is a familiar I/O medium. It is used to (1) provide data input to the CPU, (2) receive information output from the CPU, and (3) provide secondary off-line storage of data and information.

Small Computer Paper-Tape Reader/Punch

All types of paper-tape reader/punches provide a low-cost, convenient form of data storage and input/output. Punched paper tape, like punched cards, is a triple-purpose medium that is suitable for input, output, and secondary off-line storage. Small businesses frequently use paper tapes for adding machines, accounting machines, and cash registers. Certain types of paper tapes may be sent to computer centers, where they are used as input for computer-prepared reports and analyses. Small computer paper-tape readers (see Figure 2-23) provide a means of inputting programs and data to the CPU at speeds of between 10 and 300 cps. High-speed paper tape for larger computers can operate at speeds ranging from 200 to 1,000 cps, with those utilizing photoelectric reading. The reading operation is similar to that of punched cards. Sensing is accomplished at reading stations by the use of (1) electromechanical brushes or sensing pins, or (2) photoelectric cells. Generally, photoelectric reading is faster than the electromechanical sensing de-

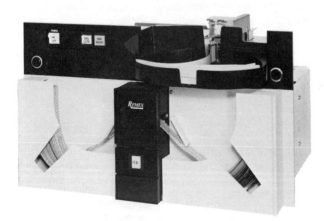

Figure 2-23. Punch/reader for small computers: Remex 6075 Series. The mechanism of the RAF 6075 Series perforator/reader punches five- and eight-track or six-track typesetter tapes at speeds up to 75 cps and bidirectionally reads tape with a thickness between 0.0026 and 0.0043 inch at speeds up to 300 cps sychronously. (Courtesy of Remex.)

vice. The process of punching paper is a relatively slow process (10 to 150 cps) when compared to the recording speeds of other output media.

Punched paper tape provides certain advantages. Paper tape is economical, lightweight, and easy to mail. It is a continuous-length medium, there is no upper-limit restriction on the length of records, and no wasted space when records are short. Tape thus provides greater data density than cards do. The equipment required for paper-tape punching and reading is small, light, relatively simple in design (thus reducing maintenance costs), and less expensive than comparable card machines.

But punched paper tapes have their disadvantages. Like cards, tape is easily torn and mutilated. Mylar and plasticized paper are sometimes used for tapes when extreme durability and tear resistance are required. Since it involves mechanically punching holes in tape, hardware failures are more apt to occur than in solid-state systems such as magnetic tape. It is more difficult to verify the accuracy of tape output than is the case with cards. Errors that are discovered cannot be corrected as easily as in the case of cards. An error in a card record requires repunching only one or a few cards, whereas an error in a tape means that the tape must be spliced or entirely repunched. Similarly, changes such as the addition to or deletion of records are more difficult to make with tape than with cards. These problems are the principal reasons that punched paper tape has not become a more widely used output medium.

2-2.4   Output Devices

Some recent small computer systems are able to support voice output in various human languages such as English, French, Spanish, and Japanese. There are also small systems that have the capability to draw maps and diagrams, and in some instances to plot tables and charts. However, the great majority of today's small computer systems include a printer as an essential output medium. In the beginning, small computers were equipped with printers adapted from large computer systems, but now various printers are designed specifically for small computer systems. They vary widely in speed, type, size, and price. The following section on printers is adapted from an excellent article in *Mini-Micro Systems* magazine, which can aid readers in selection of the "right" printer.

Printers*

A user can buy a printer from a distributor, systems house, a computer manufacturer, or directly from a printer manufacturer, but whatever his choice, he should first know what printer types are on the market, how they differ in performance and cost, and how to specify equipment to meet his needs. This section is intended to aid users to accomplish just that. It defines the basic printer categories, discusses specific selection criteria, and concludes with a summary of the techniques of printer imaging.

Printer Categories. One major classification of printers is the breakdown into impact and nonimpact printers. *Impact* printers transfer ink to paper in either of two ways. The front-striking mechanism operates like a typewriter: a character strikes a ribbon against paper to form an image. In hammer devices, a hammer strikes both the ribbon and paper against a character to form an image. *Nonimpact* printers generally use specially coated or sensitized papers that respond to thermal or electrostatic stimuli to form an image. Some use ink jets or xerography to form an image on plain paper.

Another major classification is between printers that employ *shaped characters* and those that use *matrix image formation.* Shaped characters are preformed alphanumeric symbols that strike or are struck by the ribbon and paper via a hammer mechanism. The characters can be carried on devices such as drums, chains, belts, daisy wheels, or type balls. Dot-matrix print heads use a number of print needles or ink jets to form alphanumeric symbols on the paper, with the pattern generated according to the character being formed. Some newer matrix printers employ a very fine matrix of dots—as many as 300 to the inch—producing characters that appear to the eye as shaped characters.

A final choice is between *serial printers* and *line printers.* The serial printer produces one character at a time, usually printing from left to right across a page, although units are now on the market that print in both directions. The line printer prints a group of characters simultaneously on the same line. The groups that constitute a line are printed so quickly that it appears that the entire line is printed at once. Line printers are generally faster than serial printers, but they are also more expensive.

The basic printer categories described above are combined in a variety of ways in different printers. For example, there is a shaped-character impact line printer, a shaped-character impact serial printer, a dot-matrix serial printer, and a dot-matrix nonimpact serial printer. Figure 2-24 summarizes the major selection criteria, and Figures 2-25 to 2-36 and accompanying text apply these to each major printer category.

When choosing a printer, the major selection criteria should include printer speed and cost, but the primary driving force should be the nature of the application. A 30-cps printer, for example, would be fast enough to be used in an interactive terminal but too slow to handle the volume of invoices and reports produced by the average small business system.

Any application should also dictate print quality. Clean, legible copy is a requisite in invoices, statements, and letters to customers. Lesser print quality may be acceptable if the printouts are only to be used internally.

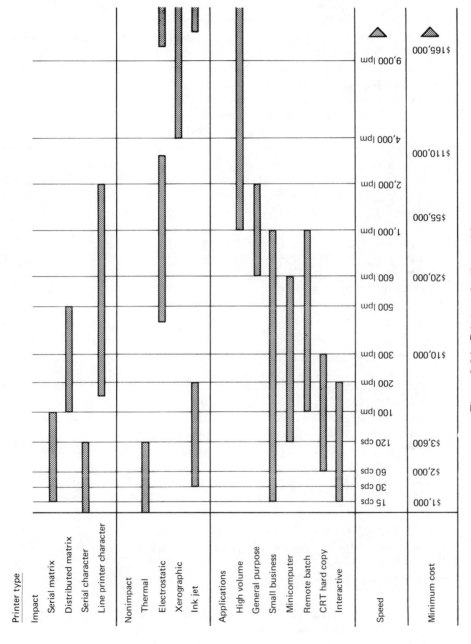

Figure 2.24. Printer selection guide.

45

Such considerations then boil the choice down to either a dot-matrix printer or a shaped-character unit.

Similarly, the nature of any application determines the level of reliability needed. Units with better reliability—increased mean time between failures or reduced mean time to repair—are invariably more expensive than less reliable units. At times, a user should consider purchasing two less expensive printers—for example, two 660-lpm printers instead of one 1,200-lpm unit—so that one can serve as a backup to the other.

Speed. Workload, obviously, determines the printer speed (the speed needed), which must be sufficiently fast to handle the data generated. But basing a purchasing decision on such a simplistic specification could lead to serious trouble. To save money, a user having a heavy workload might be tempted to purchase a printer intended for light-duty use. Such a printer, if overworked, might produce the required output, but the cost of replacing prematurely worn-out parts would soon offset any initial saving.

In data communications applications, print speed may be dictated by yet another consideration. A 30-cps printer may seem sufficient to handle one's output requirements, but if data are to be transmitted at a 1,200-baud rate, a 180-cps unit may be more appropriate, depending on the buffer capacity.

Price. The cost of printing includes not only the purchase price—$500 to $300,000—but also on the costs of maintenance and consumables: paper, preprinted or multipart forms; ribbons; and print heads. All of these items should be taken into account when computing the life-cycle cost prior to printer selection.

Vendor Support. A typical end user who buys only one or a few computer systems at most will probably deal with a systems house or a computer manufacturer. Most systems houses offer service on their printers, but in all likelihood the maintenance work will be carried out by a computer vendor. And any user who deals directly with a computer manufacturer will get a standard service contract that covers everything from the CPU to printers and terminals.

Only the largest end user—perhaps actually serving as an OEM (original-equipment manufacturer) group within a large company—will be able to purchase directly from a printer manufacturer. In this case, a user must be able to assume responsibility for spare parts, service, support, and interfacing.

Specific Printer Mechanisms. The following pages depict each printer category in diagrammatic form, describe its salient features, including its advantages and disadvantages, and list the price range and leading vendor.

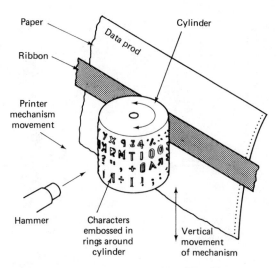

Figure 2-25. Cylinder print mechanism. (From Dataproducts Corp.)

Cylinder Printer (Figure 2-25). One of the first popular printers. A complete character set is embossed in a series of rings around the cylinder printing mechanism. The cylinder is rotated and shifted up and down on its axis to move the appropriate character into position; then a hammer strikes the cylinder.

Advantages: Cylinder printers are readily available and low in cost.

Disadvantages: Speed is low—only 10 cps. Reliability and print quality are not good; operation is very noisy.

Price: $1,000 to $2,000.

Leading supplier: Teletype Corp.

Golf-Ball Printer (Figure 2-26). An updated version of the cylinder printer; uses a spherical print mechanism. The sphere rotates on its axis to move the selected character into position, and the sphere itself strikes the paper.

Advantages: Excellent print quality; a large character set is accommodated; type fonts are interchangeable; costs are relatively low.

Disadvantages: Relatively low speed—up to 15 cps; fairly noisy in operation.

Price: $2,000 to $5,000.

Leading supplier: IBM Corp.

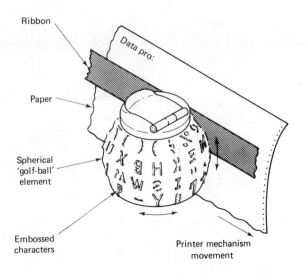

Figure 2-26. Golf ball print mechanism. (From Data-products Corp.)

Daisy-Wheel Printer (Figure 2-27). A set of spokes or arms, each with a single character embossed at its end, radiates from a wheel hub. The hub rotates to bring the desired character into position, where it is struck by a hammer mechanism.

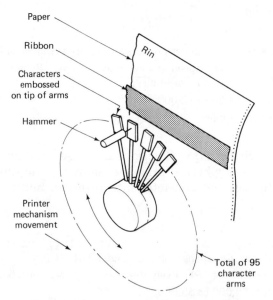

Figure 2-27. Daisy-wheel print mechanism. (From Dataproducts Corp.)

48

Advantages: Higher speed and reliability than cylinder and golf ball mechanisms: up to 30 to 55 cps; interchangeable type fonts; useful in word-processing systems where high print quality is needed.

Disadvantages: The golf-ball mechanism produces better print quality.

Price: $3,000 to $7,000.

Leading supplier: Diablo Systems, Inc.

Impact Matrix Printer (Figure 2-28).   Each symbol desired is formed from a pattern of small dots, and fonts are stored in ROM or PROM memory for character generation.   The print head in the serial printer consists of a vertical column of needle-hammers that move across a page while being selectively fired against the paper.   Print heads commonly have seven or nine needles arranged vertically, and the needles print from four to seven columns horizontally to form each matrix image.   Each complete sweep of the print head across the page produces a line of print.   In the line printer, a set of raised dots is mounted on a wide horizontal bar or comb device.   The bar slides from left to right in front of the paper, and individual needles strike each selected character dot to produce one row.   Complete characters are formed as the paper is moved to successive rows.   Vertical resolution varies from 70 to 100 points per inch; resolution improves with more needles in the print head.

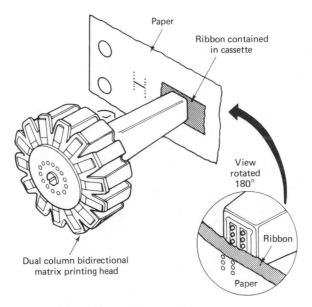

Figure 2-28. Matrix printing. (From Dataproducts Corp.)

Advantages: Some matrix printers have such fine resolution now that they appear to be printing with shaped characters; print fonts are easily changeable since character-generation patterns are stored in memory; some have graphics capability; speeds are higher than in many serial shaped-character printers; 30 to 330 cps (serial); up to 500 lpm (line).

Disadvantages: Dot-matrix characters formed with a sparse dot matrix can be hard to read; with high duty cycles, reliability drops on some print heads.

Price: $2,000 to $9,000.

Leading suppliers: Centronics Data Computer Corp. (serial); Tally Corp. (line).

Drum Printer (Figure 2-29).   A cylindrical drum, rotating at a constant speed, has a complete set of characters embossed around its circumference for each print position; a hammer strikes the required character at each print position each time the drum rotates on its horizontal axis. A position sensor linked to the hammers controls the firing of the hammers as the drum rotates. The impact must be timed precisely so that the character is brought into proper vertical position for printing on the paper without blurring, yet with sufficient density to be read easily.

Advantages: Very reliable operation; print speeds from 300 to 2,000 lpm; good cost/performance ratio for medium- to higher-duty-cycle applications.

Disadvantages: Limited choice of character fonts; possibility of vertical misregistration of characters, which produces wavy lines.

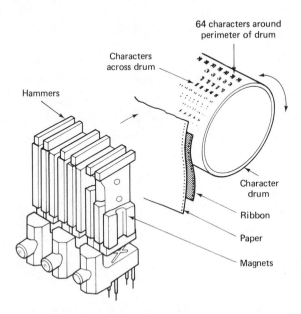

Figure 2-29. Drum printer mechanism. (From Dataproducts Corp.)

Price: $10,000 to $70,000.

Leading supplier: Dataproducts Corp.

Chain or Train Printer (Figure 2-30). An array of character slugs moves horizontally past a set of hammers—one hammer for each print position. Characters pass each hammer in sequence. In chain devices, slugs are connected and pull each other around a track. In train mechanisms, the slugs are not connected and they push each other around a track. In both cases, several complete character sets revolve horizontally at a constant speed. Hammers behind the paper fire precisely against each character to be printed as it rotates into position.

> *Advantages:* Good print quality; a variety of character sets is possible; character sets up to 128 characters can be accommodated; print speeds range up to 2,250 lpm.
>
> *Disadvantages:* The character-moving mechanisms are not as reliable as a drum, because of wear in the tracks.
>
> *Price:* $10,000 to $112,000.
>
> *Leading supplier:* IBM Corp.

Band and Belt Printer (Figure 2-31). One type of belt mechanism includes a tractor-type device in which horizontally rotating character slugs are struck by hammers situated behind the paper. Some units use a continuous steel or reinforced polyurethane belt that carries the characters that are impressed on the paper.

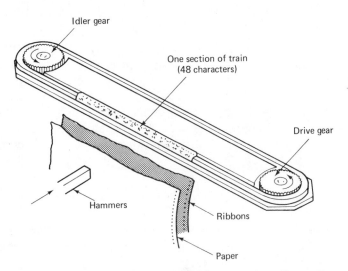

Figure 2-30. Train printer mechanism. (From Dataproducts Corp.)

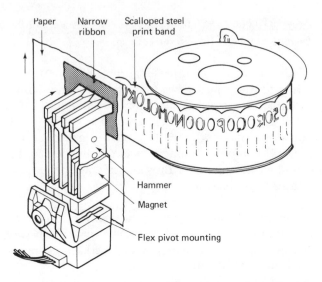

Figure 2-31. Band printing. (From Dataproducts Corp.)

Advantages: Easily interchangeable type bands for use of different character fonts; good print quality; high reliability; speeds range from 30 cps to 2,000 lpm.

Disadvantages: Some models are subject to belt and drive wear because of lubrication requirements; some have low print quality because of the hammer-mechanism design; entire steel belts must be replaced if individual characters are worn out.

Price: $3,000 to $87,000.

Leading suppliers: General Electric Corp. (low speed); IBM Corp. (high speed).

Thermal Matrix Printer (Figure 2-32).   A typical print head contains a 5 × 7 array of dot elements. As the print head moves horizontally across the specially coated paper, stopping at each column to print a character, selected elements in the array are heated; the paper changes color in the appropriate pattern for the character being generated. A different type of print head has only a vertical column of seven dot elements which scan and print each column and page, just like an impact dot-matrix print head. Print speed ranges from 30 to 100 cps.

Advantages: Very low cost; low noise level during operation; ideal for small, single-copy applications.

Disadvantages: Relatively slow speed for all but small applications; no multiple-copy capability; paper is coated or sensitized and expensive; no preprinted-forms capability.

Price: $1,000 to $5,000.

Leading supplier: Texas Instruments, Inc.

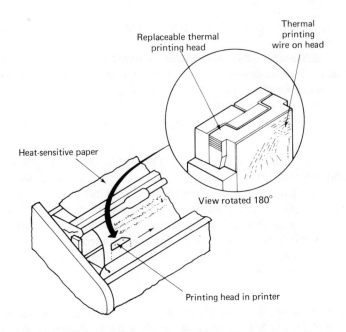

Replaceable thermal printing head

Thermal printing wire on head

Heat-sensitive paper

View rotated 180°

Printing head in printer

Figure 2-32. Thermal printing. (From Dataproducts Corp.)

Electrographic Printer (Figure 2-33).   A specially coated paper changes color when voltage is applied to the writing element. An electrolytic version uses a wet process in which moist paper is drawn between electrolytes. An electrosensitive version uses dry, layered paper. As the voltage is applied, the top layer burns away to expose the second, darker layer underneath in the desired image form.

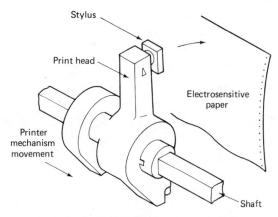

Stylus

Print head

Electrosensitive paper

Printer mechanism movement

Shaft

Figure 2-33. Electrographic printer mechanism. (From Dataproducts Corp.)

53

Advantages: Low prices; relatively high serial printer speeds—from 160 to 2,200 cps.

Disadvantages: The special paper required is expensive; no multiple copies are possible; the electrosensitive paper looks and feels like aluminum foil—it wrinkles easily and picks up fingerprints when handled.

Price: $600 to $3,000.

Leading suppliers: Scope Data, Inc. (low speed); SCI Systems, Inc. (high speed).

Direct Electrostatic Printer (Figure 2-34).   A specially coated paper is passed over an array of fine metal styli. Each stylus is selectively charged according to the output required and each character is formed by a mosaic of charged spots on the paper. The paper is then passed through a toner bath, where the charged areas attract ink particles. An alternative method of charging the paper uses a stylus that scans across the paper in contact with it. The voltage on the stylus is modulated according to the output desired and a character matrix is formed.

Advantages: Accommodates plotting as well as printing; versatility in printing fonts; lower prices than impact models of similar speeds; very high speeds possible—from 300 to 18,000 lpm.

Disadvantages: No multiple-copy capability; expensive paper; wet toner must be replenished periodically.

Price: $5,000 to $13,000 (low speed); up to $165,000 (high speed).

Leading suppliers: Versatec, Inc. (low speed); Honeywell Information Systems, Inc. (high speed).

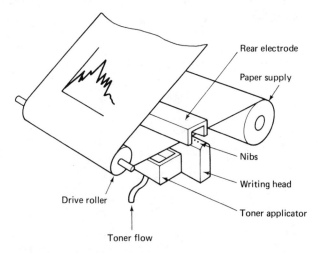

Figure 2-34. Electrostatic mechanism. (From Dataproducts Corp.)

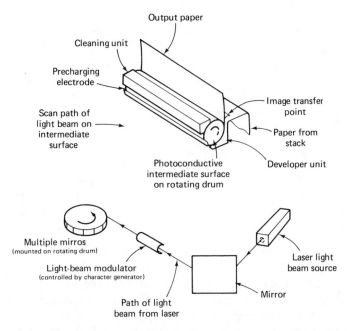

Figure 2-35. Laser xerographic mechanism. (From Dataproducts Corp.)

Xerographic Printer (Figure 2-35).   A latent image from a light source is created on an intermediate, photoconductive surface; the surface is toned with ink powder and the image is transferred electrostatically to the output paper and fused into place. One technique uses a light source and a photographic image to produce the latent image. In another approach, a laser beam is used to generate a high-quality dot-matrix character.

Advantages: Speeds range from 4,000 to 14,000 lpm; very high character resolution is possible; quiet operation; multiple combinations of character sets can be accommodated in the same line; forms can be printed simultaneously with text; 132-column-wide data can be printed on ordinary $8\frac{1}{2} \times$ 11-inch paper.

Disadvantages: No multiple-copy capability; a high level of maintenance is required to maintain copy quality; very high equipment costs; limited to high-volume applications.

Price: \$145,000 to \$310,000.

Leading suppliers: Xerox Corp. (low speed); IBM Corp. (high speed).

Ink-Jet Printer (Figure 2-36).   A controlled stream of ink droplets forms a desired image on paper. One system uses a horizontal bar with one hole per dot for the ink to pass through. Another scheme uses an on-demand ink-jet pump mechanism to produce ink images in a manner similar

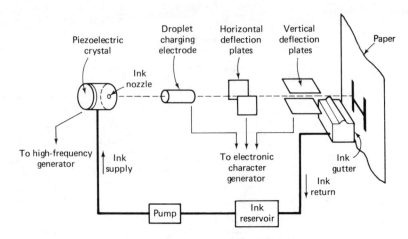

Figure 2-36. Ink jet mechanism. (From Dataproducts Corp.)

to dot-matrix needle arrays. In still another method, electric-field deflectors aim the droplets according to the image desired, deflecting the unneeded ink down into a gutter for recycling. With all three approaches, the dot structure determines the character formed, and the density of the dots—together with the degree of spattering of the ink—determines the clarity of the finished copy.

> *Advantages:* Dot-matrix character flexibility; quiet operation; very high print quality is possible; very high speed capability for large-volume printing, with speeds ranging from 72 cps to 45,000 lpm.
>
> *Disadvantages:* Copy quality is good at low speeds, poor at high speeds; no multiple-copy capability.
>
> *Price:* $5,000 to $25,000 (low speed); $5,800 per month (high speed).
>
> *Leading suppliers:* IBM Corp. (low speed); Mead Digital Systems, Inc. (high speed).

Checklist for Output Units (Printers)

1. Does the printer speed meet the report requirement needs? YES _____ NO _____

2. Does the vendor offer a serial (character) printer? YES _____ NO _____
   If yes, how fast can it print in characters per second?
   _____ cps

3. Does the vendor offer a line printer? YES _____ NO _____
   If yes, how fast can it print in lines per minute?
   _____ lpm _____ 100 lpm _____ 300 lpm
   _____ 600 lpm _____ 1,000 lpm or more

4. Does the quality of printing results meet the report requirements needs? YES ___ NO ___

5. Does the vendor offer a shaped-character printer (word-processing type) for high-quality printout? YES ___ NO ___

6. Does the vendor offer a dot-matrix printer (serial high-speed type) for lower quality printout? YES ___ NO ___

7. Can the system print reports while the user is inquiring information or entering data to the system? YES ___ NO ___

8. Can more than one printer be added to the existing system at the same time? YES ___ NO ___
   If yes, how many printers can be added? _____ printers   Minimum _____ printers   Maximum _____ printers

9. Does the vendor offer serial (character) printers and line printers? YES ___ NO ___

10. If the company's printing needs increase, can you replace a serial (character) printer with a line printer? YES ___ NO ___

11. Can the printer print multiple copies? YES ___ NO ___
    If yes, how many copies can it print? _____ copies   Minimum _____ copies   Maximum _____ copies

12. Does the printer provide both upper- and lowercase characters? YES ___ NO ___

Small Computer Plotters

Plotters convert digital values into graphic forms, such as lines, curves, and drawings. They can prepare a variety of graphic illustrations such as pictures, plots, bar graphs, and maps. Graphic plotters are generally of two types: (1) the pen-on-paper plotter, and (2) the electrostatic plotter. The pen-on-paper type of plotter draws each line or character at a time, and the plotting speed is a direct function of the amount of detail required in the drawing. The electrostatic plotter is identical to the alphanumeric electrostatic printer and differs from it only in terms of the addition of a graphics module, which allows the computer program to address each electrode individually. The plotting speed is a function of the paper movement and independent of the amount of information being plotted.

Low-cost pen plotters for small computer applications are either of the drum or flat-bed type (Figures 2-37 to 2-40). The most commonly used small computer plotters are of the drum type, where the vertical size of the plot is virtually unlimited. Most electrostatic plotters have a resolution of between 70 and 100 styli per inch, whereas pen plotters have resolutions ranging from 40 to 200 points per inch. More expensive, nonminicomputer

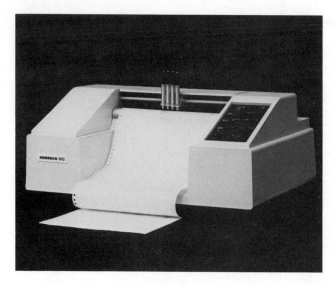

Figure 2-37. CalComp's Model 1012 Drum Plotter. CalComp's Model 1012 is a low-cost, high speed desktop drum plotter. It features a drawing speed of 10 inches per second, a resolution of 0.05 mm, four pens, and Z-fold paper 11 inches wide. Its microprocessor circuits improve operating efficiency to reduce time-sharing computer and transmission costs, making the Model 1012 ideal for remote or time-sharing environments. The plotter is compatible with the RS-232-C protocol and supports a variety of CRT terminals on-line. [Courtesy of CalComp (California Computer Products, Inc.).]

plotters have resolutions well beyond 1,000 points per inch. Several minicomputer manufacturers provide an off-the-shelf interface between a plotter and the mini. In summary, key plotter parameters are accuracy, repeatability, resolution, plot speed, size of plot (vertical and horizontal for flat-bed plotters), available minicomputer hardware interface, and plot subroutines [3].

Figure 2-38. CalComp's Model 1055 Drum Plotter. CalComp's Model 1055 drum plotter features a drawing speed of 76.2 cm (30 inches) per second, 4G acceleration, and 0.0125-mm (0.0005-inch) resolution. The plotter has four pens, allowing multiple line weights and colors within one plot without manual pen change, and scale factor adjustment, allowing for compensation for the expansion and shrinkage of plot media. Operator-selectable speed and acceleration, and return to last plotted position are standard. [Courtesy of CalComp (California Computer Products, Inc.).]

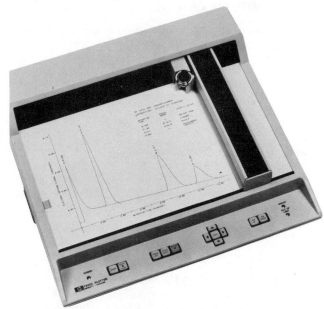

Figure 2-39. Hewlett-Packard's flat-bed-type plotter. (Courtesy of Hewlett-Packard.)

Figure 2-40. Hewlett-Packard's flat-bed-type plotter with desk-top computer. (Courtesy of Hewlett-Packard.)

2-3   COMPUTER CAPABILITIES AND LIMITATIONS

Before investing in a computer, you should be aware of what a computer can and cannot do. In general, a computer has the following capabilities:

1. *Arithmetic capability*. Digital computers have the capability of performing addition, subtraction, multiplication, and division, and of determining whether a number is positive, negative, or zero. Computers can perform arithmetic operations with nanosecond speed (billionth of a second). Human beings may need many days to solve a long mathematical equation, whereas a computer can solve such an equation in a fraction of a second. Computers are also able to handle huge volumes of repetitive and time-consuming work accurately over long periods of time, without tiring or complaining.

2. *Logic capability*. Digital computers can compare two numbers and decide whether one number is greater than, equal to, or less than the other. As a result of the comparison, computers can switch from one set of program instructions to another. With stored programs, and this logic capability, computers can perform required work without human intervention. The stored programs, however, must be prepared by a human being.

3. *Memory capability*. Digital computers can store (memorize) large volumes of information indefinitely. Human beings tend to forget items of information in days, but one can accurately retrieve information from a computer years from now.

4. *Multiple job processing capability*. Most minicomputers and large computers have the ability to process several jobs concurrently. This ability is referred to as multiprogramming or parallel processing. Two or more programs reside in primary memory at the same time and share the resources of the CPU (central processing unit). The extremely high speeds of the CPU make it appear that all the programs in primary memory are being executed simultaneously. Nevertheless, as long as there is only one CPU, the programs are being executed in sequence. Only one instruction can be executed at a time. The rapid switching of the central processing unit from one program to another program makes it appear that several programs are undergoing simultaneous execution.

5. *Remote job processing capability*. Today, many computers are designed to process information received from remote locations or to send information to remote locations. The telecommunication system is made possible by transmitting information from terminals to a remote computer through communications channels. With more emphasis being placed on broader and faster responding business information systems, the trend is toward greater use of remote job data transmission facilities. Communications processors (typically mini- or microcomputers) may be used for the following purposes: (a) remote concentration of messages, (b) message switching, and (c) front-end processing.

On the other hand, computers are subject to the following limitations:

1. *Computers cannot think.* Like any other inanimate object, a computer cannot think. Although the computer behaves like a highly efficient, fast, accurate, and intelligent "robot," it must be told when to start, stop, add and subtract, and so on. It must be instructed as to precisely what to do, at what time, and in what manner. Without proper direction, the most expensive computer is nothing but a helpless complex of components. Artificial-intelligence experts may disagree by saying that some "sophisticated" computers are capable of "thinking" by making decisions. But so far these activities are relatively limited and involve "thinking" in a very restrictive sense. Computers are still subject to human direction and control.

2. *GIGO (Garbage in, garbage out).* A computer can be no more accurate than the people who operate it, the instructions, and the data for their use. Computers can detect inaccurate data with edit programs, but generally cannot correct inaccurate data. Therefore, data fed into a computer must be accurate and complete. If the data are not clear or are not prepared properly, the results of processing will be largely wasted. Thus, it is essential to take every precaution to avoid input data errors.

3. *Physical limitations.* The main physical limitation of a computer is possible breakdown. Regardless of its electronic accuracy and speed, the computer is still a machine and is subject to an occasional breakdown. It has been estimated that up to 10% of scheduled computer time may be lost because of computer failure, power failure, maintenance time, or problems with related supportive hardware. In general, the number of breakdowns in microcomputers is less than in main-frame computers. One reason is that microcomputers have fewer connections. The degree to which something is likely to fail is directly related to the number of points that are connected to each other. When you have fewer LSI (Large Scale Integration) parts, the chance of failure should be lower. On the other hand, when you have a large number of parts, the chance of failure will be obviously greater.

Another physical limitation of a computer includes the space required by many computer systems, their supportive hardware, and the amount of wiring needed to link the system with its various components. Even though the size of microcomputers has been substantially decreased, all input and output peripherals are still required. The physical needs of the system and the availability of a suitable environment in which the system can function may become important physical limitations.

The computer's memory capacity traditionally puts a constraint on the speed of processing and the possibility of solving certain computer problems. Today, many computers have a large enough memory for solving basic problems and, if necessary, can be expanded simply by attaching another memory unit to the primary memory. The newest technology has contributed significantly to the decreasing price and increasing memory capacity, which alleviates many traditional memory constraints. However, the primary memory capacity of computers is still relatively limited when you consider the capacity of secondary mass storage devices such as disks. The memory-size limitation will remain with us until the primary memory capacity becomes compatible with the capacity of mass storage devices.

REFERENCES

[1] GEORGE SOLLMAN, "Where Are Floppy Disk Drives Going?" Shugart Associates Inc., *Mini-Micro Systems*, November 1978, p. 41.

[2] ANDREW ROMAN, "Winchester Boom to Broaden," Roman Associates International, *Mini-Micro Systems*, February 1980, p. 90.

[3] CAY WEITZMAN, Minicomputer Systems (Englewood Cliffs, N.J.: Prentice-Hall, Inc., 1974), p. 115.

3

SMALL COMPUTERS: MICRO-, SMALL BUSINESS, AND MINICOMPUTERS

3-1 WHAT IS A SMALL COMPUTER?

There is no generally accepted definition of the versatile small computer. Almost every authority who attempts a definition selects different criteria to differentiate between small computers and traditional computers. Indeed, some factors that have been used in defining a small computer appear too limited (e.g., one definition limits a small computer to less than 50 pounds; another defines a small computer as costing less than $15,000; etc.). Although it is difficult to define what a small computer is, it is rather easy to define what a small computer is not.

A small computer is not a pocket calculator. That is, it is relatively fast at making computations and can store and manipulate large complex programs. A calculator cannot handle such programs, at least yet. A small computer does not presently have a word size larger than 64 bits, nor does it cost more than $300,000, as do most medium-size and all larger computers—although pricewise it can be very difficult to draw the line between small and some medium-size computers. For all practical purposes, the small computer falls in the middle to low range of computer power, speed, and so on.

The term "small computer" denotes physical properties of some kind, and small computers can be distinguished from large computers by a number of limitations. Most people agree that the following factors are essential in categorizing computers:

Central processing unit capabilities
Memory capacity
Word length
Input/output capability
Complexity of the interface
Cost
Physical size
Overall speed

Moreover, the small computer can itself be segmented into subcategories: (1) the microcomputer, (2) the small business computer, and (3) the minicomputer (see Figures 3-1 and 3-2). This categorization is based on the charac-

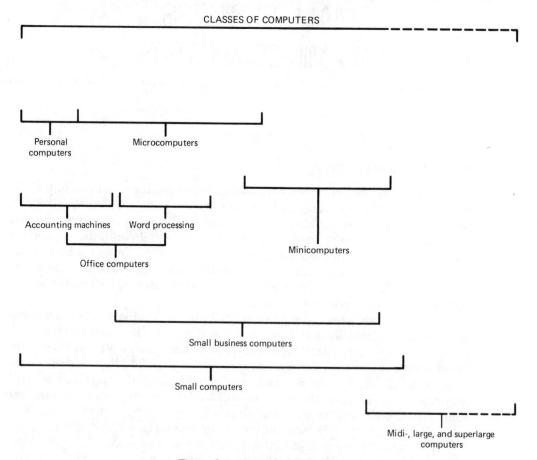

Figure 3-1. Classes of computers.

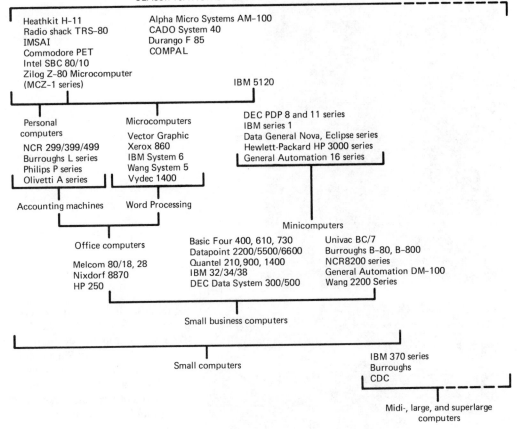

Figure 3-2. Classification of computer systems.

teristics and applications of the particular machine. Rapidly advancing technology renders specific definitions of the small computer almost impossible. Again, the most valid definitions might be achieved by considering application and function.

Despite the difficulty of giving specific definitions, an effort is made in the next section to define each of the three subcategories and describe at least the *typical computer* in each category.

3-1.1 Microcomputers and Small Personal Computers

A microcomputer can be distinguished from other types of computers by its major component, the microprocessor (see Figures 3-3 and 3-4). A microprocessor is a central processing unit (CPU) composed of a single or very limited number of integrated circuits(s) (ICs) on a small silicon chip. Additional circuits on this chip may also perform the functions of control, instruction

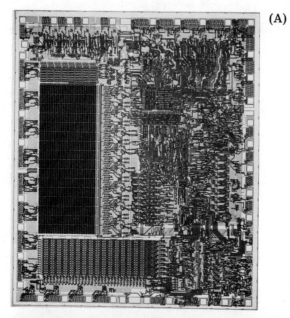

(A)

(B)

Figure 3-3. One-chip microcomputer. (A) Close-up of the Intel 8748 Single Chip Microcomputer, one of Intel's MCS-48 Single Chip Microcomputer family. Includes an 8K EPROM and 27 I/O's on one chip. (B) 8748 package on chip background. (Courtesy of Intel Corp.)

Figure 3-4. Computer Automation's Naked Mini LSI 4/10. The naked mini LSI 4/10 contains a complete minicomputer with processor, memory, and I/O on a half-card. The LSI 4/10 processor is a complete 16-bit computer, with up to 4K byte (character) of on-board RAM or RAM/PROM memory, four on-board I/O channels, and MAXI-BUS interface. 64K/128K bytes direct addressing is standard. The LSI 4/10 is fully upward-compatible (software and hardware) with all LSI 4 processors. (Courtesy of Computer Automation, Inc.)

TABLE 3-1
Examples of Microprocessors*

Manufacturer or Model Name	8-Bit-Type Model	16-Bit-Type Model
Intel	8080/8080A	8086
Motorola	6800/6802	6809
TI (Texas Instrument)	TMS 8080	TMS 9900
Zilog	Z80	Z8000
National Semiconductor	INS 8060	8900
Rockwell	PPS-8	MP-16
Mos Technology	MCS 6506/6506A	—
Data General	—	mN601
Fairchild Semiconductor	F8	F9440
Scientific Micro Systems	SMS-300	—
Signetics	2650	—
Mostek	F8, Z80	—

*The above list of microprocessors is not meant to be complete in any way. Instead, it provides a partial list for comparative purposes.

decoding, and execution, as well as input/output. Microcomputers also feature additional supporting circuitry, such as memory, input/output (I/O) interfacing, DMA* logic interrupt, and real-time clocks. The two microcomputer types are:

1. An entire computer, including CPU, memory, and input and output capability, incorporated into a single IC,
2. A computer that incorporates a microprocessor as its major component, with the addition of general memory and input and output circuits.

To distinguish between the two microcomputer types, the former is called a "one-chip" microcomputer.

Microprocessors may be further categorized as follows:

1. 4-bit calculating or instrument-type microprocessor for very small processing functions, such as a calculator or a small on-line instrument.
2. 8-bit general-purpose microprocessor. This is the most typical type of microprocessor (see Table 3-1).
3. 16-bit processor resembling a minicomputer (see Table 3-1).
4. 32-bit processor resembling a main-frame computer. (It is speculated that this processor will be able to handle a main-frame computer operating system. It will be slow, but it will run under a microcomputer.)

In other words, the basic internal data and information paths within the microprocessor chip are "4-bit slice," "8-bit CPU," "16-bit CPU," and

*DMA (direct memory access) is a valuable capability of the processor which allows the I/O to proceed concurrently with, and independently from, its own processing.

"32-bit CPU." These indicate whether the microprocessor works with "slices" of data and/or instruction words to form whole words or uses all the bits of a word at one time. Whole-word CPU architecture has the advantage of being similar to minicomputer or main-frame architecture, and is growing in popularity. Bit-slice architecture has an earlier origin and can be used to create a custom CPU with a word length that is some integral multiple of the bit-slice width. Any number of instructions can be implemented with these very flexible microprocessors [2].

The microprocessor itself, however, represents but a small part of the system. In most configurations, the CPU chip represents less than 10% of the total cost. The remainder is in memory and interface electronics to receive input and produce output. That, in turn, may represent less than half the total installed cost by the time power supplies, packaging, and cooling are added to the list. Often, a $5 chip forms the heart of a $1,000 computer.

As a result of the differences in design and organization, the assembly language for many microcomputers differs significantly from that of minicomputers. Most microcomputers have a resident assembler available from the vendor.

As for higher-level program development languages, there is a language called PL/M. It is written in the FORTRAN IV language and runs on any 32-bit host computer. It helps software designers to use existing systems to develop software for their microcomputer systems [2]. PL/M was originally designed by Intel to aid in developing software for the 8008 microprocessor systems and later was modified for the popular 8080 and 8080A. Standard programming languages are being reworked for use. Therefore, many of the microcomputer systems are not restricted to low-level programming languages. BASIC has been available for many of the systems for some time. COBOL, FORTRAN and PASCAL compilers have also been available for a few years. RPG will follow soon.

Microcomputers are developing along much the same lines as minicomputers and the earlier large mainframes. That is, the same types of operating software, development software, and applications software are being created; common types of interfaces are appearing, and peripherals of appropriate scale are being introduced. However, software utilities for microcomputers are still limited. It is almost the same situation that minicomputers were in a decade ago. Software to run multi-minicomputer networks is generally well established, whereas software to handle multi-micro-CPU configurations has only recently begun to be developed. Operating systems (OSs) for microcomputers also need reworking. CPM is still the leading OS for microcomputers.

The guidelines for microcomputers described above are generally useful, but microcomputer capacities and figures are being constantly upgraded by the vast technological advances occurring in this yet-infant market. Therefore, readers should be aware of rapid changes in the areas of microproces-

sors, the capacities of their memories, the capacities of disks, and input/
output (I/O) devices. An amazing example is the microprocessor (CPU of
microcomputer) prices. During the last few years, the price of microprocessors has decreased at the rate of about 100% per year. It started around
$300 in 1971, and has gone down to $3 (in quantities of 100) in recent
years. Further price reductions are expected to continue.

Microcomputer system price reductions have not been as great as those
for microprocessors. Price decreases for microcomputers as a whole have
been 10 to 20% in the past years. This rate will probably continue for some
time to come.

Microcomputer products currently available include:

1. Prefabricated microcomputers, configured much like minicomputers, that have
   their power, packaging, and cooling preinstalled. Examples include the PCC
   Altair 8800B and DEC's PDP-11/05.
2. Development systems, converted to end-application use, such as Motorola's
   EXORciser or Intel's MDS 800.
3. Single-board computers (SBCs), or modular card sets, from which one can configure virtually any size computer. The DEC LSI-11, Intel SBC 80 series, or
   Pro-Log's PLS series or cards are typical products.
4. Kits from which custom designs can be adapted. Kits are available from Heath-
   kit, semiconductor makers, and electronic parts distributors.
5. Custom designs, based on popular microprocessors such as the 8080A or 6800.
6. Custom, high-volume, one-chip microcomputer systems—Fairchild's F8 or Texas
   Instruments' TMS 1000 series, for example—which have program, data storage,
   input and output on one or two chips, along with the CPU [1].

In the last few years, stores that market microcomputers and microcomputer kits have opened in many American cities and towns. The profit
to be made from the sale of microcomputers (personal computers) is much
smaller than that involved with the larger computers (Figure 3-14). To make
their business profitable, these stores have to sell their machines in large volume to make up for the small profit per unit. The marketing of the Radio
Shack microcomputer through their chain stores is a good example of such
volume sales. These small computer manufacturers and outlets have to develop methods that will enable them to sell computers by the thousands. In
the near future, these microcomputer manufacturers may perfect a true
turnkey microcomputer system, so that their users will not have to worry
about programming or repair problems. When this happens, these turnkey
systems will be sold over the counter just like typewriters. A recent survey
[2] indicates that a large number of microcomputers are being introduced in
the small business environment, and their numbers are growing rapidly (see
Figures 3-5 to 3-13.) Many personal computer manufacturers are shifting
their emphasis toward small business computers. According to an SBA

Figure 3-5. Microcomputers: Xerox 860 office computer. Modular design of Xerox 860 information-processing system permits growth to handle a wide range of text-editing applications and processing of office business records and data. Five optional disk storage configurations allow it to hold up to 4,800 pages of material. A wide carriage printer is one of several optional peripheral modules. Optional software packages available with the system extend user information-processing capabilities. (Courtesy of Xerox Corp.)

(Small Business Administration) survey, there are 13 million small businesses in the United States. However, the number of small businesses that can afford $10,000 to $30,000 for a computer system is less than 13 million. Therefore, small computer manufacturers should be aware that the margin of

Figure 3-6. Microcomputers: personal computing for professionals—the HP-85. This Hewlett-Packard computer, designed for personal use in business and industry by professionals, features a central processor, typewriter-like keyboard with 20-key numeric pad, CRT display, thermal printer, cartridge tape drive, enhanced BASIC language, and interactive graphics in a fully integrated system the size of a portable electric typewriter. (Courtesy of Hewlett-Packard.)

Figure 3-7. Microcomputers: APPLE I, II, and III professional/personal computers. The APPLE III professional computer system is available with built-in disk drive, calculator-style numeric pad, keyboard, clock/calendar, serial (RS232) and Apple Silentype thermal printer interfaces, and 96K bytes (characters) of RAM (128K bytes optional). A second Apple Disk III disk drive and a 12-inch black-and-white high-resolution video monitor are also available. Apple's Software System supports their SOS (sophisticated operating system). Apple Business BASIC, Mail List Manager, and VisiCalc III. (Courtesy of Apple Computer, Inc.)

profit from sales of small business computers is limited and the small business market is finite. In any event, small businesses obviously have a need for small computers.

3-1.2 Small Business Computers

Although one might infer that the "small business computer" is designed solely for small businesses, it would be more accurate to consider it as a scaled-down general-purpose computer system capable of performing standard business data-processing operations in a stand-alone mode (i.e., without communication links to other computers). It can perform accounts receivable, accounts payable, general ledger, purchase order, inventory, payroll, and financial reporting tasks.

A small business computer (SBC) is a sophisticated electronic office machine that processes data and produces reports for users who are not necessarily computer specialists. Data may be entered by nonspecialists and are processed by a combination of user commands and stored programs. A small business computer can help a small business manager cut labor costs and gain tighter controls over operations and all the other increasing costs and complexities of doing business. Although the majority of users are small business people, it is entirely possible for a division of a large corporation to use a

71

(A)

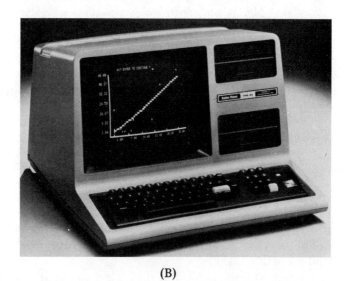

(B)

Figure 3-8. (A) and (B). Radio Shack Model TRS-80-I and TRS-80-III personal and business computers. Model I is the original TRS-80, and TRS-80 Model III is a new personal and small business computer. Radio Shack offers many types of software packages, including various business applications, personal programs and games, and word-processing capability with SCRIPSIT. The TRS-80 Model I consists of the processor (Z80), main memory (4K to 48K bytes), cassette, $5\frac{1}{4}$-inch disk drive (up to 4 drives of 98K bytes each) and printer. (Courtesy of Radio Shack, a Division of Tandy Corp.)

Figure 3-9. Radio Shack TRS-80 Model II microcomputer. The Radio Shack TRS-80 Model II microcomputer system is their top-of-the-line small business computer. Radio Shack offers business-related software for accounting functions, plus SCRIPSIT word processing. Language options available with the TRS-80 Model II include Assembler, COBOL, FORTRAN, a BASIC interpreter, and a BASIC compiler. The system consists of the processor (Z80-A), main memory (32K or 64K bytes), disk storage (one to four 8-inch disk drives) (500K each), and printer (120 cps). The printer's bidirectional head prints 9 $\times$ 7 dot-matrix upper- and lower-case letters. (Courtesy of Radio Shack, a Division of Tandy Corp.)

small business computer for its data-processing needs with better cost effectiveness than that afforded by a large central computer.

The SBC, both in price and performance, fills the gap between the two extremes of conventional accounting machines and medium-scale computer systems and is known by various names, such as business microcomputer, electronic accounting machine, office computer, word processing computer, business computer, or business minicomputer. These names are all synonyms for "small business computer."

Figures 3-15 to 3-26 illustrate typical SBC systems. The basic elements of a small business system are the same as those of a large system: the input, the processor with control or logic, memory (storage), and the output. However, the size, speed, and costs are quite different for small and large systems.

Today's SBC system typically consists of a keyboard/CRT unit for input, a processor with about 64K bytes of memory for the logic and control, a disk unit for the storage, and a serial printer.

Most systems provide sufficient storage capacity to perform calculations on a file of data with additional space for instructions that constitute application and system programs. With additional disk storage, a SBC can expand its performance and applications in such areas as accounts receivable, accounts payable, inventory controls, purchase order, job costing, and production control.

As for operating characteristics, the cycle time of the main storage ranges from a few microseconds to less than 0.0001 microsecond (100 nanoseconds; ns). The adding time of the processor ranges widely from over 200

(A)

(B)

Figure 3-10. (A) CBM (Commodore Business Machine); (B) PET (personal/professional computer). "Business" System, the 8032 Model computer. Commodore manufactures two series of computers. One series is their business-oriented computer under the name CBM (Commodore Business Computer), with full typewriter keyboard and special functions, and the other is their personal/professional computer under the name PET, with graphic characters printed on the fronts of the keys. In addition to the original 40-column, upper/lowercase computer, Commodore also offers an 80-column "business" system, the 8032 Model computer. This computer is provided with WORDPRO, a word-processing system, and is also used with such business-oriented software as VISICALC. (Courtesy of Commodore International Ltd.)

(A)

Figure 3-11. Microcomputers: portable computer systems. (A) Durango F-85 desktop computer. The Durango F-85 basic system comes with one dual diskette drive (storage capacity 946,000 bytes (characters)), one bidirectional matrix printer (speed 165 cps), one video display unit, and 64K characters of main memory. The system can be expanded to four additional video display terminals and 10 to 20 million characters of storage capacity fixed disk. Various small business application programs are available. (B) Durango F-85 desktop data processing system. (Courtesy of Durango and California Business Systems.)

(B)

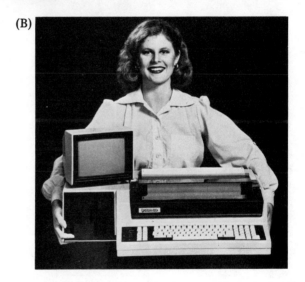

Figure 3-12. Microcomputers: portable computer systems. FINDEX— a portable computer with bubble memory ($\frac{1}{2}$ million bytes inside the case), built-in mini floppy diskette drive (200K to 400K bytes), built-in dot-matrix impact printer, and keyboard. Small business application programs are available. (Courtesy of Findex.)

Figure 3-13. Microcomputers: portable computer. The portable desktop computer, Hewlett-Packard System 45B. (Courtesy of Hewlett-Packard.)

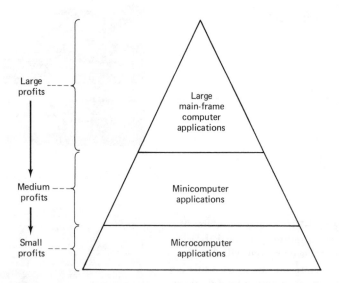

Figure 3-14. Trends and profits related to computer applications.

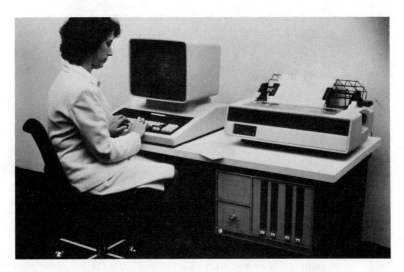

Figure 3-15. Small business computers: The Cromemco System. The Cromemco System is based on the Zilog Z-80A microprocessor with 32K bytes of RAM memory and two 8-inch floppy disk drives. Optional additions include up to 64K bytes of ROM, up to 64K bytes of ultraviolet-erasable PROM, RS-232 interfaces, disk, printer, analog-to-digital and digital-to-analog converters, BASIC, COBOL and FORTRAN compilers. (Courtesy of Cromemco and Adventures in Computing.)

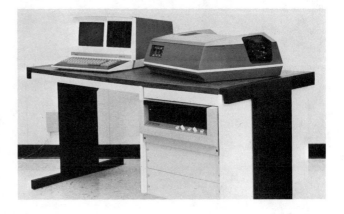

Figure 3-16. Small business computers: The Zilog MCZ-1. The Zilog MCZ-1 systems feature the use of the Z80 microprocessor and its 158-instruction set, a disk-based operating system, main storage capacity for up to 65K bytes of semiconductor memory, and two integral floppy disk drives. (Courtesy of Zilog.)

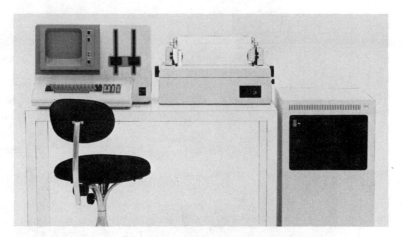

Figure 3-17. Small business computers: IBM System 5120. The IBM System 5120 comes with two internal diskette drives for recording and storing data on removable diskettes. Each diskette holds up to 1.2 million bytes (characters) of information, giving the system a built-in on-line capacity of up to 2.4 million bytes. An optional diskette unit can be included with the system, giving a total storage capacity of 3.6 or 4.8 million bytes of information. The main storage capacity ranges from 16,384 to 65,536 bytes. Either of two optional tabletop printers comes with the system. They can print at speeds up to 80 or 120 cps. This system offers a choice of BASIC and/or APL languages. (Courtesy of International Business Machines Corp.)

Figure 3-18. Small business computers: desktop computer system, the PCC 2000. The PCC 2000 is a business computer system totally contained in one unit, which includes the central processor (8085 CPU), detached, typewriter-like keyboard, 64K bytes of random-access memory, built-in video display screen, and 1.2 megabytes (million characters) of floppy disk storage. PCC's Multi-Terminal Executive, MTX, provides the PCC 2000 business computer with a business BASIC operating system which allows up to five users concurrent access to the processing power. CP/M, COBOL-80, FORTRAN-80, and other utilities are also available. (Courtesy of Pertec Computer Corp.)

78

Figure 3-19. Small business computers: J100 video computer, word processing and data processing. AM Jacquard's J100 video computer, a shared-logic small business computer, and a peripheral character printer are shown in foreground. Two satellite CRT terminals that directly access the J100's central memory are shown in the background. (Courtesy of Jacquard Systems.)

Figure 3-20. Small business computers: Basic Four 200, 410, 610, 730. The Basic System 200 represents the smallest system in the Basic Four line. It features a standard CPU with 32K bytes of memory, one 10-megabyte disk unit, one video display terminal, a 120-cps printer, and a 2.5-megabyte magnetic tape cartridge unit. A System 200 can be expanded to include up to 40K bytes of memory, 20 megabytes of disk storage, and two VDTs. (Courtesy of Basic Four, Inc.)

Figure 3-21. Small business computers: Qantel 210, 900, 950, 1400, Series 100, 200, 300. This basic System 950 represents the midway point in Qantel's product line. It consists of a standard CPU, 8K bytes of user memory, a 6 million-byte disk drive, a 1728-character CRT terminal, and a 45 or 120-cps serial printer. Expansion capabilities include a maximum of 16 terminals, four separate jobs, 12 million bytes of disk storage, two line printers, one magnetic-tape drive, and 64K bytes of user memory. (Courtesy of Qantel Corp.)

Figure 3-22. Small business computers: Small Business System by Digital Equipment Corporation. The DEC Datasystem 408 is engineered specifically for small business applications by Digital Equipment Corporation. The processor, housed in the display terminal at center, is a micro adaptation of the PDP-8 minicomputer. Its memory size is 32K bytes. Below the display terminal is a dual-diskette mass storage unit of 1 megabyte capacity on two spindles. The data printer at the left uses the dot-matrix printing technique to achieve a speed of 180 cps for tabular data listing. The printer at the right is a formed-character letter-quality printer, which affords a variety of type styles and special symbols. (Courtesy of Digital Equipment Corp.)

Figure 3-23. Small business computers: Alpha Micro Computer. The Alpha Micro Operating System (AMOS) is a disk-based operating system that employs floppy and/or hard disks. The Alpha Micro AM-1030 system can support a dual floppy disk drive, a 10-megabyte hard disk, and a 300-megabyte disk drive with up to four drives. The system can support multiple terminals. Multiuser, multitasking features of the time-share operating system enable many users to access the system simultaneously. The system allows several different jobs to run concurrently from different terminals. (Courtesy of Alpha Microsystems.)

Figure 3-24. Small business computers: Melcom 80/18. The main memory of MELCOM Model 80/18 is expandable to 96K bytes, with disk storage available from 0.5 to 40 million bytes. Up to four additional user terminals can be added. The integrated printer operates at 120 cps with an optional 600 lpm unit available. Small business application programs are available. (Courtesy of Mitsubishi Electronics of America, Inc.)

Figure 3-25. Small business computers: Cado System 20/24. Cado's operating system is permanently resident on ROM and supports a user program. It has 1.23 million bytes in standard storage capacity. The Winchester disk drive provides mass storage and is available from 13.2 million to 52 million data characters. The printer operates at 150 cps. Small business application programs are available. (Courtesy of Cado Systems and Benchmark Data Systems.)

Figure 3-26. Small business computers: Astra System Model 205. The main memory of the Astra System Model 205 is 128K bytes (characters) with floppy disk storage and a printer. Up to four additional terminals can be added. BASIC, COBOL, and Macro-Assembler languages are available. Small business application programs are available. (Courtesy of NEC Information Systems, Inc.)

milliseconds (ms) to less than 0.0002 ms (200 ns). There is a difference in calculation speed between different machines.

The rate of speed of the associated input devices will usually range from about 10 to 200 cps, and while the rate of output speed will typically range from about 10 to 500 cps.

There are more than 200 SBC models manufactured and more than 1000 independent vendors marketing them. Approximately half of the manufacturers also vend their own computers (see Figures 3-27 to 3-31). In price and performance the SBCs span a wide range. The purchase prices of these computers range from $5,000 to $100,000 and they differ greatly in their architecture, data formats, I/O equipment, and supporting programs.

As you will see in Section 3-1.3, the price range of both SBCs and minicomputers can be similar. In fact, some manufacturers utilize the same inter-

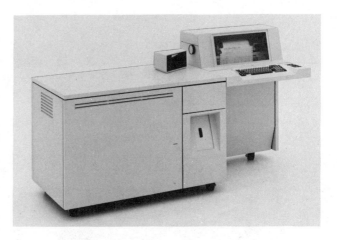

Figure 3-27. Small business computers by main-frame manufacturers: IBM System 32. The IBM System 32 is an entry-level business computer. The basic system includes 16K bytes (characters) of main memory, a nonremovable moving-head disk drive, a diskette drive, a serial matrix or line printer, and a keyboard and display unit. (Courtesy of International Business Machines Corp.)

Figure 3-28. Small business computers by main-frame manufacturers: IBM System/34. The IBM System/34 offers various combinations of display stations and printers. The IBM 5251 (1,920 characters) and 5252 dual display stations (local or remote environment) and 5256 printers (40 cps to 300 lpm) can be attached either to the central processor (via Twinax cable up to 5000 ft away) or to a remote display station. The System/34 is available in preconfigured models with a specified amount of diskette (240K to 962K bytes per diskette) and high-capacity fixed disks for auxiliary storage. Additional data can be kept on IBM diskettes with capacities as high as 1.2 million bytes per diskette and 10 diskettes per magazine. The System/34 has language options which include System/34 BASIC, COBOL, FORTRAN, and RPG II. (Courtesy of International Business Machines Corp.)

Figure 3-29. Small business computers by main-frame manufacturers: Univac BC/7. The BC/7 business computer is designed to fill the needs of first-time computer users and those using accounting machines. The three series of BC/7 are the diskette-based BC/7-600; the cartridge-disk-based BC/7-700; and the BC/7-800 multiprogramming series. The BC/7-700 systems are cartridge-disk-based and can also utilize magnetic tape for file storage and I/O, as well as diskettes for I/O. The 3048 processor of the BC/7-800 supports up to 128K bytes of MOSFET memory and up to six work stations. The BC/7 is oriented primarily toward interactive operation. The system runs under an operating system designated as the Interactive Operating System (IOS). Application programs for users are written in UNIVAC, RPG II, or ESCORT. (Courtesy of Sperry-Univac.)

nal hardware for both their "SBC" and "minicomputer" systems, although the outer packaging sometimes varies. The manufacturer-vendors have utilized these popular names for their small business systems primarily for marketing purposes, even though their particular systems (small business and minicomputer) consist of the same basic hardware (see Figures 3-32 to 3-33).

Although some minicomputers are used as small business computers and have many similar capabilities, as explained above, there are often very definite and important differences among them. Minicomputers tend to be more expensive and are generally purchased when rapid response is of primary importance, whereas SBCs are usually purchased by unsophisticated users to whom ease of programming is considerably more important than arithmetic speed. Auerbach [3] has found that marketing emphasis also determines the following general differences between minicomputers and SBCs:

1. The instruction sets of minicomputers tend to consist of rapid instructions for elementary arithmetic and logical operations; instructions in SBCs are generally slower, but include more elaborate instructions for such operations as character handling and decimal arithmetic.

2. Minicomputers require more programming for input/output control; autonomous input/output transfers are generally provided on a limited scale as optional

Figure 3-30. Small business computers by main-frame manufacturers: NCR 8140 System. The NCR 8140 small business system combines a microprocessor (memory 48K to 128K bytes) and video display (12 inches, 24 lines, 1,920 characters) in a small, compact tabletop cabinet with a cable-connected keyboard, a free-standing flexible disk (242, 944 bytes per diskette; 905, 216 bytes per diskette; up to four drives), and a visual record printer (130 to 180 cps). Optionally, it offers a high-speed printer for multipage reports (50 to 200 lpm) and data cassettes (160,000 characters, maximum for 280-ft cassette) for more flexibility in information processing and data storage. The system operates interactively. (Courtesy of NCR Corp.)

features for minicomputers. In small business computers, autonomous input/output transfers are the norm and more sophisticated features permitting the execution of a sequence of input/output operations with a single instruction are usually included as well.

3. The prices of SBCs compared to those of minicomputers necessarily reflect the manufacturer's increased marketing costs, associated with the sales and support needs of unsophisticated users.

The advantages of a small business computer, in contrast to the large computer, is increased responsiveness of the EDP function to the users' needs by providing data entry and inquiry capability on a local level. Thus, the local manager is more involved with, and has more control over, the firm's data and information system. Data processing occurs when company operations are performed; consequently, data-processing tasks can be performed more quickly and efficiently.

3-1.3 Minicomputers

In the 1960s, the word "minicomputer" became a popular term to categorize a growing number of small computers. At the time these machines were

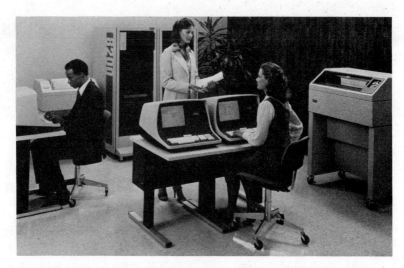

Figure 3-31. Small business computers by main-frame manufacturers: NCR 8250 System. The NCR 8250 processor is a 16-bit word mini-computer with 64K bytes of MOS (metal–oxide–semiconductor) memory, expandable in 16K-byte increments to a maximum of 128K bytes (64,000 words). The processor and memory are housed in a high-boy cabinet measuring 24 by 36 by 60 inches. The NCR 8250 System can contain one or two integrated magnetic-tape cassette handlers and one or two integrated disk drives capable of storing up to 9.8 megabytes of data each. A basic system includes an operator's CRT (12-inch screen, 1,920 character screen capacity, 9,600 bps local) and a matrix printer (50 lpm, 132-column line). Additional disk units can be included in the system, providing a maximum of 80 million bytes of storage for large file applications. (Courtesy of NCR Corp.)

introduced, the cost of most basic computer systems was less than $25,000. These minicomputers contained 4K- to 8K-word core memory using the Assembly language and FORTRAN. Application programs were very limited in the areas of data acquisition, numerical control, and communications.

In the mid-1970s, DOSs (disk operating systems) became commonplace, and many features of mainframe computer systems were adapted for standard minicomputer systems. Today, the term "minicomputer" no longer defines size, price, or performance, because the dynamic nature of the computer industry does not allow for static design. Any such definition must be flexible, changing as the minicomputer industry responds to technological and market opportunities in innovative ways. Especially innovative is the way in which minicomputers have been used in building several other large minicomputers, and multiple microprocessors have been used in some minicomputers, with each microprocessor performing a different system function within the CPU of the minicomputer.

Figure 3-32. Small business computers with minicomputer hardware: The DEC Datasystem 500 family. The DEC Datasystem 500 family is based on the 16-bit PDP 11 line. DEC Datasystem 500s are small business computers aimed at the "self-sufficient" user capable of doing the application software in-house. The Datasystem 500 family currently includes a broad array of packaged systems built around DEC's PDP 11/34A, 11/60, and 11/70 processors. The Datasystem 500s can support up to 4 million characters of main memory, 64 terminals, and 1.5 billion bytes (characters) of disk storage. (Courtesy of Digital Equipment Corp.)

According to Norman S. Zimbel of Arthur D. Little, Inc., a basic description of the "minicomputer-based business systems" includes the following:

1. Data-entry systems such as key to tape, key to disk, magnetic and optical character recognition, as well as batch- and transaction-oriented intelligent terminals.

2. Billing and accounting machines capable of off-line and on-line operation.

3. General-purpose processing systems for batch- and/or transaction-oriented processing, which may support multiple terminals and be operated either off-line or on-line in distributed processing networks.

4. Word- and text-processing machines for secretarial use or for use in publishing.

5. Computer-generated microfilm for archival storage or for support of microfilm fast-access transactions.

6. Building blocks for data networks, such as intelligent terminals, data concentrators or multiplexors, communications front ends, PABX, and arrays of minicomputers for the data-processing function.

To be more specific, a typical minicomputer has a 16-, 18-, 24-, or 32-bit word length with a memory size from 64K to 512K in modules of 4K to 8K

Figure 3-33. Small business computers with minicomputer hardware: General Automation, InstaCode 20. A typical InstaCode 20 packaged system includes a GA-240 processor with 128K bytes (characters) of memory, a 10-megabyte (million characters) cartridge disk drive, three 1920-character CRT terminals, and a 300-lpm line printer. Additional peripherals, such as 1,600-bpi/45-ips magnetic-tape units and 400-cpm card readers, are available as options. (Courtesy of General Automation, Inc.)

increment. They cost less than $300,000, with the basic equipment costing between $20,000 to $150,000. The standard peripheral equipment consists of the following: CRT, terminals, floppy disk (diskette) drives, disk pack/cartridge drives or Winchester disk, line printer, magnetic-tape cassettes or cartridges or $\frac{1}{2}$-inch magnetic tape, and data communications interface.

The memory size determines the complexity and size of programs the computer can run and the type of software that can be supported. Some minicomputer memories can be expanded to 3 megabytes (3 million characters), but the typical minicomputer offers from 64,000 to 512,000 bytes of memory. It usually features both parity check and memory protect, although these features may be optional at extra cost. If you consider parity check (for checking data accuracy) and memory protection (for preventing important data from being inadvertently erased or modified) to be important features, you may add these to most of today's minicomputers.

The primary developments in central processors and internal memories have been a result of advances in LSI semiconductor technology. The major impact to date comes from the availability of MOS LSI semiconductor memories. Several machines have been offered with memories using 1,024-bit P-channel MOS chips. These are faster than some of the core memories and provide lower cost in small capacities. However, the 4,096-bit N-channel

MOS chip is having an impact on minicomputers because it provides both higher speed and lower cost than comparable magnetic core memories. Even the cost of core memories for minicomputers has been reduced dramatically. In the case of one manufacturer's minicomputer, the cost of an additional 16K bytes of memory to increase the memory from 16K to 32K bytes was over $20,000 in early 1970. For the same manufacturer's recent memory machine, the cost of adding 16K bytes is less than $2,000.

The other impact of LSI technology affects the CPU itself as a result of programmable logic arrays (PLA) and microprocessor chips, again using MOS LSI technology.

The most commonly used storage devices are floppy disks, cartridge disks, Winchester disks, disk packs, cassette, and low-speed seven- or nine-track tape drives. Disk systems offer one unique advantage: they permit data to be accessed randomly rather than sequentially as with tape systems. As a result, disk systems are more flexible and provide higher computer system throughput than tape does. Disk performance does have a price, in some cases three to four times that of tape systems with comparable storage.

Auxiliary storage for minicomputers was very expensive until recently. A magnetic tape unit or a magnetic disk unit frequently cost more than the minicomputer itself. However, the development of magnetic tape cassettes, relatively low-cost single- or dual-platter moving-head disk units and small Winchester disk units provided significant cost improvements for auxiliary storage. The development of floppy disks or diskettes has provided modest-capacity semirandom access auxiliary storage at a unit price close to that for magnetic-tape cassettes and significantly less than that for larger capacity dual- and single-platter moving-head disks. IBM 2314-type disks and double-density 2314-type disks have been interfaced with minicomputers to provide 20 and 50 megabytes of storage per unit, respectively, in contrast to the 5 to 10 megabytes for the single- and dual-platter disk drives. The capacity of dual-platter drives is being increased to 20 megabytes, with some indications that this may go higher than 40 megabytes. Also, a few manufacturers have recently interfaced the IBM 3330-type disks, providing more than 100 megabytes per drive. However, the double-density 2314-type disk presently offers the most economical disk storage for minicomputers in terms of the cost per bit for applications requiring large capacities with the backup capability. Two or three different approaches are now available for acquiring several hundred million bytes of storage for minicomputer systems [4].

As far as internal characteristics, the basic instruction of any minicomputer may be divided into three areas: the operation to be performed, the address mode to be used, and the address field. The possible addressing options include absolute/relative addressing, direct/indirect addressing, and indexed/no-indexed addressing. Minicomputers also consist of general-purpose registers that are used as index registers, accumulators, program counters, and stack registers. The stack register enables any level of interrupt nesting possible. The interrupt structure, according to the *Encyclopedia of Computer Science* [5], is one of the key features found on most minicomputers.

The input/output structure is a major factor in determining how efficiently a computer can distribute its processing power between input/output operations and internal processing demands. The input/output operation is an integral part of most minicomputers today. Unlike most larger computers, the minicomputer I/O is limited to a few methods: (1) DMA (direct memory access), (2) processor-program-controlled I/O (through one or more hardware registers in the CPU), and (3) DMC (direct multiplexed memory access). DMC channel is the fastest and accommodates I/O data rates of up to about 1,000,000 words per second. It is usually used for block transfer to and from a disk or other external high-speed device. Processor-program-controlled I/O is the slowest of these methods and ties up the entire CPU. The basic input/output facility for a minicomputer consists of a channel shared by a number of peripheral devices (party line). The input/output channel consists of data lines and control lines that synchronize the operation of the central processor and slower-speed peripheral devices.

There have been other improvements in minicomputer peripherals. The primary one is cost reduction. Another is the increased flexibility of minicomputer input/output systems. Minicomputers now have the ability to handle larger number of peripherals simultaneously.

Most minicomputer vendors provide controllers for industry-standard I/O devices: paper-tape units, punched-card readers and punches, line printers, magnetic-tape transports, plotters, CRT displays, magnetic-tape cassettes, terminals, and teletype units. Almost all manufacturers provide mass storage devices such as disks, or tapes for their products. Floppy disks (also known as diskettes) are enjoying user popularity because they are relatively inexpensive and convenient storage devices.

There is a large range of software packages available for most minicomputers. There is also a direct correlation between memory size and the availability of sophisticated software. Available Application Languages include BASIC, COBOL, FORTRAN, RPG, PASCAL, ALGOL, Assembler, and other dialects written specifically for a computer manufacturer's own minicomputer design.

Most elaborate operating systems supporting time-sharing and real-time operations are available from most vendors. Most minicomputer operating systems are of the foreground/background type: one or more real-time programs can be executed in the foreground and one batch program can be executed in the background.

Real-time business applications include EFTS (electronic funds transfer system) used by banks; POS (point-of-sale) systems used by retail sales establishments; word processing (repetitive typing, mailing-list preparation and sorts, etc.) used by insurance firms, government agencies, and so on; and message-switching and other forms of teleprocessing systems, such as NCIC (National Crime Information Center).

As business users become a larger market for the general-purpose minicomputer, commercially oriented software is becoming readily available, including data-base management software and multiuser, multiprocessing operating system software.

As a software becomes more sophisticated, minicomputers are serving more and more as general-purpose computing machines, and the number of applications is almost limitless.

Variations of minicomputers seem unlimited, as there are more than 100 types of minicomputers being produced by about 50 manufacturers (see Figures 3-34 to 3-38). Some of the better-known minicomputer manufacturers include Digital Equipment, Data General, General Automation, Hewlett-Packard, Interdata, Microdata, IBM, BASIC FOUR, and Wang.

Emphasis upon distributed processing, in which large, centralized computers are replaced or augmented by multiple minicomputers, is causing even the largest computer manufacturer, IBM, to take a new look at the minicomputer distributed systems. Today's compact, yet surprisingly powerful minicomputers will continue to receive attention not only from big businesses but from small businesses as well.

Figure 3-34. Minicomputers: *Reality*® Series 8000 System (2000, 4000, 6000, and 8000 Series). The Series 8000 system represents the top of the line in the *Reality*® family of computer systems. It features a standard CPU with 256K bytes of memory, one 128.7-megabyte disk unit, two CRT terminals, a 300-lpm printer, and a 800-bpi/45-ips tape drive. The Series 8000 can be expanded to include up to 512K bytes of memory, 514.8 megabytes of disk storage, a 600-lpm printer, a 1600-bpi/45-ips tape drive, and 32 CRT terminals. (Courtesy of Microdata Corp.)

Figure 3-35. Minicomputers: IBM Series/1. IBM entered the minicomputer market with the Series/1 computer. The Series/1 marked the first time that IBM offered a series of minicomputers as unbundled system components rather than in the company's traditional packages. The small Series/1 includes the processor and a 4964 diskette unit. The output unit is a 120-cps 4974 printer. The display station is the 4979, one of two 1,920-character screen units. (Courtesy of International Business Machines Corp.)

Figure 3-36. Minicomputers: General Automation, InstaCode 55 System. A typical InstaCode 55 System includes a GA-470 processor with 128K bytes (characters) of memory, two 80-megabyte (million characters) disks, five 1,920-character CRT terminals, and a 600-lpm printer unit. A 1600-bpi/45-ips magnetic tape unit and a 400-cpm card reader are available as options. (Courtesy of General Automation, Inc.)

Figure 3-37. Minicomputers: PDP 11/70 and VAX-11/780. The PDP 11/70 represents the top of the PDP 11 line. However, PDP 11 users who outgrow the 11/70's capabilities can upgrade to the VAX-11/780, a 32-bit processor that can be operated in a PDP 11-compatibility mode. The TRAX is an interactive transaction processing system that runs on PDP 11/34, 60, and 70 computers. It can support up to 64 terminals on the PDP 11/70. (Courtesy of Digital Equipment Corp.)

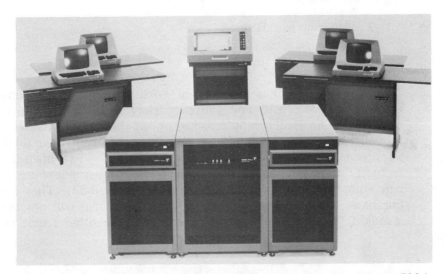

Figure 3-38. Minicomputers: The Basic/Four System 730. The System 730 is the top of the Basic Four line. Created for businesses that need on-line, multitasking transaction processing, a base system consists of a 96K system memory, four video display terminals, two 75-megabyte disk drives, and one 300-lpm printer. The system can be expanded to a 256K system memory, up to 300 megabytes of disk drive in 75-byte increments, 16 terminals, and two 300- or 600-lpm printers. (Courtesy of Basic Four Corp.)

3-2 HOW MICRO-, MINI-, AND SMALL BUSINESS COMPUTERS ARE MARKETED

Small computers are marketed by a variety of companies. An investigation of small computers through current newspapers, manufacturers' literature, and computer magazines will reveal a multitude of articles, advertisements, and brochures for small computers. This is quite understandable because more than 1000 computer vendors of various sizes are marketing small computers today. In Appendix II, Table C, names and addresses of mini-, micro-, and small business computer manufacturers are summarized. Although there are many ways in which small computers are marketed by this great variety of vendors, the majority of vendors can be defined according to the following five categories: (1) manufacturers, (2) "assembled" manufacturers, (3) manufacturers' dealers (distributors), (4) independent system houses, and (5) computer stores.

Each category does business in a somewhat different way. An overview of each category is presented in the following section.

3-2.1 Manufacturers

The first category consists of different small computer manufacturers. This category is subdivided into three groups:

1. Main-frame manufacturers
2. Minicomputer manufacturers
3. Microcomputer manufacturers

The first group is made up of *Fortune* 500-type companies such as Burroughs, IBM, NCR, and Univac. They have large product lines and resources. The small computer is just one of their many products. NCR and Burroughs, however, obtain a very sizable portion of their total corporate sales revenues from small business computers. The main-frame manufacturers market direct to end users, serving as a single-source vendor for hardware, software, and maintenance (see Figure 3-39). They offer flexible purchase, lease, or rental plans, but most of them will not modify their standard "boiler plate"-type contract. On the other hand, most of the

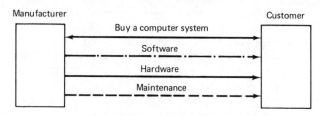

Figure 3-39. Manufacturers.

mini- and microcomputer manufacturers (groups 2 and 3) offer only a purchase plan. This means that you may have to go to a third party to obtain a lease or rental plan. The main-frame manufacturers provide highly reliable computers, but they are generally higher-priced than the other two groups. One of the obvious reasons for this is that the main-frame manufacturers have established well-known names in the computer industry, which gives them an edge over the other two groups. The main-frame manufacturers provide a wide range of computer sizes, but they are relatively further behind in the art of applying the most current technology to their computers.

The second group consists of minicomputer manufacturers such as DEC (Digital Equipment Corporation), Data General, Computer Automation, General Automation, Hewlett-Packard, Wang Laboratory, and others. The third group is a new breed in the computer industry. It is composed of microcomputer manufacturers such as Intel, National Semiconductor, Motorola, Texas Instruments, Zilog, and others. The second and third groups for the most part specialize in manufacturing hardware and providing operating systems. They do not usually provide application programming support, which small businesspeople need most. They tend to shy away from application programs and direct end-user services.

In an effort to solve this problem, most of the mini- and microcomputer manufacturers have arranged dealers for their products, sometimes referred to as distributors. Their dealers take the responsibility for providing application programs, installing hardware and software, and training end users. The manufacturer's dealers (distributors) are discussed in Section 3-2.3.

3-2.2   "Assembled" Manufacturers

The second category of small computer vendors is that of the "assembled" manufacturers. They provide a complete computer hardware system which they assemble themselves from different components produced to their specifications by various other manufacturers. These manufacturers include Datapoint, Qantel, Cado, Compal, and Randal Data Systems. They market these total hardware systems under their own company names. The basic relationship among assembled manufacturers, OEM (original-equipment manufacturers), and customers is shown in Figure 3-40. Assembled manufacturers' total computer hardware systems are usually maintained by a separate organization which services different equipment of various origins. Buyers of assembled computer systems should insist on a one-company maintenance contract. Under a multiple maintenance company type of agreement, when something goes wrong each maintenance company is likely to point its finger to the other maintenance companies. For example, the CPU maintenance company may decide that an error originates in the I/O devices. The I/O device maintenance company, in turn, may identify the cause as a software problem. The software maintenance company when

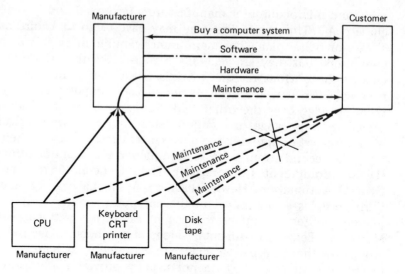

Figure 3-40. "Assembled" manufacturers.

contacted will point back to the CPU. Obviously, this situation would be improved by dealing with a single maintenance company.

Assembled manufacturers are generally able to offer the user very attractive hardware prices and efficient hardware systems. However, most of these manufacturers do not provide application programming services. They usually refer their customers to an independent system house (fourth category) or a dealer. Some assembled manufacturers make arrangements to have dealers (distributors) when they become relatively large themselves.

When a hardware system is purchased from an assembled manufacturer, the user may find it is necessary to have contracts with several different organizations, such as the assembled manufacturer (hardware), an independent system house (application programs), a maintenance company (various equipment), and a finance company (leasing or financing for the computer system). Users are advised to obtain the fewest number of contracts possible. For example, the user can insist on having one contract for all hardware, software, and maintenance with one company, such as a dealer or assembled manufacturer. In turn, the dealer or manufacturer can make its contracts with other organizations.

3-2.3 Manufacturers' Dealers (Distributors)

The third category comprises the manufacturers' dealers, sometimes referred to as distributors. They are dealers for minicomputer, microcomputer, and or assembled manufacturers. A dealer purchases a computer from a particular manufacturer at a dealer's discount and sells it to an end user at list price. A dealer usually has a programming staff who prepare special application programs. It is common for dealers to form associations under an individual manufacturer in order to exchange vital information. Many manufacturers play a clearinghouse role for the dealers in exchange of information on application programs. In this way, interchange of application program package information that has been developed for the same type of computer system can take place.

Access to such vital information broadens a dealer's application program market areas and helps to reach a larger customer base. Thus, dealers can offer many turnkey application programs for the same type of computer system. They will install the equipment, train your personnel, and get the system ready to start processing your special applications. Under this arrangement, dealers provide most of your needs except for hardware maintenance and finance (see Figure 3-41).

The small computer buyer should exercise caution when doing business with a small dealer: being small businesspeople themselves, they have a high mortality rate. Many of them have just launched their own businesses, and you are relying on them for your ongoing application program support. Most dealers have fewer than 20 employees. They are still in the infant stage in the lucrative small computer industry.

3-2.4   Independent System Houses

The fourth category of small computer vendors is the independent system houses, which also sometimes act as independent dealers. They specialize in providing application program expertise to the end user without restricting themselves to any particular computer manufacturer's products. Conse-

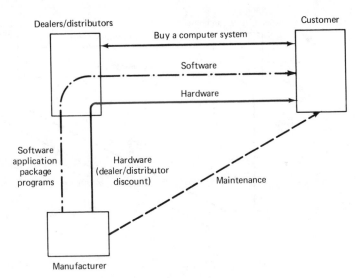

Figure 3-41. Dealers/distributors.

quently, the user has the option of choosing whatever hardware is preferred. After the user chooses the hardware, the system house staff can write custom application programs for that hardware. If the user wishes to have only standard accounting applications, most system houses have package programs available that can, with minor modifications, do the job. The system house people will provide a study of your company's needs, design a customized system, write custom programs, install these programs, train your personnel, and get you ready to start processing your applications.

Under this arrangement, the user is rarely able to obtain a one-company contract (see Figure 3-42). The user will probably find it necessary to have contracts with three separate organizations: an independent system house for application programs, a computer manufacturer for hardware and maintenance, and a finance company for financing the computer system.

Many system houses are still in the infant stage. Their mortality rate is probably highest among the five categories. The user should be aware there can be risk involved when relying on a small independent system house to take the major responsibility of providing a custom program and ongoing application program support. When the user has decided to engage a small system house to develop a custom application program, thorough documentation should be insisted upon as part of the contract. In addition, the custom programs should be written in a well-known high-level language such as BASIC, COBOL, FORTRAN, or RPG (see Chapter 8). By acquiring thorough documentation and programs written in a high-level language, the user has a much better chance to find another system house to support the system in case the original system house goes out of business.

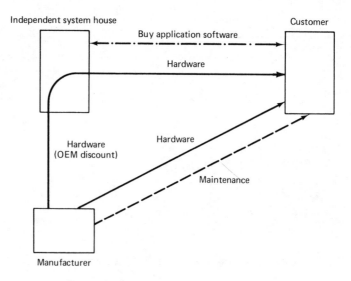

Figure 3-42. Independent system house.

3-2.5 Computer Stores

The fifth category of small computer vendors is composed of the computer stores. They have grown like mushrooms in number, their aim being the sale of personal computers and microcomputers. Their sales trend also indicates the inception of the small business computer, its size ranging to even the minicomputer level. There are two types of computer stores. The first type follows the traditional store concept in that it sells various computers produced by different manufacturers. The second type of computer store markets only its own brand of computers, such as Radio Shack and DEC (Digital Equipment Corporation). DEC is a full-fledged minicomputer manufacturer, but it is experimenting with the retail-store sales approach.

The major drawback of computer stores is the lack of technical support both in software and hardware, with a few exceptions. Their customers are usually referred to an independent system house for application program development and support (see Figure 3-43). If something goes wrong with the computer, the customer has to bring it back to the store and leave it for repairs. Many computers have to be shipped to the original point of manufacture for repair, which can take time.

Under this type of purchase arrangement, the user will find it extremely useful to have a great deal of knowledge in hardware and software programming, so that most problems can be remedied without outside assistance. Otherwise, the user will usually find it necessary to have contracts with several organizations, such as an independent system house for application programs, a maintenance company for hardware maintenance, the computer

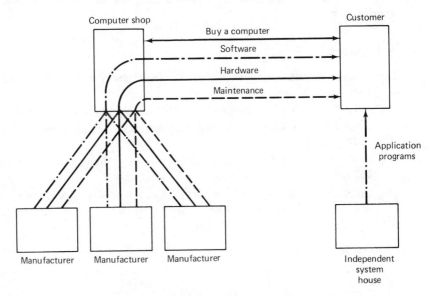

Figure 3-43. Computer shops.

store or the original computer manufacturer for the operating system, and a finance company if the computer is financed.

The approach currently being applied by computer stores still presents many barriers to small businesspeople who are trying to adapt the computer system to real business applications. In the future, if application software packages can be developed into "perfect turnkey" systems, computer stores will be able to sell a large quantity of small business computers over the counter, just as typewriters are sold now.

3-3 TABLE OF SMALL BUSINESS COMPUTER SYSTEM VENDORS

Table C in Appendix II is provided as a guide to finding vendors of small business computer systems, and was prepared specifically with nontechnical buyers in mind.

Information in the table was collected and summarized from various sources, including requests for proposals, vendor brochures, computer magazines, and other sources.

Because of constant technological advancement and almost daily change taking place in the computer industry, readers are advised to check the most recent information available from vendors, especially price ranges and application software.

Readers should be aware that it is impossible, owing to the volatile nature of the market, to list all vendors of small business computer systems.

In Table C, systems are listed according to the alphabetical order of vendor names.

REFERENCES

[1] "Micro Computer Overview," *Mini-Micro Systems*, Vol. 10, Nos. 11–12 (November–December 1977), p. 34.

[2] *Datapro Report on Minicomputers*, (Delran, N.J.: Datapro Research Corp., 1980).

[3] *Auerbach Report on Minicomputers*, (Pennsauken, N.J.: Auerbach Publishers, Inc., 1979).

[4] L. C. HOBBS and RICHARD A. MCLAUGHLIN, "Minicomputer," *Datamation*, July 1974, p. 52.

[5] CHESTER L. MEEK and ANTHONY RALSTON, eds., *Encyclopedia of Computer Science*. 1st ed. New York: Petrocelli/Charter, 1976.

4

ANALYSIS OF BENEFITS
OF COMPUTERIZATION

Computer-based electronic data-processing and management information systems are rapidly becoming an essential part of even relatively small businesses. The introduction of mini/micro computers only a few years ago has been a primary technological factor in this development. The economic (and profitability) opportunities afforded by these systems are indeed significant. Furthermore, as the cost factors and the power of these systems continue to improve, EDP systems will continue to increase in importance. This chapter presents a summary overview of the potential values of computer-based EDP in small to medium-sized business applications. It also discusses some of the key methods for evaluating computer economic benefits, such as payback period, average rate of return, and time-adjusted rate of return (discounted-cash-flow method). These economic evaluation methods are demonstrated in the California Wholesale Company case in Section 4-3.

4-1   IDENTIFYING THE VALUES OF COMPUTER UTILIZATION

The application of computer-based electronic data processing may involve various aspects of a business organization. These include:

Administration and accounting
Marketing and sales

Product/service development, manufacturing, and inventory control

Estimation of production costs

Many firms first considering an EDP system look toward the administration and accounting function only for EDP utilization. Although economic benefits can be obtained with this limited view, substantial profitability advantages will be realized with a much broader viewpoint. For instance, consider a typical firm in which the sales dollar is distributed as follows:

$$
\begin{array}{lr}
\text{Cost of goods (or services) sold} & = \quad 65\% \\
\text{Administration and accounting expense} = & 15\% \\
\text{Before-tax profit (BTP)} & = \quad 20\% \\
\hline
\text{Gross sales} & 100\%
\end{array}
$$

If we assume that the introduction of an efficient EDP system can reduce current cost rates by about 10%, the increased profitability of the firm is as follows:

$$
\begin{array}{ll}
\text{Increased profit from reduced cost} \\
\text{cost of goods sold} & = \dfrac{10\%}{100} \times \dfrac{65\%}{100} = \; 6.5\%
\end{array}
$$

$$
\begin{array}{ll}
\text{Increased profit from reduced} \\
\text{administration and accounting} & = \dfrac{10\%}{100} \times \dfrac{15\%}{100} = \; 1.5\% \\
\text{expense}
\end{array}
$$

$$
\begin{array}{ll}
\text{Net increase in gross profit} \\
\text{(\% of sales)} & = \hspace{3cm} 8.0\%
\end{array}
$$

$$
\begin{array}{ll}
\text{Increase in profit} \\
\text{(\% of profit)} & = \dfrac{8\%}{20\%} \times 100\% = 40.0\%
\end{array}
$$

The leverage here is both obvious and substantial. Relatively small instruments (cost reductions) can yield substantial benefits. Assigning EDP to the administration and accounting function only, although useful, may not yield the major potential contribution to increase in profitability. Reducing the cost of goods (or services) sold is, and should be, the primary area for EDP consideration. It is also evident that the risks of introducing EDP can be significant. If, for any reason, the EDP system does not deliver anticipated cost benefits, reverse leverage can severely damage a firm's profitability. When a firm's before-tax profit values are in the 5 to 10% area, the risks are even greater. It is essential, therefore, that a firm's management pay very careful attention to a number of aspects of EDP acquisition, development, and implementation.

First, the EDP needs of the firm must be very carefully analyzed, and alternative systems must be carefully examined to ensure acquisition of an appropriate and cost-efficient system. These tasks are performed by the feasibility study (Chapter 1) and the EDP economic benefit study (discussed later in this chapter). The business operations of every firm have unique aspects which make it unlikely that the standard "canned" programs will yield specifically desired results. Indeed, some firms' decisions to implement an EDP system without the benefit of adequate initial analysis and system planning have resulted in near catastrophic failures owing to high EDP costs, loss of market share, and lack of cost/profitability control. In other words, each firm's EDP needs tend to be unique. These unique features must be understood in detail before hardware and software procurement proceeds. The system must be selected and/or designed to fit the firm's needs, both functionally and economically. The process of identifying the needs and potential benefits requires time, effort, computer information, and management skill.

Studies of successful EDP systems [1] show that a firm's EDP costs should not exceed about 1 to 2% of its gross-sales figure. In some cases, EDP costs can run as high as 4%. A firm with $12 million in gross sales should therefore consider an EDP budget of about $120,000 per year. The annual EDP budget for this firm should not exceed about $240,000 unless very special circumstances are evident. These studies also show that internal support costs (other than vendor or equipment costs) range from a low of about 35% to a high of about 65%. Our $12 million firm, then, should consider a vendor-related annual investment of no more than about $42,000 to $78,000. A smaller firm of say less than $100,000 gross sales is not in the market for acquisition of significant amounts of EDP equipment, at least until the costs for such equipment are reduced. Leasing, rental, time-sharing, or service agencies may be a better solution for these smaller firms. Various computer firms provide the opportunity for a small firm to utilize EDP equipment and services for low monthly costs of less than $1,000.

The cost-reduction and profitability benefits of EDP systems fall into two categories. They are:

1. Tangible cost reductions, e.g.:
   a. Reduced clerical costs
   b. Reduced inventory and carrying costs
   c. Reducing average days outstanding of accounts receivable
   d. Savings by better management of accounts payable
   e. Reduction of redundant tasks
   f. Cost growth avoidance as sales increase

2. Intangible profit increases, e.g.:
   a. Faster problem identification
   b. Improved customer service

      c. Improved management information integrity

      d. Improved sales analysis capability

Both tangible and intangible factors are important when considering alternative EDP systems. Initial feasibility studies should carefully address both areas in some detail. After defining alternative system designs, a firm's managers can be asked to provide estimates of sales and/or cost improvements expected as a result of implementation of each of the alternative systems. The managers should also provide a probability of success value with each estimate. The expected profitability can then be estimated with the help of simple straightforward decision theory analyses. The result of these studies will be (1) a clear understanding of the firm's EDP needs, (2) a good specification for the desired system, (3) involvement of the firm's personnel to ease changeover problems, and (4) a clear, well-documented EDP implementation plan, schedule, and effectiveness measurement methodology [2]. The following sections discuss the methods for evaluating EDP economic benefits and demonstrate these methods, which comprise the "planning phase" shown in Figure 4-1. In this chapter only the planning phase of Figure 4-1 is covered. The system analysis and design phase (user requirements and request for proposal) is discussed in Chapter 6.

4-2 METHODS FOR EVALUATING EDP ECONOMIC BENEFITS

Acquisition of EDP equipment and software represents a significant investment of a firm's capital resources. Many financial factors must be considered in the acquisition decision. The firm's financial posture (cost of capital), cost of the acquisition, and anticipated benefits of the acquisition must be analyzed in some depth to arrive at wise EDP investment decisions. There are a few accepted alternative techniques that can be employed in any investment decision of this type. They are (1) pay-off period (break-even analysis), (2) average rate of return (financial statement method), and (3) time-adjusted rate of return (discounted-cash-flow method). All of these financial analysis techniques have individual advantages and disadvantages. Methods 2 and 3 have the advantages that the EDP investment decision can be both compared directly with other investment opportunities, and evaluated in terms of its impact on the firm's risk posture. All three techniques require the estimation of income, savings, and expenditures over a significant period of time. In general, a time period of at least 3 years should be addressed. A 5-year cycle is recommended. Any standard textbook in the field of managerial finance presents the details of each technique. Therefore, these concepts are discussed briefly in this section, and brief descriptions, formulas, and simple examples are presented. In Section 4-2.1, these methods are demonstrated in a fictitious case referred to as "California Wholesale Company."

1. Investigative phase

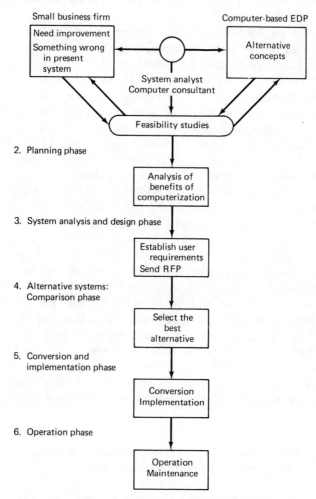

Figure 4-1. Systematic EDP system development cycle for small business.

4-2.1 Payback-Period Method

This method, which is extremely simple, provides a rough approximation of how soon an investment will "pay for itself." To use the payback method, we divide the total original investment by the average annual income that the particular investment project is expected to produce. Assume that a firm is considering the computer system investment of $50,000 for a period of 8 years; net earnings or cash inflows (after taxes and financing costs but before depreciation) will amount to $80,000. The average cash inflow will then be

$10,000 ($80,000 ÷ 8), and the payback period will be 5 years ($50,000 ÷ $10,000 = 5).

The payback method has several drawbacks. *First*, it reflects only the return on the original investment, that is, its liquidity, and cannot measure the project's profitability. Therefore, profits arising *after* the investment has been recovered tend to be ignored. Furthermore, the economic life of the system is disregarded. For example, assume that two computer systems A and B have identical payback periods; system A's earnings will cease 2 years after the payback period, but system B's earnings will continue for several more years. The more profitable nature of system B will not be evident from the data supplied by the payback method. *Second*, the method does not recognize the time value of money flows. To use our earlier example, if the earnings for system B ($80,000 in all) were $30,000 for the first year, $20,000 the second year, and $5,000 for the subsequent years, the firm can attain sizable new earnings by immediately reinvesting these funds each year. If the cash inflow for system A were $5,000 for the first 6 years, $20,000 for the seventh year, and then $30,000 the eighth year, the return on reinvestment would naturally be less. Furthermore, the payback method does not arrange systems in order of preference; it is concerned simply with how fast the investment will be recovered, not with the fact that larger sums should be reflected in the early returns on the project.

The major weaknesses of the payback method are that it ignores both profitability and the time value of money. Simply because a project has a short payback period does not automatically assure the decision maker that it should be selected over an alternative with a longer payback, especially when the project with the short payback also has a short economic life.

4-2.2 Average-Rate-of-Return Method (Financial Statement Method or Time-Unadjusted Return-on-Investment Method)

The first concept necessary for an understanding of the investment process is the rate of return. We shall see later that this can be a rather tricky notion, but for the conditions to which we are limiting ourselves here, it is, fortunately, quite straightforward. The rate of return is a measure of the *relationship between the amount an investor gets back from his investment and the amount invested*. Thus, if we were to invest $100 this year and obtain $120 next year, we would have earned a rate of return of 20% for the year [3].

If one invests $100 this month and receives $105 in return next month, he has earned 5% *per month*. Note that the rate of return is a rate per *month, year, or whatever time period* one might specify.

In the absence of any period quoted, the rate is assumed to be annual. In general, when an investor foregoes $X (investment) now and receives in return $\$Y$ gross income after some time period, his or her rate of return R is:

$$\text{rate of return } R = \frac{\$Y - \$X}{\$X} = \frac{\text{gross income} - \text{investment}}{\text{investment}} = \frac{\text{net income}}{\text{investment}}$$

per time period. The following table gives examples of such calculations:

Investment [Amount Invested Now ($X)]	Gross Income [Amount Received Later ($Y)]	Time Period Between Investment and Receipt	Rate of Return
$100	$150	1 year	50%/year
100	105	1 month	5%/month
100	200	5 years	20%/year (100%/5 years)

When the time period is more than 1 year, the comparable annual rate can be found by dividing the rate of return by the number of years in the time period:

$$100\% \text{ per 5 years} = 100 \div 5 = 20\% \text{ per year}$$

Or we can use the formula for average rate of return on average investment:

$$\text{average rate of return} = \frac{\text{average net income}}{\text{average investment}}$$

Consider the following computer investment:

Economic life of a computer system	7 years
Total anticipated net income for the 7-year period	$70,000
Investment in a computer system	$60,000
Salvage value	$10,000
Depreciable value	$50,000

The average rate of return is calculated as follows:

$$\frac{\text{average net income}}{\text{average investment}} = \frac{\$70,000/7 \text{ years}}{\$10,000 + \frac{1}{2}(50,000)} = \frac{\$10,000}{\$35,000}$$

$$= 0.285 \quad \text{or} \quad 28.5\% \text{ average rate of return}$$

The average net income ($10,000) is computed by dividing the total antici-pated net income ($70,000) by the number of years comprising the economic life of the asset (the computer system), 7 years. The average investment is computed by taking the sum of the salvage value of the computer system ($10,000) and one-half of the depreciable value of the computer system ($50,000). The investment is averaged because depreciable computer systems do not require a permanent investment, but are gradually recovered through depreciations. Thus, only the salvage value is considered a permanent investment.

In our example, 28.5% is the average rate of return over the economic life of the computer system. However, the rate of return in the early years might be as low as 2.3%; in the middle years, as high as 40 to 50%; and in the last years, 10 to 15%. A drawback to this method is that it is based on the assumption that each year's cash inflow is worth as much as every other year, and ignores the fact that the value of the investment may decrease as it depreciates until it reaches zero (or a salvage value) at the end of its economic life.

Another fault in this method is that it ignores the time value of money. Since this method is one of approximation, it cannot be used when an extreme degree of accuracy is required. However, for the practical problem of ranking alternatives, the method does an admirable job [4].

4-2.3 Time-Adjusted Rate-of-Return Method (Discounted-Cash-Flow Method)*

This method recognizes that, because of the existence of interest, a dollar today has more importance to the investor than has a dollar 5 years in the future. The time-adjusted rate of return requires consideration of the timing of the investment and the funds flow, and provides a profitability ranking in a comparison among alternatives. A definition for this time-adjusted rate of return is "the rate of interest that will discount future net cash inflows from the proposed project down to the amount of the investment in the project" [5].

For the purpose of illustration, the following hypothetical computer system investment is used.

The Computer-Need Company is thinking of purchasing a new micro/minicomputer system that will save $10,000 in cash operating costs per year, after taxes, and will cost $46,390. The useful life is estimated to be 8 years, after which the computer system will have zero disposal value.

1. Use the payback formula (net investment ÷ annual earning) to arrive at a factor rate:

$$\$46,390 \div \$10,000 = 4.639$$

*The rate of return determined by this method is called the time-adjusted rate of return, internal rate of return (used mainly in Keynesian economics), or project rate of return. The method itself is also known as the compound-interest method, the financial method, or the investor's method.

2. Refer to Table A in Appendix II for the present value of an annuity of $1.00. Since the investment is for a period of 8 years, follow the line along to the right for 8 periods, and find the figure or the closest figure to 4.639. This is 4.639 under the 14% column. Therefore, the time-adjusted rate of return is 14%.

3. We then compare this rate with a desired rate of return and/or the cost of Computer-Need Company's capital to decide if the investment should be made. The cost of capital varies depending on individual company's position and opportunity.

As long as the cash flow is the same every year and the factor figure is known, management can easily determine, from a table for the present value of an annuity, what rate can be expected for whatever number of years may be involved in the life of the capital project. Conversely, if management desires a certain rate, this table will also show how long the life of the system must be in order to yield that rate.

Although this method does provide a sophisticated answer to the investment question, it has some disadvantages. Alternatives with different useful lives are not compared quite as easily as the steps set forth above would suggest, varying annual funds flow would make the comparison more difficult, and generally the assumption is that the funds flow is received totally at the end of the period rather than throughout the period [6].

When yearly earnings are not identical, however, a separate trial-and-error computation must be made to obtain the proper rate of return for each uneven cash flow. To illustrate, assume that the cash flow for Computer-Need Company is $15,000 for the first 4 years, and then $5,000 for the subsequent 4 years. One approach would be to start with the rate that is normal for the particular type of investment project. It was 14% from the foregoing hypothetical computer system investment.

At 14% the annuity percent would be 4.639. To find the annuity for $15,000, we look up the 14% column (Table A) to the line for four periods, where we find a 2.914 annuity percent. The difference between 4.639 and 2.914, or 1.725, represents the percent for $5,000 for the last four periods. The computation is shown in Table 4-1(a). The substantial difference (+$5,945) between the amount of the investment and the present value indicates that the 14% rate is not correct. This result is somewhat obvious from the fact that the big cash inflow in the beginning of four periods contributed most to the present value.

We can, therefore, try a figure as high as 20%, as in Table 4-1(b). The substantial difference (-$1,315) indicates that the 20% rate is still not a proper rate. Since the difference is negative in this instance, we then lower the rate to 19%, as in Table 4-1(c). The insignificance of the difference indicates that this is the proper rate.

The time-adjusted rate-of-return method (discounted-cash-flow method) makes possible a great degree of accuracy, because the time value of money, salvage values, and after-tax cash flows are taken into consideration.

TABLE 4-1
Time-Adjusted Rate-of-Return Method (Discounted-Cash-Flow Method)

Period	Annual Cash Flow		(a) Annuity Rate at 14%		Present Value of Annual Cash Flow
Years 1–4	$15,000	X	2.914	=	$43,710
Years 5–8	5,000	X	1.725	=	8,625
			4.639		$52,335
Amount of investment					46,390
Difference					$ 5,945

Period	Annual Cash Flow		(b) Annuity Rate at 20%		Present Value of Annual Cash Flow
Years 1–4	$15,000	X	2.589	=	$38,835
Years 5–8	5,000	X	1.248	=	6,240
			3.837		$45,075
Amount of investment					46,390
Difference					-$ 1,315

Period	Annual Cash Flow		(c) Annuity Rate at 19%		Present Value of Annual Cash Flow
Years 1–4	$15,000	X	2.639	=	$39,585
Years 5–8	5,000	X	1.318	=	6,590
					$46,175
Amount of investment					46,390
Difference					-$ 215

There are difficulties in the practical application of these methods. There is, for example, the problem not only of forecasting the inflows over the length of life of the asset, but also of determining the actual life. Inherent in both is the problem of uncertainty.

We have seen that many small firms do not bother with the refinements of the time-adjusted rate of return (discounted-cash-flow method). Would they be better off to do so? In many instances such refinements and accuracy would produce benefits that exceed the added costs in terms of management time and training.

4-3 APPLICATIONS OF COMPUTER ECONOMIC EVALUATION METHODS

In Section 4-2 we discussed the various methods for evaluating computed economic benefits. Let us apply these methods to the hypothetical California Wholesale Company case.

The management of the company decided to investigate the benefits of computerization. The manager, Mr. Able, was assigned the task of finding the computer economic benefits and the feasibility of the company's computerization. The manager collected the following pertinent information for the company:

Useful life of a computer	5 years
Purchasing value of a computer	$40,000
Purchasing value of software	20,000
	$60,000
Residual value of a computer system	$6,000
Discount rate (rate of return of the company)	16%
Allowable payback period of the company	5 years

The manager expects that over the next 5 years with the aid of the computer the company will incur the tangible and intangible savings shown in Table 4-2.

4-3.1 Payback-Period Method

This method requires only the total original investment and the average annual income in order to produce the payback period.

The total original investment for the computer system is $60,000 ($40,000 for hardware and $20,000 for software).

TABLE 4-2
Tangible and Intangible Cost-Savings Summary

Savings	Year 1	2	3	4	5
Tangible					
Increase in sales	$ 4,000	$ 4,000	$ 8,000	$ 8,000	$ 8,000
Inventory reduction	10,000	10,000	15,000	15,000	15,000
Salary	600	600	600	600	600
Other	400	400	400	400	400
Total tangible	15,000	15,000	25,000	25,000	25,000
Cumulative total tangible	15,000	30,000	55,000	80,000	105,000
Intangible					
Improved customer service	5,000	20,000	20,000	20,000	20,000
Sales forecast improvement	3,000	5,000	7,000	9,000	10,000
Total intangible	8,000	25,000	27,000	29,000	30,000
Cumulative total intangible	8,000	33,000	60,000	89,000	119,000

The average cash inflow over the 5 years is computed as follows:

$$(\$15,000 + \$15,000 + \$25,000 + \$25,000 + \$25,000) \div 5 \text{ years}$$

$$= \$21,000 \text{ per year}$$

so the payback period will be

$$\$60,000 \div \$21,000 = 2.86 \text{ years}$$

The payback period, 2.86 years, is well within the allowable payback period of the company (5 years).

Figure 4-2 indicates the break-even point as 3.25 years, which is a little different from our computation for the payback period of 2.86 years. The

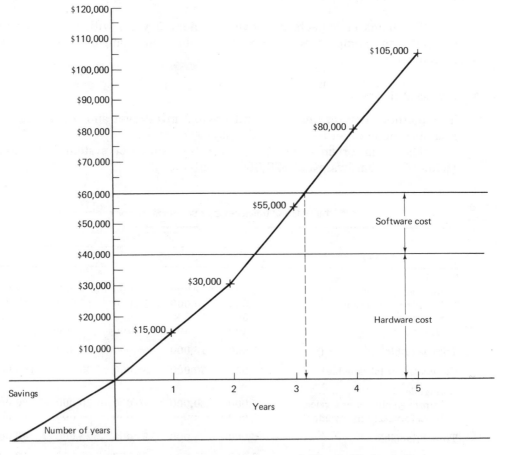

Figure 4-2. Break-even analysis for the California Wholesale Company.

reason for the difference is that the average-rate-of-return method takes the average earnings over the 5-year period, but the break-even analysis immediately reflects the varying cash inflows each year.

Small cash inflows in the first and second years and larger cash inflows in the third, fourth, and fifth years are reflected in the break-even analysis point, but not so on the average rate of return.

The difference is really insignificant, as both figures indicate that the payback periods are well below the company's allowable payback period (5 years). Therefore, the manager can report preliminary results to top management, showing that the results of the payback and break-even-point methods indicate a positive sign for a computer investment.

Since the payback method cannot measure the investment's profitability, the manager should not compile final recommendations until further analyses are carried out. Among these should be the average rate of return or time-adjusted rate of return. This will determine the profitability of computer investment for the company.

4-3.2   Average-Rate-of-Return Method

The average-rate-of-return method is used to determine if the investment proposals under consideration will generate enough earnings and if so, to what extent.

We will now compute the average rate of return for the California Wholesale Company. The average rate of return is calculated as follows:

$$\frac{\text{average net income}}{\text{average investment}} = \frac{(\$15{,}000 + \$15{,}000 + \$25{,}000 + \$25{,}000 + \$25{,}000)/5}{\$6{,}000 + \frac{1}{2}(\$54{,}000)}$$

$$= \frac{\$21{,}000}{\$33{,}000}$$

$$= 0.636 \quad \text{or} \quad 63.6\%$$

The average net income ($21,000) is computed by dividing the total anticipated income ($105,000) in years 1–5 by the number of years comprising the economic life of the computer (5 years).

The average investment is computed by the sum of the salvage value of the computer ($6,000) and one-half of the depreciable value of the computer ($60,000 – $6,000).

In the California Wholesale Company case, the average rate of return over the next 5 years is 63.6%, which exceeds the discountable (rate of return of the company) of 16%. This means that anticipated earnings from this computer investment exceeds anticipated earnings from other capital investments. Therefore, the manager can make a further preliminary report to upper management that economic benefits from computer investments outweigh other investments and therefore justify such an investment.

The average-rate-of-return method, however, ignores the varying cash inflows over the years and the time value of money. Therefore, this method is one of approximation, so it is not advisable to apply it when an extreme degree of accuracy is required.

The next method, the time-adjusted rate of return, will take the varying cash inflows and the time value of money into consideration for its computation.

4-3.3 Time-Adjusted Rate-of-Return Method

The time-adjusted rate-of-return (discounted-cash-flow) method measures the rate of return that can be expected in the future, based on an investment made today. It is an effective means of appraising various investment alternatives [3]. Let's figure out the time-adjusted rate-of-return of the California Wholesale Company case.

Their cash flow is $15,000 for the first and second years, and then $25,000 for the third, fourth, and fifth years. Since yearly earnings are not identical over the 5-year period, we have to perform a separate computation for each uneven cash flow in order to obtain the proper rate of return.

We can start with the rate of 16% that the company considers as the minimum rate of return. Then we refer to Appendix II, Table A, for the percent value of an annuity along the 5-year period line.

At the rate of 16%, the annuity percent would be 3.274. To find the annuity percent for $15,000, we look up the 16% column to the line for two periods, where we find a 1.605 annuity rate. The difference between 3.274 and 1.605, or 1.669, represents the percent for $25,000 for three periods. The computation is then performed as in Table 4-3(a).

TABLE 4-3
Time-Adjusted Rate-of-Return (Discounted-Cash-Flow) Method

Period	Annual Cash Flow		(a) Annuity Rate at 16%		Percent Value of Annual Cash Flow
Years 1–2	$15,000	X	1.605	=	$24,075
Years 3–5	25,000	X	1.669	=	41,725
			3.274		$65,800
Amount of investment					− 60,000
Difference					+$ 5,800

Period	Annual Cash Flow		(b) Annuity Rate at 20%		Percent Value of Annual Cash Flow
Years 1–2	$15,000	X	1.528	=	$22,920
Years 3–5	25,000	X	1.463	=	36,575
			2.991		$59,495
Amount of investment					60,000
Difference					−$ 505

The substantial positive difference ($5,800) between the present value and the amount of the investment indicates that the rate of return is not 16%, but should be much higher. We then try a much higher rate, say 20%, as in Table 4-3(b). The insignificance of the difference indicates that 20% is the proper rate. The annuity rate, 20% (rate of return), exceeds the company's discount rate of 16%. Therefore, the manager, Mr. Able, now can make a positive final recommendation for computer investment to the management of the company.

REFERENCES

[1] J. D. COUGAR, *Guidelines for Small Business Computer Selection*, prepared for Hewlett-Packard Corp., 1977. J. F. CLINTON, "Notes Developed for a Seminar on Mini-computer Applications," 1977.

[2] J. S. CAMPBELL, R. A. POST, C. F. LEAVER, and K. D. ANDERSON, *Computer-Based EDP Evaluation and Selection*, 1978, unpublished paper, General Dynamic, Pomona, California.

[3] S. WINTON KORN and THOMAS BOYD, *Accounting for Management Planning and Decision Making* (New York: John Wiley & Sons., 1975), pp. 607–608.

[4] MARTIN B. SOLOMON, JR., *Investment Decisions in Small Business* (Lexington, Ky.: University of Kentucky Press, 1963).

[5] NAA (National Association of Accountants) Research Report 35, *Return on Capital as a Guide to Managerial Decisions*, December 1959, p. 58.

[6] NAA (National Association of Accountants) Research Monograph 2, *Accounting Information in Managerial Decision-Making for Small and Medium Manufacturers* by Gary A. Luoma, December, 1967, p. 22.

5

PROS AND CONS
OF COMPUTER SYSTEMS
AND OUTSIDE SERVICES

5-1 COMPUTER SERVICES AND SELECTION CRITERIA

What type of computer service is best for your organization? Is it an in-house computer, a service center, a time-sharing service, or a combination of these?

5-1.1 Various Computer Services

Today there are many different ways in which a firm may obtain the computing power it requires, and each method has advantages and disadvantages. In this chapter we describe and analyze the various approaches according to selection factors. Following are some of the approaches that most small firms will consider:

1. In-house computers
2. Computer service bureaus
3. Time-sharing services/remote computing services
4. Any combination of approaches 1, 2, and 3
5. Facilities management
6. Computer-time rental from other users
7. Shared facilities

The first three approaches are the most common, particularly with first-time EDP users. The last three approaches are used less frequently.

The basic distinctions among these approaches are relatively simple. In the first case, the computer is located on the firm's premises and is fully under the customer's control. In the second case, the computer is located elsewhere and is operated by an independent service company (or sometimes by a bank or accounting firm). In the third case, the computer, although located on the premises of an independent service company, is directly accessible via a terminal to the customer firm. The fourth case is simply any combination of the foregoing three approaches. The fifth case involves contracting with a service company to take over complete responsibility for an organization's data-processing operations. The computer itself may be located either on the customer's premises or at the service company. In the sixth case, companies that have excess time available on their in-house computers sell that time to others at reasonable prices. In the seventh case, two or more companies form a jointly owned corporation that installs a computer and contracts to provide data-processing services to each of the contributing companies, and perhaps to others as well.

In addition to the aforementioned approaches, there are numerous variations of EDP services. However, the in-house computer, computer service centers, and time-sharing services are the three basic approaches used today. It is worth noting that many companies find it worthwhile to use two or more of the basic approaches to EDP at the same time. For example, numerous companies with in-house computer installations also make use of either computer service bureaus or time-sharing services to facilitate the handling of:

1. Periodic overloads in the volume of data to be processed.
2. Projects that require specialized programs, equipment, or handling procedures [1].

To select the best approach for an organization, criteria and constraints should be established. To set criteria and constraints, one should define the factors that affect criteria and constraints for comparison purposes. Each decision regarding the most suitable approach to EDP for an organization should be based upon careful consideration of the factors discussed below. Each will have a different effect in different organizations. However, all of them are important enough to be considered as selection factors.

5-1.2 Factors to Consider for the Selection Criteria

The factors discussed below affect an organization, particularly if careful consideration is not given to them in the selection stage. We will raise some important questions regarding each factor. It is suggested that you do the same before you decide on the type of service you wish to have.

The list of questions for each factor is certainly not exhaustive. Therefore, if you have any questions applicable to your organization, you should by all means ask them. You may save much trouble and money in the future.

1. *Availability, reliability, and backup of the system.* Will the system or service you select be available when you need it? Is the location of the computer satisfactory? It may be on your premises, in the same city, or miles away from your organization. Can you be reasonably sure that the system operates reliably? Will the computer be repaired promptly whenever it fails? In the event that the system you use is incapacitated for an extended period, do you have a program-compatible system available near you? If your answer to any of these questions is no, you may encounter not only inconvenience but also undue expense, such as losing important customers [1].

2. *Availability, reliability, and technical support of the software.* Are the packaged programs that will be needed to satisfy your applications already available? What modifications do you need to make to these programs? If packaged programs are not available due to the specialized nature of your applications, is the supplier of the computer service willing and able to prepare a program for your applications? Who will own the application programs that the supplier may develop for you? Is the supplier equipped and willing to provide the technical assistance you are likely to need in the future? Will there be someone available to resolve the everyday problems that are likely to arise when you use the system?

3. *Variable, fixed, and total costs of EDP services.* *Variable costs:* What costs will be incurred in direct proportion to the amount of work done by the computer services you use?

Fixed costs: What costs will be incurred on a regular basis, irrespective of the volume of work done by the computer?

Total cost: What costs will be incurred for your total data-processing services? [1]

4. *Security of information and hardware.* Will your vital and confidential information be safe against unauthorized access? Will your computer system be as safe as possible against natural catastrophies such as earthquake, fire, or flood? [1]

5. *Expandability of the EDP service.* When your organization grows to the point where the EDP service must be expanded, will the computer service permit convenient expansion without any need for substantial reprogramming? Will the computer service handle increasing workload volumes and additional applications without undue extra charges?

6. *Speed of processing (response, turnaround, and throughput times).* What will be the response time of the processing? Response time is the yardstick by which a user can measure the timeliness of the output he or she receives from the computer service center. It is the elapsed time between submission of input data by a user and receipt of the resulting report. It is a "door-to-door" measurement. What will the turnaround time be? Turn-

around time is the elapsed time between data arrival at the computer center and the availability of output for pickup. What will be the throughput time? Throughput is the time required for work to flow through the machine room.

7. *Need for additional personnel.* Will it be necessary to add any individuals with data-processing knowledge and/or experience to your staff in connection with the new system? If so, how many, and where will you find them? What will salary costs be?

8. *Ease of installation, implementation, and maintenance.* What problems and costs will be encountered in installing or converting the system? If your organization buys the computer, what services will the vendor supply in terms of facility and site preparation, physical planning, and system checkout? What is the warranty duration, and what are the repair practices that will apply? How quickly will the vendor respond to a service call? Will the vendor respond to a service call during a night shift? What problems and costs will be encountered in installing and testing programs? What problems and costs will be encountered in operating the system on a day-to-day basis?

5-2   IN-HOUSE COMPUTER: ADVANTAGES AND DISADVANTAGES

The in-house approach to computer utilization involves locating the computer on the premises of the end user.

The computer processing is completely controlled by the user without outside help. The computerized business operates its equipment through its own staff. The staff usually consists of data-entry operators, computer operators, programmers, and analysts. The effectiveness of an in-house system depends greatly on the competence of the staff. In the recent small business computer environment, programmers and system analysts are less frequently employed as in-house computer staff. This is mainly due to the trend of installing turn key systems.

The user has the option to rent, lease, or buy the computer under this approach. These three alternatives may also be combined for different components of the system. For instance, a company may own its CPU, but lease or rent all the peripherals.

Communication between managers and the data-processing department is also important. A system cannot function at peak efficiency unless management knows what it wants and conveys this need to the computer staff. In other words, the mere presence of an in-house computer does not automatically facilitate effectiveness.

Furthermore, a system must be cost-effective to be worth having. In-house systems generally operate more efficiently at higher work volumes. This capacity is always present, whether or not it is being utilized.

As with any of the computer approaches, there are trade-offs that make the in-house approach attractive and at the same time unattractive. The advantages of having an in-house computer include:

1. *The system is under your control.* The computer, software, and staff are all within the company. Control of all processing and storage of data is in the company's hands.
2. *The system operation is reliable.* The system is as reliable as management cares to make it. Since reliability is very important, most businesses with in-house capabilities will minimize the time that the system is down by providing whatever maintenance is required.
3. *Variable costs are low.* All forms, cards, additional storage costs, and so on, are relative low in cost.
4. *The system is secure.* All file storage is accessible only to selected people within the company. Data are not handled by outsiders.
5. *Human-machine interaction.* Many recent small business computers are available with data base languages which allow the user to query the data base with "what if" types of questions.
6. *Capacity.* In times of emergency, overtime runs can be handled to facilitate data overloads.

Some of the disadvantages of having a computer in the house are:

1. *Fixed costs are high.* The maintenance and payments for the computer are costly.
2. *Expansion is often difficult.* The problem with the in-house approach is one of compatibility. If, for instance, a business needs to expand current capabilities, additional equipment must be compatible with existing equipment.
3. *Space is needed for equipment.* Equipment and staff must have physical space. The equipment space must be clean and situated for security.
4. *Additional personnel may be needed.* Although most small business computers do not require a special operator, additional personnel may be required.
5. *Economy decreases with smaller work loads.* Many businesses experience fluctuations in sales or service demands over the course of a year. Processing needs fluctuate accordingly. Smaller workloads are not as economical as full ones.
6. *Systems tend to become obsolete.* The computer industry is progressing at such a rapid pace that computer innovations can make a relatively new computer obsolete.
7. *Risk of choosing the wrong equipment.* If a system is leased or purchased, there is always the possibility that the equipment chosen will later be found not to satisfy a company's processing needs. A company must then obtain additional capabilities in some form.
8. *Communication problems.* If communication is poor between management and the data-processing staff, processing may be inefficient.

5-3   TIME-SHARING AND REMOTE COMPUTING SERVICES: ADVANTAGES AND DISADVANTAGES [2] [4]

Time-sharing and remote computing services include both time-sharing and remote batch. The main computer is located elsewhere and is connected to the user through a terminal. Time-sharing and remote computing services, then limited to batch processing, actually started almost two decades ago. Time-sharing and remote batch were developed for users seeking greater versatility, expertise, and the ability to accomplish complex tasks. They offer users the opportunity to process data without the requirements of hardware and large staffs (as in some cases of in-house computing).

Time-sharing is a service in which the user has immediate access to the data. The user has a terminal on his premises and is able to make inquiries directly to the access computer. Aside from the cost of using the terminal, the user must pay the telephone charges from the terminal to the time-sharing company's point of access, which in some cases can be exorbitant. The expense of transmitting data from the point of access to the central computer is usually assumed by the time-sharing company. That distance can exceed thousands of miles in some instances, such as in intercontinental time-sharing.

Remote batch processing differs from time-sharing in that the user does not have immediate access to the data. The end user communicates with remote data collection centers, each of which services a particular locale. This initial connection can be made by telephone. The end user conveys information to these data collection points as often as has been arranged for. The collection point, which usually serves many businesses within the area, then disseminates information to the service center's CPU, which is in a centralized area. The data collection point connects to the CPU usually by small computers. Information can be stored, manipulated, and/or turned into reports by the central computer. The batch mode of processing, remote or not, denotes some time delay between initial transmission of information and response to that information, and indeed there is a delay under this approach.

Time-sharing and remote computing services provide standard program packages, but also specialize in custom applications, the cost varying with the complexity of the application and what is included in the software package.

Advantages of time-sharing and remote computing include:

1. *Flexibility.* The expansion or reduction in a company's workload over time can be handled because the user can increase or decrease time-sharing use.

2. *Low processing cost.* The customer pays only for the time used.

3. *Direct communication.* There is a direct line between the user and the computer.

4. *Human–machine interaction.* This interaction allows the user to ask "what if" types of questions and to obtain immediate answers to these questions.

5. *Nationwide operation.* The size of the major time-sharing services ensures that they offer a large amount of experience and knowledge regarding business needs.

6. *Fast response.* Turnaround time is fast, resulting in quicker decision making by management. In a competitive market, this is important.

7. *High-level languages and utilities are available.* The user has access to many of the high-level languages and utilities, subject only to the limitations in the time-sharing service's computers and software.

8. *Personnel are not necessary.* Additional data-processing staff is not required.

9. *Low fixed costs.* Large initial hardware costs are avoided.

10. *Applications.* There is a growing library of application systems and packages. Time-sharing services expand their applications to keep up with the competition.

11. *Advanced equipment.* The equipment is constantly updated to satisfy more demanding users.

12. *Reduced risk in choosing wrong equipment.* If a business plans to convert to an in-house computer in the future, it may be wise to consider using time-sharing and remote computing services first to determine what types of equipment and software work best in a particular situation.

Major disadvantages of time-sharing and remote computing are as follows:

1. *Reliability.* There is no control over system breakdowns.

2. *Data security.* As data are stored in an outside computer system with other use data, the question of security is a major worry.

3. *Data storage costs.* Based on the number of characters to be stored, large amounts of data can run into high costs.

4. *Slow input/output.* Generally speaking, these terminals operate at much slower speeds than their in-house equivalents. Ten to 15 cps is typical, although users may be able to choose 120 cps, and 240 cps and higher with CRTs.

5. *Deterioration of response times.* Peak load times sometimes bring slower response times. Even a 1-second delay is noticeable and irritating to the end user at a terminal. Occasionally, users even have problems getting onto the computer.

6. *High cost of extra capacity.* Since the user is charged for all the terminal connect time and resources used during that period, any extra capacity is expensive.

5-4   COMPUTER SERVICE BUREAUS: ADVANTAGES AND DISADVANTAGES [3] [5]

A computer service bureau is generally a small business formed and operated by people who have worked in the computer field. Generally, they have a medium-scale general-purpose computer and do normal programming for business applications. Client firms contract with them for data-processing applications, which are usually performed in batch mode. Communications between the client firm and the computer are off-line, courier or mail, rather than on-line through terminal equipment as in time-sharing.

Service rendered to client firms generally falls into either of the following two categories:

1. Repetitive, recurring service, usually applications-oriented and consisting of general accounting and reporting systems.
2. Overflow, nonrecurring service, usually time-oriented and consisting of peak-load and conversion efforts.

Computer service bureaus are independent organizations that satisfy all of the user's processing needs. Processing and report generation are performed by the service bureau's equipment, using their software and staff. Most service bureaus will develop programs to fit the user's specific needs.

The physical process of a business/service center relationship is as follows. The business must organize and determine which data are to be processed by computer and what type of information is desired from the processing of that data. Service bureaus usually provide consultants to discuss these points with management. It is often the case that the new user has no experience with computerized processing and needs careful guidance and some straightforward answers.

Typically, a company mails or courier-sends invoices, packing slips, work orders, and so on, to the service bureau. The service bureau then keys the data into their system, where processing occurs. Reports are generated, to be mailed or hand-carried back to the business. The transmission of information, reports, and so on, between service bureau and customer can be a very time-consuming process. There is the usual trade-off of time versus cost.

The user is charged for the quantity of processing, the type of applications, the information desired, all of which enters into the costs of analysis, keypunching, and programming. Computer service bureaus have been used primarily by companies with small volume needs, little computer experience, and as a support to in-house computing and time-sharing.

Computer service bureaus are beginning to specialize. In some cases, this specialization has been industry-oriented. For example, a given center might specialize to a major extent in hospital data processing. In this case, the center would offer hospital administrators a unique blend of specific knowledge with respect to that particular enterprise, together with data-processing systems and operating expertise. In other cases, specialization is concentrated in a single area, such as payroll processing. In this case a computer service bureau may develop a particular expertise in the processing of payrolls and offer to process payrolls for a broad range of industries.

Following are the principal advantages of computer service bureaus:

1. *Low fixed costs.* There is no initial investment, and no maintenance.
2. *Expandable.* Increasing business workload can be handled if the business is willing to pay the extra costs.
3. *No additional personnel.* Unlike in-house systems, there are no additional staff requirements. Management need not have previous computer experience.

4. *No room required for equipment.* Hardware is not on the business premises; therefore, there are no space requirements.
5. *No operating problems.* Most service bureaus do everything, taking all responsibility.
6. *Application packages available.* Low developmental costs for custom packages.
7. *Low processing cost.* The customer pays only for the time and manpower used.
8. *Wide range of languages and utilities available.* The user may have access to many of the higher-level languages and utilities, subject only to the limitations of the service bureau's computers and software.
9. *Reduced risk in choosing wrong equipment.* If a business plans to convert to an in-house computer in the future, it may be wise to consider using a service bureau first to determine what types of equipment and software work best in a given situation.

Important disadvantages of computer service bureaus include:

1. *Security is low.* Not only are data stored on someone else's premises, but information must be carried back and forth between user and service bureau. Security risks are present.
2. *High variable costs.* The costs of all supplies and variable processing costs are at the discretion of the service center.
3. *Low turnaround time.* Turnaround time can exceed 1 week in some situations.
4. *No control.* Control is out of the user's hands. Once the information leaves the user's premises, the service bureau takes control of everything.
5. *Reliability.* There is no control over system breakdowns.

5-5 SUMMARY COMPARISON OF THREE APPROACHES TO SELECTION FACTORS

Selection Factor in Question	In-house (Purchase, Lease, or Rent a Computer)	Computer Service Bureau	Time-Sharing and Remote Computing Services
I. Availability, reliability, and backup of the system			
1. Will the system be available when you need it?	a	c	b
a. Yes, the computer is completely under your control.			
b. Usually, when you need it you have immediate access to the terminals.			
c. Most of the time, but not always when you need it; needs careful consideration.			

Selection Factor in Question	In-house (Purchase, Lease, or Rent a Computer)	Computer Service Bureau	Time-Sharing and Remote Computing Services

2. Where is the computer located?
   a. On your premises.
   b. In the same city.
   c. Miles away.
	a	b	b or c

3. Can you be reasonably sure that the system operates reliably?
   a. Very high reliability.
   b. Not under your direct control.
	a	b	b

4. Is there a backup system?
   a. You arrange yourself.
   b. Not under your control.
	a	b	b

II. Availability, reliability, and technical support of the software			

1. Are business application programs available?
   a. Yes, at most of service centers.
   b. No, but you could buy programs from a small computer manufacturer or independent software firm.
	b	a	a

2. Are programming services available?
   a. Yes, nearly all.
   b. No, use your own programmer.
	b	a	a

3. Is there technical support?
   a. Varies greatly in quality and quantity.
   b. Generally poor (computer manufacturer).
	b	a	a

III. Variable, fixed, and total costs of EDP services			

1. Variable cost includes the cost of supplies (cards, forms, disks, etc.), power, and rental charges.
   a. Low.
   b. Low, but depends on how much time you use.
   c. High.
	a	c	b

2. Fixed cost includes payments for the computer, maintenance, etc.
   a. Very low (or none).
   b. High.
	b	a	a

3. Total costs.
   a. Economical when the workload is small.
   b. Economical when the workload is heavier.
	b	a	a

Selection Factor in Question	In-house (Purchase, Lease, or Rent a Computer)	Computer Service Bureau	Time-Sharing and Remote Computing Services
IV. Security of information and hardware			
1. Will your vital information be safe against unauthorized access?	a	c	b
a. Under your direct control, as safe as you are able to make it.			
b. Data and programs are usually safeguarded by the system, but access by many parties increases risk.			
c. Processing is under complete control of an outside agency; safety unsure.			
V. Expandability of the EDP services			
1. Will your computer service method permit convenient expansion?	b	a	a
a. As your work load expands, you can simply use more.			
b. Varies greatly among small business computers.			
VI. Speed of processing			
1. What is the processing speed?	b	c	a
a. Instant response.			
b. On-line or batch.			
c. One day or more.			
VII. Need for additional personnel			
1. Will it be necessary to add any individuals with DP knowledge?	a, b or c	a	c
a. None.			
b. An operator.			
c. A programmer.			
VIII. Ease of installation, implementation, and maintenance			
1. What do you install at your premises?	c	a	b
a. None.			
b. Terminals.			
c. Small computer.			
2. What problems will be encountered in implementing the common business systems?	a or c	b or c	b or c
a. None; implement the "turnkey" system.			
b. None; use the existing programs and library packages.			
c. Few; converting or modifying the existing program.			

Selection Factor in Question	In-house (Purchase, Lease, or Rent a Computer)	Computer Service Bureau	Time-Sharing and Remote Computing Services
3. What problems will be encountered in implementing the specialized system? a. Many problems in the course of designing the system, writing the programs, testing programs, etc.	a	a	a
4. What problems will be encountered in operating the system? a. None; they will operate for you. b. Few; they will operate the computer system, you operate a simple data terminal. c. Few; you operate a small computer.	c	a	b

REFERENCES

[1] *DataPro Research Report: Approaches to Electronic Data Processing* (Delran, N.J.: DataPro Research Corp., 1978).

[2] *DataPro Research Report: All About Time-Sharing and Remote Computing Services* (Delran, N.J.: DataPro Research Corp., 1976).

[3] *DataPro Research Report: Computer Service Centers* (Delran, N.J.: DataPro Research Corp., 1974).

[4] *Auerbach Computer Technology Reports: Timesharing* (Pennsauken, N.J.: Auerbach Publishers, Inc., 1978).

[5] *Service Bureau Selection and Evaluation* (Pennsauken, N.J.: Auerbach Publishers, Inc., 1975).

HOW TO SELECT
AND INSTALL A COMPUTER

Smaller firms rarely conduct a formal EDP economic benefit study for EDP procurement decisions. Usually, they simply request a proposal from a number of vendors to see what a system will cost. Little, if any, attention is focused on the firm's actual needs, potential benefits, and the risks. Realization of proper results in computer utilization requires a "systematic" approach throughout the analysis, selection, and implementation of an EDP system. Risks cannot always be eliminated, but they can be realistically assessed. The "systematic" approach need not be expensive. An additional cost of about $2,000 to $10,000 is typical compared to the subjective judgment or vendor proposal technique. This means an additional one-time investment of about 10% of the system cost to yield profitability increases of 20 to 100% and to help eliminate the risk of choosing the wrong computer. Choosing the wrong computer in relation to the actual needs involved may result in losing your entire business.

"Systematic" EDP system development is really a necessity in relation to the total investment and risks. EDP system evaluators discuss the "systematic approach from various viewpoints. The studies have revealed, however, that the approaches are essentially similar and result in similar evaluatory techniques. It is presented here as a six-phase process, shown in Figure

6-1. It should be noted that vendor and equipment selection does not occur until late in the fourth phase (alternative system comparison). The investigative and planning phases are necessary precursors to the system analysis and design phase. When the planning phase and system analysis design phase are complete, selection of equipment (or services) can be based on the firm's real needs as well as the unique aspects of the firm's operations. The suggested systematic approach provides a number of obvious benefits.

The firm's management knows what it needs and wants.

Costs and benefit goals are well established prior to substantial financial commitments.

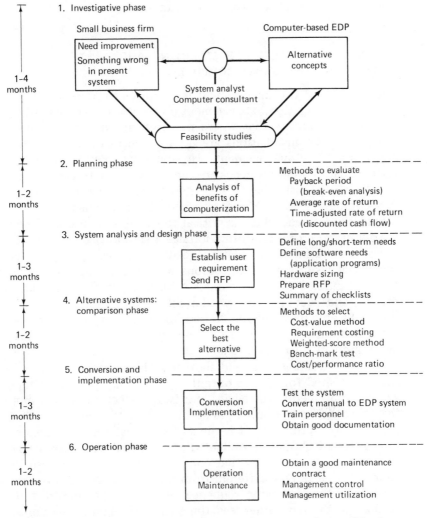

Figure 6-1. Systematic EDP system development cycle for small business.

Data required for vendor and/or equipment selection are developed based on the firm's actual requirements.

Contractual/obligation requirements are developed by, and are under the control of, the firm's management.

The EDP system is under clear management control throughout the planning, requirement, selection, implementation, and operational cycles (i.e., the firm gets what it is paying for).

In Section 6-1, the theoretical six-phase process (Figure 6-1) is converted into 10 actual steps to follow when selecting and installing your first computer. Small computer buyers can simply follow these steps to complete the installation cycle discussed in the following section.

6-1 TEN PRACTICAL STEPS FOR SELECTING AND INSTALLING YOUR FIRST COMPUTER

The blessing of top management is the primary prerequisite of a successful computer installation. Management must set the objectives of computer use. Our studies indicate that where management involvement and support are high, computer installations are usually successful. A manager of a small business is "the" management. He should be able to describe to a vendor or system analyst what his needs are and what he wants a computer to do.

Table 6-1 lists the 10 suggested steps for selecting and installing your first computer. First, long-term (5 to 10 years) business information needs should be defined, which is critical to future operations. Then, short-term (1 to 2 years) business information needs should also be defined. Identifying short-term business information needs comprises specific definition of the functional requirements of various applications such as billing, inventory control, and accounts receivable. A businessperson should know the terms, pricing, and customer and vendor information that he or she requires and should be able to define the desired format of output reports. As long as the required information is in a file, the computer can generate a report according to individual specifications.

After defining long- and short-term business information requirements and the desired format for output reports, consideration of computer (hardware) requirements can begin. Software selection is even more important than hardware selection. Finding the right size of hardware does not constitute a serious problem. It is the software that varies tremendously. Therefore, software should be evaluated and selected with extreme care. Prospective buyers are cautioned that computer salespeople will usually present an approach that is very different from the one outlined above. They generally encourage the following sequence of events: (1) ordering the computer because of the long order lead time, (2) defining information needs, and (3) identifying appropriate software or writing custom application programs.

TABLE 6-1

Ten Practical Steps for Selecting and Installing Your First Computer

1. Define information need (see Chapters 1, 4, 5, 10, and 12).
   a. Long-term business needs (5–10 years).
   b. Short-term business needs (1–2 years).

2. Define software need (see Chapters 6, 8, and 9).
   a. Define all required reports and describe desired format.
   b. Select application areas; inventory control, invoicing, order processing, general ledger, accounts receivable, etc.
   c. Define record layout, file layout, number of files.[a]

3. Define hardware need (see Chapters 2, 3, and 6).
   a. Amount of primary memory.
   b. Number and size of disks.
   c. Number and speed of printers.
   d. Number of terminals.

4. Send out request for proposal (RFP) (see Chapter 6).

5. Select vendor and computer system (hardware and software)[a] (see Chapter 7).

6. Test system thoroughly before acceptance (see Chapters 6 and 7).
   a. Individual program test(s).
   b. Job-stream test.
   c. Entire system test with live data.

7. Convert existing files to computerized files[a] (see Chapter 6).

8. Train personnel (see Chapter 6).

9. Obtain good documentation (see Chapters 6 and 11).
   a. System documentation.
   b. Application program documentation.
   c. Operation documentation.
   d. User documentation.

10. Obtain a good maintenance contract[b] (see Chapter 11).

[a] Indicates areas in which system analysts can be helpful.
[b] Indicates area in which an attorney can be helpful.

Blindly following the computer salesperson's approach is not recommended. A computer should not be ordered until objectives have been clearly defined.

Careful identification of long- and short-term objectives will eliminate most problems in defining hardware needs (hardware size). One should establish requirements for:

Amount of primary memory
Size and number of disks
Speed and number of printers
Number of terminals
Other equipment, such as card readers, tapes, etc.

A misjudgment in any one of these areas (especially the first four) is potentially dangerous. Underconfiguration of a hardware system (i.e., insufficient memory size and/or disk capacity, too few terminals, or a slow printer) can mean automatic failure in a particular application. A system should not be underconfigured in terms of either hardware or software. The problems, delays, and cost involved in upgrading a system and writing programs or restructuring files would be tremendous compared to the relatively minor expense of providing for sufficient and extra capacity in the first place.

Preliminary preparation, in terms of defining requirements for software and hardware, is essential before embarking on the process of vendor selection.

After the functional requirements of software and hardware have been defined, an RFP (request for proposal) can be sent out to several potential vendors. In an RFP, vendors can be requested to respond specifically to the following questions: (1) Can they satisfy your requirements? (2) How much will the system cost? (3) What kind of hardware does the business need to meet its objectives? Therefore, vendor responses will be structured according to the business needs rather than in the form of advertisements that say, for example: "Our computer is one of the best in the industry, and it will solve all your data-processing problems." Prospective buyers should insist that proposals be as specific as possible. For example, after evaluating hardware size requirements, a buyer arrives at the following hardware configuration:

64K memory
Two 5-megabyte disks
Three terminals
One 300-lpm printer

One should then ask vendors whether their system will support this hardware configuration. More specifically, they should be asked whether their *operating system* will support such a configuration. Quite often the answer is "no"; if the answer is "yes," ask them to specify the maximum configuration that the system can support in the future. If there is no provision for future growth, one should not buy that system.

When the various vendors have responded to the system specification, the field of candidate systems can be narrowed still further. There are several techniques that may be employed for this purpose:

1. EDP system evaluation: no-cost-and-no-time method

   a. Subjective judgments
   b. Vendor proposal and literature review

2. EDP system evaluation: small-cost-and-time method

   a. Cost/value technique
   b. Requirement costing technique

3. EDP system evaluation: fair-amount-of-cost-and-time method

   a. Weighted-score method
   b. Cost/effectiveness ratio

4. System (hardware) performance evaluation: fair-amount-of-cost-and-time method

   a. Application bench-mark test
   b. Kernel program
   c. Synthetic program
   d. Cost/performance ratio method
   e. Expanded cost/performance ratio method

5. System (hardware) performance evaluation: large-amount-of-cost-and-time method

   a. Simulation method

These methods are discussed in full in Chapter 7.

Implementation is another important area because many small business-people do not anticipate all aspects of computerization-associated expenses. For example, there is a significant communications gap in that both vendor and buyer generally assume, without verification, that the other party will assume the responsibility for implementation. If there is no provision for implementation, the buyer should understand that the vendor will not be responsible for implementation.

Unfortunately, a buyer has probably not even thought about many implementation tasks, for example:

Who is going to convert existing files to computerized files?
Who is going to design the forms?

Who is responsible for designing the system test?
Who is responsible for running the system test?
Who is going to train the personnel?
Who is going to develop the documentation?

A buyer needs a good contract that states specifically who is going to do all of the above, when, and the amount of time required. Identification of the person who will spend the necessary amount of time with a buyer to determine implementation requirements is a critical element in a contract.

Program testing and system testing is one of the most critical aspects of implementing a computer system because without programs the system will never produce the output you asked for. Since testing is quite unpredictable in terms of the results, it is difficult to establish a day-to-day detailed testing schedule in advance. However, the time required for testing and debugging the programs and systems should be as closely estimated as possible, and then that time should be doubled to establish the scheduled time for testing. A liberal allowance should be made for testing time because this is one of the most likely areas to fall behind the supplementation deadline. To test properly the programs and system, good test data must be available. The data used should be both correct and incorrect, to test the normal processing routines as well as the error routines of the system. In addition, the data should be designed to test the limits of the programs and system: that is, the data should contain both minimum and maximum values to test the programs and system.

Three levels of testing are required to do a thorough job of program and system testing. These are:

1. Individual program testing
2. Job-stream testing
3. System testing with live data

The individual program testing is usually handled by the programmers who have written the programs. Programs should be compiled and executed correctly. All known errors should be removed from the programs prior to using test data. Program testing should include testing with all conceivable invalid data.

After each program has been individually tested, "job-stream" programs in the system should be tested as a unified group. This is called "job stream" or "link" testing. Programs within the system that depend upon another program should be tested together to see whether one program transfers correct information to another program. It is possible that several programs depend on one another. Therefore, job-stream testing is quite important.

After the job-stream testing is completed, the entire system must be run through a series of tests. In most system testing, the test data are designed and prepared by the consultant or system analyst to satisfy the objectives of the systems testing. Therefore, the consultant or system analyst must determine what constitutes satisfactory system performance, that is, at what point the system can be declared complete. After all the initial testing has been satisfactorily done, another complete system test should be run using "live data," that is, actual data that have previously been processed through the existing system (probably a manual system). The potential buyer of the system is strongly recommended to conduct rigorous "live data" tests before accepting the system.

System testing is one of the most important steps needed in ensuring that a reliable customized system is being placed in production, yet it is often one of the most neglected areas. This is one reason for errors in the system that are not discovered until actual production is begun. Therefore, it is important that system testing be performed completely before launching the actual production for a customized package.

Personnel training may not constitute as large a problem as conversion to computerized files. Nonetheless, it is a problem area. Most manufacturers provide $\frac{1}{2}$-day training on terminals and the computer. Adequate training requires considerably more time. In fact, several training sessions may be required to train personnel properly, so that they can function not only on normal tasks but also on special tasks. The most difficult group to train will usually be in the operations area; for example, operating personnel responsible for inventory production planning may not have as much self-discipline as those in the accounting department.

Documentation is a vital part of system implementation and maintenance. Significant information about the programs and the system must be recorded clearly and concisely and then stored. Too many small businesses have neglected or completely ignored documentation. In these cases, when it becomes necessary to initiate or maintain a minor program modification, many hours of effort are required to reconstruct the input, output, and processing operations. There are four important areas to consider in documentation:

1. System documentation
2. Application program documentation
3. Operations manual or operations documentation
4. User manual or user documentation

System documentation should include the following:

System name or title

System narrative or abstract. Should describe the main features of the system and each function that the system performs. For example, the narrative for an accounting system would include descriptions of setting up the accounts, entering transactions, and preparing income statements. It should also describe the software used in the system, such as programming languages, operating systems, and utilities.

System flowchart. Should show the information flow and the processing flow for an entire system.

File description. Should describe the purpose of the files and file organization, such as sequential, indexed sequential, or random file.

Adequate application program documentation is essential for continued operation and maintenance of the system. The consequences of missing documentation are considerable, particularly if one cannot locate the original software house and must maintain a system with little or no documentation. The contents of the program documentation should include:

Program name or title
Program narrative or abstract
Record layouts
System flowchart and file layout
Detailed description
Program logic or program flowchart
Program listing (source program listing)
Test data

Computer operations are an important aspect of documentation. An operations manual provides the computer operator with instructions on how to run the programs and the machine(s) in the system. A perfectly designed system and set of programs are useless if they cannot be run properly on the computer. Thus, it is essential that accurate and complete operational instructions be prepared for computer operators. It is also necessary to provide an operator with step-by-step procedures to follow in any special operation either within a program or within the entire system. The operational documentation is the convenient run book for the computer operator.

The documentation prepared for the users of the system is called user documentation. It describes the output from the system and illustrates any data preparation that the user must perform for entry into the system. Therefore, source documents and their uses should be thoroughly described in the user documentation. If the source documents and other materials must be submitted to the computer by a certain date and time, those deadlines should also be included in the documentation. For small business applications, screen menus on a CRT (cathode ray tube) should give users sufficient operational instructions.

Maintenance could be another problem area if you are buying a microcomputer system, because maintenance available for microcomputers is as inadequate as minicomputer maintenance was several years ago. You should find out who provides it, the vendor or a contract maintenance firm. Particularly if you are in an out-of-the-way geographic location, you should find out where you are serviced from, and what the response time is. Maintenance can include a variety of services. Ask the vendor to enumerate them. Are parts replaced free of charge? How long must you wait between placement of a service call and arrival of a technical representative? Are there additional costs, such as traveling expenses? If so, how are these costs calculated? In determining expected downtime, find out the distance between your firm and a spare-parts depot.

A service representative can respond to your call in a short time if he is located nearby, so a list of the cities housing service centers is important. Additional information that affects a firm's service capabilities include the number of service representatives employed and the levels of employee experience. Do customer engineers have prior experience with small business computers? How are customer engineers trained (formal class, on-the-job training, etc.)?

The maintenance contract and other computer-related contracts are getting more and more complex in certain aspects as the number of small businesspeople increasingly use computers. It is advisable to consult an attorney before any computer contracts are signed (see Chapter 11).

Here are some of the questions to be answered before signing a maintenance contract.

> How fast will the vendor respond to system malfunction?
>
> How fast will the vendor respond to the program error?
>
> How long is the MTTR (mean time to repair) for this vendor?
>
> If the vendor goes bankrupt, who will maintain the system?
>
> Do you have an arrangement for use of a backup computer in case of a breakdown that requires more-than-normal repair time?

6-2 HOW TO PREPARE A REQUEST FOR PROPOSAL

6-2.1 Description of a Request for Proposal

Let's take a look at the evaluation selection steps in a typical request for proposal (RFP) process. The term RFP originated in the Department of Defense, and it says: when we buy something, we're going to put out a description of what we need and request the vendors to give us proposals. We're going to have the vendors give them to us in the format we specify so that the proposals can be compared without having to extrapolate between apples and oranges. We will be looking at apples and apples, so the different descriptions and prices can be put side by side, allowing us to evaluate technical information of which we might otherwise never become fully cognizant.

The RFP is a tool designed to solicit proposals and/or quotations for outside competitive procurement of data-processing hardware, software, and services. The quality of the RFP should be measured in terms of its ability to:

1. Adequately inform all bidders of the background and requirements of the intended procurement and to enable them to prepare a meaningful response.
2. Define requirements in a manner that will maximize the number of bidder responses.
3. Define requirements in such a manner that the issuer can be assured of a high-quality product or service.
4. Specify required deliverables and means of measuring performance which are specific and quantitative so that both the issuer and the bidder can understand and accept proper responsibility for the products and services required.
5. Develop bidding requirements in such a manner that the cost to respond does not place an undue financial burden on the prospective bidder while providing the issuer with sufficient data for proper evaluation.

One example of the RFP process is included at the end of this chapter. The RFP description will vary depending upon who writes it. But the first step is to study the company and determine what is to be automated. Then this information should be written up in the RFP, which is the most crucial step in the whole process. If insufficient or ambiguous information goes into the RFP, one is going to get an invalid response from the vendor.

The next step is to send the RFP out to selected vendors, which again is a critical step in the process. A reputable consultant is one among many sources that can aid in determining reputable vendors. Once a group of vendors are selected, send the RFP out to them and get their proposals back. Then review the proposals step by step, which will permit an overall evaluation. Be certain to check the user references included in the responses, then collect all the data and prepare a comparative analysis, comparing the vendors to each other. Finally, using the comparison method (see Chapter 7), together with the user references, select the "best" alternative.

6-2.2 User-Requirement Definition

As we discussed in Section 6-1, the support of top management is the primary prerequisite of a successful computer installation. Management must set the objective of computer use. In the case of small businesses, the president of the company must be involved in determining user requirements. He or she should be able to describe to a consultant, systems analyst, or vendor the firm's needs and what he or she wants a computer to do.

After management objectives have been established, the next step is to look in detail at the company needs. One of the things that can be done is to collect examples of inputs, examples of what is stored in established company files, and examples of outputs. Some of the output reports may be prepared by an outside processing service such as a CPA or computer service bureau. In essence, one must define the data that are being processed in the organization.

Then one should define its timeliness: how fast does the input have to be converted into the output? If it has to be done instantaneously, a more expensive system is required than if the input could be batched in once a week and converted into a particular type of output. After defining timeliness, one should collect the volumes of inputs and outputs, and file sizes. Typically, it may take 2 to 3 weeks to go through an organization and collect these data. Next, one should project these volumes and file sizes out over the life of the short- and long-term business cycle. Typically, a 2- to 5-year projection cycle is used for this study. Looking at a business that has a number of accounts receivables, so many inventory items, and so many checks to be written and payed, one should ask: "What is it going to be in 2 years and what is it going to be in 5 years?" Projecting these volumes and file sizes can be a tough process. But top management should project the company future growth rate as accurately as possible. A system analyst or system consultant, in turn, can convert growth rate into volumes growth rate and file-size growth rate. If one does not project these volumes and file sizes out over a certain period of time, the vendor who is looking at the RFP is not going to be able to configure a system that will work not just today, but 5 years from today. What this means is that if the vendor has a family of machines that cannot easily grow to accommodate the volumes in 5 years, he might have to propose a smaller version of a larger family of small computers, so that it will allow room within that family of machines to grow up to what the 5-year projections are. To aid in defining user and/or company needs the checklists shown in Figures 6-2 to 6-7 are most useful.

USER-REQUIREMENT SPECIFICATION FORM

<u>General Information</u>

Company Name _____ Phone _____

Address _____

City/State _____ Zip Code _____

Contact _____

Decision Maker(s) _____

Figure 6-2

Type of Business: Wholesaler _____   Retail _____

                          Manufacturer _____   Service _____

                          Construction _____   Other _____

Type of Product _____

Type of Customers _____

Number of Companies _____

Business Volumes:	Today	In 2 Years	In 5 Years
Annual Sales	_____	_____	_____
Number of Employees (Payroll)	_____	_____	_____
Number of Transactions	_____	_____	_____
Number of Customers (Accounts Receivable)	_____	_____	_____
Number of Vendors (Accounts Payable)	_____	_____	_____
Number of Items (Inventory Control)	_____	_____	_____

Present Accounting Method:

Applications:	Areas of Interest	Present Method	Solution
General Ledger	_____	_____	_____
Accounts Receivable	_____	_____	_____
Accounts Payable	_____	_____	_____
Payroll	_____	_____	_____
Inventory Control	_____	_____	_____
Job Estimation	_____	_____	_____
Word Processing	_____	_____	_____
Other	_____	_____	_____
_____	_____	_____	_____
_____	_____	_____	_____
_____	_____	_____	_____
_____	_____	_____	_____

Figure 6-2. (*Continued*)

USER-REQUIREMENT SPECIFICATION FORM

APPLICATION: GENERAL LEDGER

1. Functions and Features

Essential

__________ Maximum Number of Charts of Accounts
__________ Number of Digits in Chart of Accounts
__________ Double-Entry System
__________ Chart-of-Account Maintenance
__________ Multiple Postings within Periods
__________ Transaction Entry and Posting
__________ Report Generator
__________ Cumulative General Ledger
__________ Company Information Change
__________ End-of-Period Processing

Desirable

__________ Multiple Companies
__________ Subaccounts for Departments
__________ Subaccounts for Profit Centers
__________ Ratios on Financial Reports
__________ Budgets on Financial Reports
__________ Account Inquiry
__________ Multiple Reports within Periods

2. Reports and Displays

Essential

__________ Master File List (Chart-of-Accounts List)
__________ Transaction Register
__________ Cash Disbursements Journal
__________ Cash Receipts Journal

Figure 6-3

_____ Trial Balance

_____ Balance Sheet

_____ Income Statement (Profit and Loss Statement)

Desirable

_____ Profit-Center Income Statement

_____ Department Income Statement

_____ Depreciation Schedule

_____ Cash-in-Bank Report

Figure 6-3. *(Continued)*

USER-REQUIREMENT SPECIFICATION FORM

APPLICATION: ACCOUNTS RECEIVABLE

1. Functions and Features

Essential

_____ Maximum Number of Customers

_____ Maximum Number of Invoices

_____ Customer Billing

_____ Sales Entry and Posting

_____ Receipts Entry and Posting

_____ Customer Information Update

_____ Sales Analysis

Figure 6-4

_____ Open Item or Balance Forward

_____ End-of-Period Processing

Desirable

_____ General Ledger Interface

_____ Inventory Control Interface

_____ Returns and Allowances

_____ Cyclic Billing

_____ Sales Commission

_____ Miscellaneous Messages

_____ Automatic Late Charge

2. Reports and Displays

Essential

_____ Alphabetic Customer List

_____ Cash Receipts Journal

_____ Sales Journal

_____ Statements and Remittance

_____ Aged Accounts Report

_____ Sales Analysis by Customer

_____ Sales Analysis by Region

_____ Invoices

Desirable

_____ Delinquent Report

_____ Monthly Sales Summary

_____ Sales Analysis by Salesperson

_____ Commission Report

_____ Mailing Labels

Figure 6-4. (*Continued*)

USER-REQUIREMENT SPECIFICATION FORM

APPLICATION: ACCOUNTS PAYABLE

1. Functions and Features

Essential

________________ Maximum Number of Vendors

________________ Maximum Number of Voucher/Month

________________ Individual Selection of Payment

________________ Deferral of Payment

________________ Month-to-Date Total by Vendors

________________ Recurring Payment

________________ Manual Check Entry

________________ Credit Entry

________________ Vendor Maintenance

________________ Voucher Entry and Posting

________________ End-of-Period Processing

Desirable

________________ General Ledger Interface

________________ Partial Payment

________________ Automatic Payment

________________ Override of Automatic Payment

________________ Year-to-Date Total by Vendors

2. Reports and Displays

Essential

________________ Vendor Analysis Report

________________ Voucher Register

________________ Cash Requirement Report

________________ Checks

________________ Check Register

Figure 6-5

Desirable

           _____   General Ledger Distribution Cross Reference

           _____   Precheck Writing Report

           _____   Vendor Alphabetic List

           _____   Aged Payables Report

           _____   End-of-Month Report

Figure 6-5. (*Continued*)

USER-REQUIREMENT SPECIFICATION FORM

APPLICATION: PAYROLL

1. Functions and Features

Essential

                                System can handle the following pay types:

           _____   Hourly Pay Type

           _____   Salaried Pay Type

           _____   Other Pay Type

                                System can handle the following pay rates:

           _____   Regular Pay Rate

           _____   Overtime Pay Rate

           _____   Shift Differential Pay Rate

           _____   Bonuses

           _____   Other

                                System can handle the following pay periods:

           _____   Weekly Pay Period

           _____   Biweekly Pay Period

           _____   Semimonthly Pay Period

           _____   Monthly Pay Period

           _____   Other Pay Period

           _____   Maximum Number of Employees

Figure 6-6

_____ Calculation of Net Pay

_____ Tax Calculation

_____ Tax Table Maintenance

_____ Print Paychecks

_____ Manual Check Handling

_____ Check Voiding

_____ Attendance Entry and Posting

_____ Tax Withholdings

_____ Maximum Number of Automatic Deductions

_____ Government Reporting

_____ Employee File Maintenance

_____ End-of-Period Processing

Desirable

_____ General Ledger Interface

_____ Multiple-State Tax Table

_____ Multiple-Department Attendance by One Employee

_____ Maximum Number of One-Time Deductions

_____ Labor Distribution

2. Reports and Displays

Essential

_____ Master File List (Employees List)

_____ Attendance Register

_____ Earning Report

_____ Deduction Report

_____ Overtime and Sick Pay Report

_____ Paychecks

_____ Check Register

_____ W-2 Forms or Report

_____ 941-A Forms or Report

Figure 6-6. (*Continued*)

Desirable

_____   Alphabetic Employee List

_____   Precheck Register

_____   Labor Distribution Report

_____   Period Summary Report (Monthly Summary)

_____   Governmental Reports

_____   Certified Payroll Reports

Figure 6-6. *(Continued)*

USER-REQUIREMENT SPECIFICATION FORM

APPLICATION: INVENTORY CONTROL

1. Functions and Features

Essential

_____   Order Entry (Prebilling)

_____   Invoicing (Postbilling)

_____   Maximum Number of Inventory Items

_____   Finished Goods Inventory

_____   Raw Materials Inventory

_____   Automatic Reorder Items

_____   Reorder-Point Adjustment

_____   Multiple Price Levels

_____   Invoice Entry and Posting

_____   Receiving Entry and Posting

_____   Inventory Item Maintenance

_____   Credit and Return Handling

_____   Adjustments to Quantity Backorder

_____   End-of-Period Processing

Figure 6-7

Desirable

_____	Accounts Receivable Interface
_____	General Ledger Interface
_____	Bill-of-Materials Processing (BOMP)
_____	Materials Requirements Planning (MRP)
_____	Quantity Adjustments Prior to Invoicing and Billing
_____	Backorder Reporting
_____	Selective Billing
_____	Partial Billing

2. Reports and Displays

Essential

_____	Picking Tickets
_____	Customer Invoices
_____	Sales Report
_____	Inventory Status Report
_____	Below-Minimum-Inventory Report
_____	Inventory Master Price Listing

Desirable

_____	Shipping Report
_____	Receipt Adjustment Report
_____	Backorder Report
_____	Open-Order Report by Item
_____	Open-Order Report by Customer

Figure 6-7. (*Continued*)

6-2.3 Hardware and File Sizing

Careful preparation of the user requirement forms in Section 6-2.2 will eliminate most problems in defining hardware needs (hardware sizing). One should establish requirements for the following hardware units:

CPU (e.g., amount of primary memory)
Size and number of disks

Speed and number of printers

Number of terminals

Other equipment, such as card readers, tapes, etc.

A misjudgment in any one of these areas is potentially dangerous. As discussed earlier in this chapter, underconfiguration of a hardware system (i.e., insufficient memory size and/or disk capacity, too few terminals, or a slow printer) can cause system failure and lead to business failure. A system should not be underconfigured in terms of either hardware or software. The problems and cost involved in upgrading a system later would be enormous compared to the relatively minor expense of providing sufficient and extra capacity in the first place.

One should ask each vendor to specify the maximum configuration that the system can support in the future. If there is no provision for future growth, one should not buy that system.

Establishing hardware requirements can be accomplished by studying results of user requirements and converting them into the appropriate size of hardware unit.

Now let us say the study of user requirements in Section 6-2.1 revealed that ABC Company has 1,000 active accounts receivable customer accounts with an anticipated growth of 50% in the next 5 years. Figure 6-4 shows how to determine a realistic file size and disk storage capacity requirements.

Readers should be aware of the fact that the accounts receivable master file in Figure 6-8 is one of many files requiring maintenance when running a computerized system. Just to run an accounts receivable system, it requires at least an accounts receivable customer master file, invoice master file, and receipt master file. Therefore, we must carry out the same file-size computation procedure as shown in Figure 6-8 for the rest of the files before we can make a final selection of disk size. If we are considering other files, such as inventory-control-related files, accounts-payable-related files, payroll-related files, and general-ledger-related files, ABC Company probably needs cartridge

1. Determining Record Size for an Accounts Receivable Customer Master File

Data Elements (Fields)	*Storage Requirements*
Alphanumeric Fields	
Customer Number	5
Customer Name	28
Street Address	28
City Address	28
State Address	28
ZIP Code	5
Telephone Number	10
Salesperson Number	2

Figure 6-8. Determining File Size for Disk Requirement

Data Elements (Fields)	Storage Requirements
Terms Code	2
UPS Zone Number	2

Numeric Fields*	
Current Balance	6
30-Day Balance	6
60-Day Balance	6
Unapplied Cash	6
Credit Limit	6
Period-to-Date Sales	6
Period-to-Date Cost	6
Year-to-Date Sales	6
Year-to-Date Cost	6
Last Activity Date	6
Open-Order Amount	6
Total	204 characters/record

2. Determining File Size for an Accounts Receivable Customer Master File

Number of Characters per Customer	204
Number of Customers in Accounts Receivable Master File	×1,000
Number of Characters in Accounts Receivable File	204,000
Number of Characters for Anticipated Growth (50%)	+102,000
Minimum Realistic File Size Capacity Required for Accounts Receivable Customer Master File	306,000

3. Determining Disk Size for an Accounts Receivable Customer Master File (Hardware Selection)

The 306,000-character AR customer master file requires a minimum of a *single-sided double-density floppy disk* or a *dual-sided single-density floppy disk* which can hold 314,000 to 500,000 characters.

Thus, smaller diskettes, such as a mini floppy diskette (about 100,000 characters) or a single-sided single-density floppy disk (300,000 characters or less), will not hold this accounts receivable customer master file.

*Amount of storage required for numeric fields varies depending on the hardware (computer).

Figure 6-8. (*Continued*)

disks (5 to 20 megabytes capacity) or even a hard disk pack (10 to 500 megabytes capacity).

After the functional requirements of software (user requirements) and hardware (hardware sizing) have been defined, the RFP can be sent to several potential vendors. In the RFP, vendors can be requested to respond specifically to the following questions:

1. Can they satisfy your requirements?
2. How much will the system cost? (See Section 6-2.4.)
3. What kind of hardware does the business need to meet its objectives?

Therefore, vendor responses will be structured according to the business needs rather than in the form of vendors' advertisements. Prospective buyers should insist that proposals be as specific as possible (see ABC Company's sample RFP). After receiving vendors' responses, evaluation of the systems can proceed according to the evaluation methods discussed in Chapter 7.

6-2.4 Cost Estimate for an In-House Computer

After defining user requirements and hardware sizing, a closer estimate should be made of both the real and hidden costs of computerization. Real costs are associated with the purchase and rental of a computer system as identified in the vendor proposal. Hidden costs include items necessary for the support of a system. Such support costs are site cost, personnel, conversion, maintenance/backup, and financial cost. The hidden costs must be identified for each potential owner and included in the total cost analysis in relation to automation. Sometimes these hidden costs are spelled out on a vendor's proposal, but if they are not included, they are often overlooked by users. If these costs are not brought to the vendor's attention, they will usually be left out.

Computer costs differ from system to system, and one organization's cost to run and maintain a computer can be entirely different from another's. Some of the hidden costs may not pose an undue expense to a relatively large organization, but these costs may become a crucial expense in a smaller organization. Accounting for these costs may not be easy. For instance, full-time responsibility for managing and overseeing the computer operations may not be specifically assigned to anyone, but somebody should be in a position to accept responsibility. As a result, management cost should be included.

Figure 6-9 provides a checklist for comparing total cost on a one-to-one system basis. Each system is different from every other; adding up all the items will help you evaluate both the real and hidden costs of installing and operating every computer system you are analyzing.

Individual costs on the checklist, such as hardware costs, software costs,

	One-Time Cost	Cost per Month
Hardware Costs		
Central Processor Unit (CPU)		
Storage Devices (floppy disk, cartridge, etc.)		
Input Devices (data-entry terminals, etc.)		
Output Devices (printers)		
Communications (modems, phone lines)		
Remote-Site Terminals		
Other		
Software Costs		
System Software		
Application Software		
Program Modifications		
Conversion Costs		
Consultant		
File Creation		
Data Conversion		
Parallel Operation Hardware Cost		
Parallel Operation Personnel Cost		
Maintenance/Backup		
Hardware Maintenance Costs		
Software Maintenance Costs		
Equipment and Supplies for Backup		
Outside Services (nearest computer)		
Documentation		
Other		
Subtotal	_____	_____
Personnel Costs		
Computer Terminal/Operations Personnel		
Managers (% of time to supervise computer operations)		
Data-Preparation Personnel		
Other		
Supply Costs		
Floppy Disks		
Cartridge Disks		

Figure 6-9. Cost Estimate for an In-House Computer

	One-Time Cost	Cost per Month
Supply Costs (Continued)		
Tapes		
Report Paper		
Preprinted Forms (checks, invoices, etc.)		
Other		
Site Costs		
Space		
Environment (air conditioners, dedicated power line, spike control, etc.)		
Security		
Other		
Financial Costs		
Hardware Insurance Costs		
Legal Fees		
Consultant Fees		
Financial Charges		
Other		
Subtotal	_____	_____
Grand Total	=========	=========

Figure 6-9. (*Continued*)

conversion costs, maintenance costs, and others, will be important parameters in the evaluation methods discussed in Chapter 7.

6-3 SAMPLE REQUEST FOR PROPOSAL FOR ABC COMPANY

In this section, ABC Company case is utilized to demonstrate a sample RFP (request for proposal). The sample RFP letter and forms can be utilized as a base, in part or as a whole, in preparing an actual RFP.

The materials employed to complete this RFP are drawn and summarized from various chapters, especially Chapters 2, 6, and 9. The hardware system checklists are excerpted from Chapter 2. The software system checklists are summarized from Chapter 9.

The instructions given earlier in this chapter should be studied before preparing an RFP.

Following is a sample letter from the computer system consultant hired by the ABC Company to request bid proposals from appropriate vendors. All subsequent material, to the end of the chapter, forms a part of the RFP.

XYZ Vendor
123 Ready St.
Bonanza City, CA

Dear XYZ Vendor:

Bid proposals are being requested from interested computer vendors in behalf of the ABC Company. The ABC Company wishes to acquire a small business computer to assist management in collecting pertinent business information and making sound decisions. This company specializes in manufacturing leisure-related products for a worldwide market.

The applications that the company wishes to acquire are standard financial systems: general ledger, accounts receivable, accounts payable, payroll, and an inventory control. It is desired that these application programs form an integrated set that will allow interface among these application areas, in order to minimize human intervention for other than auditing purposes. All hardware and software systems that are proposed for the company must be operational and available for demonstration.

More detailed information is attached concerning the company, its present accounting method, user requirements on individual application programs, and minimum hardware system requirements.

Interested vendors are requested to send bid proposals to the attached address no later than March 26 of this year. If you wish to submit a bid proposal, please follow the format outlined in attachment A, which describes how to submit your proposal and provides minimum bid proposal forms for your convenience.

Sincerely,

Mr. Smart Ableman
Computer System Consultant
123 Go Street
Happy City, CA

USER-REQUIREMENT SPECIFICATION FORMS

User requirement specifications have been prepared by ABC Company management with the assistance of Mr. Ableman, computer system consultant.

The specifications will serve as a checklist for vendors in preparing a proposal and for ABC Company management in making comparisons of vendors' application packages.

Each of the specific application forms is divided into two categories: (1) functions and features and (2) reports and displays.

Each of these two categories is divided into two groups, (a) essential and (b) desirable. The essential section lists the mandatory features that ABC Company requires. The desirable section lists the optional features that ABC Company would like to acquire without too much additional expense.

USER-REQUIREMENT SPECIFICATION FORM

General Information

Company Name __ABC Company__   Phone __598-4238__

Address __1234 Temple Avenue__

City/State __Pomona, California__   Zip Code __91768__

Contact _____

Decision Maker(s) __Mr. John Doe, President__

Type of Business: Wholesaler _____   Retail _____

       Manufacturer __✓__   Service _____

       Construction _____   Other _____

Type of Product __Leisure-related products__

Type of Customers __International businesses__

Number of Companies __Four__

Business Volumes:

	Today	In 2 Years	In 5 Years
Annual Sales	$4 million	$5 million	$6 million
Number of Employees (Payroll)	35	40	45
Number of Transactions	95/day	110/day	120/day
Number of Customers (Accounts Receivable)	120	140	170
Number of Vendors (Accounts Payable)	200	220	300
Number of Items (Inventory Control)	1000	1200	1700

Present Accounting Method:

Applications:	Areas of Interest	Present Method	Solution
General Ledger	✓	manual	
Accounts Receivable	✓	manual	
Accounts Payable	✓	manual	
Payroll	✓	bank service	
Inventory Control	✓	tub file	

Job Estimation _____ _____ _____

Word Processing _____ _____ _____

Other _____ _____ _____

_____ _____ _____ _____

_____ _____ _____ _____

_____ _____ _____ _____

_____ _____ _____ _____

USER-REQUIREMENT SPECIFICATION FORM

Application: General Ledger

1. *Functions and Features*

Essential

150	Maximum Number of Charts of Accounts
6	Number of Digits in Chart of Accounts
✓	Double-Entry System
✓	Chart-of-Account Maintenance
✓	Multiple Postings within Periods
✓	Transaction Entry and Posting
✓	Report Generator
✓	Cumulative General Ledger
✓	Company Information Change
✓	End-of-Period Processing

Desirable

✓	Multiple Companies
✓	Subaccounts for Departments
	Subaccounts for Profit Centers
✓	Ratios on Financial Reports
	Budgets on Financial Reports
✓	Account Inquiry
✓	Multiple Reports within Periods

156

2. *Reports and Displays*

Essential

✓	Master File List (Chart of Accounts List)
✓	Transaction Register
✓	Cash Disbursements Journal
✓	Cash Receipts Journal
✓	Trial Balance
✓	Balance Sheet
✓	Income Statement (Profit and Loss Statement)

Desirable

	Profit-Center Income Statement
✓	Department Income Statement
	Depreciation Schedule
✓	Cash-in-Bank Report

USER-REQUIREMENT SPECIFICATION FORM

Application: Accounts Receivable

1. *Functions and Features*

Essential

170	Maximum Number of Customers
100/day	Maximum Number of Invoices
✓	Customer Billing
✓	Sales Entry and Posting
✓	Receipts Entry and Posting
✓	Customer Information Update
✓	Sales Analysis
✓	Open Item or Balance Forward
✓	End-of-Period Processing

Desirable

✓	General Ledger Interface
✓	Inventory Control Interface
✓	Returns and Allowances

157

____✓____	Cyclic Billing
_____	Sales Commission
____✓____	Miscellaneous Messages
_____	Automatic Late Charge

2. *Reports and Displays*

Essential

____✓____	Alphabetic Customer List
____✓____	Cash Receipts Journal
____✓____	Sales Journal
____✓____	Statements and Remittance
____✓____	Aged Accounts Report
____✓____	Sales Analysis by Customer
____✓____	Sales Analysis by Region
____✓____	Invoices

Desirable

____✓____	Delinquent Report
____✓____	Monthly Sales Summary
_____	Sales Analysis by Salesperson
_____	Commission Report
____✓____	Mailing Labels

USER-REQUIREMENT SPECIFICATION FORM

Application: Accounts Payable

1. *Functions and Features*

Essential

____300____	Maximum Number of Vendors
____120____	Maximum Number of Vouchers/Month
____✓____	Individual Selection of Payment
____✓____	Deferral of Payment
____✓____	Month-to-Date Total by Vendors
____✓____	Recurring Payment
____✓____	Manual Check Entry

___✓___	Credit Entry
___✓___	Vendor Maintenance
___✓___	Voucher Entry and Posting
___✓___	End-of-Period Processing

Desirable

___✓___	General Ledger Interface
___✓___	Partial Payment
_____	Automatic Payment
_____	Override of Automatic Payment
___✓___	Year-to-Date Total by Vendors

2. *Reports and Displays*

Essential

___✓___	Vendor Analysis Report
___✓___	Voucher Register
___✓___	Cash Requirement Report
___✓___	Checks
___✓___	Check Register

Desirable

___✓___	General Ledger Distribution Cross Reference
___✓___	Precheck Writing Report
___✓___	Vendor Alphabetic List
___✓___	Aged Payables Report
___✓___	End-of-Month Report

USER-REQUIREMENT SPECIFICATION FORM

Application: Payroll

1. *Functions and Features*

Essential

System can handle the following pay types:

___✓___	Hourly Pay Type
___✓___	Salaried Pay Type
_____	Other Pay Type

System can handle the following pay rates:

√	Regular Pay Rate
√	Overtime Pay Rate
	Shift Differential Pay Rate
√	Bonuses
	Other

System can handle the following pay periods:

	Weekly Pay Period
√	Biweekly Pay Period
	Semimonthly Pay Period
√	Monthly Pay Period
	Other Pay Period
80	Maximum Number of Employees
√	Calculation of Net Pay
√	Tax Calculation
√	Tax Table Maintenance
√	Print Paychecks
√	Manual Check Handling
√	Check Voiding
√	Attendance Entry and Posting
√	Tax Withholdings
10	Maximum Number of Automatic Deductions
√	Government Reporting
√	Employee File Maintenance
√	End-of-Period Processing

Desirable

√	General Ledger Interface
√	Multiple-State Tax Table
√	Multiple-Department Attendance by One Employee
5	Maximum Number of One-Time Deductions
	Labor Distribution

2. *Reports and Displays*

Essential

_____✓_____	Master File List (Employees List)
_____✓_____	Attendance Register
_____✓_____	Earning Report
_____✓_____	Deduction Report
_____✓_____	Overtime and Sick Pay Report
_____✓_____	Paychecks
_____✓_____	Check Register
_____✓_____	W-2 Forms or Report
_____✓_____	940 and 941 Forms or Report

Desirable

_____✓_____	Alphabetic Employee List
_____✓_____	Precheck Register
_____	Labor Distribution Report
_____✓_____	Period Summary Report (Monthly Summary)
_____✓_____	Governmental Reports
_____	Certified Payroll Reports

USER-REQUIREMENT SPECIFICATION FORM

Application: Inventory Control

1. *Functions and Features*

Essential

_____✓_____	Order Entry (Prebilling)
_____	Invoicing (Postbilling)
_____1700_____	Maximum Number of Inventory Items
_____✓_____	Finished Goods Inventory
_____	Raw Material Goods Inventory
_____✓_____	Automatic Reorder Items
_____✓_____	Reorder-Point Adjustment
_____✓_____	Multiple Price Levels
_____✓_____	Invoice Entry and Posting
_____✓_____	Receiving Entry and Posting

____✓____	Inventory Item Maintenance
____✓____	Credit and Return Handling
____✓____	Adjustments to Quantity Backorder
____✓____	End-of-Period Processing

Desirable

____✓____	Accounts Receivable Interface
____✓____	General Ledger Interface
_____	Bill-of-Materials Processing (BOMP)
_____	Materials Requirements Planning (MRP)
____✓____	Quantity Adjustments Prior to Invoicing and Billing
____✓____	Backorder Reporting
____✓____	Selective Billing
____✓____	Partial Billing

2. *Reports and Displays*

Essential

____✓____	Picking Tickets
____✓____	Customer Invoices
____✓____	Sales Report
____✓____	Inventory Status Report
____✓____	Below-Minimum-Inventory Report
____✓____	Inventory Master Price Listing

Desirable

____✓____	Shipping Report
____✓____	Receipt Adjustment Report
____✓____	Backorder Report
____✓____	Open-order Report by Item
_____	Open-order Report by Customer

APPLICATION PROGRAM FILE ORGANIZATION AND SYSTEM FLOW

After reviewing and studying ABC Company's file requirements and system flow, the computer system consultant prepared the application program file organization, file sizes, and each application program's system flow.

The number next to each file shown on the flowcharts represents the current number of records in each file (minimum file size).

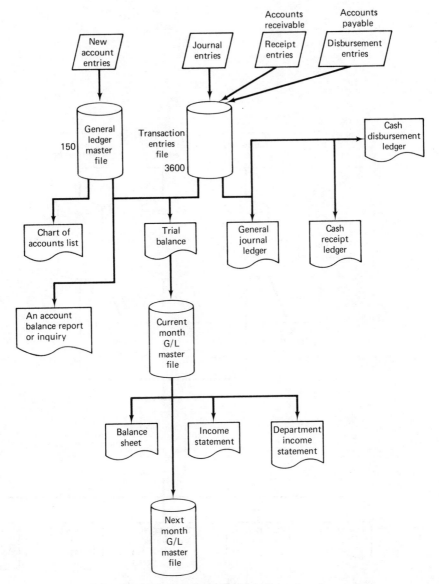

General ledger system flow.

In no way should this particular sample file organization be construed so as to limit the vendor's creativity in configuring their file organization; as long as the proposed system will generate essential reports and displays and include essential functions and features as specified in the user-requirement specification.

The file organization, system flow, and reports can be used as a guideline for the vendor in preparing their bid proposal.

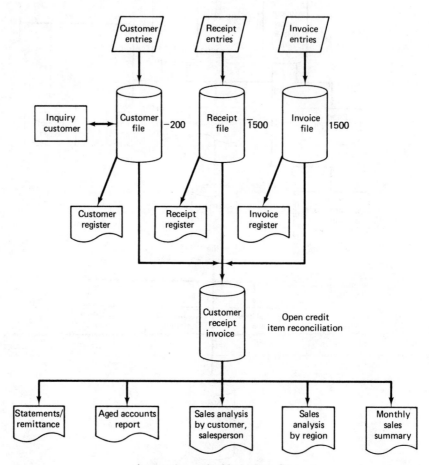

Accounts receivable system flow.

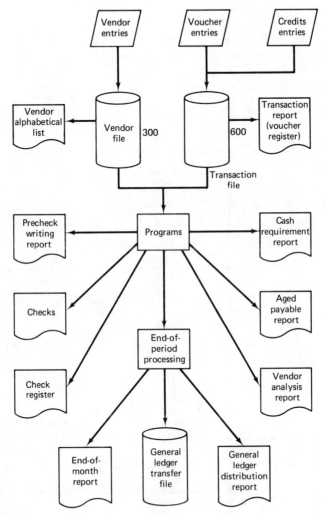

Accounts payable system flow.

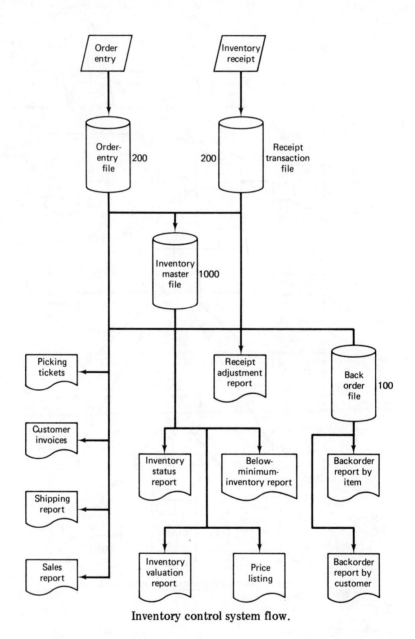

Inventory control system flow.

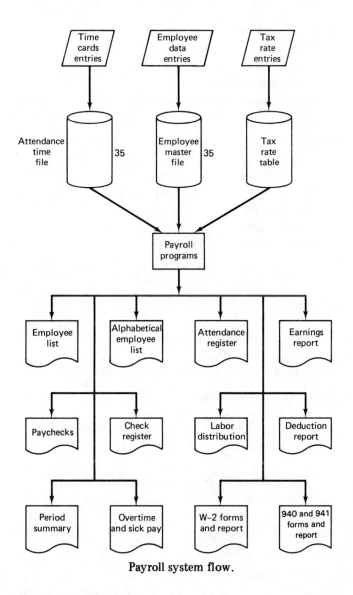

Payroll system flow.

MINIMUM HARDWARE/SOFTWARE SYSTEM

ABC company considers the following hardware components and system software to be requisites for the "minimum" acceptable system:

Hardware components

    Micro/mini central processing unit (64K)

    Floppy disk (314K characters)

    Serial printer (120 cps)

    CRT terminal (two are preferred)

    Any additional components required for a complete installation

Software

    Operating system

    Utilities (copy, sort, merge, etc.)

    Standard programming language (BASIC)

    Report-generator capability

    Data-base language preferred

    Source code should be provided

ATTACHMENT A

    I. How to Submit your Proposal

   II. Personnel to Contact

  III. Minimum Bid Proposal Forms

      1. Vendor Information

      2. A Proposed Hardware System

      3. A Proposed System's Cost Estimate: One-Time Cost and Recurring Cost

      4. Proposed Hardware System Checklists

      5. Proposed Software System

      6. Proposed Software System Checklists

      7. Maintenance

      8. Vendor's Policy

I. How To Submit Your Proposal

Vendors should answer all the questions on our attached preprepared forms and checklists, and add to the proposal all necessary additional information. It is essential to include sample output reports of all financial systems in your proposal. All proposals should include firm prices. If after reviewing the forms and checklists you wish to discuss specific requirements and clarify any of the questions, please contact Mr. Ableman, computer system consultant, at the address listed.

II. Personnel To Contact

ABC company has retained a computer system consultant,

> Mr. Smart Ableman
> 123 Go Street
> Happy City, CA
> (714) 598-4333

to assist in our evaluation and acquisition of a computer hardware and software system. All queries about your bid proposal should be directed to Mr. Ableman at the address listed.

III. Minimum Bid Proposal Forms

1. Vendor Information

Company Name _____ Phone _____

Address _____

City/State _____ ZIP Code _____

Contact _____ Title _____

Vendor's Speciality: ( ) Manufacturing   ( ) Dealer

　　　　　　　　　　　( ) System House   ( ) Other _____

Number of Years in Business _____

Client Name _____ Phone _____

Address _____

City/State _____ ZIP Code _____

Client Name _____ Phone _____

Address _____

City/State _____ ZIP Code _____

2. A Proposed Hardware System

Hardware	Make (Model)	Capacity or Speed	Price per Unit	Number of Units	Expandability
CPU	_____	_____	_____	_____	_____
Secondary Storage	_____	_____	_____	_____	_____
Output	_____	_____	_____	_____	_____
Input	_____	_____	_____	_____	_____
Other	_____	_____	_____	_____	_____
Other	_____	_____	_____	_____	_____

3. A Proposed System's Cost Estimate: One-Time Cost and Recurring Cost

	One-Time Cost	Cost per Month
Hardware Costs		
Central Processor Unit (CPU)		
Storage Devices (floppy disk, cartridge, etc.)		
Input Devices (data-entry terminals, etc.)		
Output Devices (printers)		
Communications (modems, phone lines)		
Remote-Site Terminals		
Other		
Software Costs		
System Software		
Application Software		
Program Modifications		
Conversion Costs		
Consultant		
File Creation		
Data Conversion		
Parallel Operation Hardware Cost		
Parallel Operation Personnel Cost		
Maintenance/Backup		
Hardware Maintenance Costs		
Software Maintenance Costs		
Equipment and Supplies for Backup		
Outside Services (nearest computer)		
Documentation		
Other		
Subtotal	_____	_____
Personnel Costs		
Computer Terminal/Operations Personnel		
Managers (% of time to supervise computer operations)		
Data-Preparation Personnel		
Other		
Supply Costs		
Floppy Disks		
Cartridge Disks		

	One-Time Cost	Cost per Month
Supply Costs (Continued)		
Tapes		
Report Paper		
Preprinted Forms (checks, invoices, etc.)		
Other		
Site Costs		
Space		
Environment (air conditioners, dedicated power line, spike control, etc.)		
Security		
Other		
Financial Costs		
Hardware Insurance Costs		
Legal Fees		
Consultant Fees		
Financial Charges		
Other		
Subtotal	_____	_____
Grand Total	==========	==========

4. Proposed Hardware System Checklists

    A. Checklist for CPU

    B. Checklist for Mass Storage Units (Disk Storage)

    C. Checklist for Input Units (Keyboard Display Terminals)

    D. Checklist for Output Units (Printers)

A. Checklist for CPU

1. Can the main memory accommodate the largest application program and operating system simultaneously? YES _____ NO _____

2. How much memory is available in the CPU? _____K
   Minimum _____K Maximum _____K _____

3. Can the present computer system be incorporated into a larger system without modifying or changing the existing software? YES _____ NO _____

4. What type of memory does the CPU have?
   _____ Core _____ MOS

5. Does the CPU have automatic restart logic in the event of a power failure? YES _____ NO _____

6. Can a segment of memory be added without replacing the entire existing CPU?   YES ____   NO ____

7. If the CPU has MOS memory, is there a power battery-pack protection feature in the system?   YES ____   NO ____

8. Does the CPU have self-diagnostic logic built in to warn a maintenance person when the system is beginning to fail?   YES ____   NO ____

9. Does the system require a dedicated line for the computer?   YES ____   NO ____

10. Does the system require a static-electricity-free room?   YES ____   NO ____

11. Does the system require a temperature-controlled room?   YES ____   NO ____

12. Does the system require a special dust-free room?   YES ____   NO ____

13. Does the system require a room with a raised floor to house the computer's air-conditioning and water-cooling system?   YES ____   NO ____

14. Which type of electrical power service is required to operate the computer system, 110 V or 220 V?   _____

B. Checklist for Mass Storage Units (Disk Storage)

1. Can the mass storage unit store all the programs and data necessary to operate the system?   YES ____   NO ____

2. What is the disk-drive capacity?
   _____K   Minimum _____K
   Maximum _____ K

3. Can the disk storage be removed from the disk drive?   YES ____   NO ____

4. Can the information stored on the mass storage be backed up or copied easily?   YES ____   NO ____

5. How long does it take to back up a disk to other storage media? _____minutes Minimum _____minutes Maximum _____ minutes

6. What types of mass storage media can be used for backup? Diskette _____   Cartridge disk _____
   other _____

7. Can a disk drive be added to the existing system? If yes, how many? _____   YES ____   NO ____

8. What types of mass storage disks can be added?
   Diskette _____   Cartridge disk _____
   Disk pack _____   _____

9. Can the system accommodate a Winchester disk drive? If yes, is it an 8-inch disk drive or a 14-inch disk drive?
   _____ inch   YES ____   NO ____

C. Checklist for Input Units (Keyboard Display Terminals)

1. Can the operating system accommodate more than one terminal? YES ___ NO ___

2. How many keyboard display terminals can be added to the existing system? _____ terminals
   Minimum _____ units   Maximum _____ units

3. If more than one terminal is operating at a time, can each terminal be processing a different task? YES ___ NO ___

4. Does the input terminal have the intelligence to edit the input data so the CPU can be released for more important tasks? YES ___ NO ___

5. Does the input terminal have special functions such as a moving cursor, flashing light on screen, and other easy-to-use functions? _____ YES ___ NO ___

6. Does the input terminal have numeric 10-pad keys? YES ___ NO ___

7. How many characters can be displayed at one time on a keyboard display terminal? _____ characters
   Fewer than 1,000 _____ 1,920 _____ 1,980 or more _____

8. Does the system provide input terminal key control features? YES ___ NO ___

9. Does the system provide foreground/background capability? (For example, can the system print reports while the user is inquiring information from keyboard display terminal?) YES ___ NO ___

10. How fast can the keyboard display terminal transfer data to and from the central processing unit?
    _____ cps
    Fewer than 120 cps _____
    Between 120 and 480 cps _____
    960 or more cps _____

11. Can the system support a keyboard printer? YES ___ NO ___

12. How far can the keyboard display terminal be away from the central processing unit?
    Different room _____ less than 100 ft
    Different building _____ less than 250 ft
    Different city _____ more than 500 ft

D. Checklist for Output Units (Printers)

1. Does printer speed meet the report requirement needs? YES ___ NO ___

2. Does the vendor offer a serial (character) printer? YES ___ NO ___
   If yes, how fast can it print in characters per second?
   _____ cps

3. Does the vendor offer a line printer?   YES _____   NO _____
   If yes, how fast can it print in lines per minute?
   _____lpm   _____100 lpm   _____300 lpm
   _____600 lpm   _____1,000 or more lpm

4. Does the quality of printing results meet the report re-
   quirements needs?   YES _____   NO _____

5. Does the vendor offer a shaped character printer (word-
   processing type) for high-quality printout?   YES _____   NO _____

6. Does the vendor offer a dot-matrix printer (serial high-
   speed type) for lower quality printout?   YES _____   NO _____

7. Can the system print reports while the user is inquiring
   information or entering data to the system?   YES _____   NO _____

8. Can more than one printer be added to the existing sys-
   tem at the same time?   YES _____   NO _____
   If yes, how many printers can be added? _____
   printers   Minimum _____ printers   Maximum
   _____ printers

9. Does the vendor offer serial (character) printers and
   line printers?   YES _____   NO _____

10. If the company's printing needs increase, can you re-
    place a serial (character) printer with a line printer?   YES _____   NO _____

11. Can the printer print multiple copies?   YES _____   NO _____
    If yes, how many copies can it print? _____ copies
    Minimum _____ copies   Maximum _____ copies

12. Does the printer provide both upper- and lowercase
    characters?   YES _____   NO _____

5. Proposed Software System

A. Application Software	Price	Modification Yes	No	Prevailing Rates for Additional Programming
General Ledger				
Accounts Receivable				
Accounts Payable				
Inventory Control				
Payroll				
Job Cost				

B. What are the languages available under a proposed system?

BASIC _____   COBOL _____   FORTRAN _____

OTHER _____

C. What are the utilities available under a proposed system?

Copy utility for backup ————————— Sort utility ————————

Merge utility ———————— Other utility ————————

D. Does the proposed system support a report generator?

Yes ———————————————— No ————————————————

E. Does the proposed system support a data-base language?

Yes ———————————————— No ————————————————

F. What is the operating system available under the proposed system?

Name of the operating system (example: CPM) ————————

6. Proposed Software System Checklists

A. Checklist for General Ledger
B. Checklist for Accounts Receivable
C. Checklist for Accounts Payable
D. Checklist for Inventory Control
E. Checklist for a Payroll System

A. Checklist for General Ledger

1. Does the system utilize a standard double-entry accounting system procedure and automatically maintain a zero balance at all times? YES ——— NO ———

2. Does the system handle multiple ledgers or multiple companies? YES ——— NO ———

3. How many charts of accounts can the system support? ————————————

4. Does the system provide enough flexibility in numbering charts of accounts? YES ——— NO ———

5. Can the system provide major and minor account numbers? YES ——— NO ———

6. Can the system support a report-generator program? YES ——— NO ———

7. Can the system provide an *account balance report* if the user wishes to stay *current* on a particular account? YES ——— NO ———

8. Can the system provide month-to-date and year-to-date totals? YES ——— NO ———

9. Can the system provide comparative data, ratios, and budget figures on the financial statements? YES ——— NO ———

10. Can the system provide comparative data on the company's financial position 1 year ago?   YES ____   NO ____

11. Does the system provide the ability to designate period beginning and ending dates?   YES ____   NO ____

12. Does the system handle transaction entries at any time regardless of the ending period?   YES ____   NO ____

13. Can the system be interfaced with an accounts receivable system?   YES ____   NO ____

14. Can the system be interfaced with an accounts payable system?   YES ____   NO ____

15. Can the system be interfaced with a payroll system?   YES ____   NO ____

16. Can the system be interfaced with an inventory control system?   YES ____   NO ____

17. Can the system be interfaced with all accounting systems?   YES ____   NO ____

18. Can the integrated system be used stand-alone if the user desires?   YES ____   NO ____

B. Checklist for Accounts Receivable

1. Is the system designed for the open-item billing method, the balance-forward billing method, or a combination?   _____

2. How many customer accounts can the system support?   _____

3. How many outstanding invoices can the system keep under the open-item method?   _____
(For instance, if the outstanding receivables average 60 days, the system needs to keep 2 months of invoices in storage before it purges them.)

4. Does the system produce acceptable statements?   YES ____   NO ____

5. Does the system allow multiple billing statement cycles?   YES ____   NO ____

6. Can the system produce compatible statement and invoice formats?   YES ____   NO ____

7. Does the system provide the ability to incorporate miscellaneous messages on the customer statement?   YES ____   NO ____

8. Does the system provide the ability to create statements only if desired?   YES ____   NO ____

9. Can the system provide recurring billing?   YES ____   NO ____
(This provides the ability to bill a customer a given amount every billing cycle.)

10. Does the system provide a late-charge calculation?   YES ____   NO ____

11. Does the system provide the option of selecting either custom forms or computer tab paper for printing statements and reports?   YES ____   NO ____

12. Can the user format the output reports? YES _____ NO _____

13. Can the system be interfaced with a general ledger system? YES _____ NO _____

14. Can the system be interfaced with an inventory control system? YES _____ NO _____

15. Can the dollar amounts on each invoice be charged to multiple general ledger account numbers? YES _____ NO _____

16. Can the system handle partial payment for an invoice? YES _____ NO _____

17. Can the system handle a received check that is in payment for three separate invoices? YES _____ NO _____

18. Can the system accept incoming purchase orders as pro forma invoices prior to the issuance of the true invoices? YES _____ NO _____

C. Checklist for Accounts Payable

1. What is the maximum number of vendors allowed in the system? _____

2. What is the maximum number of vouchers allowed in the system? _____

3. Can the system provide automatically recurring payment? YES _____ NO _____

4. Can an automatic payment system be overriden by a manual payment system? YES _____ NO _____

5. Does the system allow for individual selection or deferment of payments? YES _____ NO _____

6. Can the system handle partial payments? YES _____ NO _____

7. Can the system maintain month-to-date and year-to-date totals by vendors to see how the company's payments are distributed? YES _____ NO _____

8. Is the check format or content compatible with the business? YES _____ NO _____

9. Can the accounts payable system be interfaced with the general ledger system? YES _____ NO _____

10. Can the cash-in-bank account be debited as checks are written? YES _____ NO _____

11. Can the voucher be distributed to the appropriate accounts of the general ledger? YES _____ NO _____

D. Checklist for Inventory Control

1. Does the system support invoicing (post-billing)? YES _____ NO _____

2. Does the system support order entry (pre-billing)? YES _____ NO _____

3. What is the maximum number of inventory items allowed in the system? _____

4. Does the system support only finished goods inventory?   YES _____   NO _____

5. Does the system support raw material goods inventory in addition to finished goods inventory?   YES _____   NO _____

6. Can the system support bill-of-materials processing (BOMP)?   YES _____   NO _____

7. Can the system support materials requirements planning (MRP)?   YES _____   NO _____

8. Does the system automatically reorder items when supplies reach a low point?   YES _____   NO _____

9. Can the reorder point be easily raised or lowered when needed?   YES _____   NO _____

10. Does the system have the ability to override the item's price if necessary?   YES _____   NO _____

11. Does the system have multiple-price-level capability?   YES _____   NO _____

12. Does the system have the ability to credit returned items?   YES _____   NO _____

13. Does the system provide for adjustments to quantity backordered?   YES _____   NO _____

14. Does the system provide quantity adjustments prior to invoicing and billing?   YES _____   NO _____

15. Does the system provide backorder reporting?   YES _____   NO _____

16. Does the system provide full backorder retention and control?   YES _____   NO _____

17. Does the system provide selective billing capability, which can bill only selected orders?   YES _____   NO _____

18. Can the system provide partial billing?   YES _____   NO _____

19. Can the system forecast consumer buying trends?   YES _____   NO _____

20. Can the system determine at what rate a certain product is being sold?   YES _____   NO _____

21. Can the inventory control system be interfaced with the accounts receivable system?   YES _____   NO _____

22. Can the system automatically transfer the information on the invoices created by the inventory control system to the customer statement subsequently generated by the accounts receivable system?   YES _____   NO _____

E. Checklist for a Payroll System

1. Can the system hold all information for the total number of employees that may work for you in a given year?   YES _____   NO _____

2. Can the system handle hourly, salaried, and commission pay types?   YES _____   NO _____

3. Can the system handle various pay periods as needed? (i.e., daily, weekly, biweekly, semimonthly, monthly, quarterly, and yearly)   YES ____   NO ____

4. Can the system handle varying pay rates as needed? (i.e., regular, overtime, special)   YES ____   NO ____

5. Does the system come with all the tax calculation routines that will be needed?   YES ____   NO ____

6. Does the system provide tax tables? Are the tax tables updated by the user or is there a subscription service that provides yearly updates?   YES ____   NO ____

7. Does the system provide labor distribution?   YES ____   NO ____

8. Does the system make provisions for special exceptions? (i.e., floating employees, pay rate changes in midperiod)   YES ____   NO ____

9. Does the system have the capability to handle bonuses and other special pay types with or without taxes?   YES ____   NO ____

10. Are manual check handling and check voiding provided?   YES ____   NO ____

11. Are a sufficient number of deductions provided?   YES ____   NO ____

12. Does the system provide for one-time deductions such as union initiation fees?   YES ____   NO ____

13. Will the system print payroll checks? Is the check format acceptable? Can the format be easily modified? Can check printing be restarted from any point in a run in the event of a forms jam?   YES ____   NO ____   YES ____   NO ____   YES ____   NO ____

14. Does the system provide for reporting to all levels of government? Are the various report formats easily modified?   YES ____   NO ____

15. Can the system automatically produce W-2 and 941-A forms?   YES ____   NO ____

16. Does the system support a multiple-states tax table?   YES ____   NO ____

17. Does the system stand alone or is it integrated into a complete general ledger system?   YES ____   NO ____

18. Does the system post gross earning, FICA, state tax, other withholdings, various deductions, and net pay to the appropriate accounts of the general ledger?   YES ____   NO ____

7. Maintenance

1. Who will provide maintenance service for the system?

Vendor _____ Third party _____

Name of the company _____

2. How often is preventive maintenance performed?

_____

Monthly _____   Quarterly _____

Semiannually _____   Throughout the year _____

3. How much will preventive maintenance cost? _____

Less than 5% of system cost _____

5–10% of system cost _____

Over 10% of system cost _____

4. What is the average response time? _____

1–5 hours _____   5–8 hours _____   24 hours _____

1–2 days _____   2–3 days _____   More than 3 days _____

5. What is the average time [mean time to repair (MTTR)] to repair the system?

Less than 2 hours _____   2–5 hours _____

5–8 hours _____   24 hours _____

1–3 days _____   More than 3 days _____

6. How much will an emergency repair call cost?

_____

7. What kind of backup arrangement do you provide?

_____

8. Will a specific field engineer be assigned to the company?

Yes _____   No _____

9. Is the field engineer trained to work on small business computer systems?

Yes _____   No _____

Factory-trained _____   Factory-/field-trained _____

Manual only _____

8. Vendor's Policy

1. Installation Charge _____

2. Transportation Charge _____

3. Cancellation Penalty _____

4. Performance Guarantee _____

5. Acceptance Period (days) _____

6. Policy on Replacement Computer _____

7

METHODS OF EVALUATING
A COMPUTER SYSTEM OR
OUTSIDE COMPUTER SERVICE

In Chapter 6 the various steps of acquiring a system were discussed, so it is assumed in this chapter that the reader has already acquired the necessary information to select the "best" system. The necessary information includes the user's system specification need, available hardware and software costs, and vendors' responses on the RFP (request for proposal).

A standard method of selecting any system from a myriad of systems with similar features is to formulate a system specification which represents the minimum requirements that are essential for an application. This approach, by establishing requirement(s) that cannot be met by all systems, reduces to a manageable level the number of supplier candidates.

When the various vendors have quoted prices according to the system specifications, the customer proceeds to narrow down the field of candidate systems. There are certain techniques for doing this, which may be utilized individually or collectively. This chapter discusses these techniques.

7-1 EDP SYSTEM EVALUATION

7-1.1 No-Cost-and-Less-Time Method

Subjective Judgment

Subjective judgment is one technique of computer selection frequently used, particularly when the evaluator is pressed for time.

As an example, assume that system specifications have been generated for a minicomputer, and that the response from all suppliers has been narrowed to candidate manufacturers A, B, and C, and that the selection is to be made from among these three candidates. Various avenues of subjective judgment are possible:

1. Manufacturer B has replied with an offer of a BASIC compiler in addition to the FORTRAN compiler that was specified in the system description. Manufacturer B is selected for this reason; however, manufacturers A and C offer the same BASIC compiler option (at one-half manufacturer B's price) but did not include it since it was not named in the system specifications.

2. The modular construction of manufacturer C is more appealing to the purchaser than those featured by manufacturers A and B. Although capability to perform to system specifications is marginal, manufacturer C is selected because of the appeal of the system construction.

3. Manufacturers B and C offer peripheral options of magnetic tape, punched tape, cassette, and card reader. Manufacturer A offers all these options plus floppy disk. The manager of the section where the system will be installed likes floppy disk storage and issues direction to purchase manufacturer A's system on that basis.

Thus, subjective judgment, when used as a technique for selection, applies the decision maker's values (sometimes prejudice) to the presence or absence of specific features in a particular system.

When other criteria for selection are lacking, subjective judgment must be applied. For example, if two suppliers bid for a system giving the same features, cost, maintenance package, and so on, a subjective decision has to be made.

At other times this technique, when used by itself, can result in a poor selection. In the examples given, the decisions were made subjectively. In case 1, the decision was not a good one, because the BASIC compiler was not part of the system specifications and could have been purchased at lower cost from either of the other two manufacturers. In case 2, where actual performance capability is jeopardized for quasi-esthetic reasons, the hazards of subjective judgment are considerably more obvious.

Consequently, subjective decision making is a technique that should not be used exclusively when choosing a costly system.

One of the most widely used methods of obtaining information on system performance/features is a review of the available literature. A good place to start a search for candidate systems that meet the user's criteria is with the publications of Datapro Research Corp. (see Chapter 1). This firm publishes a listing of all major manufacturing lines with information regarding performance characteristics, peripheral information, and costs. These publications cost approximately $400 per year for the major system version. Datapro also offers publications on mini systems and software. Auerbach Publishers offers a similar service. These publications are available in most libraries with large collections in the business field.

Information on existing and future systems can be located in many manufacturers' journals. IBM, Hewlett-Packard, and Bell Systems are examples of manufacturers who publish periodicals to which many companies subscribe. Information may also be obtained by referring to trade magazines such as *Mini-Micro Systems*, *Small Business Computer*, *Datamation*, and *Infosystems*, which are available in many libraries.

Once having determined from the literature the types of computer systems that potentially meet the established needs, two typical actions normally follow:

1. The regional sales representative and applications engineer are contacted for system brochures and technical discussions.
2. Present users (both local and distant) of the systems under consideration are located.

Generally, sales representatives can arrange visits to companies that use the systems of interest. Some of the best data regarding the performance, maintenance, and service of a system can be acquired through existing users. Visits are usually more productive if sales representatives do not accompany the potential buyer because most users will not speak as frankly under those conditions.

Literature review and user consultation are very good techniques for evaluating potential systems. However, the final selection should be based on a combination of other techniques, described next.

7-1.2 Small-Cost-and-Time Method

Cost–Value Technique

The cost–value technique of computer selection provides the means to evaluate proposals on the basis of both cost and technical performance. Generally thought to be superior to both cost-only and weighted-score methods, the cost–value method combines the best features of both and, in addition, has the ability to consider life-cost elements.

This method requires the prospective customer to attach a dollar value to each of the desired attributes of the computer system. These estimated values should represent actual costs to the customer either to purchase the item from a third party or to generate the item internally. If a vendor item is offered at lower cost than the established value, *the difference between the vendor cost and the established estimated value is deducted from the vendor's total cost proposal.* For vendor items not offered or those for which the cost exceeds the established estimated value, no value is deducted from the vendor's cost. After each proposal is evaluated against the list of desired items and their values, the vendor proposing the lowest cost should generally be selected.

This method requires not only an accurate technical specification for the desired system, but also a clear understanding of the values of the system. Items considered in this type of evaluation include basic hardware, peripherals, software, maintenance, technical support, training, operating personnel, and facilities.

Example: West Coast Electronic Company. A set of system requirements has been generated to illustrate both the cost/value method and the requirements-costing technique. A set of sample data have also been generated to demonstrate the basic mechanics of the cost/value technique.

The system selected will be utilized primarily for the accounting and engineering departments of the West Coast Electronic Company. Programs prepared for this system will generally be small; thus, primary memory requirements will be small.

The BASIC language will be required in the system. Since the system will be utilized by several personnel, some form of program storage will be required. This should be of a removable type so that each programmer can physically retain his or her own programs. Printer output will also be required for keeping records. Business accounting programs will be the primary application. If a vendor cannot supply the desired accounting package, the vendor will be removed from competition. Vendor support will also be required.

Associated with these requirements, the desired item values given in Table 7-1 have been determined by the user with the assistance of a qualified computer consultant.

Vendors A and B have bid the costs listed in Table 7-2 to satisfy the user requirements.

Next, the cost/value technique is applied. If a vendor's item is offered at less cost than the user's established estimated value, the vendor's item cost is deducted from this value. The differences between the vendor's item costs

TABLE 7-1
Estimated Costs of Desired Items

User's Desired Items	Established Estimated Value
Printer	$2,500
Mass storage device (10 megabytes)	$8,000
BASIC language	Required
Accounting package	$4,000
Vendor support (training and maintenance)	$2,000

TABLE 7-2
Vendor's Bids

	Vendor's Bid	
	Vendor A	Vendor B
Vendor's total system cost	$28,900	$25,200
Printer	Standard	$2,000
Mass storage device (10 megabytes)	$7,000	$10,200
BASIC language	Standard	Standard
Accounting package	$2,500	$3,800
Support (training and maintenance)	$2,500	$1,000

and the user's estimated values are summarized in Table 7-3. If the vendor's item cost exceeds the user's estimated value, zero value is assigned to the table. After the differences between costs and values are totaled, the total difference is deducted from the vendor's total system cost. The result is

TABLE 7-3
Cost/Value Difference Summary

	Vendor A	Vendor B
(1) Vendor's total system cost	$28,900	$25,200
Printer	− 2,500	− 500
Mass storage device (10 megabytes)	− 1,000	0
BASIC language	0	0
Accounting package	− 1,500	− 200
Support (training and maintenance)	0	− 1,000
(2) Total cost/value difference to be deducted	− 5,000	− 1,700
(3) Final value: (1) − (2) = (3)	$23,900	$22,500

the final cost value, which is used for the system selection. The vendor proposing the lowest value is considered to be the best.

Using the final value of this example, vendor B would be selected. Although vendor B has the lowest final value, the overall difference between vendors A and B is very small. A comment that is frequently made at this point is: "If there is such a small difference, would you not consider some other items to change the value?" Edward O. Joslin's response is: "The answer is an emphatic NO! If there was anything else that should have been considered, then it should have had a pre-established value prepared for it, and it should have been considered along with the other desirable items." [1]

This method is simple and easy for small businesspeople to apply. One drawback to this method is that the user has to define the right dollar amount for the items desired, and he or she may not be knowledgeable enough to do it wisely. It is, therefore, advisable that small business managers seek the assistance of a qualified computer consultant while establishing their system requirements and setting the desired item values.

Requirements-Costing Technique* (Recommended)

This technique is similar to the cost/value technique in that it utilizes the estimated value of the system desired as a basis for evaluating the vendor proposal. All elements of a proposal can be reduced to a dollar value that represents cost to the potential customer. This single value becomes the final selection criterion for the proposed system. As in the cost/value technique, the desired items are estimated at a value which represents the cost to the customer to generate that item internally or acquire the item from a third party.

Implementation of the requirements-costing technique requires the customer to *establish a mandatory or minimum system.* Any vendor who does not meet the minimum requirement is not considered for selection. In addition to the minimum system, *the customer establishes an estimated dollar value for each of the items desired.* These values are then compared to the cost proposed by the vendor. For each desirable item that is not offered or is offered at a cost that exceeds the estimated value, *the estimated value is assessed against the vendor cost* (added to the proposed cost). If the vendor offers a desired item at a cost that is below the estimated value, *only the actual cost is assessed against the vendor.* In this manner, all costs of meeting all the requirements over the entire stated system life are considered in the evaluation. The system having the *lowest total requirements cost* over the entire system life is the system selected.

*Based on Edward O. Joslin, *Requirements Costing: A Superior Computer Evaluation Methodology* (Pennsauken, N.J.: Auerbach Publishers, Inc., 1975), DP Administration, Selection and Evaluation of Hardware, 2-04-01. By permission of Auerbach Publishers, Inc.

Items considered in this technique are the same as those considered in the cost/value technique. This system of evaluation can be effective in the selection process; however, it can be effective only in proportion to the effort to specify needs and estimate costs properly. The customer can often better understand his or her real needs and potential payoffs after a comprehensive and painstaking selection process.

Requirements-costing techniques attempt to achieve maximum value per dollar invested. It is of paramount importance to consider all costs in the evaluation process, not just the mandatory requirements. Total cost can be expressed by the following equation:

total cost = mandatory costs + other costs + desirable feature costs

Mandatory Costs. Life-cycle costing must include the mandatory equipment, software, support, and so on. Cost-of-money factors must be evaluated to adjust payments made in later years to the present value of money. This would be very important in "lease vs. buy" decisions. Inflation effects should also be considered in deriving the present value of money. These are very important considerations for the life cost of the system (usually 5 to 8 years).

Other Costs. System operating expenses must then be calculated for each system being evaluated over the expected life of the equipment. These expenses include staffing to operate the equipment, electrical power required, air conditioning (if needed), and space. Again, the present value of money over the life of the equipment, as well as inflation effects, should be taken into consideration.

Desirable-Features Costs. Perhaps the most controversial costs with vendors are the desirable-features costs. Hence, it becomes vital to specify in detail the features that are desired (but not mandatory) and the dollar value the buyer places on these features. The vendor will be penalized if these features are not included in the basic equipment, or if additional charges will be made to add these features.

It must be remembered that "desirable features" means just that. For instance, a software program may be offered as part of the vendor's basic equipment, but it could be bought elsewhere or it could be prepared by the staff of the buyer. It is important to note that the value of a desirable feature (such as this software program) should be the lowest-cost alternative available to the user.

The lowest-cost alternative for each of the desirable features becomes the preestablished value and serves as the basis of the assessment or penalty charge to the vendor who may fall short of meeting the full requirement of the desirable feature. The degree to which the vendor falls short of meeting this requirement is proportioned to the penalty charged. Hence, if a vendor does not offer this feature, he is charged the full assessment. If his equipment only provides 40% of the capability required, he is assessed 60% of the value of the feature. Also, if he adds an additional charge for this feature, he is assessed the full amount of the charge.

Considerable time and effort are required to arrive at an accurate value assessment for each of the desirable features. This understanding is invaluable. The desirable features of candidate computers in capability dollar value is summarized in Table 7-4. How well the candidate computers fulfill the preestablished value of desirable features is shown in terms of dollar value. The preestablished value represents the user's maximum credit value for each desirable feature.

Requirement costing assessments are compiled in Table 7-5. If the computer provides 100% of the capability for a desirable feature, it is not assessed the value for requirement costing.

TABLE 7-4
Desirable Features of Candidate Computers in Capability Dollar Value

Desirable Feature	Maximum Credit Value	Computer			
		W	*X*	*Y*	*Z*
Printers	$4,000	$2,000	$ 500	$0	$ 0
Mass storage	5,000	5,000	0	0	5,000
Report generator	3,000	2,000	800	0	3,000
Software package	5,000	3,000	3,100	0	5,000
Vendor support	3,000	0	1,200	0	0

TABLE 7-5
Requirement Costing Assessments

	Maximum Credit Value for Desirable Features	Computer			
		W	*X*	*Y*	*Z*
(1) Mandatory items (systems cost)		$22,000	$14,700	$18,000	$43,000
(2) Other costs (power, air conditioning, staffing, etc.)		1,000	500	2,300	4,300
(3) Desirable features		Assessed Values			
Printers	$4,000	$ 2,000	$ 3,500	$ 4,000	$ 4,000
Mass storage	5,000	0	5,000	5,000	0
Report generator	3,000	1,000	2,200	3,000	0
Software package	5,000	2,000	1,900	5,000	0
Vendor support	3,000	3,000	1,800	3,000	0
(4) Total cost: (1) + (2) + (3) = (4)		$31,000	$29,600	$40,300	$51,300

Thus, zero dollar value is assigned to the particular desirable feature on the requirement-costing table. If the computer provides only 30% of the capability required, it is assessed 70% of the preestablished value of the feature. If the computer does not provide the capability for a certain desirable feature, it is assessed 100% of the preestablished value of the feature. For example, the candidate computer W does not provide vendor support. Therefore, it is charged 100% of the vendor support feature, which is a $3,000 value.

In summary, Table 7-5 indicates that computer X system should be selected. The cost data presented support that decision. However, the result for this example is applicable only for this particular system need and system configuration.

The cost data also suggest another important point. The system required is a very small, limited-capacity type of system. Including a computer such as computer Z would have been a mistake if an actual analysis were being done. The Z system, as described, was obviously too powerful for the desired task. The basic system cost kept the Z system from being competitive.

Because this method requires that the customer clearly understand the specified system, it provides the best cost data with which to make a selection.

7-1.3 Fair-Amount-of-Cost-and-Time Method

Weighted-Score Method (Recommended)

The weighted-score method is perhaps the easiest method for a potential computer system buyer to use. Simply stated, the attributes that the buyer feels are necessary and desirable are assigned a value in descending order of importance. The sum of assigned values equals 100. Thus, if an applications software package is considered to be most important, it will be assigned the highest value. The weights assigned are subjective, but each competing system is evaluated and scored according to the value assigned to that attribute.

The weighted-score technique of computer system evaluation employs a mixture of quantitative and qualitative judgments to reach a decision. In this method various weights in the form of points or percentages are assigned to various system features considered desirable by the evaluator. The systems under consideration are then rated against the items chosen for evaluation. The scores are totaled and the system or vendor with the highest score is selected.

One distinct advantage of this technique is its flexibility. The list of attributes can be expanded or reduced depending on the user's needs (for instance, business vs. scientific). A note of caution is required. There would be, perhaps, a tendency to oversimplify the list or to assign too high a value to an attribute. Factors that may be overlooked involve the long-term operational availability of the system, including reliability and vendor support both for maintenance and consultant services.

The fact that the weighted-score technique is easy to apply may be its greatest drawback. The weights assigned are highly subjective, as is the value assigned for a competing system. Because of this, one can always question a weight as to its relative importance and question the values assigned. On the other hand, with careful selection of the attributes, the technique can indicate those systems that most closely meet the user's needs.

Thomas H. Athey [2] improved and expanded this weighted-score method. His overall method builds on important concepts from operations research, decision theory, economics, marketing, behavioral science, and system theory, and results in a major integrating device called MECCA (Multi-dimensional Evaluation Comparison of Courses of Action). This method is used as both a guide for the analyst in his or her study of a problem area and as a very effective communications device for decision makers. The MECCA approach is demonstrated in Cases A and B of Appendix I.

Description of the Method. The weighted-score method of computer selection is performed in four steps.

1. An exhaustive list of selection parameters is formulated.
2. The selection parameters are ranked according to importance and weighting factors for each are calculated.
3. Each candidate computer is scored on how well it measures up to each selection parameter.
4. The individual scores for each computer selection parameter are multiplied by the corresponding weighting factors, and these products are summed for each candidate computer. The candidate with the highest sum is generally selected.

The choice of selection parameters is the most important step in this method. The list should be prepared by a manager (user) and a computer consultant familiar with all aspects of the specific application, and it should be approved by users, operators, and management. Selection parameters must be directly related to system performance and cost.

The ranking and weighting of selection parameters can be the most difficult step in the method, especially if the agreement of a number of people is required. The "sum of the points" method may be effective for this purpose. This method consists of a systematic comparison of all the parameters in a group environment, and sums up the points for each parameter.

The scoring of candidate systems should be based on concrete data obtained from literature review, bench-mark tests, and user visitations and should be performed by those familiar with computer systems and the specific application to be implemented.

Pros and Cons of the Method. The weighted-score method will do a reasonably good job of selection if sufficient care is devoted to the listing, ranking, and weighting of selection parameters. It is not as reliable as a requirements-costing technique (Section 7-1.2) because it is not as closely related to life-cycle cost. It is, however, a much simpler method to employ.

Example. XYZ Corporation. XYZ Corporation has decided to purchase a small computer system for one of their field offices. The computer will be used as a data-entry device to the IBM 370 at the home office and to retrieve product availability from the IBM 370. They also wish to maintain local account records, print status reports, and perform some minimal accounting.

The hardware they will require is the computer, two terminals, a mass storage device, and a line printer. There is a strong possibility that they would want to add more terminals and do more data processing at the field office in the future.

The possible candidates for this computer have been narrowed down to computers A, B, C, and D. The weighted-score method of selection will be used.

Step 1: Compilation of Selection Parameters. Parameters are specific criteria of the overall system objectives and are used as a basis to determine the value of candidate computers. Parameters should be established by the user, preferably with the assistance of a computer consultant. The following list of selection parameters could be used:

1. *Basic capability*
   Computer: memory size, speed, number of registers
   Software: assemblers, compilers, application software
   Peripherals: terminals, mass storage, line printers
2. *Growth capabilities*
   Memory: maximum size
   Terminals: maximum number
   Mass storage: maximum number of words
   Applications: range of application software available
3. *Cost*
   Price: initial cost of hardware and software
   Implementation: cost of training, installation, initial data base, application software
   Operation: cost to operate system (operators, power, maintenance)
4. *Support*
   Training
   Maintenance
   Software: help with application software and program debugging

Step 2: Ranking and Weighting of Selection Parameters. Assigning a weight factor for each parameter is an important step in this process. You should assign the value very carefully, preferably with the assistance of a computer consultant or other expert.

The top-level parameters are ranked and weight factors applied in percentages:

(1) Basic capability	(30%)	0.30
(2) Cost	(30%)	0.30
(3) Growth capability	(20%)	0.20
(4) Support	(20%)	0.20
	(100%)	1.00

Then the second-level parameters are ranked and weighted. The final weight factors are calculated by multiplying first- and second-level factors as in Table 7-6. For example, the final weight factor for the second-level parameter called "computer" is 0.150. It is computed by multiplying the

TABLE 7-6
Final Weight Factors for Each Parameter

Parameter		Weight Factor
(1) Basic capability (30%)		
Computer (50%)	$0.50 \times 0.30 =$	0.150
Software (30%)	$0.30 \times 0.30 =$	0.090
Peripherals (20%)	$0.20 \times 0.30 =$	0.060
		0.300
(2) Cost (30%)		
Operation (45%)	$0.45 \times 0.30 =$	0.135
Price (35%)	$0.35 \times 0.30 =$	0.105
Implementation (20%)	$0.20 \times 0.30 =$	0.060
		0.300
(3) Growth capability (20%)		
Terminals (35%)	$0.35 \times 0.20 =$	0.070
Applications (30%)	$0.30 \times 0.20 =$	0.060
Mass storage (20%)	$0.20 \times 0.20 =$	0.040
Memory (15%)	$0.15 \times 0.20 =$	0.030
		0.200
(4) Support (20%)		
Maintenance (50%)	$0.50 \times 0.20 =$	0.100
Training (25%)	$0.25 \times 0.20 =$	0.050
Software (25%)	$0.25 \times 0.20 =$	0.050
		0.200

first-level parameter "basic capability" (30%) by the second-level parameter "computer" (50%):

$$0.50 \times 0.30 = 0.150$$

Thus, the second-level parameter "computer," under "basic capability," weighs 15% toward the final computer selection process.

Step 3: Candidate Computer Scoring. In step 3, the user rates candidate computers by their relative performance and assigns relative scores to each parameter of the candidate computers. The user and computer consultant should set up performance scores for each parameter and create the relative performance chart. Performance scores can then be assigned to candidate computers according to the relative performance chart. A sample relative performance chart for this case is created in Table 7-7. Candidate computers are rated on their capability to fulfill the selection parameters.

TABLE 7-7
Relative Performance Chart

| Parameter | Performance Score by Percentage | | |
	0	50	100
(1) Basic capability			
Computer	Low score in bench-mark test	Middle score in bench-mark test	High score in bench-mark test
Software	No business applications	Individual applications	Integrated applications
Peripherals	No peripherals	2 (terminal, printer)	5 or more
(2) Cost			
Operation	Greater than $3,000	$2,000	Less than $1,000
Price	Greater than $50,000	$30,000	Less than $10,000
Implementation	Greater than $10,000	$5,000	Less than $500
(3) Growth capability			
Terminals	No terminal	2 terminals	6 terminals
Applications	No additional programs	5 vital programs	20 vital programs
Mass storage	No growth	10 megabytes	100 megabytes
Memory	No growth	10K bytes	1,000K bytes
(4) Support			
Maintenance	No service	8 a.m.–5 p.m. within 2 days	24 hr within 5 hr
Training	No training	1 week of training	3 weeks of intensive training
Software	No support	Limited support	Unlimited support

TABLE 7-8
Candidate Computer Scoring (0 to 100)

	Computer			
Parameter	A	B	C	D
(1) Basic capability				
Computer	85	50	95	60
Software	60	90	100	50
Peripherals	90	80	90	80
(2) Cost				
Operation	90	85	85	90
Price	50	100	50	75
Implementation	60	90	90	60
(3) Growth capabilities				
Terminals	90	75	100	75
Applications	75	80	95	50
Mass storage	60	80	100	60
Memory	100	50	90	60
(4) Support				
Maintenance	95	85	85	90
Training	85	90	90	100
Software	80	90	90	90

In the case of cost factors, the lower the cost is, the higher the performance score will be. Candidate computers A, B, C, and D are scored and their capabilities summarized in Table 7-8. These scores are assigned by the user and/or computer consultant based on the information available from vendors, their customers, bench-mark test results, literature, subjective judgments, and other sources. These scores tend to be subjective, reflecting the evaluator's personal point of view. Thus, evaluators should be aware of the importance of impartiality and assign scores with extra care.

Step 4: Weighted-Rating-Score Computation. The final step for the weighted-score method is the weighted-rating-score computation. Individual scores (from Table 7-8) are multiplied by weight factors (from Table 7-6) and summed for each candidate. The computations in Table 7-9 are sample weighted-rating computations for computer A's basic capability and cost sections.

The final results of weighted-rating-score computations are summarized in Table 7-10. At the bottom of the table, the weighted rating scores have been totaled for comparison.

Computer C proves to be the best alternative, since it received the highest total score (89.1) on the weighted-rating-score computation. As far as the cost and support areas are concerned, computer C is rated as just average. However, the basic capability and growth capability areas of computer C are

TABLE 7-9
Weighted-Rating-Score Computation for Computer A

Parameter	Individual Score	X Factor =	Weighted Rating Score
(1) Basic capability			
Computer	85	X 0.150 =	12.8
Software	60	X 0.090 =	5.4
Peripherals	90	X 0.060 =	5.4
(2) Cost			
Operation	90	X 0.135 =	12.2
Price	50	X 0.105 =	5.3
Implementation	60	X 0.060 =	3.6

TABLE 7-10
Weighted-Rating-Score Summary for Candiate Computers

Parameter	Weight Factor from Table 7-4	Computer A	B	C	D
(1) Basic capability					
Computer	0.150	12.8	7.5	14.3	9.0
Software	0.090	5.4	8.1	9.0	4.5
Peripherals	0.060	5.4	4.8	5.4	4.8
Subtotal	0.300	23.6	20.4	28.7	18.3
(2) Cost					
Operation	0.135	12.2	11.5	12.8	12.2
Price	0.105	5.3	10.5	5.3	7.9
Implementation	0.060	3.6	5.4	5.4	3.6
Subtotal	0.300	21.1	27.4	23.5	23.7
(3) Growth capability					
Terminals	0.070	6.3	5.3	7.0	5.3
Applications	0.060	4.5	4.8	5.7	3.0
Mass storage	0.040	2.4	3.2	4.0	2.4
Memory	0.030	3.0	1.5	2.7	1.8
Subtotal	0.200	16.2	14.8	19.4	12.5
(4) Support					
Maintenance	0.100	9.5	8.5	8.5	9.0
Training	0.050	4.3	4.5	4.5	5.0
Software	0.050	4.0	4.5	4.5	4.0
Subtotal	0.200	17.8	17.5	17.5	18.0
Grand total	1.000	78.7	80.1	89.1	72.5

rated very high, and computer C exceeds in these areas compared to the other three computers. In the beginning, it was stated that one of the important requirements of a small computer system for XYZ Corporation was growth capability. Computer C meets that requirement. Therefore, according to this method computer C should be selected as the best alternative for XYZ Corporation.

Cost/Effectiveness Ratio

Description of the Method. The cost/effectiveness ratio method is simply an extension of the weighted-scoring method of selection. The calculation is performed by dividing total system cost by points earned in the weighted-score method. The points used in this calculation should include only "effectiveness" points (subtract any cost-associated points before dividing).

Example. Using the results of the weighted-score method from Table 7-10, the calculation would be as shown in Table 7-11.

In this example, cost-associated points (cost subtotal from Table 7-10) are subtracted from total weighted-score points (grand total from Table 7-10). Then the total system costs are divided by the differences. The results are the cost/effectivenss ratios summarized in Table 7-11.

Computer B proves to be the best alternative, because it received the best cost/effectiveness ratio (760). Using this method, computer B would be selected rather than computer C, derived from the weighted-score method.

TABLE 7-11
Cost/Effectiveness Ratio Method

	Computer			
	A	*B*	*C*	*D*
Total weighted scoring points (grand total from Table 7-10)	78.7	80.1	89.1	72.5
Cost-associated points (cost subtotal from Table 7-10)	− 21.1	− 27.4	− 23.5	− 23.7
Difference	57.6	52.7	65.6	48.8
Total system cost (including operation and implementation	$66,000 ÷57.6	$40,000 ÷52.7	$62,000 ÷65.6	$53,000 ÷48.8
Cost/effectiveness ratio	1,150	760	945	1,086

7-2 SYSTEM HARDWARE EVALUATION

7-2.1 Fair-Amount-of-Cost-and-Time Method

Application Bench-Mark Test (Recommended)

The application bench-mark method of evaluating computer system performance is useful for measuring several aspects of system capability. The bench-mark test results on various small business computers are available at reasonably small cost from organizations such as the Association of Small Computer Users [3], and usually at no cost from various computer manufacturers. The reader should be aware that manufacturer's bench-mark test results may tend to favor their own machines. The bench-mark reports available from the Association of Small Computer Users are believed to be impartial and very informative for small business computer buyers. If the bench-mark test result is not available for the particular system the user wants to examine, a bench-mark test can be conducted by the user with the assistance of a computer consultant. Of course, this will cost somewhat more. The procedure and example of conducting a bench-mark test is discussed later in this section. The cost and time involved to conduct the bench-mark test on several computers could be beyond the amount the user wishes to invest.

The bench-mark program would be written in a specific, high-level language and would normally represent an instruction and input/output sequence typical of the evaluator's intended application of the system. The bench-mark program would then be run on the computer system(s) under consideration. Compilation and execution times, and output quality, can then be compared.

Several extensions of the basic bench-mark comparison are possible. The program can be written in assembly language as well as in a high-level language. The two runs can then be compared. Such a comparison will give a more specific demonstration of each computer's internal capabilities and provide a method of comparing compiler performance between systems. A number of bench-mark programs could also be prepared and run individually and then loaded and run in the multiprogramming mode (assuming, of course, that the systems under consideration have multiprogramming capability). This comparison would demonstrate each system's ability to perform in high-load situations.

To be effective, bench-mark programs must be carefully developed to represent accurately the components of the intended application. Sufficient time on peripheral equipment must be included if it is typical of the true application. In addition, adequate portions of primary and secondary memory should be occupied during the run of such a situation would be encountered in actual use.

Bench-mark evaluation incorporates a few of the simpler and more discrete methods of comparison. Among these are cycle and add time and instruction mix.

Cycle and add time, evaluated by itself, is of limited value in modern computer systems. The parameters related to cycle and add time do not take into account the organization of the machine. The add operation cannot always be considered typical of all computer instructions. Capabilities such as efficiency of the software, look-ahead features, and number of addresses required to perform a given instruction are ignored by this method. The cycle and add time parameters were of greater significance when most programming was done in assembly language. They are of less significance today since high-level language programs (BASIC, FORTRAN, COBOL, PASCAL, etc.) must interact with a significantly greater portion of the machine's segments.

Instruction-mix evaluation is an extenison of cycle and add time measurement. One can tabulate and assign comparative weight to execution time for various instruction types according to their relative importance in system performance. Business applications would assign heavier weights to editing, table look-up, and data movement. A scientific application would weight arithmetic operations more heavily. As with cycle and add time, many factors are not considered when comparing only instruction mix. Input/output capabilities are omitted, as are other elements, such as work size, data pathing, and software.

The cycle-time and instruction-mix segments of the bench-mark test will not be extremely helpful to the small businessperson selecting a small business computer. This applies especially if solutions are being sought to problems in such application areas as accounts receivable and inventory control. However, certain important information may be learned from the overall application bench-mark results. A few companies now publish results of the bench-mark test as applied to various small business computers for potential buyers. The following is an example of the bench-mark test procedure and results.

Bench-Mark Test Example for Computer Systems A, B, and C. Three SBCs (small business computers) were chosen from 20 original computers for the final selection test. These three computers are very competitive in many aspects, including price, support, training, and maintenance. Therefore, the final decision depends heavily on the results of this bench-mark test.

Equivalent configurations were obtained from the vendors of these competitive systems. Vendors were encouraged to run selected bench marks in the language of their choice. All three vendors chose to make their run in BASIC.

The bench-mark programs were evaluated for compatibility of instructions. After ensuring that the alterations in some programs caused no change in program output, the program data were keyed on diskettes through a keyboard.

The *input processing speeds* were measured in the following manner:

> The stopwatch and the first stroke of data were simultaneously pressed and when all data were correctly keyed to the diskette, the stopwatch was stopped.

The *program processing and output speed* were measured in the following manner:

> *Business application program test.* The stopwatch and the run or execute key were pressed simultaneously and when the results were completely printed on the printer, the stopwatch was stopped.
>
> *Scientific/engineering program test.* The stopwatch and the run or execute key were pressed simultaneously and when the results appeared on the screen, the stopwatch was stopped.

The bench-mark program set consisted of four *real application program tests* and two *hardware speed tests*, as explained in the following sections.

Real Application Program Tests. The following bench marks test the running time of actual programs that the user might want the computer to perform.

1. *Payroll program.* Fifty employee records were created for a payroll master file. Each employee record contained 12 fields: employee number, employee name, social security number, pay rate, hours worked, union dues, medical insurance, other deductions, year-to-date FICA, year-to-date SDI, year-to-date withholding, and net pay. The payroll master file is updated sequentially for all 50 employee records for weekly paychecks.

2. *Accounts receivable program.* Fifty customer records were created for an accounts receivable file. Each customer record contains 11 fields: customer number, name, telephone number, documentation number, documentation date, sales amount, salesperson number, payments, credit limit, sales month-to-date, and sales year-to-date. The accounts receivable file is updated randomly 50 times by customer number for sales amounts and payments. Printed reports are: aged trial balance, customer statements, sales summary, and cash summary.

3. *Inventory control program.* Fifty inventory item records were created for an inventory master file. Each inventory item record contains 12 fields: item number, item name, bin number, list price, cost price, sales price, quantity on hand, maximum quantity, reorder level, last received date, last received quantity, and last order date. The inventory master file is updated randomly 50 times by item number for sales orders and received items. Printed reports are a detailed inventory report and a summary inventory report.

4. *Scientific/engineering program.* This program contains a variety of calculations, including addition, subtraction, multiplication, division, and exponentiation, as well as other standard scientific and mathematical functions.

Hardware Speed Tests. The two hardware speed tests are run as follows:

1. *I/O (input/output) intensive program.* This program reads numbers from 1 to N on diskette, retrieves every other number and prints the numbers on a printer. N values were 500, 1,000, 2,000, and 4,000.

2. *CPU intensive program.* The program contains a variety of calculations, including addition, subtraction, multiplication, division, and exponentiation, and other basic mathematical functions. This program runs through an iterative process N times, with N values of 500, 1,000, 2,000, and 4,000.

Conclusion of the Bench-Mark Test. The bench-mark report (Table 7-12) clearly indicates that system B has superior speed in the I/O intensive test and system C has superior speed in the CPU intensive test. As far as

TABLE 7-12
Bench-Mark Report: Total Time for Each System

		System A		System B		System C	
		Min	Sec	Min	Sec	Min	Sec
		Real Applications Programs Test					
Input processing speed							
A-1	Payroll program	60	31	52	15	59	42
A-2	Accounts receivable	31	14	26	25	43	21
A-3	Inventory program	56	45	44	15	43	14
A-4	Scientific/engineering	2	45	3	55	1	55
Programming processing and output speed							
B-1	Payroll program	12	40	11	09	15	05
B-2	Accounts receivable	14	32	13	09	18	51
B-3	Inventory program	11	42	11	03	16	45
B-4	Scientific/engineering	24	45	29	41	22	01
		Hardware Speed Tests					
I/O intensive							
C-1	$N =$ 500	2	41	1	54	2	32
C-2	$N =$ 1,000	2	59	2	05	2	45
C-3	$N =$ 2,000	3	47	3	02	3	35
C-4	$N =$ 4,000	5	02	4	45	4	54
CPU intensive							
D-1	$N =$ 500		21		31		14
D-2	$N =$ 1,000		42		55		33
D-3	$N =$ 2,000	1	24	1	56	1	17
D-4	$N =$ 4,000	2	59	4	05	2	32

business applications are concerned, system B has a hedge over systems C and A on program processing and output speed as well as input processing speed. If the company is primarily concerned with business applications, system B should be selected. However, if scientific and engineering activities are a more important part of the company's computer applications, system C would be a better candidate for the company than either system A or system B.

Kernel Program

The kernel program is useful to system engineers and other computer specialists for testing system performance and specific hardware features, such as add time, cycle time, addressing logic, registers, and other characteristics. It is not advisable for the nontechnical person to utilize this technique without the assistance of a computer specialist. This method is included here mainly for the reader's reference and understanding. A kernel program is normally a manually coded and timed program utilizing a variety of instructions, some of which may not be used in existing applications. The time for execution of these instructions is taken from published data. The relative total time for the system under consideration can then be compared. The program itself is not run on the computers being evaluated. Kernel programs do take into account special registers, addressing logic, and other elements not considered in instruction-mix or cycle-and-add-time measurements. However, they do not adequately consider input/output functions, use of other than primary memory, or compilation or loading time. Multiprogramming and multiprocessing are also very difficult to evaluate through kernel programs. Since this method of evaluation is primarily manual, there are limitations to the number and length of kernel programs that can be applied to the computer selection process. In addition, it is possible that a kernel program could be written to emphasize the strengths of one CPU and, when applied to another, would point out its weakness, thus swaying the decision [4].

A kernel evaluation can be used to examine a program bottleneck (critical path) or system hardware performance, whichever the evaluator considers pertinent to the evaluation.

Concerning a program bottleneck, a good place to begin doing a kernel analysis is to analyze a program that needs improvement in order to better utilize the computer system. Considering program XYZ as this program (see Table 7-13), the evaluator goes through the segments of code, locating the critical paths. There can be more than one kernel in a program to analyze.

Looking at program XYZ, the evaluator notices that process A is executed 100 times, which is 87% of the executions involved in this program. However, the critical path could be different when you consider execution

TABLE 7-13
Program XYZ

	Number of Executions (%)		Percent of Execution Time
Initial input	5	(4%)	5
Edit data	5	(4%)	10
Process A	100	(87%)	5
Process B	5	(4%)	78
End of job routine	1	(1%)	2
	116	(100%)	100

time. This program shows process B as taking 78% of the total processing time and, therefore, would be considered the critical path.

Considering system hardware performance, the kernel program can be coded to rate different computers. To simplify matters, consider the kernel program as one instruction:

$$\text{ANSWER} = [(G \times 4 + 7) + 9 \times (8 \div 4)] \div 2$$

Three different computer systems are analyzed. Table 7-14 gives the performance results of systems A, B, and C. By comparison, system B rates first, system C second, and system A is third. This means that system B should be picked if that program is the one utilized for most of the business's applications on the computer. A word of caution, however: most analysts fail to consider storage arrangements, compiler times, or I/O device times because of the painstaking and time-consuming tasks necessary to acquire such information.

The kernel method could be extended to utilize the total system time (compiler, I/O device, storage, retrieval, and program times) rather than just the program execution time. However, it is very difficult to measure systems performance, especially under multiprogramming and/or multiprocessing mode.

TABLE 7-14
Execution Times (msec) of Systems A, B, and C

	A	B	C
Load G to accumulator	0.05	0.049	0.055
Multiply by 4	0.02	0.19	0.19
Add 7 to accumulator	0.17	0.16	0.16
Store in A	0.09	0.11	0.12
Load 8 to accumulator	0.05	0.049	0.055
Divide by 4	0.30	0.25	0.28
Multiply by 9	0.20	0.19	0.19
Divide accumulator by 2	0.30	0.25	0.28
Add A to accumulator	0.17	0.16	0.16
	1.58	1.408	1.49

By analyzing all programs and other appropriate times, a total time for all programs and operations in the system will give the best overall system solution.

Synthetic Programs

Synthetic programs combine methods similar to those employed in both kernel programs and bench-mark programs. They are similar to kernel programs in that they do not necessarily represent an existing application. The similarity to bench-mark programs is due to high-level-language coding and the fact that the program is actually run on the machines being evaluated.

Synthetic programs have the potential of being one of the most useful methods of comparing computer system performance. The programs could be designed to exercise each system's full range of operations, including input/output capabilities, compilation and execution time, and primary and supplementary memory capabilities. Industry-wide standard programs could be developed to test system performance from general operating characteristics to very specific features. Of course, establishment of such programs would be costly and require much consideration to evaluate accurately all aspects of the many systems available today [4].

In summary, the methods described thus far in Section 7-2.1 completely ignore many elements that are usually considered before final selection of a computer system. Among the omissions are cost, supplier support, installation requirements, system reliability, and possibilities for system alteration and expansion. *The cited methods, particularly the bench-mark and synthetic programs, are useful in measuring and comparing system hardware performance.* If their limitations are not disregarded, such operational methods can be employed to provide a very informative view of prospective computer systems.

Cost/Performance Ratio* (Recommended)

The cost/performance method (price/performance ratio) is based on assigning values to various parameters associated with a specific computer's hardware and software performance. These values are then used in two equations to calculate the hardware performance ratio P_h and software performance ratio P_s. These two ratios are then used to calculate the overall cost/performance ratio for the computer under consideration. The variables are weighted in such a manner that a "good" computer will have a ratio of about 1. The larger the value, the less performance per dollar.

*Cost/performance equations from J. L. Butler, "Comparative Criteria for Minicomputers," *Instrumentation Technology*, Vol. 17 (October 1970). By permission of Instrumentation Technology.

Hardware Performance. The parameters that are considered in the hardware performance ratio equation are separated into several categories. The first group contains basic constraints on the machine and are as follows:

M main memory storage capacity of the basic machine in bits

F number of bits in the address field of single-word instructions

W word length (bits)

R number of general-purpose registers

T main memory read/write cycle time

N number of extras in the basic price, including real-time clock, power-failure protection, automatic restart after power failure, memory parity checking, memory protection

The next group of hardware parameters includes arithmetic capability A_h, logic capability L_h, and input/output capability I_h. A_h is assigned a value between 0 and 100 according to the following guidelines:

0   no arithmetic capability

25   hardware "add" and complement

50   hardware "add" and "subtract"; software "multiply" and "divide" (fixed point, slow)

75   hardware "add" and "subtract"; hardware "multiply" and "divide" (fixed point, fast)

90   hardware "add" and "subtract"; hardware "multiply" and "divide" (fixed point); software floating-point arithmetic

100   hardware fixed-point and floating-point arithmetic

L_h is given a number between 0 and 100 according to the following criteria:

0   no logic capability

25   "And" and "Or" and "Exclusive Or"

50   "And," "Or" and "Exclusive Or"

75   all of the above plus word test and conditional branch instructions

90   all of the above plus bit test and bit manipulation instructions

100   all of the above plus arithmetic rational test instructions

I_h is assigned a value between 0 and 100 as follows:

0   no I/O

25   programmed I/O through internal registers only

75   same as above plus the DMA standard

100   all of the above plus multiple I/O processors

The above foregoing parameters are used in the following equation to calculate P_h:

$$P_h = \frac{\text{Basic system cost (\$)}}{0.1M \left(1 - \dfrac{W - F}{2W}\right) + \dfrac{20}{T} (A_h + L_h + I_h) + 100N + 50R}$$

The term $0.1M[1 - (W - F/2W)]$ takes into consideration the fact that the effective memory size is reduced for machines that use many double-word instructions. The assumption is made that the larger the address field in single-word instructions, the fewer the double-word instructions that will be needed. Eight-bit word machines will often have an address field, $F = 0$.

The next major term, $(20/T) (A_h + L_h + I_h)$, is a measure of the arithmetic, logic, and input/output power of the machine.

The term $100N$ is used to assign a value to those machines that include extra features in the basic price.

The term $50R$ gives a value to the number of general-purpose registers, because the larger R is, the easier the computer is to program.

Software Performance. Software is as important as hardware in a computer and is given equal weight in the calculation of the overall cost/performance ratio. The parameters included in the software cost/performance-ratio equations are:

D	off-line diagnostic routines supplied: No = 0 Yes = 1
B	debugging routines supplied: No = 0 Yes = 1
L	loader routines supplied: No = 0 Yes = 1
A	number of assemblers
C	number of compilers
S	power of on-line operating system

The power of the on-line operating system, S, is given a rating between 0 and 100 and shows only how much the system does, not how well it does its function. The factors that are considered when assigning a value for S are:

1. Will the system handle a bulk memory device?
2. Does it have interrupt-handling capability?
3. Are I/O-driver routines included?
4. Does it have memory mapping capability?
5. Are miscellaneous routines included?
6. Does it have multiprogramming capability?

These parameters are used in the following equation to calculate P_s:

$$P_s = \frac{\text{Basic system cost (\$)}}{500(D + B + L) + 1,000A + 2,000C + 50S}$$

Total Cost/Performance Ratio. The formula for total cost/performance ratio gives equal weight to P_h and P_s and is calculated by

$$P = \frac{P_h + P_s}{2}$$

Cost/Performance Ratios of Four Small Computers. The values of P_h, P_s, and P were calculated for four computers. Systems A, B, C, and D were evaluated. The values assigned to each parameter and the calculated values of P_h, P_s, and P are shown in Table 7-15. The calculations for each computer are given in Table 7-16.

Using the calculated performance value (P) as the criterion, system D provides the most performance per dollar, system C is rated second, system A is third, and system B is fourth. These ratings agree with the design objective for these machines. System B is designed to be an electronic accounting machine, a small business computer, or a programmable terminal. It is essentially an electronic accounting machine. It can be programmed only in its own assembly language. Its software packages are designed for billing, accounting, inventory control, and financial management applications.

System A is a small, general-purpose computer intended for business data processing and use with intelligent terminal systems. It has only an Assembler and no high-level-language capability. System C and D computers are designed for use with several high-level languages. They can be in timesharing computer systems, and a large variety of software packages are available. Thus, system C and D computers designed for general use rated higher than the special-purpose machines. Between these two systems, the D system provides much better hardware performance (1.473) over the C system (2.313). The C system shows a little better software performance (2.143) over the D system (2.290), but the overall result indicates that the D system overall performance (1.88) is much better than the C system (2.23).

Expanded Method of Cost/Performance Ratio

The cost/performance ratio method just described considers only hardware and system software factors. Other factors to be considered are application programs, software, and vendor support.

The importance of support costs and the availability of application programs are a significant consideration in the evaluation and selection of a

TABLE 7-15
Parameter Values for Price/Performance Ratios

	Hardware Parameters											System Parameters							
System	\$	M	F	W	R	T	N	A_h	L_h	I_h	P_h	D	B	L	A	C	S	P_s	P
A	30.3	192K	8	24	5	2 μs	1	100	0	25	2.105	0	0	1	1	0	35	9.328	5.72
B	17.9	96K	8	16	0	1.2 μs	1	75	25	100	1.693	0	0	1	0	0	6	22.375	12.03
C	8.6	32K	0	8	14	3.2 μs	0	50	75	100	2.313	1	1	1	1	0	30	2.143	2.23
D	33.9	38K	0	8	16	1.6 μs	2	50	75	100	1.473	1	1	1	1	5	46	2.290	1.88

Basic system cost (\$)

$$P_h = \frac{0.1M\left(1 - \frac{W-F}{2W}\right) + \frac{20}{T}(A_h + L_h + I_h) + 100N + 50R}$$

$$P = \frac{P_h + P_s}{2}$$

Basic system cost (\$)

$$P_s = \frac{500(D + B + L) + 1{,}000A + 2{,}000C + 50S}$$

where

$\$$ = cost ($\times 10^3$)
M = basic core total bits (K)
F = bits in portion of single-word instruction
W = word length (bits)
R = number of general-purpose registers
T = core memory read/write cycle time (μs)
N = real-time clock, power-failure protection, automatic restart, memory parity check, memory protection, other
A_h = number proportional to arithmetic capability
L_h = number proportional to logic capability
I_h = number proportional to I/O capability
P_h = hardware

where
D = off-line diagnostic Y/N supplied
B = debugging routines Y/N
L = load for routines Y/N
A = number of assemblers
C = number of compilers
S = on-line bulk memory, interrupt capability, I/O-driver routines included, memory mapping, miscellaneous routines, multiprograms
P_s = software
P = final performance

Calculation of P_h

$$P_h = \frac{\text{Basic system cost (\$)}}{0.1M \left(1 - \dfrac{W - F}{2W}\right) + \dfrac{20}{T}(A_h + L_h + I_h)\, 100N + 50R}$$

System A

$$P_h = \frac{\$30,315}{0.1(192,000)\left[1 - \dfrac{24 - 8}{2(24)}\right] + \dfrac{20}{2.0}(100 + 0 + 25) + 100(1) + 50(5)}$$

$$= 2.105$$

System B

$$P_h = \frac{\$17,900}{0.1(96,000)\left[1 - \dfrac{16 - 8}{2(16)}\right] + \dfrac{20}{1.2}(75 + 25 + 100) + 100(1) + 50(0)}$$

$$= 1.683$$

System C

$$P_h = \frac{\$8,571}{0.1(32,000)\left[1 - \dfrac{8 - 0}{2(8)}\right] + \dfrac{20}{3.2}(50 + 75 + 100) + 100(0) + 50(14)}$$

$$= 2.313$$

System D

$$P_h = \frac{\$33,888}{0.1(384,000)\left[1 - \dfrac{8.0}{2(8)}\right] + \dfrac{20}{1.6}(50 + 75 + 100) + 100(2) + 50(16)}$$

$$= 1.473$$

Calculation of P_s

$$P_s = \frac{\text{Basic system cost (\$)}}{500(D + B + L) + 1,000A + 2,000C + 50S}$$

System A

$$P_s = \frac{\$30,315}{500(0 + 0 + 1) + 1,000(1) + 2000(0) + 50(35)}$$

$$= 9.328$$

TABLE 7-16 *(Continued)*

System B

$$P_s = \frac{\$17{,}900}{500(0 + 0 + 1) + 1{,}000(0) + 2{,}000(0) + 50(6)}$$

$$= 22.375$$

System C

$$P_s = \frac{\$8{,}571}{500(1 + 1 + 1) + 1{,}000(1) + 2{,}000(0) + 50(30)}$$

$$= 2.143$$

System D

$$P_s = \frac{\$33{,}888}{500(1 + 1 + 1) + 1{,}000(1) + 2{,}000(5) + 50(46)}$$

$$= 2.290$$

Calculation of P

$$P = \frac{P_h + P_s}{2}$$

System A

$$P = \frac{2.105 + 9.328}{2} = 5.716$$

System B

$$P = \frac{1.683 + 22.375}{2} = 12.03$$

System C

$$P = \frac{2.313 + 2.143}{2} = 2.228$$

System D

$$P = \frac{1.473 + 2.290}{2} = 1.882$$

computer system. Information on these factors is difficult to get from vendors. The best way to get information on these factors will probably be the reports published by reputable research institutes or publishers, such as the Datapro reports.

Application Programs. The application program performance ratio P_a can be calculated by multiplying the reciprocal of the user rating (4 is the highest score) for applications programs of four (as reported, for example, in Datapro's *User Ratings of Minicomputers and Small Business Computers* [5]). Thus, the best computer would have a value of 1 for P_a; and $P_a = 4/R_a$, where R_a is the user rating for applications programs.

Vendor Support. The vendor support performance ratio P_v is calculated by dividing the annual maintenance charge for the basic system by the sum of the ratings for responsiveness of maintenance service, effectiveness of maintenance service, and technical support (as reported, for example, in Datapro's *User Ratings of Minicomputers and Small Business Computers*). We also divided it by the main memory size in kilobits to compensate for the size of the system. P_v is calculated as follows:

$$P_v = \frac{\text{Annual maintenance fee (\$)}}{M_k\,(R_r + R_e + R_t)}$$

where R_r = user rating for responsiveness of maintenance service
R_e = user rating for effectiveness of maintenance service
R_t = user rating for technical support
M_k = memory size, kilobits

Total Cost/Performance Ratio with P_a and P_v. The total cost/performance ratio P_t can be calculated as

$$P_t = \frac{P_h + P_s + P_a + P_v}{4}$$

The smaller the P_t value, the greater the performance per dollar spent on the system.

Total Cost/Performance Ratios of Four Small Computers. The values of R_a, R_r, R_e, and R_t found in Datapro's *User Ratings of Minicomputers and Small Business Computers* are shown in Table 7-17, together with the calculated values of P_a, P_v, and P_t for the same four computers rated previously using the cost/performance ratio, P (see Table 7-18 for calculations).

The four computers are ranked in the same order, using P_t as found when evaluating them according to P.

The calculations show that the best vendor support value is obtained for system D; next in rank is system C with system A third, and system B fourth.

The best application programs performance rating is calculated for system D, with system B and system A tied for second place, and system C ranked last among the four small computers.

TABLE 7-17
Parameters for Calculating Application Programs and Vendor Support Performance Ratios

System	R_a	P_a	R_r	R_e	R_t	M_k	Annual Maintenance Fee ($)	P_v	P_t
A	3.0	1.333	3.2	3.1	2.8	192	1,992	1.140	3.476
B	3.0	1.333	3.5	3.2	3.0	96	996	1.070	6.615
C	2.9	1.379	2.7	2.8	2.4	32	588	2.326	2.040
D	3.3	1.212	3.0	3.2	2.8	384	2,220	1.091	1.404

$$P_a = \frac{4}{R_a} \qquad P_v = \frac{\text{Annual maintenance fee (\$)}}{M_k(R_r + R_e + R_t)}$$

$$P_t = \frac{P_h + P_s + P_a + P_v}{4}$$

where
  R_a = user rating for application programs
  P_a = application program performance ratio
  R_r = user rating for responsiveness of maintenance service
  R_e = user rating for effectiveness of maintenance service
  R_t = user rating for technical service
  P_v = vendor support performance ratio
  P_t = total cost/performance ratio
  M_k = main memory size (kilobits)

Source: Values for R_a, R_r, R_e, and R_t are from *User Ratings of Minicomputers and Small Business Computers* (Delran, N.J.: Datapro Research Corp., November 1980), pp. 70C-010-40a–e.

7-2.2 Large-Amount-of-Cost-and-Time Method: Simulation

The simulation technique makes use of a simulator, which is a computer program that contains the relevant operational characteristics of different computers in a series of tables. The information concerning the user's computer job mix is fed into the simulator and the program calculates how different computer systems will perform running that mix. Empirical formulas are used to analyze multiprogramming and multiprocessing capabilities of various configurations of computers. This type of simulator is called an empirically oriented simulator.

Another type is the event-oriented simulator, which uses a computer program to model the computer system under consideration. The span of operations that would be executed during a given time period is represented in this simulation program. Several event-oriented simulators have been developed and have provided performance predictions very close to a computer's later performance. This type of simulation is very costly and has generally been limited to large-scale projects such as the design of a completely new computer system. Empirical table-look-up simulators have had mixed success. It is difficult to give adequate consideration to multiprogramming and the effects of software in such simulators. These simulators have been

Calculation of P_a

$$P_a = \frac{4}{R_a}$$

System A

$$P_a = \frac{4}{3.0} = 1.333$$

System B

$$P_a = \frac{4}{3.0} = 1.333$$

System C

$$P_a = \frac{4}{2.9} = 1.379$$

System D

$$P_a = \frac{4}{3.3} = 1.212$$

Calculation of P_v

$$P_v = \frac{\text{Annual maintenance fee (\$)}}{M_k(R_v + R_e + R_t)}$$

System A

$$P_v = \frac{\$1,992}{192(3.2 + 3.1 + 2.8)} = 1.140$$

System B

$$P_v = \frac{\$996}{96(3.5 + 3.2 + 3.0)} = 1.070$$

System C

$$P_v = \frac{\$588}{32(2.7 + 2.8 + 2.4)} = 2.326$$

System D

$$P_v = \frac{\$2,220}{384(3.0 + 3.2 + 2.8)} = 0.642$$

213

TABLE 7-18 *(Continued)*

Calculation of P_t

$$P_t = P_h + P_s + P_a + P_v$$

System A

$$P_t = \frac{2.105 + 9.328 + 1.333 + 1.140}{4} = 3.476$$

System B

$$P_t = \frac{1.683 + 22.375 + 1.333 + 1.070}{4} = 6.615$$

System C

$$P_t = \frac{2.313 + 2.143 + 1.379 + 2.326}{4} = 2.040$$

System D

$$P_t = \frac{1.473 + 2.29 + 1.212 + 0.642}{4} = 1.404$$

most successful in predicting the performance of computers used on business-oriented job mixers. This type of data processing produces a large volume of input and output which is easy to estimate.

The parameters in event-oriented simulators can be varied to determine the optimum computer system configuration. Using this approach, bottlenecks can be detected and various proposed solutions analyzed before changes are actually made.

Simulation is a good method of selecting an optimum computer system, but it is expensive to produce custom-tailored programs. The empirical simulators have had mixed success.

Pitfalls in Using Simulation

Nothing is perfect. Bad simulations, however, have their special brand of imperfection—errors that are rarely discovered until too late. There are two sources of error in simulation, each of them extremely difficult to detect unless the proper precautions are taken.

The first source of error is "bad logic," an inaccurate representation of the system simulated. Unlike most logic models run on a computer, a simulation model cannot be tested or debugged because there are no test data available for comparing the simulation results.

The second source of error is improper evaluation of the simulation results. Simulation is an experiment. No matter how loudly one proclaims the results, it does not change this fact. Every experiment is subject to sampling error. Every result of a simulation run has an associated "confidence interval." Therefore, the results should be thoroughly analyzed by a statistician.

7-3 SUMMARY OF AVAILABLE METHODS [6]

None of the computer selection approaches can be applied rigidly to all problems, although some of them can be more generally applied than others. The methods and their respective weaknesses will be reviewed in turn.

1. *Subjective judgment* should probably be the method used *only* by a *very knowledgeable* buyer of a relatively inexpensive machine with limited application needs. This is analogous to a wealthy person selecting among a Lincoln, a Cadillac, and a Mercedes to give as a birthday present.

2. The *literature review* can be used as a first step (by semitechnical personnel) to select candidate systems for further in-depth evaluation. No final decision should be made on the basis of a literature search by itself; this task should be undertaken as part of initial feasibility studies and immediately after the job requirements have been defined.

3. The *cost/value* and *requirements-costing* evaluation techniques are very strong methods which are probably best for the experienced user of EDP machines. The smaller EDP user could hire a consultant to assist in establishing values for the required functions. The larger EDP user might well have the in-house capability of establishing values for the required functions.

4. The *weighted-score* and *cost/effectiveness ratio* evaluation approaches must be applied very carefully, because of the possibility of slanting the results. If good system requirements are developed to support the weights, these techniques can be effective and valuable tools.

5. The *application bench mark* will do very little for the EDP system evaluation except, possibly, permit comparison of machines that are otherwise very similar. This evaluation method should always be made with other machine evaluation techniques.

6. The *cost/performance ratio* evaluation method *can* be the best approach but only if certain critical actions are taken to expand the decision equation to fit precisely the application being considered. The weight or value of each parameter must be adjusted by correcting the constants embedded in the equation, and the equation must be expanded to include the total life-cycle cost of the machine. These costs should also be connected to a common time basis (such as present value), considering the firm's cost of capital, opportunities lost, and alternative financing and/or procurement techniques.

7. *Simulation* of the alternative EDP candidates is a powerful, useful, and relatively accurate selection technique. The concepts of simulation

cost/benefit analyses should be inherent in any EDP selection and design effort. On the negative side, the cost of developing *detailed* operations and economic algorithms cannot generally be justified for small to medium-size firms. However, simplified cost/benefit relationships and estimates can and must be developed at low cost and in a short period to ensure procurement of EDP system and hardware that meet the firm's needs. Systematic structured analysis of the firm's EDP needs is a necessary and high-payoff endeavor.

REFERENCES

[1] EDWARD O. JOSLIN, *Requirements Costing: A Superior Computer Evaluation Methodology* (Pennsauken, N.J.: Auerbach Publishers, Inc., 1975), p. 9.

[2] THOMAS H. ATHEY, *A Systematic Systems Approach* (Englewood Cliffs, N.J.: Prentice-Hall, Inc., in press).

[3] Association of Small Computer Users, *Bench Mark Report*, Vol. 1, Nos. 1–12 (Boulder, Colo.: Association of Small Computer Users, 1979).

[4] HENRY C. LUCAS, JR., *Computer Based Information Systems in Organizations* (Chicago: Science Research Associates, Inc., 1971), pp. 122–125.

[5] *User Ratings of Minicomputers and Small Business Computers* (Delran, J.J.: Datapro Research Corp., November 1980).

[6] J. S. CAMPBELL, R. A. POST, C. F. LEAVER, and K. D. ANDERSON, "Computer-Based EDP Evaluation and Selection" (Unpublished paper, General Dynamics, Pomona, California, 1978).

SELECTING SYSTEM
SOFTWARE

8-1 WHAT IS SOFTWARE?

The business manager should clearly recognize that software is equally, if not more important than hardware. Appropriate software can constitute the difference between a smoothly running system and a hit-and-miss installation. The ultimate user(s) should have some knowledge of system and application software. System software usually consists of the operating system, compilers, utilities, and optional file or data-base management systems. Applications software consists of programs developed for specific jobs in a business.

8-1.1 Operating System

Operating system software comprises those programs that control execution of computer programs and those programs that may provide scheduling, debugging, accounting, input/output control, storage assignment, compilation, data management, and related services. This software controls the hardware processing and decides when certain functions are to take place: input/output (I/O) operations, time distribution to real time, CPU processing of user applications and utility programs, and multiple programming schedules, for example. This software is very important in the creation and mainte-nance of an efficient and easy-to-use computer system (see Figure 8-1).

As an example, if the hardware a firm determined its needs consisted of a CPU, two 40-megabyte disks, three CRT terminals, and a 300-lpm printer, the prospective buyer should ask the vendor whether or not his system software could ·support the required hardware. Buyers should verify that system software will support the hardware they are purchasing. If it does not, they should consult system software specialists or other vendors to determine if there is an available system to support the hardware.

Regardless of the efficiency of application programs, only the operating system program can utilize the maximum capabilities of the hardware. How-ever, the hardware and the operating system should be considered as an

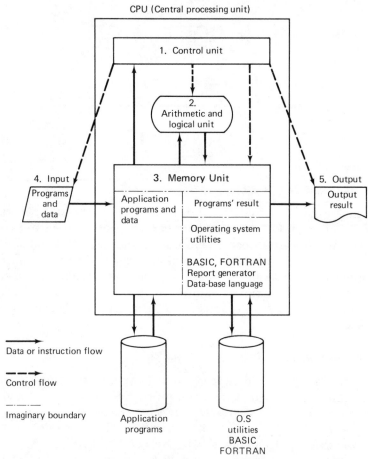

Figure 8-1. Software programs and data flow in the schematic diagram of a computer system.

integrated computer system and not exclusively as either hardware or as an operating system. Certain vendors may have more than one operating system. A particular hardware configuration may or may not be appropriate to the vendor-recommended operating system.

To determine if the operating system will support the hardware, the vendor should be required to make hardware configuration estimates. The vendor should specify that the suggested operating system does indeed support the minimum-hardware configuration. The vendor should also specify the maximum configuration for future growth of the proposed system. No one should buy a system without expansion capabilities, because a growing business creates the need for a viable and expandable system.

The foregoing specifications and estimates should be included in the written contract between vendor and business manager. This contract should include the hardware configuration, system software, and the maintenance agreement. Vendors may not honor verbal agreements. All desired terms should be written.

Verify that specifications, operating systems, and configurations specified by the vendor are defined for the intended processing unit. If they are not, there is potential for a sizable loss to the business manager when he or she has to change to another larger processing unit or an entirely new system. Following is a checklist for evaluating an operating system.

Checklist for Operating System

1. Does the operating system support the required hardware configuration?
2. Does the operating system support more than one terminal? If so, how many?
3. Can the operating system be used for a larger system without modification when your business grows?
4. Can you enter data while the system is printing a mailing list or paychecks?
5. Does the operating system have the capability of handling virtual memory? Virtual memory is a great extension of main memory.

8-1.2 Compilers

Compilers are usually located in the processing unit. The compiler translates human-prepared (higher-level) languages (e.g., BASIC and COBOL) into the machine language that actually operates the computer.

The system should be able to handle a high-level language such as BASIC, FORTRAN, RPG, COBOL, or PASCAL. It would be most unwise to limit a system's languages to lower-level languages such as Assembler or some macro languages. Few programmers handle assembly or macro languages well. Use of a higher-level compiler language effectively creates a potential reservoir of outside programming rather than limiting assistance to that provided by the vendor selling the system. The ultimate user may even become efficient enough in a higher-level language to develop programs without the help of programmers.

The type of processing mode a system uses will affect the choice of compiler. For instance, BASIC is more suitable for on-line data-processing systems. On the other hand, COBOL and RPG are better equipped for batch processing. FORTRAN is equipped for on-line as well as batch processing.

At the present time, many minicomputers use BASIC, FORTRAN, RPG, COBOL, and PASCAL effectively. The COBOL and RPG compilers currently available for microcomputers need improvement, however, and it may be a few years before truly efficient ones exist.

The buyer should decide which processing mode the system will use and how appropriate the vendor's language compilers are for the system(s) being considered. One might also ask recent customers of the vendor about the specific compiler languages under consideration. Questions might be directed to the following areas: (1) the clarity of system error messages, (2) problems or "bugs" in the language, (3) capacity or range of the language, (4) types of programs that run well in this language, and (5) number of errors in the application programs supplied by the vendor.

After the buyer has decided upon the compiler languages, he should then direct his attention to the vendor's utility programs.

Checklist for Compilers (Computer Language)

1. Does the system support a high-level language? If so, what language?
2. Does the system support the BASIC language if you are considering a small business computer?
3. Is the language suitable for an on-line data-processing system or batch processing? Choose the language that suits your processing mode.

8-1.3 Utility Programs

Utilities are a series of programs that simplify daily use of a system. These programs provide useful routines that can be used repeatedly in the operating systems and applications programs, eliminating the need for certain operations to be rewritten in various programs. Considerable programmer time and money will be saved if the utility programs can do what is desired in certain parts of application programs.

These programs include copy routines, key item routines for records, merging routines to create one file, and text editor programs that allow users or programmers to change (modify) parts of a program without rewriting the entire program or section.

The report-generator program is very important to the small business computer system. It can be very useful as an extension of utility programs or file management systems. It gives users report functions without requiring a host of programmers. It allows users to generate reports any time and to arrange the report heading and items just the way they like to see them. For instance, some report-generator programs support functions that involve counting the number of items and/or summing the dollar values of sales or invoices.

Again, prospective buyers should ask the vendor's customers about the utility programs and report-generator programs they have to use, if the programs work well and efficiently, and if bugs in the programs have been corrected. These programs should be discussed with the vendor and all agreements and future modifications should be written into the contract.

Checklist for Utility Programs

1. Do the utility programs allow users to copy one file to another?
2. Do the utility programs allow users to merge two files into one?
3. Do the utility programs have a text-editor capability that allows users or programmers to change (modify) parts of a program without rewriting the entire program?
4. Do the utility programs allow users to sort files by key items alphabetically and/or numerically (ascending or descending order)?
5. Do the utility programs support a report-generator function?

8-1.4 File Management System

The buyer and vendor should also discuss file management.

A file is a group of similar logical records that are stored as one logical file for the user (e.g., a list of inventory items and their vendors). There are two basic types of files.

In one type of file each logical record features portions of information (data items or fields) of nonvarying length. Each logical record has the same length regardless of the number of characters used for each field. This is sometimes called a fixed-length file.

The other type of file consists of logical records with fields of varying length depending on the amount of information. This is called a variable-field-length file. It is considerably more complex to store and revise information in variable-length files than in fixed-length files. Thus, it is more difficult for the vendor to write and more expensive for the buyer to purchase error-free programs for variable-length files.

A good file management system performs five major functions:

1. Addition of new records to specific files (provision for file growth is absolutely essential).
2. Removal of undesirable or old records (deletions) from a file without disturbing the sequence of the file or any information on other records in the file.

3. Accessibility of information or records in a file. A user or application program should be able to reference any record in any file and obtain one or more data fields of information. If the file is not accessible, data cannot easily be utilized. (One should remember, however, that information may never be requested, even though the file is accessible.)

4. Ability to change information in a specific data field of a record without re-creating the entire record from scratch. Any field should be accessible for revision without the rest of that record, or any other record in the file, being affected.

5. The final function is that of listing files. This should include the following lists: the order in which the files are stored, specific data field(s), numerical or alphabetical sequence, and partial listings or subsets of the foregoing (e.g., all last names beginning with A).

Files are stored either sequentially by a certain field (alphabetical or numerical) or by random access, which means that the file can be created in any type of order by certain data field(s) using random storage techniques. It is preferable to have both storage methods, but if one must choose between them, random access is the obvious choice because one could arrange files in any logical order, including sequential.

Checklist for File Management Systems

1. Does the system support a file management program?
2. Do the five file maintenance functions operate smoothly?

   a. Adding new information to specific file
   b. Deleting undesirable information from a file without disturbing the file
   c. Changing information in specific data collections without re-creating the entire record
   d. Inquiring concerning information in a file
   e. Listing a partial file or an entire file according to a designated sequence, such as numerical or alphabetical order

3. How much time is required to list or reorder files?
4. Is there any way to recover files?
5. How much time is required to obtain the desired information?
6. Is there a report generator in the file management system?
7. How many records can a user access simultaneously?
8. Can the file be expanded?
9. Can a record be located using more than one field (multiply key access)?
10. Is processing sequential, index-sequential, or random?
11. Does the file system save space?
12. Does the system reduce redundant information to a minimum?

A data base may be considered as a mass grouping, or pool, of generally nonredundant information (data) that is accessible to more than one application program. The data are independent of the application programs, and vice versa. An assemblage of data bases constitutes a data-base management system.

The data-base management system is considerably more sophisticated than a file management system. There are no files that fit only one or two application programs. Instead, there is a pool of information that can be referenced by many application programs from the various departments of the business. For example, both personnel and payroll staff may access and use some of the same information in a data base.

One could create files (by collecting the necessary information from the data base) and lists, or access individual records or combinations of records from the data base, without ever writing a program. For example, one could list all inventory items by part number and, by writing a simple program, total the number of each item sold for deletions, and add decisions regarding inventory updates.

This type of system might be most appropriate for on-line inquiry operations with a minicomputer system. However, a data base could also be processed in batch mode. Many small computer-based data-base management systems (SC-DBMSs) have been developed since the mid-1970s. The cost of SC-DBMSs today ranges from less than $1,000 to over $50,000.

The data-base system should be designed for growth and for maintaining independence between data and application programs. There should be no need to change application programs to obtain the data utilized.

Checklist for Data-Base Management Systems

1. Does the system support a data-base management system?
2. Does your application require a data-base management system?
3. What is the minimum and maximum cost to create the data base?
4. Is there a method, such as a password, for ensuring the privacy or security of data against unauthorized use?
5. How much time is required to locate desired data?
6. How many key words and/or conditions does the data-base management system allow users to put in an inquiring sentence?
7. How well does the data base work?
8. Is expansion possible?
9. Are users of a similar data base available who are willing to discuss their experience?

The age-old problem that constantly interferes with human relationships, the problem of communicating accurately, is also present in the human/computer relationship—perhaps to an even greater degree. Although computer languages have been designed to reduce this difficulty, it still exists and is as great a problem as ever, although computers are more flexible now than they have ever been.

The problem is twofold in nature: (1) the computer does exactly what it is told to do (i.e., it cannot think for itself); and (2) it uses a machine language that is completely foreign to human languages. Higher-language programmers have sought to overcome these two basic difficulties. The essential difficulty of constructing what is called a higher-level language (FORTRAN, BASIC, COBOL, etc.) can only be appreciated by someone who has actually attempted to construct one; however, one can begin to appreciate the problem by considering the length of time required to learn a foreign language. In addition, imagine how difficult it would be to learn a foreign language if there were no one to teach it.

Perhaps an appreciation of how far the industry has come in the design and utilization of computer languages for business purposes can be seen by reviewing the length of time it has taken to achieve the present state of the art. (It is definitely still an art, although much scientific work has been accomplished in this field.)

Although the first recognized computer came into existence during World War II, it was not until the early 1950s that simpler methods of programming arose. Prior to that, programming had been very difficult and extremely frustrating. In general, computer programs addressed only small problems that required very large numbers of calculations. These calculations generally related to engineering, and all programming was in machine language.

Machine language is "bit and byte"-oriented, oriented toward the basic storage capacity unit of the computer. Machine language programming is written in one of several codes, each of which is oriented to the machine rather than to types of problems or to human beings.

Here is an example of a machine language and how it works. Entering data directly in binary form (called a "bit") is a simple way to program a computer that wastes virtually no memory. Data are entered in binary form by simply flipping switches either *on* or *off*. For instance, if the switches are respectively: OFF, OFF, OFF, ON, OFF, OFF, OFF, ON this would be a binary number 00010001, which the computer would read as a "00010001." When the program is running and it reads 00010001, it will interpret it to mean: "Add the number 1 to the number located in the first register." For example, suppose the first register holds the number 14; then when the instruction 00010001 is read, "1" will be added to 14. The register will then hold the number 15.

If the Assembler instruction were being used, the code for our earlier statement would be "INC 1." When this instruction is acted upon, the register will again hold the number 15. This simple transition from machine (or binary) language to assembly language took years to formulate in the world of computers.

When we move from Assembler to higher-level languages, the basic method of operation is changed. The higher-level language is no longer restricted to a register application where the data must be moved from one hardware location to another. When a higher-level language is used, the same operations occur, but now the programmer does not always know or care what happens at the Assembler level; he only knows that the higher-level language does the job.

The higher-level language is oriented toward our normal way of doing addition. An example in BASIC would be: "A = B + 1." If B equals 14, then after the statement A = B + 1 is completed, A will equal 15. In another level of language, COBOL, the same instruction could be: "ADD 1 to B giving A." (COBOL can be made to look like BASIC by using the word "COMPUTE": for example, "COMPUTE A = B + 1.") Thus, registers are not important to the higher-level programmer.

The other higher-level languages, with the exception of RPG, are similar for this particular statement. Let's summarize these so that we can get an idea of how they look when they are compared:

Machine Language	Assembler Language	BASIC	FORTRAN	COBOL
00010001	INC 1	A = B + 1	A = B + 1	ADD 1 to B giving A

Note that they all add the number "1" to another number.

Although these languages have obvious similarities, they also have many differences. These differences arise because each language was originally designed for different purposes, and is used with different considerations in mind.

Computers really became useful when higher-level languages were developed in about the mid-1950s. FORTRAN, which is an acronym for FORmula TRANslator, was the first really useful and powerful high-level language to be developed. It was specifically oriented toward mathematical utilization of the computer. However, many businesses began to use it because of the numerous advantages it offered in comparison to the then-current Assembler languages. Again, however, the limitations of FORTRAN, when used in a business environment, were very extensive, and it became apparent that another language would be necessary. Within a few years, the CODASYL (Conference on Data Systems Language) was formed to produce that new language.

COBOL was the result of the CODASYL committee's deliberation. This new language, implemented by most computer manufacturers in the early 1960s, became to the business community what FORTRAN was to the scientific community.

A rapid succession of languages followed on the heels of COBOL, each created to fulfill an immediate need. BASIC was implemented in 1965 as a simple language that students, who were usually working on-line to a large computer, could use easily. Furthermore, BASIC's capability of immediate corrections made program experimentation possible. The fact that students were exposed first to BASIC was to have far-reaching effects on the computer industry, because one's first experience usually creates a long-term familiarity and attachment.

RPG was introduced by IBM in 1964 as a less tedious alternative to assembly language for writing programs that tabulate and summarize data from sequential files. In 1971, an improved version called RPG II was introduced, and RPG III is the newest introduction. Many programmers support this language because it is easy to use, if one does not object to adhering to a fixed logic. It has generally been used by small- and medium-scale data-processing installations.

PASCAL is one of the newest high-level languages in the small computer field. PASCAL has been accepted at many universities for several years and is now being used more and more in industry. It was introduced by Niklaus Wirth as a vehicle for teaching concepts of systematic program design or "structured programming" and as a basis for writing software such as compiler programs [1]. Structured programming is a way to reduce the time needed to develop large programs and to improve the possibility that, once developed, they will work correctly.

"PASCAL can be an extremely powerful tool for writing interactive business application programs on microcomputers and minicomputers. PASCAL provides data structuring facilities generally superior to those of COBOL, and its control constructs allow a systematic and modular approach to program design that reduces development effort and improves reliability ..." [2].

Probably the most important recent development in computer languages has been the gradual borrowing of one language's assets by another. This has been particularly true of the BASIC language.

Although BASIC was designed originally for students to learn to use easily, it now has all the capabilities, depending on the dialect, of practically any other language. Virtually every mini- and microcomputer manufacturer has a version of BASIC, most of them being very good and some of them being very powerful and easy to use.

Thus, BASIC has become the defacto language of small computers and, from all indications, will probably remain in the forefront for many years to come.

One question that may have occurred to some readers is: Why so many different ways of telling a computer what it's supposed to do? The answer is fairly simple, although the decision as to which language to use in a specific application may not be as simple. What follows is an attempt to give some direction to the search for the optimum language that will fulfill your needs.

As mentioned earlier, FORTRAN was originally designed to handle large quantities of numbers—called "number crunching" in the trade—whereas COBOL was designed to move considerable amounts of data from one place to another with very little number crunching. BASIC was designed for easy programming, with very limited number-size and data-movement capabilities, whereas PRG performs well in report production. If each of these languages has corresponding advantages and disadvantages, which is best?

In investigating the hardware aspects of this question, one quickly realizes that a complete computer costing under $10,000 practically mandates a dialect of BASIC—which isn't a really bad choice in most cases. When the price rises to about $20,000 or more, COBOL and FORTRAN become alternative choices. At a price greater than $50,000, virtually any language is available, or at the very least a restricted dialect of most languages can be purchased. So at the present state of the small computer business, the best language is generally BASIC (even though PASCAL is getting lots of attention), although larger systems have the other languages available.

If BASIC is the best choice (or only choice, in some cases), why are we even discussing the other languages? The answer is simple—it is likely that the other languages will be available on small computers very soon. This means that very good software packages may follow and that more knowledgeable systems analysts and programmers may enter the small business computer field [3].

REFERENCES

[1] NIKLAUS WIRTH, "The Programming Language PASCAL," *Acta Informatica*, Vol. 1 (1971), pp. 35–63.

[2] KEN BOWLES, *PASCAL versus COBOL: Where PASCAL Gets Down to Business* (Peterborough, NH: BYTE Publications, Inc., August 1978).

[3] DOUG FLEW, *Computer Languages for Small Business Computers*, unpublished paper, California State Polytechnic University, Pomona, 1978.

DEVELOPING OR SELECTING
APPLICATION SOFTWARE

9-1 WHAT IS APPLICATION SOFTWARE?

Application software consists of programs developed to perform specific jobs for a business. The analysis of specific jobs the system should perform must be well understood before participating in any discussion with vendors.

Application programs include order processing, inventory control, purchasing, general ledger system, accounts payable, accounts receivable, and payroll system.

There are two ways to obtain application programs. One alternative is to purchase or lease package programs already developed by the vendor. A second alternative is to create custom programs to suit the specific needs of the user for each application.

If package programs are chosen, one should not try to modify them (except for minor changes, such as names or headings). The most important factor in this recommendation is that the warranty made by the vendor may be voided if major changes are made and an error occurs in the program.

The custom approach is very time-consuming and because of the amount of programmer time (at \$20 to \$40 per hour) needed to develop custom programs, adds considerable cost to application software. It is also possible that the programmers might misunderstand the buyer or the vendor regarding requirements and thus develop an incorrect program. This could result in either the expenditure of more time and money to patch the custom program, or disregarding the custom program and spending additional money to purchase the package program for that application.

The vendor's experience and reputation are important regardless of which approach is taken. This does not require choosing a vendor who has been around for 10 years, or one who has installed a great many programs. Look for the vendor that by reputation installs and services programs effectively and cooperatively. A good vendor will assist prospective buyers in gaining knowledge and provide answers and consultation regarding application software.

The vendor should provide reference of users. In discussions with users, prospective buyers might ask such questions as:

What problems have they encountered with the programs?

Is it possible to observe the operation?

Does the system run the way the user and observers think it should?

Does the vendor provide quality maintenance quickly?

Does the vendor charge extra for errors found in the programs?

Does the user get a discount on modified or updated versions of the program?

This discussion of software should acquaint the business manager with some of the problems, and methods of avoiding problems, in choosing and implementing systems or application software into the computer system.

9-2 PROS AND CONS OF PACKAGE PROGRAMS VS. CUSTOM PROGRAMS

Before the development of mini- or microcomputers the only organizations that owned computers were large business firms. Most organizations were large enough to employ a data-processing staff. This staff would usually conduct systems studies, selection and evaluation of systems, systems designing, and all programming, including application software.

The application programs were considered customized (or in-house) software. They were called customized programs because they were designed to specifically handle the data, operations, and reports for the company that employed the data-processing staff working on those particular applications. (Customized programs may now be developed in-house by independent software houses or by individuals contracted to write application programs for the business organization.) All files and record designs and reports were also built into these programs. They were tailored to the specific needs of the user. With the advent of technology, mini- and microcomputers came on the scene and opened up the use of computers to almost anyone. Hardware vendors also started selling hardware and software separately (this is called unbundling). Together with this, the growth of software houses and individual programmers designing and programming software packages developed rapidly.

A software package is computerized application program (such as inventory control, accounts payable, or payroll) that is already designed, written, documented usually, and ready to run. It can be purchased or leased by an organization or person in lieu of developing a program to do the identical things. Software packages are usually designed to be used as is; each item of information is input separately with its own identifying parameter; output is usually rigid, although there is some freedom in the way data are printed, reports are sequenced, or totals occur. Packages may range in price from $15 to $100,000 and are available to perform many typical business functions. A word of caution: not all packages are designed to do what they are stated to do. Make sure the package is checked out thoroughly before being leased or purchased. Figure 9-1 illustrates a general rule of thumb: package software is usually suitable for back-office business and customized software is preferable for front-office business. Management is usually less concerned with input format, handling of data, or output reports as long as each application in the back office generates the information they need. The customer is not directly involved, so special forms or reports are not absolutely necessary. Since the only information required is for decision making, and most package programs generate the basic information needed by management to do their job, packaged software is adequate for this purpose.

On the other hand, front-office business usually involves the direct relationship of the customers to the business. Therefore, any use of application programs in front-office business usually requires a customized approach that will give all necessary information to management and customers on specialized forms. The design of customer bills, customer accounts receivable, and ordering receipts are critical to both management and the customer.

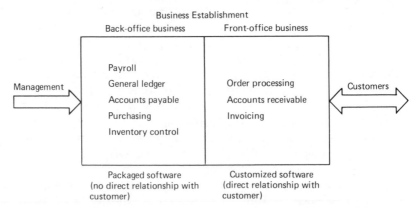

Figure 9-1. Package software for back-office business and customized software for front-office business.

Most packages are constructed to handle generalized information and output forms and therefore do not lend themselves well to front-end business applications. This is the general trend only; some businesses may not consider this appropriate for their organizations.

9-2.1 Package Programs: Advantages and Disadvantages

Following is a discussion of some of the advantages of package programs.

1. *Immediate use of program.* The user gets immediate use of the package if no alterations of the system or modification of the package is required. This provides the user with the results required, and he need not worry about when a customized program might be finished.

2. *Less programming time needed* (no programming if no modifications are required).

With little or no programming required, the user saves the programming costs associated with that particular program. This allows the savings to be invested elsewhere for greater return on investment or reduction of other areas of costs.

3. *Overall lower costs.* The lower overall cost of a package program as compared to a customized program results in savings to the user. For example, no costs are involved in the design or coding of a package program. No input or output file layout, record layout, or report formats need to be created by the user. Approximately 60% of the total cost of developing a program stems from the design and coding phases.

4. *Packages usually cost only 10% of customized program development costs.* When comparing the total cost of package programs versus customized programs, the package software total cost will generally run around 10 to 25% of a customized program's total cost. The principal savings result from no design or coding phases for the package program. The costs associated with both package and custom programs are discussed later in the chapter.

5. *Generally speaking, better documentation than in-house or customized programs.* Documentation for package programs is usually more fully developed as a selling aid to show the customer/user the ease of use and beneficial aspects of the package(s).

6. *Usually, easy to use.* Package programs are usually easier to use and operate because they are designed to complete the tasks as generally as possible so that many customers will want to purchase the package. When a package program is run, intricate explanations for every step of the program are included. This makes use of the program fairly easy for everyone.

Possible disadvantages of package programs include:

1. *No perfect program package for specific needs.* Since packages are designed to meet many customers' needs, there are usually no perfect packages to fit the job. Approximately 80% of all packages require some modification, however slight. This would result in a package that may or may not do the entire job it was purchased to do.

2. *Possibly inefficient package.* Package programs may be very inefficient in operation or in the programming techniques used. The program may take a long time to run, causing computer resources to be tied up longer than they should be. This, in turn, leads to extra costs that usually are not considered when the package is purchased. The programming techniques used may also cause longer than necessary run times, and they may make poor use of the customer's equipment in terms of space or equipment used.

3. *Nonflexible.* The package may be nonflexible, in that input and output formats are already designed and usually cannot be changed unless program modifications are made. However, the sequence of the reports generated can usually be switched to satisfy the customer. The characteristics of a package program discussed in the introduction would apply here.

4. *May require more hardware than you need or have.* When the package is finally run on the user's system, it may be found that larger hardware resources are needed to run the program. This may amount to more resources than the user's business needs can support. If this situation arises, the entire cost of the package becomes a loss to the user and, in addition, he is back where he started from.

5. *Little or no vendor maintenance.* Once a package is purchased or leased and all training and documentation are completed, the user is usually given little or no vendor maintenance. This is especially true if the vendor did not design the package but is merely handling it for someone else. A good practice before purchasing or leasing is to find out who designed, owns, and has the right to sell it.

6. *Unknown owner of package.* If the user does obtain a package from someone other than the owner, he may have to pay the owner compensation for its use. This situation might develop where the vendor sells the package to the user without authorization by the owner or without letting the user know that he does not have the owner's permission.

7. *Misrepresentation of package ability.* The ability of the package to do what the salesperson or brochure states may be misrepresented to the customer. It is the user's responsibility to make sure the program does what it is supposed to do. If you cannot test the program or go through the documentation before purchase, a good practice is to put into the contract the statements from the brochure and/or the sales representative. (See more concerning this area in Chapter 11.) One other caution: some minor package programs may be sold that are riding on the reputation and ability of a "big brother" package, and then may not work as intended. Check these minor packages as thoroughly as possible before buying.

9-2.2 Custom Programs: Advantages and Disadvantages

We now point out some of the advantages of custom programs compared to packaged software.

1. *Designed the way the user wants and needs.* By having a customized program designed, the user can specify and fit the program to do what he

wants and needs it to do. The file layout, input, output, reports, and methods of computations are developed by the user's staff.

2. *May adjust programs to existing hardware resources.* If the program is customized, it can be made to accommodate existing hardware resources, since the resources are known before the program is designed. This is a savings because most problems can be programmed in various ways to produce the same results given the limits and capabilities of the hardware resources available. The unsuspected need for more hardware resources than are available is eliminated.

3. *Can consider growth of company in the programs.* When customizing programs, the specific anticipated growth needs of the company can be planned into the programs being designed. This can ensure maximum useful life of a program, thus saving money that would have to be spent purchasing or leasing updated versions of package programs as conditions warranted.

4. *More user involvement during development stage.* The user becomes more involved because of the development stage and can therefore use this knowledge to make the program more fully meet his needs.

5. *Users can train along with the system.* As users train along with the system, they become very knowledgeable about the program's capabilities and limitations. They can therefore better utilize the program, perhaps getting greater profit and less cost from it than originally planned.

6. *If developed in-house, staff can easily maintain, modify, or update.* When in-house staff people design a program, they have complete knowledge of how it functions and can easily accommodate maintenance, modification, or update with less design and programming time. This takes much less effort than trying the same thing on a package program with little knowledge of how it was put together.

On the other hand, there are various disadvantages to custom programs.

1. *Costs usually exceed package program costs.* A major drawback is the high cost of developing a custom program over purchasing or leasing a similar package program. Usually, only very specialized custom programs actually cost less than purchasing package programs.

2. *Time delay of program.* Designing and coding a program can take from a few weeks to many months or more to complete, depending on the size and complexity of the program. When the program is needed immediately, time delays can cost the company a great deal in terms of money, profits, and operation costs.

3. *Need of good communication to develop a good system.* A major failure area involves custom programs not doing what they are supposed to be designed to do, a problem that stems from poor communication between designers and users of the program. Without good understanding between users and designers, no program can be developed to handle properly what the user wants it to handle. This problem can lead to bad feelings between designers and users of a system.

TABLE 9-1
Custom vs. Package Costs in the Program Development Cycle

Type of Cost	Custom (%)	Package (%)
Problem definition, determining objectives, and analysis of problem	7–15	7–15
Package evaluation	—	7–20
Package price	—	30–50
Information gathering	—	4–11
Program design	10–25	—
Program coding	25–35	—
Program testing	3–8	3–8
File conversion	10–15	10–15
Documentation	6–10	2–4
Implementation	10–20	5–15
Training	2–5	4–6
Periodic test and review	2–5	2–5

4. *Program tends to be developed around existing hardware.* By developing programs to work on existing hardware, techniques for designing or using file structures or more efficient processing might not be used. This can sometimes result in slow running, inefficient (space wasting), or totally unusable programs that cause the company to experience lower profits, higher operating costs, and decreased customer satisfaction.

5. *If developed in-house, documentation may not be prepared.* When customized programs are developed (especially in-house), the documentation tends to be left until after the program is implemented and running. At this point there is often a tendency not to produce it, because the users have other work they want done and know the workings of the program anyway. But later, the absence of previous personnel who designed or used the program may cause turmoil when there is no documentation to follow.

The decision whether to purchase a package program or to develop a custom program requires full knowledge of the costs and benefits associated with each alternative. Chapter 4 discusses the costs and benefits of computerization, which include programming costs and benefits. These cost/benefits can easily be analyzed to assist in making decisions on package or custom programs.

Table 9-1 compares custom and package costs involved in the program development cycle.

9-3 NINE STEPS TO ENSURE SELECTION OF GOOD PACKAGE APPLICATION PROGRAMS

There are some steps that help to reduce the risks involved when a package program is being selected. Many package program failures result from inadequate system specification and poor evaluation of packages. The following discussion should aid management in creating successful methods for obtaining good packages.

Selection of packages includes many important steps that will help reduce risks and losses in buying or leasing software. Among the more important steps are the development of system criteria, the evaluation of packages and vendors, and user references. The recommended selection steps are as follows:

1. *Appoint a qualified consultant or selection team* (to be used for remaining steps if possible) *to select and purchase the best package(s).*

2. *Prepare a minimum-criteria list.* Included in such a list are aspects of the package that may meet your problems and objectives, technical specifications and operation information of the package and effects on hardware resources, implementation and maintenance information, and the price of the package for the period selected. This list should contain only *minimum* criteria critical to your system.

3. *Develop a description of your system and attach it to the minimum-criteria list. Vendors of packages must then be located and this information given to them. Request written responses plus brochures of packages that meet your list.* Packages can often be examined at the following types of businesses: hardware vendors, software houses, service businesses, and consultant services. Information on various packages can be located in such publications as manufacturers' software catalogs, *Datamation, Infosystem, EDP Analyzer, Software Digest, International Computer Programs Quarterly*, Auerbach's *Software Reports*, Computer Information Center Service reports, *The NCC National Computer Program Index*, and Datapro Research Corp. reports.

4. *Do a preliminary screening of all vendor responses to see if their packages meet the minimum-criteria list.* Any packages that do not should be eliminated. From this screening, compile a list of "desirables" that you think you might like to have, based on vendor responses and your needs.

5. From the list of minimum and desirable criteria, screen the remaining packages and again *eliminate any packages that do not fulfill your requirements.*

6. *Evaluation of vendors of remaining packages is appropriate at this point. Questions that might be asked of vendors include:*

   a. Does the vendor have any software development experience, or does he just handle software for others?

   b. What is their main line of business?

   c. Are the sales figures of the company available?

   d. Is a profit and loss statement available?

   e. What are the geographical areas of coverage?

   f. What type of technical personnel are available for questions or service?

   g. What do the training and education programs consist of?

   h. Does the vendor have an emergency support program?

   i. What guarantees and warranties are specified in the contract?

    j. Will the vendor supply information as to the number of present users, and user references?

    k. How long has the company been in business?

    l. How many people does the company employ?

    m. Is the vendor the originator of the design and coding of the package?

    n. What are the backgrounds of principal members of the firm (business, sales, technical, application)?

    o. Will the vendor help install the package?

    p. What type of documentation is available on the package?

    q. Will the vendor support or maintain the system after purchase?

A decision may be made to eliminate more packages because of poor vendor evaluations, which sometimes indicates poor vendor packages.

7. *Invite the remaining vendors to give lectures, seminars, or demonstrations of their packages.*

8. Obtain user references from top vendors. If a vendor refuses to give references, eliminate that vendor's package. Contact users and ask about the package, and if at all possible visit several sites to watch the package in operation. Questions to ask the user might pertain to overall satisfaction, details regarding any problems, throughput and efficiency, ease of installation, ease of use, documentation, vendor technical support, training, full price of package, package changes, and any changes the user thinks should be made to the package. Again, this may result in some packages being eliminated from consideration.

9. *Use one of the selection techniques described in Chapter 7* to rate each package on the requirement list. Whatever method of evaluation is chosen, apply the weights and rankings of each criterion before evaluating, to eliminate subjective bias. Select the highest-scoring package remaining from the weighted-score evaluation.

In summary, software packages provide an alternative to developing custom programs for all your application needs. A detailed and well-planned selection and evaluation of packages is a necessity to decrease risks and prevent package selection failures.

9-4 COMMON BUSINESS APPLICATION PROGRAM PACKAGE EVALUATION

The following sections discuss each of the common business applications: general ledger, accounts receivable, accounts payable, inventory control, and payroll. Each application is described and its functions and features discussed. The most important functions and features are summarized under a checklist for each application. Basic file organization and system flow are included. Sample output reports are shown to illustrate typical reports that can be generated by small business computer systems.

9-4.1 General Ledger

The general ledger is regarded as a financial history describing what has happened during a given accounting period. The purposes of the automated general ledger system are (1) to keep a record of financial transactions and balances of those transactions (*general ledger*), and (2) to generate an accurate and timely *balance sheet* and *income statement* (also called a *profit and loss statement*).

The general ledger balances all transactions. When all accounts are in balance in the general ledger, the necessary financial reports, such as the income statement and the balance sheet, are reproduced. Then the current period transactions are cleared to the "totals to date" so the process may take place for the next period.

An income statement reports on the operating expenses of the business. It consists of all income and expense accounts and is often referred to as a profit and loss statement. From these reports, the management can determine the current financial status of the company and make decisions as to the future financial direction of the company.

Functions and Features

The automated general ledger system must utilize standard double-entry accounting system procedure and automatically maintain a zero balance at all times. The double-entry accounting procedure uses debits and credits as a means of assuring that all accounts are in balance by requiring that each transaction affect both a debit and a credit. For every debit entry there must be a corresponding credit entry of an equal dollar amount, and vice versa. Tables 9-2 and 9-3 illustrate the effect of accounting entries increasing or decreasing an account, depending on whether entered as a debit or as a credit.

In Table 9-2, a cash sale of $500 would increase the revenue account "Sales" as a credit and would increase the asset account "Cash" as a debit. The debits and credits are increased equally (by $500) for this transaction.

In Table 9-3, the receipt of a $200 invoice for computer supplies would increase the expense account "Supplies" as a debit and increase the liability account "Accounts Payable" as a credit. Again, the debits and credits are increased equally (by $200).

TABLE 9-2
Effect of a Cash Sale

Assets Account	"Cash"	Revenue Account	"Sales"
Debit	*Credit*	*Debit*	*Credit*
Increase	Decrease	Decrease	Increase
$500			$500

TABLE 9-3
Effect of an Invoice for Supplies

Expense Account	"Supplies"	Liability Account	"Accounts Payable"
Debit	Credit	Debit	Credit
Increase	Decrease	Decrease	Increase
$200			$200

In a similar fashion, all transactions should balance between debits and credits. To verify the balance, a trial-balance report will be generated before producing important reports such as the balance sheet and income statement.

The automated general ledger system should allow the user to check for omissions and illogical entries.

Setting up the proper chart of accounts for a company is an essential part of the automated general ledger system. Many small businesses fail to establish a proper chart of accounts, even with assistance from a CPA, owing to a lack of understanding of the automated general ledger system and the company's real business needs. An up-to-date, properly established chart of accounts should provide not only the general financial status of the company, but also specific department account information.

Multiple ledgers for multiple company capability are important if the company has more than one division and/or subsidiary. The system should allow the company to keep each division's ledger separate and still produce a consolidated company financial statement. This feature is getting more popular with the use of small business computer systems.

The flexibility in numbering the chart of accounts and the maximum number of charts of accounts available are important features to be considered in the automated general ledger system selection process. Some systems do not have any flexibility in establishing a chart of accounts. They may have only a preassigned chart-of-account numbers such as 100s for asset accounts, 200s for liabilities accounts, 300s for capital accounts, 400s for income accounts, and 500s for expense accounts. Yet most systems provide some flexibility for the user to manipulate chart-of-account numbers. Most systems allow the user to set up the major and minor account numbers, and some provide for division or department account numbers to be set up. The user should ensure that the company's chart of accounts is compatible with the chart of accounts of the automated general ledger system to be adopted.

As far as the maximum available number of charts of accounts is concerned, it can vary from 100 to an almost unlimited number in different automated general ledger systems. The user should select the system that can adequately accommodate the company's present chart-of-account numbers and have enough flexibility to change for the company's future growth and modifications.

Report formatting is another useful feature to be considered in the

238

automated general ledger system selection process. Report formatting should be user-definable. If the user wishes to format the financial statement differently for various purposes, he or she should be able to reformat the statement without changing the figures. This type of system allows the user to create and customize financial reports. Technically speaking, this is called a report-generator program. To create a new report, such as a balance sheet or income statement, the user must first create a "format" for that report. A format is a set of instructions typed in by the user, which tells the report-generator program how to make up and print out a unique financial report for the user. The user can assign titles and account numbers which indicate what type of account it is, and the system will generate a report with the assigned titles and account numbers.

Some general ledger systems can provide a single account balance report. This is a very useful tool that allows the user to stay *current* on an important account balance even though the system has not yet reached the end of the accounting period (usually a month). When the user decides to obtain an account balance report, he or she enters a desired account code into the system. The system will look up the ending balance for that particular account, add and subtract all applicable transactions for the period to date, and compute the current ending balance for the account. This balance, of course, is only as current as the most recent transaction input.

The end of each month and the end of the year are special times for the general ledger system. This is when various specific tasks must be completed to allow the period to be closed and financial reports summarizing the month's or year's activity to be generated. Most systems can perform housekeeping functions such as generating month-to-date and year-to-date totals. Some systems can provide the user with comparative data, ratios, and/or budget figures on the financial statements. Comparative data on the financial position month-to-date and year-to-date one year ago can be generated by some systems at the ending period. Some systems provide the ability to designate period beginning and ending dates. This gives the user the option of having other than 12 monthly periods, such as 13 periods a year. Transaction entry at any time, regardless of the period-ending date, can be a convenient feature. If closure for one period is not completed, the user can still enter transactions into the system for the next period. Posting to the general ledger takes transactions from the current period in the general journal and posts them to the appropriate accounts. Posting should not be permitted if the journal is out of balance. However, you should be able to override the out-of-balance feature if you are making an entry to bring the general ledger back into balance.

Some automated general ledger systems may be interfaced with all other accounting systems, such as the accounts receivable, accounts payable, payroll, and inventory control systems. This approach is called an "integrated" system. Each of the application systems interfaces with every other system. For instance, an inventory control system posts invoiced sales to an accounts receivable system, which in turn posts receipts to a general ledger system. An accounts payable system and payroll system post payments and paychecks, respectively, to the general ledger system. Then the general ledger system summarizes all this information into the company's financial reports. This integrated system approach is getting more popular, even in the small business computer field.

An individual account system or "stand-alone" approach performs in a different manner. This approach is appropriate for a small-volume business in which only a few transactions occur each period. It does not provide the benefit of "automatic" data transfer to other accounting systems. Therefore, the user has to reenter all the transactions into the general ledger system. These extra human interventions may cause entry errors and a loss of control.

Many small specialized businesses tend to take a middle approach between the fully integrated and stand-alone methods. For example, a construction firm application program may integrate only with an accounts payable system and a general ledger system. A wholesale distributor application program may integrate only with an accounts receivable system and an inventory control system. A manufacturing firm application program may integrate with a raw materials inventory control system, a payroll system, and a job estimate or job cost system. A property management application program may integrate with an accounts receivable system and a general ledger system.

To survive in the competitive business field, it is wise for the small company with limited capital to begin by using this "middle" approach. If this approach proves successful, it can be expanded later into an integrated system.

Checklist for General Ledger

1. Does the system utilize a standard double-entry accounting system procedure and automatically maintain a zero balance at all times?   YES _____   NO _____

2. Does the system handle multiple ledgers or multiple companies?   YES _____   NO _____

3. How many charts of accounts can the system support? _____

4. Does the system provide enough flexibility in numbering charts of accounts?   YES _____   NO _____

5. Can the system provide major and minor account numbers?   YES _____   NO _____

6. Can the system support a report-generator program?   YES _____   NO _____

7. Can the system provide an *account balance report* if the user wishes to stay *current* on a particular account?   YES _____   NO _____

8. Can the system provide month-to-date and year-to-date totals?   YES _____   NO _____

9. Can the system provide comparative data, ratios, and budget figures on the financial statements?   YES _____   NO _____

10. Can the system provide comparative data on the company's financial position 1 year ago?   YES _____   NO _____

11. Does the system provide the ability to designate period beginning and ending dates?   YES _____   NO _____

12. Does the system handle transaction entries at any time regardless of the ending period?   YES _____   NO _____

13. Can the system be interfaced with an accounts receivable system?   YES _____   NO _____

14. Can the system be interfaced with an accounts payable system?   YES _____   NO _____

15. Can the system be interfaced with a payroll system?   YES _____   NO _____

16. Can the system be interfaced with an inventory control system?   YES _____   NO _____

17. Can the system be interfaced with all accounting systems?   YES _____   NO _____

18. Can the integrated system be used stand-alone if the user desires?   YES _____   NO _____

Files for General Ledger System

The general ledger system operates with a general ledger master (chart of accounts) file and the transaction (or journal) file (see Figure 9-2). The master file allows for the creation and maintenance of a chart of accounts. The transaction file allows for the recording of journal entries to be posted to the chart of accounts at the end of each accounting period. The general ledger master file contains the chart of accounts, which includes the current balance of each account, monthly budget amounts, year-to-date amount, and monthly and yearly comparative amounts. The transaction file contains transactions, which include account number, source code, reference, date, and amount. These two files are interfaced at the end of an accounting period (usually a month) by the trial balance, which matches accounts in the master file with appropriate transaction entries from the transaction file. The system then lists each account, transactions, and totals, and updates the master file to produce a current-month master file. Financial reports are then generated from the current-month master file. The reports produced are the income statement (profit and loss statement), the balance sheet, and under some systems, the profit-center income statement and/or department income statement.

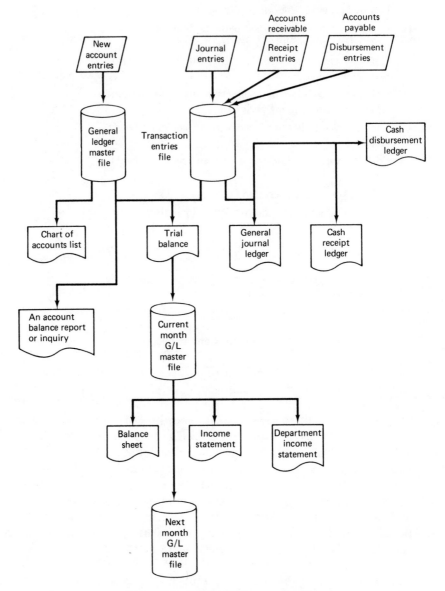

Figure 9-2. General ledger system flow.

General Ledger Output Reports

Reports and other output that may be provided by the general ledger system include:

1. Chart-of-accounts list (master file list)
2. Single-account balance report or account inquiry by display
3. Transaction register
4. Cash receipts ledger
5. Cash disbursements ledger
6. Trial balance
7. Income statement (comparative figures and ratios)
8. Balance sheet
9. Department income statement
10. Profit-center income statement

Figures 9-3 to 9-10 show sample general ledger reports.

```
                          TAYLOR OFFICE EQUIPMENT
                             GENERAL LEDGER
                            MASTER FILE LIST
                                03/01/79
```

ACCOUNT	DESCRIPTION	TYP	M/S	COL	CURRENT	Y-T-D	BUDGET
100	ASSETS	1		1			
101	CASH	2	M	1			
102	CASH - OPERATING	2	S	1	49.56	2,721.21	0.00
109	CASH ON HAND	2	S	1	0.00	150.00	0.00
111	ACCOUNTS RECEIVABLE	2		1	10,070.20	27,371.25	0.00
121	PREPAID EXPENSES	2		1	0.00	490.00	0.00
131	INVENTORY	2		1	-5,878.20	19,731.99	0.00
170	TOTAL CURRENT ASSETS	4		2			
171	FURNITURE & EQUIPMENT	2		1	0.00	4,255.37	0.00
172	ACCUMULATED DEPRECIATION	2		1	-180.40	-786.00	0.00
180	DEPOSITS	2		1	0.00	750.00	0.00
198	TOTAL FIXED ASSETS	4		2			
199	TOTAL ASSETS	6		3			
200	LIABILITIES & CAPITAL	1		1			
201	ACCOUNTS PAYABLE	2		1	-2,046.56	-12,363.58	0.00
210	TAXES PAYABLE	2	M	1			
211	FICA TAX PAYABLE	2	S	1	-127.60	-632.35	0.00
212	FEDERAL TAX PAYABLE	2	S	1	-374.30	-1,382.21	0.00
213	STATE TAX PAYABLE	2	S	1	-74.28	-229.86	0.00
214	SALES TAX PAYABLE	2	S	1	-239.12	-903.96	0.00
250	TOTAL CURR LIABILITIES	4		2			
251	NOTE PAYABLE-BANK	2		1	800.00	-1,400.00	0.00
289	TOTAL-LONG TERM LIAB.	4		2			
290	TOTAL LIABILITIES	6		3			
291	CAPITAL STOCK	2		2	0.00	-25,000.00	0.00
296	RETAINED EARNINGS	2		2	0.00	-8,773.26	0.00
297	CURRENT EARNINGS	2		2	0.00	0.00	0.00
298	TOTAL CAPITAL	6		3			
299	TOTAL LIAB. & CAPITAL	8		3			

Figure 9-3. General ledger chart-of-account list (master file list). (Courtesy of Retail Sciences, Inc., Peachtree Software Product.)

```
                              TAYLOR OFFICE EQUIPMENT
                                 GENERAL LEDGER
                                MASTER FILE LIST
                                   03/01/79

ACCOUNT    DESCRIPTION                    TYP   M/S   COL      CURRENT          Y-T-D         BUDGET
-------    ------------------------       ---   ---   ---   ------------   ------------   ------------

  300      INCOME                          1           1
  301      SALES                           2     M     1
30101      SALES                           2     S     1     -11,618.00     -23,236.00    -208,100.00
30102      SALES                           2     S     1      -3,060.00      -6,120.00    -203,100.00
  311      SERVICE                         2     M     1
31101      SERVICE                         2     S     1           0.00           0.00     -14,100.00
31102      SERVICE                         2     S     1           0.00           0.00     -15,100.00
  321      RETURNS & ALLOWANCES            2     M     1
32101      RETURNS & ALLOWANCES            2     S     1           0.00           0.00       2,800.00
32102      RETURNS & ALLOWANCES            2     S     1           0.00           0.00       3,100.00
  399         NET SALES                    4           1
  400      COST OF GOODS SOLD              1           1
  401      BEGINNING INVENTORY             2     M     1
40101      BEGINNING INVENTORY             2     S     1           0.00           0.00           0.00
40102      BEGINNING INVENTORY             2     S     1           0.00           0.00           0.00
  411      PURCHASES                       2     M     1
41101      PURCHASES                       2     S     1       1,560.32       3,120.64     212,000.00
41102      PURCHASES                       2     S     1       2,008.00       4,016.00     216,700.00
  421      FREIGHT                         2     M     1
42101      FREIGHT                         2     S     1          56.00         112.00       4,600.00
42102      FREIGHT                         2     S     1           0.00           0.00       4,000.00
  431      ENDING INVENTORY                2     M     1
43101      ENDING INVENTORY                2     S     1       2,653.48       5,306.96     -60,000.00
43102      ENDING INVENTORY                2     S     1       3,224.78       6,449.56     -66,000.00
  499         GROSS PROFIT                 6           1
  501      SALARIES                        2     M     1
50101      SALARIES - DEPARTMENT 1         2     S     1         900.00       1,800.00      20,000.00
50102      SALARIES - DEPARTMENT 2         2     S     1       1,200.00       2,400.00      29,300.00
  509      PAYROLL TAXES                   2           1           0.00           0.00       4,400.00
  511      RENT                            2           1         500.00       1,000.00      10,200.00
  512      OFFICE EXPENSES                 2           1          38.56          77.12       2,400.00
  513      TELEPHONE                       2           1         120.00         240.00       1,900.00
  514      UTILITIES                       2           1          25.00          50.00       2,300.00
  521      ADVERTISING                     2           1           0.00           0.00      12,400.00
  522      INSURANCE                       2           1           0.00           0.00         600.00
  523      PROFESSIONAL FEES               2           1         125.00         250.00       1,300.00
  531      DEPRECIATION                    2           1         180.40         360.80       1,700.00
  532      INTEREST EXPENSE                2           1          82.00         164.00         200.00
  533      MISCELLANEOUS EXPENSES          2           1           5.16          10.32         400.00
  596         TOTAL EXPENSES               6           1
  599           NET INCOME                 8           1

** TOTAL RECORDS IN FILE =  70

               OUT OF BALANCE - CURRENT -          -0.00
                               Y-T-D   -           0.00
```

Figure 9-3. (*Continued*)

244

```
                          TAYLOR OFFICE EQUIPMENT
                            GENERAL LEDGER
                         TRANSACTIONS REGISTER
                               03/01/79

 ACCOUNT     DESCRIPTION                   REFER.   S    DATE        AMOUNT
 -------     ------------------------      --------  -   --------   ------------

   102       JOHN MOODY                     30628    1  04/12/78        625.00
   102       S. W. WELLS                    30645    1  04/25/78        582.40
   102       DANIEL B. JOHNSON             30639    1  04/01/78      3,640.00
   102       VOID                           VOID     1  04/01/78          0.00
   102       STEVENS - A6015                429      2  04/15/78     -1,560.32
   102       NOTE PAYABLE - NBG             430      2  04/15/78       -882.00
   102       SOUTHERN BELL                  431      2  04/15/78       -120.00
   102       GEORGIA POWER                  432      2  04/15/78        -25.00
   102       YELLOW FREIGHT                 433      2  04/15/78        -56.00
   102       ROBERT YOUNG - CPA             434      2  04/21/78       -125.00
   102       SALARIES                      435-439   2  04/30/78     -1,524.36
   102       HAYDEN REALTY                  428      2  04/15/78       -500.00
   102       BANK CHARGE - MARCH            STMT     5  04/12/78         -5.16
   111       SALE - JAMES WILSON            30641    6  04/03/78        561.60
   111       JOHN MOODY                     30628    6  04/12/78       -625.00
   111       BAKER HARDWARE                 30642    6  04/12/78        133.12
   111       TJ WRIGHT & SON                30643    6  04/12/78      2,600.00
   111       BROWNS CLEANING SERVICE        30644    6  04/15/78      2,340.00
   111       DANIEL JOHNSON                 30639    6  04/15/78     -3,640.00
   111       ADJUSTMENT TO BAKER            30642    6  04/30/78          0.48
   111       SALE - JASPER                  30645    6  04/21/78      8,700.00
   131       ENDING INVENTORY               APRIL    6  04/30/78     -5,878.20
   172       DEPREC. - APRIL                531      3  04/30/78       -180.40
   201       ANDERSON OFFICE SUPPLY         10074    6  04/07/78        -38.56
   201       ACCOUNTS PAYABLE               6114     6  04/19/78     -2,008.00
   211       FICA TAX PAYABLE               PAYROLL  6  04/19/78       -127.60
   212       FEDERAL TAX PAYABLE            PAYROLL  6  04/30/78       -374.30
   213       STATE TAX PAYABLE              PAYROLL  6  04/30/78        -74.28
   214       GA SALES TAX UNIT              S/J      6  04/30/78       -239.12
   251       NOTE PAYABLE                   430      3  04/15/78        800.00
   30101     SALE - JAMES WILSON            30641    6  04/03/78       -540.00
   30101     SALE - BAKER HARDWARE          30642    6  04/19/78       -128.00
   30101     SALE - BROWN CLEANING          30644    6  04/20/78     -2,250.00
   30101     SALE - JASPER                  39645    6  04/21/78     -8,700.00
   30102     SALE - TJ WILSON & SON         30643    6  04/13/78     -2,500.00
   30102     SALE - SW WELLS                30645    6  04/13/78       -560.00
   30102     VOID                           VOID     6  04/13/78          0.00
   41101     EQUIP PURCHASE                 A6015    6  04/03/78      1,560.32
   41102     STEVENS - EQUIP PURCH          6114     6  04/19/78      2,008.00
   42101     YELLOW FREIGHT                 433      6  04/19/78         56.00
   43101     ENDING INVENTORY               APRIL    6  04/30/78      2,653.48
   43102     ENDING INVENTORY               APRIL    6  04/30/78      3,224.78
   50101     SALARIES                      435-436   6  04/30/78        900.00
   50102     SALARIES                      437-439   6  04/30/78      1,200.00
   511       HAYDEN REALTY                  4288     7  04/01/78        500.00
   512       ANDERSON OFFICE                10074    7  04/07/78         38.56
   513       SOUTHERN BELL                  431      7  04/20/78        120.00
   514       GEORGIA POWER                  432      7  04/20/78         25.00
   523       ROBERT WARREN - CPA            434      6  04/21/78        125.00
   531       DEPRECIATION - APRIL           531      3  04/15/78        180.40
   532       INTEREST ON NOTE - NBG         430      3  04/15/78         82.00
   533       BANK SERVICE CHARGE-MARCH      STMT     7  04/12/78          5.16



 ** TOTAL TRANSACTIONS IN LIST =    52

                            TOTAL DEBITS       32,661.30
                            TOTAL CREDITS     -32,661.30
                                              ---------------
                            OUT OF BALANCE          0.00
```

Figure 9-4. General ledger report: transaction register. (Courtesy of Retail Sciences, Inc., Peachtree Software Product.)

245

```
                    C A S H  R E C E I P T S  L E D G E R
   REPORT GL- 4          JOHN DOE COMPANY              POSTED ON 01/23/80
   CONTROL SOURCE        DATE    REFERENCE        AMOUNT    GL ACCT. # JUL.
   ------------------------------------------------------------------------
        137          07/11/79  J. DOE        $    647.82      50 10 20
        138          07/11/79  J. BRIDGER    $     29.50      20 10 10
        139          07/11/79  L. RANGER     $     91.00      50 10 20
        140          07/15/79  P. T. BARNUM  $    586.25      50 10 20
        141          07/18/79  J. C. SMITH   $     35.00      20 10 20
        142          07/23/79  W. CODY       $     47.50      50 10 30
        143          07/24/79  W. B. HICKOCK $    532.99      10 10 20
        144          07/27/79  C. JANE       $    387.00      20 10 10

                                  TOTAL     $   2362.06**
```

Figure 9-5. General ledger report: Cash receipts ledger.   (Courtesy of Adventures in Computing, Inc.)

```
                         TAYLOR OFFICE EQUIPMENT
                            GENERAL LEDGER
                          CASH DISBURSEMENTS
                              03/01/79

      ACCOUNT    DESCRIPTION              REFER.  S    DATE        AMOUNT
      -------    -----------------------  ------- -  --------   ------------

        102      STEVENS - A6015            429    2  04/15/78     -1,560.32
        102      NOTE PAYABLE - NBG         430    2  04/15/78       -882.00
        102      SOUTHERN BELL              431    2  04/15/78       -120.00
        102      GEORGIA POWER              432    2  04/15/78        -25.00
        102      YELLOW FREIGHT             433    2  04/15/78        -56.00
        102      ROBERT YOUNG - CPA         434    2  04/21/78       -125.00
        102      SALARIES                 435-439  2  04/30/78     -1,524.36
        102      HAYDEN REALTY              428    2  04/15/78       -500.00

      ** TOTAL TRANSACTIONS IN LIST =   8

                                 TOTAL DEBITS          0.00
                                 TOTAL CREDITS     -4,792.68
                                                 --------------
                                 OUT OF BALANCE    -4,792.68
```

Figure 9-6. General ledger report: cash disbursements.   (Courtesy of Retail Sciences, Inc., Peachtree Software Product.)

```
                              TAYLOR OFFICE EQUIPMENT                    PAGE   1
                                 GENERAL LEDGER
                                 TRIAL BALANCE
                                   04/31/78

  -----------ACCOUNT------------ -BEGINNING- ------------------------TRANSACTION---------------------- ---ENDING---
  NUMBER     DESCRIPTION          BALANCE    DESCRIPTION          DATE  SRC  REFERENCE    AMOUNT          BALANCE
  ------     -----------          -------    -----------          ----- ---  ---------   -----------    ------------

   100    ASSETS

   101    CASH                      0.00

   102    CASH - OPERATING       2,721.21
                                            JOHN MOODY           04/12  1    30628          625.00
                                            S. W. WELLS          04/25  1    30645          582.40
                                            DANIEL B. JOHNSON    04/01  1    30639        3,640.00
                                            VOID                 04/01  1    VOID             0.00
                                            STEVENS - A6015      04/15  2    429          1,560.32-
                                            NOTE PAYABLE - NBG   04/15  2    430            882.00-
                                            SOUTHERN BELL        04/15  2    431            120.00-
                                            GEORGIA POWER        04/15  2    432             25.00-
```

Figure 9-7. General ledger report: trial balance.   (Courtesy of Retail Sciences, Inc., Peachtree Software Product.)

TAYLOR OFFICE EQUIPMENT
GENERAL LEDGER
TRIAL BALANCE
04/31/78

NUMBER	ACCOUNT DESCRIPTION	BEGINNING BALANCE	TRANSACTION DESCRIPTION	DATE	SRC	REFERENCE	AMOUNT	ENDING BALANCE
			YELLOW FREIGHT	04/15	2	433	56.00-	
			ROBERT YOUNG - CPA	04/21	2	434	125.00-	
			SALARIES	04/30	2	435-439	1,524.36-	
			HAYDEN REALTY	04/15	2	428	500.00-	
			BANK CHARGE - MARCH	04/12	5	STMT	5.16-	
							49.56 *	2,770.77 *
109	CASH ON HAND	150.00						
111	ACCOUNTS RECEIVABLE	27,371.25	SALE - JAMES WILSON	04/03	6	30641	561.60	
			JOHN MOODY	04/12	6	30628	625.00-	
			BAKER HARDWARE	04/12	6	30642	133.12	
			TJ WRIGHT & SON	04/12	6	30643	2,600.00	
			BROWNS CLEANING SERVICE	04/15	6	30644	2,340.00	
			DANIEL JOHNSON	04/15	6	30639	3,640.00-	
			ADJUSTMENT TO BAKER	04/30	6	30642	0.48	
			SALE - JASPER	04/21	6	30645	8,700.00	
							10,070.20 *	37,441.45 *
121	PREPAID EXPENSES	490.00						
131	INVENTORY	19,731.99	ENDING INVENTORY	04/30	6	APRIL	5,878.20-	
							5,878.20- *	13,853.79 *
170	TOTAL CURRENT ASSETS						4,241.56 **	54,706.01 **
171	FURNITURE & EQUIPMENT	4,255.37						
172	ACCUMULATED DEPRECIATION	786.00-	DEPREC. - APRIL	04/30	3	531	180.40-	
							180.40- *	966.40- *
180	DEPOSITS	750.00						
198	TOTAL FIXED ASSETS						180.40- **	4,038.97 **
199	TOTAL ASSETS						4,061.16 **	58,744.98 **
200	LIABILITIES & CAPITAL							
201	ACCOUNTS PAYABLE	12,363.58-	ANDERSON OFFICE SUPPLY	04/07	6	10074	38.56-	
			ACCOUNTS PAYABLE	04/19	6	6114	2,008.00-	
							2,046.56- *	14,410.14- *
210	TAXES PAYABLE	0.00						
211	FICA TAX PAYABLE	632.35-	FICA TAX PAYABLE	04/19	6	PAYROLL	127.60-	
							127.60- *	759.95- *
212	FEDERAL TAX PAYABLE	1,382.21-	FEDERAL TAX PAYABLE	04/30	6	PAYROLL	374.30-	
							374.30- *	1,756.51- *
213	STATE TAX PAYABLE	229.86-	STATE TAX PAYABLE	04/30	6	PAYROLL	74.28-	
							74.28- *	304.14- *
214	SALES TAX PAYABLE	903.96-	GA SALES TAX UNIT	04/30	6	S/J	239.12-	
							239.12- *	1,143.08- *
250	TOTAL CURR LIABILITIES						2,861.86- **	18,373.82- **
251	NOTE PAYABLE-BANK	1,400.00-	NOTE PAYABLE	04/15	3	430	800.00	
							800.00 *	600.00- *
289	TOTAL-LONG TERM LIAB.						800.00 **	600.00- **
290	TOTAL LIABILITIES						2,061.86- **	18,973.82- **
291	CAPITAL STOCK	25,000.00-						
296	RETAINED EARNINGS	8,773.26-						
297	CURRENT EARNINGS	0.00						
298	TOTAL CAPITAL						0.00 **	33,773.26- **
299	TOTAL LIAB. & CAPITAL						1,999.30 **	5,997.90 **
300	INCOME							
301	SALES	0.00						

Figure 9-7. *(Continued)*

247

NUMBER	DESCRIPTION	BEGINNING BALANCE	DESCRIPTION	DATE	SRC	REFERENCE	AMOUNT	ENDING BALANCE
30101	SALES	23,236.00-						
			SALE - JAMES WILSON	04/03	6	30641	540.00-	
			SALE - BAKER HARDWARE	04/19	6	30642	128.00-	
			SALE - BROWN CLEANING	04/20	6	30644	2,250.00-	
			SALE - JASPER	04/21	6	39645	8,700.00-	
							11,618.00- *	34,854.00- *
30102	SALES	6,120.00-						
			SALE - TJ WILSON & SON	04/13	6	30643	2,500.00-	
			SALE - SW WELLS	04/13	6	30645	560.00-	
			VOID	04/13	6	VOID	0.00	
							3,060.00- *	9,180.00- *
311	SERVICE	0.00						
31101	SERVICE	0.00						
31102	SERVICE	0.00						
321	RETURNS & ALLOWANCES	0.00						
32101	RETURNS & ALLOWANCES	0.00						
32102	RETURNS & ALLOWANCES	0.00						
399	NET SALES						14,678.00- **	44,034.00- **
400	COST OF GOODS SOLD							
401	BEGINNING INVENTORY	0.00						
40101	BEGINNING INVENTORY	0.00						
40102	BEGINNING INVENTORY	0.00						
411	PURCHASES	0.00						
41101	PURCHASES	3,120.64						
			EQUIP PURCHASE	04/03	6	A6015	1,560.32	
							1,560.32 *	4,680.96 *
41102	PURCHASES	4,016.00						
			STEVENS - EQUIP PURCH	04/19	6	6114	2,008.00	
							2,008.00 *	6,024.00 *
421	FREIGHT	0.00						
42101	FREIGHT	112.00						
			YELLOW FREIGHT	04/19	6	433	56.00	
							56.00 *	168.00 *
42102	FREIGHT	0.00						
431	ENDING INVENTORY	0.00						
43101	ENDING INVENTORY	5,306.96						
			ENDING INVENTORY	04/30	6	APRIL	2,653.48	
							2,653.48 *	7,960.44 *
43102	ENDING INVENTORY	6,449.56						
			ENDING INVENTORY	04/30	6	APRIL	3,224.78	
							3,224.78 *	9,674.34 *
499	GROSS PROFIT						5,175.42- **	15,526.26- **
501	SALARIES	0.00						
50101	SALARIES - DEPARTMENT 1	1,800.00						
			SALARIES	04/30	6	435-436	900.00	
							900.00 *	2,700.00 *
50102	SALARIES - DEPARTMENT 2	2,400.00						
			SALARIES	04/30	6	437-439	1,200.00	
							1,200.00 *	3,600.00 *
509	PAYROLL TAXES	0.00						
511	RENT	1,000.00						
			HAYDEN REALTY	04/01	7	4288	500.00	
							500.00 *	1,500.00 *
512	OFFICE EXPENSES	77.12						
			ANDERSON OFFICE	04/07	7	10074	38.56	
							38.56 *	115.68 *

Figure 9-7. *(Continued)*

248

TAYLOR OFFICE EQUIPMENT
GENERAL LEDGER
TRIAL BALANCE
04/31/78

| ACCOUNT | | -BEGINNING- | TRANSACTION | | | | | ---ENDING--- |
NUMBER	DESCRIPTION	BALANCE	DESCRIPTION	DATE	SRC	REFERENCE	AMOUNT	BALANCE
513	TELEPHONE	240.00	SOUTHERN BELL	04/20	7	431	120.00 120.00 *	360.00 *
514	UTILITIES	50.00	GEORGIA POWER	04/20	7	432	25.00 25.00 *	75.00 *
521	ADVERTISING	0.00						
522	INSURANCE	0.00						
523	PROFESSIONAL FEES	250.00	ROBERT WARREN - CPA	04/21	6	434	125.00 125.00 *	375.00 *
531	DEPRECIATION	360.80	DEPRECIATION - APRIL	04/15	3	531	180.40 180.40 *	541.20 *
532	INTEREST EXPENSE	164.00	INTEREST ON NOTE - NBG	04/15	3	430	82.00 82.00 *	246.00 *
533	MISCELLANEOUS EXPENSES	10.32	BANK SERVICE CHARGE-MARCH	04/12	7	STMT	5.16 5.16 *	15.48 *
596	TOTAL EXPENSES						3,176.12 **	9,528.36 **
599	NET INCOME						1,999.30- **	5,997.90- **

*** TOTALS :		BEGINNING	CURRENT	ENDING
	DEBITS	80,827.22	32,661.30	113,488.52
	CREDITS	80,827.22-	32,661.30-	113,488.52-
*** OUT OF BALANCE :		0.00-	0.00	0.00-

Figure 9-7. (*Continued*)

TAYLOR OFFICE EQUIPMENT
GENERAL LEDGER
INCOME STATEMENT
04/31/78

	THIS MONTH	RATIO	YEAR-TO-DATE	RATIO
INCOME				
SALES	$14,678.00	100.0	$44,034.00	100.0
SERVICE	$0.00	0.0	$0.00	0.0
RETURNS & ALLOWANCES	$0.00	0.0	$0.00	0.0
NET SALES	$14,678.00	100.0	$44,034.00	100.0
COST OF GOODS SOLD				
PURCHASES	$3,568.32	24.3	$10,704.96	24.3
FREIGHT	$56.00	0.4	$168.00	0.4
ENDING INVENTORY	$5,878.26	40.0	$17,634.78	40.0
GROSS PROFIT	$5,175.42	35.3	$15,526.26	35.3
SALARIES	$2,100.00	14.3	$6,300.00	14.3
PAYROLL TAXES	$0.00	0.0	$0.00	0.0
RENT	$500.00	3.4	$1,500.00	3.4
OFFICE EXPENSES	$38.56	0.3	$115.68	0.3
TELEPHONE	$120.00	0.8	$360.00	0.8
UTILITIES	$25.00	0.2	$75.00	0.2
ADVERTISING	$0.00	0.0	$0.00	0.0
INSURANCE	$0.00	0.0	$0.00	0.0
PROFESSIONAL FEES	$125.00	0.9	$375.00	0.9
DEPRECIATION	$180.40	1.2	$541.20	1.2
INTEREST EXPENSE	$82.00	0.6	$246.00	0.6
MISCELLANEOUS EXPENSES	$5.16	0.0	$15.48	0.0
TOTAL EXPENSES	$3,176.12	21.6	$9,528.36	21.6
NET INCOME	$1,999.30	13.6	$5,997.90	13.6

Figure 9-8. General ledger report: income statement, with comparative figures and ratios. (Courtesy of Retail Sciences, Inc., Peachtree Software Product.)

```
                         TAYLOR OFFICE EQUIPMENT
                            GENERAL LEDGER
                           INCOME STATEMENT
                              04/31/78

              --------------------- T H I S   Y E A R ---------------------   ------ L A S T   Y E A R ------
              THIS MONTH    RATIO    YEAR-TO-DATE    RATIO     BUDGET        THIS MONTH     YEAR-TO-DATE
              ----------    -----    ------------    -----     ------        ----------     ------------

INCOME
SALES         $14,678.00    100.0    $44,034.00      100.0    $411,200.00    $27,060.00     $79,020.30
SERVICE           $0.00       0.0        $0.00         0.0     $29,200.00      $2,420.00      $6,620.00
RETURNS & ALLOWANCES $0.00    0.0        $0.00         0.0      $5,900.00-         $0.00          $0.00
              -----------    -----   -----------     -----                  -----------    -----------
  NET SALES   $14,678.00    100.0    $44,034.00      100.0    $434,500.00    $29,480.00     $85,640.30

COST OF GOODS SOLD
PURCHASES      $3,568.32     24.3    $10,704.96       24.3    $428,700.00    $30,400.00     $88,050.00
FREIGHT           $56.00      0.4       $168.00        0.4      $8,600.00       $225.00        $563.00
ENDING INVENTORY $5,878.26   40.0    $17,634.78       40.0    $126,000.00-   $10,150.00-    $26,783.90-
              -----------    -----   -----------     -----                  -----------    -----------
  GROSS PROFIT $5,175.42     35.3    $15,526.26       35.3    $123,200.00     $9,005.00     $23,811.20

SALARIES       $2,100.00     14.3     $6,300.00       14.3     $49,300.00     $3,300.00      $9,900.00
PAYROLL TAXES      $0.00      0.0        $0.00         0.0      $4,400.00       $211.60        $634.80
RENT             $500.00      3.4     $1,500.00        3.4     $10,200.00       $550.00      $1,650.00
OFFICE EXPENSES   $38.56      0.3       $115.68        0.3      $2,400.00       $136.80        $332.77
TELEPHONE        $120.00      0.8       $360.00        0.8      $1,900.00       $180.00        $495.10
UTILITIES         $25.00      0.2        $75.00        0.2      $2,300.00       $160.50        $368.18
ADVERTISING        $0.00      0.0        $0.00         0.0     $12,400.00       $225.00        $675.00
INSURANCE          $0.00      0.0        $0.00         0.0        $600.00       $162.00        $486.00
PROFESSIONAL FEES $125.00     0.9       $375.00        0.9      $1,300.00         $0.00          $0.00
DEPRECIATION     $180.40      1.2       $541.20        1.2      $1,700.00        $24.45         $73.35
INTEREST EXPENSE  $82.00      0.6       $246.00        0.6        $200.00        $10.12         $30.36
MISCELLANEOUS EXPENSES $5.16   0.0       $15.48        0.0        $400.00        $14.80         $32.40
              -----------    -----   -----------     -----                  -----------    -----------
  TOTAL EXPENSES $3,176.12    21.6     $9,528.36       21.6     $87,100.00     $4,975.27     $14,677.96

              -----------    -----   -----------     -----                  -----------    -----------
  NET INCOME   $1,999.30     13.6     $5,997.90       13.6     $36,100.00     $4,029.73      $9,133.24

              ===========    ======  ===========     ======   ===========    ===========    ===========
```

Figure 9-8. *(Continued)*

```
                    TAYLOR OFFICE EQUIPMENT
                       GENERAL LEDGER
                       BALANCE SHEET
                         04/31/78

                          ASSETS
                    ------------------------

CASH                      $2,920.77
ACCOUNTS RECEIVABLE      $37,441.45
PREPAID EXPENSES            $490.00
INVENTORY                $13,853.79
    TOTAL CURRENT ASSETS              $54,706.01

FURNITURE & EQUIPMENT     $4,255.37
ACCUMULATED DEPRECIATION    $966.40-
DEPOSITS                   $750.00
    TOTAL FIXED ASSETS                 $4,038.97

    TOTAL ASSETS                                  $58,744.98

                                                 ===============


                    LIABILITIES & CAPITAL
                    ------------------------

ACCOUNTS PAYABLE         $14,410.14
TAXES PAYABLE             $3,963.68
    TOTAL CURR LIABILITIES            $18,373.82

NOTE PAYABLE-BANK           $600.00
TOTAL-LONG TERM LIAB.                    $600.00

TOTAL LIABILITIES                                 $18,973.82

CAPITAL STOCK            $25,000.00
RETAINED EARNINGS         $8,773.26
CURRENT EARNINGS          $5,997.90
TOTAL CAPITAL                         $39,771.16

    TOTAL LIAB. & CAPITAL                         $58,744.98

                                                 ===============
```

Figure 9-9. General ledger report: balance sheet, with comparative figures. (Courtesy of Retail Sciences, Inc., Peachtree Software Product.)

```
                              TAYLOR OFFICE EQUIPMENT
                                 GENERAL LEDGER
                                 BALANCE SHEET
                                   04/31/78

     ** THIS MONTH THIS YEAR **                        ** THIS MONTH LAST YEAR **


                                    ASSETS
                          ----------------------------

CASH                        $2,920.77                      $6,401.80
ACCOUNTS RECEIVABLE        $37,441.45                     $12,271.79
PREPAID EXPENSES              $490.00                        $310.00
INVENTORY                  $13,853.79                     $22,500.00
   TOTAL CURRENT ASSETS                  $54,706.01                    $41,483.59

FURNITURE & EQUIPMENT       $4,255.37                      $2,445.00
ACCUMULATED DEPRECIATION      $966.40-                       $73.35-
DEPOSITS                      $750.00                        $575.00
   TOTAL FIXED ASSETS                     $4,038.97                     $2,946.65

   TOTAL ASSETS                          $58,744.98                    $44,430.24

                                     ==============                    ==============


                              LIABILITIES & CAPITAL
                          ----------------------------

ACCOUNTS PAYABLE           $14,410.14                      $1,846.15
TAXES PAYABLE               $3,963.68                         $0.00-
   TOTAL CURR LIABILITIES                $18,373.82                     $1,846.15

NOTE PAYABLE-BANK             $600.00                      $4,100.00
TOTAL-LONG TERM LIAB.                       $600.00                     $4,100.00

TOTAL LIABILITIES                        $18,973.82                     $5,946.15

CAPITAL STOCK              $25,000.00                     $25,000.00
RETAINED EARNINGS           $8,773.26                         $0.00
CURRENT EARNINGS            $5,997.90                     $13,484.09
TOTAL CAPITAL                            $39,771.16                    $38,484.09

   TOTAL LIAB. & CAPITAL                 $58,744.98                    $44,430.24

                                     ==============                    ==============
```

Figure 9-9. (*Continued*)


```
                              TAYLOR OFFICE EQUIPMENT
                                 GENERAL LEDGER
                            DEPARTMENT INCOME STATEMENT
                                   04/31/78

DEPARTMENT NUMBER 02
                      --------------------- T H I S   Y E A R ------------------------   ------ L A S T   Y E A R ------
                        THIS MONTH    RATIO    YEAR-TO-DATE    RATIO     BUDGET          THIS MONTH      YEAR-TO-DATE

INCOME
SALES                   $3,060.00     100.0    $9,180.00      100.0    $203,100.00      $13,200.00      $38,760.00
SERVICE                     $0.00       0.0        $0.00        0.0     $15,100.00       $1,220.00       $3,220.00
RETURNS & ALLOWANCES        $0.00       0.0        $0.00        0.0      $3,100.00-          $0.00           $0.00

   NET SALES            $3,060.00     100.0    $9,180.00      100.0    $215,100.00      $14,420.00      $41,980.00

COST OF GOODS SOLD
PURCHASES               $2,008.00      65.6    $6,024.00       65.6    $216,700.00      $14,900.00      $42,750.00
FREIGHT                     $0.00       0.0        $0.00        0.0      $4,000.00         $100.00         $240.00
ENDING INVENTORY        $3,224.78     105.4    $9,674.34      105.4     $66,000.00-      $4,400.00-     $11,413.90-

   GROSS PROFIT         $2,172.78-    -71.0    $6,518.34-     -71.0     $60,400.00       $3,820.00      $10,403.90

SALARIES - DEPARTMENT 2 $1,200.00      39.2    $3,600.00       39.2     $29,300.00       $1,500.00       $4,500.00

   TOTAL EXPENSES       $1,200.00      39.2    $3,600.00       39.2     $29,300.00       $1,500.00       $4,500.00


   NET INCOME           $3,372.78-   -110.2   $10,118.34-    -110.2     $31,100.00       $2,320.00       $5,903.90

                      ==============  ======  ==============  ======  ==============  ==============  ==============
```

Figure 9-10. General ledger report: department income statement. (Courtesy of Retail Sciences, Inc., Peachtree Software Product.)

9-4.2 Accounts Receivable

The purpose of the accounts receivable system is essentially to post sales and receipts, bill customers, and keep track of outstanding receivables. The main objectives of an automated accounts receivable system are as follows:

1. Posting sales and receipts
2. Keeping track of outstanding customer accounts
3. Sending periodic statements to notify customers regarding their status
4. Improving billing services
5. Improving cash flow methodology
6. Providing reports for management, such as an aged accounts receivable report

Functions and Features

An accounts receivable system can be open-item, balance-forward, or a combination of the two. Under the balance-forward system, once an invoice has been billed it is discarded and the outstanding balance for the appropriate customer will be carried forward. Many service companies prefer to use the balance-forward system. On the other hand, under an open-item system, the invoice is retained until payment is received against that particular invoice. Most manufacturing and wholesale industries employ the open-item system. When a combination of the two systems is in effect, either open-item or balance-forward can be selected, on a customer-by-customer basis. Very few accounts receivable systems can support a combination of the two.

Most accounts receivable systems assume monthly billing, but some allow cyclical billing. The latter feature gives the user flexibility in selecting different billing dates for different customers. Under this system, multiple "statement cycles" can be established, thereby avoiding having all statements coming out on the same day and swamping the system and staff. For example, statements for one-fourth of the customers can be created each week. This feature is very useful for a company that sends out a very large number of bills every month.

An accounts receivable system may be interfaced with the general ledger system. This would allow the accounts receivable, cash receipts, and other items to be posted automatically to the appropriate accounts of the general ledger system.

Some accounts receivable systems are designed to interface with the inventory control system. Under this type of system, orders are entered into the inventory control system, and the invoice information is passed on to the accounts receivable system. Most wholesale distributors prefer to use such an accounts receivable system.

Most accounts receivable systems produce statements and some also produce invoices. Statements may be printed either on custom forms or on standard computer tab paper. When printed on continuous computer tab paper, statements should carry the correct headings. Statements can be printed on forms already imprinted with the company name and address and the computer system will print only the appropriate information on the forms. Remittance instructions may also be printed on part of the statement, if desired.

If the accounts receivable system produces invoices, the statement and invoice formats should be compatible. All receipts should be input prior to issuing statements; otherwise, the statements cannot reflect the latest payments from the customers. Finance charges, if any, should also be computed before printing statements.

The open-item accounts receivable system should be able to close each month to allow accumulation and transmission of dollar values to the general ledger system. The dollar amounts of unmatched receipts should not flow through the general ledger system. The month-end closing process should cause all paid invoices and their corresponding receipts to be purged or erased. Thus, no receipts will stay in the system for more than a month. However, invoices should remain in the system until the month they are paid.

Checklist for Accounts Receivable

1. Is the system designed for the open-item billing method, the balance-forward billing method, or a combination?   _____

2. How many customer accounts can the system support?   _____

3. How many outstanding invoices can the system keep under the open-item method?   _____
   (For instance, if the outstanding receivables average 60 days, the system needs to keep 2 months of invoices in storage before it purges them.)

4. Does the system produce acceptable statements?   YES ____   NO ____

5. Does the system allow multiple billing statement cycles?   YES ____   NO ____

6. Can the system produce compatible statement and invoice formats?   YES ____   NO ____

7. Does the system provide the ability to incorporate miscellaneous messages on the customer statement?   YES ____   NO ____

8. Does the system provide the ability to create statements only if desired?   YES ____   NO ____

9. Can the system provide recurring billing?   YES ____   NO ____
   (This provides the ability to bill a customer a given amount every billing cycle.)

10. Does the system provide a late-charge calculation?   YES ____   NO ____

11. Does the system provide the option of selecting either custom forms or computer tab paper for printing statements and reports?   YES ____   NO ____

12. Can the user format the output reports?   YES ____   NO ____

13. Can the system be interfaced with a general ledger system?   YES ____   NO ____

14. Can the system be interfaced with an inventory control system?   YES ____   NO ____

15. Can the dollar amounts on each invoice be charged to multiple general ledger account numbers?   YES ____   NO ____

16. Can the system handle partial payment for an invoice?   YES ____   NO ____

17. Can the system handle a received check that is in payment for three separate invoices?   YES ____   NO ____

18. Can the system accept incoming purchase orders as proforma invoices prior to the issuance of the true invoices?   YES ____   NO ____

Files for Accounts Receivable

There are at least two files associated with an accounts receivable system. the customer master file and transaction file (receipts file). If the system employs an open-item system, there will also be an invoice file or open-item file, and if the system handles sales commissions, there will be a salespersons' file. Some systems may require a sales analysis file if the user wishes to have various sales analysis reports (see Figure 9-11).

Accounts Receivable Output Reports

Reports that may be present in an accounts receivable system include:

1. Alphabetical customer list
2. Cash receipts journal
3. Sales journal
4. Statement and remittance
5. Aged accounts report
6. Sales analysis by customer
7. Sales analysis by salesperson
8. Sales analysis by item
9. Monthly sales summary

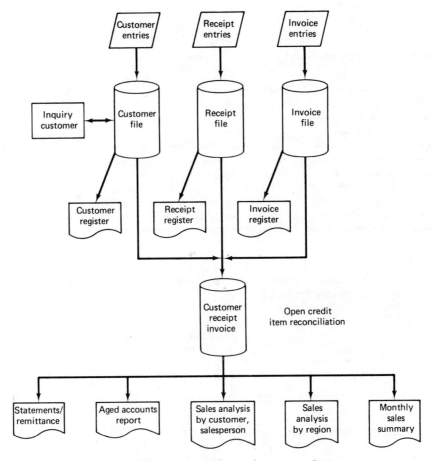

Figure 9-11. Accounts receivable system flow.

10. Delinquent report
11. Commission report
12. Finance charge report
13. Invoices

Figures 9-12 to 9-20 show sample accounts receivable reports.

9-4.3 Accounts Payable

The purpose of the accounts payable system is to keep track of cash requirements and to pay vendors as required. The accounts payable system can be an efficient management tool for keeping track of financial activities of vendors, cash flow, and discounts. The accounts payable system should be

```
                              TAYLOR OFFICE EQUIPMENT
                               ACCOUNTS RECEIVABLE
                             CUSTOMER ACCOUNT LISTING
                                   07/15/80

ACCOUNT      CUSTOMER NAME              ADDRESS                              PHONE         TYPE       BALANCE
-------   -------------------------  ---------------------------------   -------------  ---------   -------
ALLEN     ALLEN & COMPANY            4436 ROSWELL RD. NE.   ATLANTA, GA. 30342   (404)255-9999  REGULAR     157.73
COX       COX PROPERTIES, INC.       1334 PERIMETER PK.     DUNWOODY, GA. 30338  (404)394-6666  BAL FWD    3316.89
EVANS     EVANS OFFICE SUPPLY        2550 PIEDMONT RD. NE   ATLANTA, GA. 30324   (404)262-8888  REGULAR      71.73
HARLEN    HARLEN INSURANCE AGENCY    2336 PEACHTREE RD. NE  ATLANTA, GA. 30305   (404)238-1212  AUTO BILL    36.39
JOHNDE    JOHNSON DELIVERY SERVICE   430 PHARR RD. NE       ATLANTA, GA. 30308   (404)262-2555  REGULAR     119.60
KELLY     KELLY SUPPLY COMPANY       2055 LAWRENCEVILLE HWY. DECATUR, GA. 30033  (404)634-1555  BAL FWD     582.72
LENOX     LENOX MAMAGEMENT SERVICE   3400 PEACHTREE RD. NE  ATLANTA, GA. 30326   (404)237-2323  BAL FWD    2263.30
MARSH     MARSHALL, ALLEN & BOOSE    510 N. DRUID HILLS RD. ATLANTA, GA. 30324   (404)634-6666  BAL FWD     162.58
MCMILL    MCMILLAN & ASSOCIATES      1100 LENOX RD. NE      ATLANTA, GA. 30326   (404)233-7777  AUTO BILL   163.44
ROYAL     ROYAL IMPORTERS, LTD.      344 AIRPORT IND. PARK  COLLEGE PARK, GA. 30337 (404)763-3333 REGULAR   401.62
SDI       SOUTHERN DIST., INC.       4350 BUFORD HWY. NE    CHAMBLEE, GA. 30341  (404)633-5555  REGULAR      88.88
WALLWH    WALLACE WHOLESALE, INC.    780 FULTON IND. BLVD   ATLANTA, GA. 30330   (404)641-8888  BAL FWD    1166.21
                                                                                                          =========
          TOTALS                                                                                           8531.09

                           *** END OF CUSTOMER ACCOUNT LISTING ***
```

Figure 9-12. Accounts receivable report: alphabetical customer list. (Courtesy of Retail Sciences, Inc., Peachtree Software Product.)

```
                              CASH RECEIPTS JOURNAL
DATE: 06/11/76                    VAN DYKE DISTRIBUTORS

BANK ACCOUNT G/L #3000000001

CUSTOMER                 CHECK    +---TRANSACTION--+   ORIGINAL
NUMBER NAME              NUMBER   NUMBER TYPE  DATE    BALANCE    PAYMENT   DISCOUNT ADJUSTMENT G/L NUMBER  AMOUNT

300 JOHN SMITH, INC.     H564     000008 DI 06/11/76   290.00    290.00     0.00     0.00
                         H564     000108 DI 06/11/76    14.38     14.38     0.00     0.00
                         H564     000111 DI 06/11/76  4006.91   2195.62     0.00     0.00

       * * CUSTOMER TOTAL * *                                   2500.00     0.00     0.00

500 CHICAGO AUTO PARTS INC. 11437 000003 DI 06/11/76   200.00    200.00     0.00     0.00
                         11437    000004 DM 06/11/76   300.00    300.00     0.00     0.00
                         11437    000006 DI 06/11/76   120.00    120.00     0.00     0.00
                         11437    000105 DI 06/11/76   236.35    236.35     0.00     0.00
                         11437    000110 DI 06/11/76    23.50     23.50     0.00     0.00
                         11437    000113 DI 06/11/76  1557.05   1120.15     0.00     0.00

       * * CUSTOMER TOTAL * *                                   2000.00     0.00     0.00

       * * BANK ACCOUNT 3000000001 TOTAL * *                    4500.00

       * * FINAL TOTAL * *                                      6643.37     0.00    26.50
```

```
                                                         MONTHLY CASH JOURNAL
                                                              G/L RECAP

           G/L RECAP                          DATE: 06/11/76   VAN DYKE DISTRIBUTORS

G/L NUMBER   REF    DEBIT     CREDIT          G/L NUMBER   REF     DEBIT     CREDIT
1000000001   B1    3202.37    0.00            1000000001   B1     3202.37    0.00
2000000001   CASH    0.00     0.00            2000000001   CASH     0.00     0.00
3000000001   A/R   4500.00  7738.87           3000000001   A/R    4500.00  7738.87
3000000002   CR1     0.00     0.00            3000000002   CR1      0.00     0.00
3000000003   CR2     0.00     0.00            3000000003   CR2      0.00     0.00
3000000004   CR3     0.00     0.00            3000000004   CR3      0.00     0.00
3000000005   CR4     0.00     0.00            3000000005   CR4      0.00     0.00
3000000006   CR5     0.00     0.00            3000000006   CR5      0.00     0.00
4000000001   DISC   10.00     0.00            4000000001   DISC    10.00     0.00
4000000002   ADJ1   15.00     0.00            4000000002   ADJ1    15.00     0.00
4000000003   ADJ2    0.00     0.00            4000000003   ADJ2     0.00     0.00
4000000004   ADJ3   11.50     0.00            4000000004   ADJ3    11.50     0.00
4000000005   ADJ4    0.00     0.00            4000000005   ADJ4     0.00     0.00
                  ---------- ----------                        ---------- ----------
                   7738.87   7738.87                            7738.87   7738.87

                                              13 G/L ACCOUNT(S) LISTED
```

Figure 9-13. Accounts receivable report: cash receipts journal. (Courtesy of Nixdorf Computer Inc.)

MINI-COMPUTER BUSINESS APPLICATIONS, INC.

SALES JOURNAL

CUST-#	NAME	DOC-# DOC-DATE	DOC TYP	APPLY-TO DUE-DATE	SALE-AMT MISC-CHGS	SALES-TAX FREIGHT	TOTAL-AMT COST	SLSMN COMM-AMT REFERENCE
000100	John Q. Williams Company	3000 07/17/79	I	3000 08/16/79	2,130.85 23.65	123.88 125.84	2,404.22 1,524.94	400 21.30 Order # W7601
	OPTIONAL DISTRIBUTIONS: 3100-100 Sales - Product Line A				562.17			
	3110-200 Sales - Product Line B				842.01			
	3110-200 Sales - Product Line 2				465.28			
	3120-100 Sales - Product Line C				281.39			
000100	John Q. Williams Company	3001 07/11/79	C	2000 07/11/79	59.26CR .00	3.40CR .00	62.66CR 33.18CR	400 .59CR Credit Memo to 002000
	OPTIONAL DISTRIBUTIONS: 3100-100 Sales - Product Line A				59.26CR			
000200	21st Century Enterprises	3002 07/03/79	I	3002 08/02/79	715.45 25.00	44.42 .00	784.87 512.67	100 7.15 Order # 21-8564
	OPTIONAL DISTRIBUTIONS: 3120-100 Sales - Product Line C				715.45			
000200	21st Century Enterprises	3003 07/19/79	D	887 07/19/79	286.12 .00	17.16 .00	303.28 158.24	100 2.86 Debit Memo to 000887
	OPTIONAL DISTRIBUTIONS: 3110-100 Sales - Product Line B				286.12			
000200	21st Century Enterprises	3004 07/24/79	I	3004 08/23/79	1,239.18 .00	74.35 36.45	1,349.98 952.14	100 12.39 Order # 21-9451
	OPTIONAL DISTRIBUTIONS: 3100-200 Sales - Product Line 1				707.40			
	3110-100 Sales - Product Line B				531.78			
000400	Beverly Beauty Supply	3005 07/02/79	I	0 08/01/79	1,305.87 54.29	.00 31.99	1,392.15 1,045.87	500 13.05 P.O. # 885619
	OPTIONAL DISTRIBUTIONS: 3100-100 Sales - Product Line A				562.97			
	3120-100 Sales - Product Line C				742.90			
000400	Beverly Beauty Supply	3006 07/21/79	I	0 08/20/79	1,562.93 .00	85.96 45.95	1,694.84 1,125.45	500 15.62 Verbal per Anne Beech
	OPTIONAL DISTRIBUTIONS: 3110-100 Sales - Product Line B				1,562.93			
000600	Mallory Company, The	3007 07/18/79	I	0 08/17/79	1,496.00 38.12	92.04 37.77	1,663.93 1,135.19	200 14.96 7/12/79 Letter - J.W. Wilson
	OPTIONAL DISTRIBUTIONS: 3100-100 Sales - Product Line A				789.24			
	3120-100 Sales - Product Line C				706.76			
	GRAND TOTALS:				8,677.14 141.06	434.41 278.00	9,530.61 6,421.32	86.74

8 ENTRIES

Figure 9-14. Accounts receivable report: sales journal. (Courtesy of Mini-Computer Business Applications, Inc.)

257

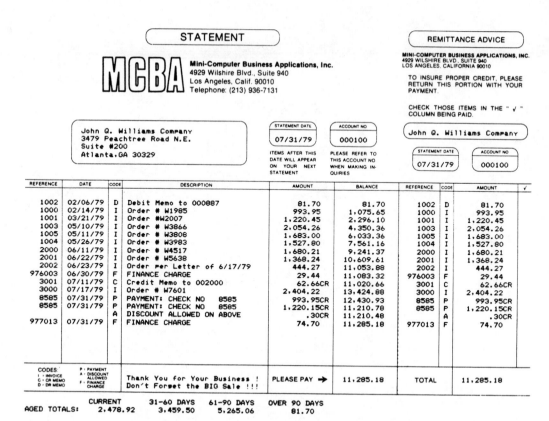

Figure 9-15. Accounts receivable report: statement and remittance. (Courtesy of Mini-Computer Business Applications, Inc.)

able to maintain a complete record for each vendor, and help to determine which vouchers to pay by the due date or discount date, or within certain cash requirements. It should also be able to automatically print checks and a check register if needed. The accounts payable system may be designed to interface with the general ledger system to provide automatic monthly journal entries to the general ledger. However, the accounts payable system should also be able to run independently so that it may be used with the existing manual accounting system as well.

Functions and Features

The accounts payable system should assist the user in deciding which vendors to pay by generating appropriate reports. These reports can be the open voucher report, the cash requirements report, and the aged payable report. After analyzing these reports and considering the amount of cash the user has available, the vendors and vouchers to be paid can be selected.

ACCOUNT	CUSTOMER NAME	PHONE	INVOICE	DUE DATE	CURRENT	1-30	31-60	OVER 60	TOTAL	OPEN CR
ALLEN	ALLEN & COMPANY	(404)255-9999	812	5/ 4/80				26.92		
			884	5/28/80			130.81			
					0.00	0.00	130.81	26.92	157.73	0.00
COX	COX PROPERTIES, INC.	(404)394-6666	---	6/30/80					3316.89	
EVANS	EVANS OFFICE SUPPLY	(404)262-8888	1030	6/ 9/80			21.47			
			1066	6/21/80		27.50				
			1245	7/15/80	22.76					
					22.76	27.50	21.47	0.00	71.73	0.00
HARLEN	HARLEN INSURANCE AGENCY	(404)238-1212	1260	7/20/80	36.39					
					36.39	0.00	0.00	0.00	36.39	0.00
JOHNDE	JOHNSON DELIVERY SERVICE	(404)262-2555	1230	7/10/80						-20.13
			1263	7/21/80	36.75					
			1275	7/25/80	102.98					
					139.73	0.00	0.00	0.00	139.73	-20.13
KELLY	KELLY SUPPLY COMPANY	(404)634-1555	---	7/ 9/80					582.72	
LENOX	LENOX MAMAGEMENT SERVICE	(404)237-2323	---	7/ 7/80					2263.30	
MARSH	MARSHALL, ALLEN & BOOSE	(404)634-6666	---	6/30/80					162.58	
MCMILL	MCMILLAN & ASSOCIATES	(404)233-7777	0	7/ 6/80						-90.00
			1218	6/29/80		90.00				
			1219	7/ 6/80		33.49				
			1236	7/12/80		39.95				
			1395	7/30/80	90.00					
					90.00	163.44	0.00	0.00	253.44	-90.00
ROYAL	ROYAL IMPORTERS, LTD.	(404)763-3333	1084	6/27/80		36.37				
			1242	7/14/80		365.25				
					0.00	401.62	0.00	0.00	401.62	0.00
SDI	SOUTHERN DIST., INC.	(404)633-5555	1206	6/17/80		159.95				-150.00
			1251	7/17/80						
			1271	7/23/80	38.95					
			1292	7/30/80	39.98					
					78.93	159.95	0.00	0.00	238.88	-150.00
WALLWH	WALLACE WHOLESALE, INC.	(404)641-8888	---	7/14/80					1166.21	
TOTALS					367.81	752.51	152.28	26.92	8791.22	-260.13

*** END OF AGEING REPORT ***

Figure 9-16. Accounts receivable report: aged accounts report. (Courtesy of Retail Sciences, Inc., Peachtree Software Product.)

Some systems pay vouchers automatically, depending on the due date and discount. In such a system, an override feature should be provided that allows the user to optionally defer payment or select those bills that are to be paid individually.

The accounts payable system should be able to print a check for each vendor, listing all vouchers paid by check. The user should also have the option of printing a check register that will list the check number and vouchers paid for each vendor. Some systems allow the user to pay only part of a voucher amount. This partial payment is a valuable feature that should be considered.

An accounts payable system may be interfaced with the general ledger system. Cash in the bank account can be credited as checks are written, and

SALES ANALYSIS BY CUSTOMER

DATE: 06/11/76   VAN DYKE DISTRIBUTORS

CUSTOMER NUMBER NAME	PROD CODE	AVERAGE COST	TOTAL SALES	GROSS PROFIT	PROFIT PERCENT
100 ESSEX ENTERPRISES	2	1. 100	6. 75	1. 25	22. 72
	3	17. 000	23. 00	6. 00	35. 29
	01	4. 600	5. 25	0. 65	14. 13
** TOTAL **			35. 00	7. 90	29. 15
200 LINCOLN PARK OFFICE MACH.	1	2. 350	5. 00	2. 65	112. 76
	3	17. 000	25. 00	8. 00	47. 05
	5	0. 000	0. 00	0. 00	0. 00
	01	31. 600	379. 50	189. 90	100. 15
	04	124. 550	400. 00	150. 90	60. 57
** TOTAL **			809. 50	351. 45	76. 72
300 JOHN SMITH, INC.		2. 950	2. 95	0. 00	0. 00
	1	2. 500	6. 40	1. 40	28. 00
	2	2. 950	14. 05	2. 25	19. 06
	3	12. 000	13. 00	1. 00	8. 33
	01	203. 600	987. 55	173. 15	21. 26
	02	12. 065	2737. 50	927. 75	51. 26
	03	12. 510	318. 75	131. 10	69. 86
	04	2. 400	283. 70	137. 25	93. 71
** TOTAL **			4363. 90	1373. 90	45. 94
400 NORTHWESTERN UNIVERSITY	1	2. 350	6. 40	1. 70	36. 17
	2	8. 500	30. 00	4. 50	17. 64
	3	11. 750	26. 00	2. 50	10. 63
	5	525. 000	600. 00	75. 00	14. 28
	01	4. 600	26. 25	3. 25	14. 13
** TOTAL **			688. 65	86. 95	14. 45
500 CHICAGO AUTO PARTS INC.	1	101. 250	139. 00	37. 75	37. 28
	2	8. 500	55. 00	12. 50	29. 41
	3	17. 000	25. 00	8. 00	47. 05
	01	22. 600	161. 78	93. 98	138. 61
	02	12. 065	1623. 00	416. 50	34. 52
	05	0. 000	0. 00	0. 00	0. 00
** TOTAL **			2003. 78	568. 73	39. 63
600 RATOC OFFICE FURNISHINGS	1	2. 491	85. 00	42. 65	100. 70
	2	8. 333	33. 00	8. 00	32. 00
	3	12. 000	14. 00	2. 00	16. 66
	5	525. 000	625. 00	100. 00	19. 04
	01	4. 500	72. 00	18. 00	33. 33
** TOTAL **			829. 00	170. 65	25. 92
700 MISSOURI DRUM & BRAKE INC	1	2. 457	84. 00	49. 60	144. 18
	2	1. 100	6. 20	1. 80	40. 90
	3	17. 000	26. 99	9. 99	58. 76
	01	18. 050	139. 50	67. 30	93. 21
	02	12. 065	2227. 50	417. 75	23. 08
** TOTAL **			2484. 19	546. 44	28. 19

Figure 9-17. Accounts receivable report: sales analysis by customer and by customer type. (Courtesy of Nixdorf Computer Inc.)

vouchers can be distributed to the appropriate accounts of the general ledger system. If the system provides automatic distribution to the general ledger accounts, there will be a limit on the number of accounts to which any one voucher may be distributed. Thus, the user should be sure that the number chosen is sufficient for the needs of the business.

Checklist for Accounts Payable

1. What is the maximum number of vendors allowed in the system?

DATE: 06/11/76   VAN DYKE DISTRIBUTORS

SALESMAN ID	NAME	PROD CODE	AVERAGE COST	TOTAL SALES	GROSS PROFIT	PROFIT PERCENT
1	SMITH	2	1. 100	6. 75	1. 25	22. 72
		3	17. 000	23. 00	6. 00	35. 29
		01	4. 600	5. 25	0. 65	14. 13
	** TOTAL **			35. 00	7. 90	29. 15
2	DOE	1	2. 350	5. 00	2. 65	112. 76
		3	17. 000	25. 00	8. 00	47. 05
		5	0. 000	0. 00	0. 00	0. 00
		01	31. 600	379. 50	189. 90	100. 15
		04	124. 550	400. 00	150. 90	60. 57
	** TOTAL **			809. 50	351. 45	76. 72
3	ADAMS		2. 950	2. 95	0. 00	0. 00
		1	2. 500	6. 40	1. 40	28. 00
		2	2. 950	14. 05	2. 25	19. 06
		3	12. 000	13. 00	1. 00	8. 33
		01	203. 600	987. 55	173. 15	21. 26
		02	12. 065	2737. 50	927. 75	51. 26
		03	12. 510	318. 75	131. 10	69. 86
		04	2. 400	283. 70	137. 25	93. 71
	** TOTAL **			4363. 90	1373. 90	45. 94
4	JONES	1	2. 350	6. 40	1. 70	36. 17
		2	8. 500	30. 00	4. 50	17. 64
		3	11. 750	26. 00	2. 50	10. 63
		5	525. 000	600. 00	75. 00	14. 28
		01	4. 600	26. 25	3. 25	14. 13
	** TOTAL **			688. 65	86. 95	14. 45
5	BROWN	1	101. 250	139. 00	37. 75	37. 28
		2	8. 500	55. 00	12. 50	29. 41
		3	17. 000	25. 00	8. 00	47. 05
		01	22. 600	161. 78	93. 98	138. 61
		02	12. 065	1623. 00	416. 50	34. 52
		05	0. 000	0. 00	0. 00	0. 00
	** TOTAL **			2003. 78	568. 73	39. 63
6	BABBIT	1	2. 491	85. 00	42. 65	100. 70
		2	8. 333	33. 00	8. 00	32. 00
		3	12. 000	14. 00	2. 00	16. 66
		5	525. 000	625. 00	100. 00	19. 04
		01	4. 500	72. 00	18. 00	33. 33
	** TOTAL **			829. 00	170. 65	25. 92
7	GUTHRIE	1	2. 457	84. 00	49. 60	144. 18
		2	1. 100	6. 20	1. 80	40. 90
		3	17. 000	26. 99	9. 99	58. 76
		01	18. 050	139. 50	67. 30	93. 21
		02	12. 065	2227. 50	417. 75	23. 08
	** TOTAL **			2484. 19	546. 44	28. 19

Figure 9-18. Accounts receivable report: sales analysis by salesperson. (Courtesy of Nixdorf Computer Inc.)

2. What is the maximum number of vouchers allowed in the system? _____

3. Can the system provide automatically recurring payment?   YES _____   NO _____

4. Can an automatic payment system be overridden by a manual payment system?   YES _____   NO _____

5. Does the system allow for individual selection or deferment of payments?   YES _____   NO _____

6. Can the system handle partial payments?   YES _____   NO _____

SALES ANALYSIS BY ITEM

DATE: 06/11/76　　　　　　　　　　　　VAN DYKE DISTRIBUTORS

ITEM NUMBER	DESCRIPTION	UNIT	QUANTITY SOLD	AVERAGE COST	AVERAGE PRICE	SALES EXTENSION	GROSS PROFIT	PROFIT PERCENT
PRODUCT CODE								
1000	PAPER CLIPS	CS	19.0	4.526	5.89	112.00	26.00	30.23
6236	STAPLES	GR	5.0	163.800	198.56	992.80	173.80	21.22
7055	FILE CABINET	EA	10.0	31.600	66.17	661.78	345.78	109.42
	** TOTAL **					1766.58	545.58	44.68
PRODUCT CODE 02								
2017	CARBON PAPER-3C	RM	400.0	12.065	16.47	6588.00	1762.00	36.51
	** TOTAL **					6588.00	1762.00	36.51
PRODUCT CODE 03								
8001	DLX STAPLER	EA	15.0	12.510	21.25	318.75	131.10	69.86
	** TOTAL **					318.75	131.10	69.86
PRODUCT CODE 04								
4003	PENCIL-2H	DZ	60.0	0.365	1.22	73.20	51.30	234.24
10003	HERM M-10 TYPEWRITER	EA	3.0	124.550	203.50	610.50	236.85	63.38
	** TOTAL **					683.70	288.15	72.84
PRODUCT CODE 05								
5015	RING BINDERS	CS	0.0	0.000	0.00	0.00	0.00	0.00
	** TOTAL **					0.00	0.00	0.00
	** FINAL TOTALS **					11202.77	3101.87	38.29

Figure 9-19. Accounts receivable report: sales analysis by item. (Courtesy of Nixdorf Computer Inc.)

FINANCE CHARGE REPORT

DATE: 06/11/76　　　　　　　　　　　　VAN DYKE DISTRIBUTORS

LINE	CUSTOMER NUMBER NAME	PHONE	CURRENT A/R BAL	OVERDUE BALANCE	OLDEST INVOICE	CURRENT FINANCE	FC PERCENT	NEW FINANCE
1	100 ESSEX ENTERPRISES	312/121-1212	319.86	285.00	39	0.00	1.50	4.28
2	300 JOHN SMITH, INC.	312/982-2222	4294.69	280.00	160	0.00	1.50	4.20
3	400 NORTHWESTERN UNIVERSITY	312/234-6666	796.18	50.00	117	0.00	1.50	0.75
4	500 CHICAGO AUTO PARTS INC.	312/234-1231	2426.90	290.00	74	0.00	1.50	4.35
5	700 MISSOURI DRUM & BRAKE INC	314/456-1231	2365.59	75.00	51	0.00	1.50	1.13
6	800 JOHNSON RETAIL STORES INC	312/321-7777	142.76	150.00	158	0.00	1.50	2.25
			10345.98	1130.00		0.00		16.96

Figure 9-20. Accounts receivable report: finance charge report. (Courtesy of Nixdorf Computer Inc.)

7. Can the system maintain month-to-date and year-to-date totals by vendors to see how the company's payments are distributed?   YES ____   NO ____

8. Is the check format or content compatible with the business?   YES ____   NO ____

9. Can the accounts payable system be interfaced with the general ledger system?   YES ____   NO ____

10. Can the cash-in-bank account be credited as checks are written?   YES ____   NO ____

11. Can the voucher be distributed to the appropriate accounts of the general ledger?   YES ____   NO ____

Files for Accounts Payable

There are mainly two files associated with an accounts payable system: the vendor file and the transaction file (vouchers and credits file); see Figure 9-21. If the system can be interfaced with the general ledger system, the general ledger master file should be included.

Accounts Payable Output Reports

For the accounts payable system to be an effective management tool, it should be able to generate hard-copy reports. Some examples of these are:

1. Vendor alphabetic list
2. Vendor analysis report
3. Voucher register (open voucher)
4. Cash requirement report
5. Aged payable report
6. Precheck writing report
7. Checks
8. Check register
9. General ledger distribution report
10. End-of-month report

Figures 9-22 to 9-30 show sample accounts payable reports.

9-4.4 Inventory Control

An inventory control system can help a company better manage its inventory, reduce overstocks, stockouts, and on-hand product quantities. In an average small business firm, inventory carrying costs are estimated to be

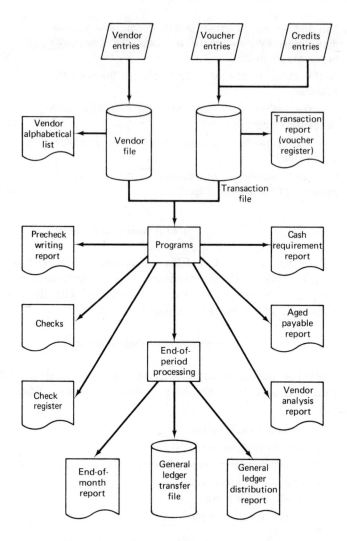

Figure 9-21. Accounts payable system flow.

about 25 to 50% of the total value of the inventory. As a result, it is extremely desirable to keep optimum inventory levels. There must be enough goods to fill orders quickly, but having too many goods on hand can tie up capital that can be used elsewhere in the company. Another inventory consideration is that customer shifts in buying patterns may cause some items in stock to become outdated, and perishable goods will deteriorate. A large inventory of such goods can mean a great loss for the firm. In the past, the very complex matter of what and how much of each item to stock was left in the hands of employees, who had their experience to use for sound

VENDOR ID	NAME / ADDRESS	PHONE	AMOUNTS		LAST CHECK		AUTO VOUCHER ENTRY		ACCOUNT	AMOUNT
ALLEN	ALLEN EQUIPMENT CO. 4436 ROSWELL RD. NE. ATLANTA, GA. 30342	404-255-9999	YTD PURCH: YTD PAYMT: CURR. BAL:	$83,026.96 $56,038.29 $26,988.67	NO. : AMT. : DATE:	753 $7,600.00 06/16/80				
ATLMAG	ATLANTA MAGAZINE ADVERTISING OFFICE COMMERCE BUILDING ATLANTA, GA. 30313	404-394-4943	YTD PURCH: YTD PAYMT: CURR. BAL:	$700.00 $350.00 $350.00	NO. : AMT. : DATE:	$0.00				
BANKAM	BANKAMERICARD/VISA FIRST NAT. BANK OF ATLAN. 2400 PIEDMONT RD. NE. ATLANTA, GA. 30324	404-231-7643	YTD PURCH: YTD PAYMT: CURR. BAL:	$6,503.29 $5,603.29 $900.00	NO. : AMT. : DATE:	799 $875.00 06/31/80				
COX PR	COX PROPERTIES, INC. 17-C PERIMETER PARK 256 PERIMETER CENTER PKWY DUNWOODY, GA. 30338	404-394-6666	YTD PURCH: YTD PAYMT: CURR. BAL:	$16,000.00 $14,000.00 $2,000.00	NO. : AMT. : DATE:	800 $2,000.00 06/31/80	DUE DAY : 31 DISC. DAY: 21	DISC.	51100	$2,000.00 $0.00 $40.00
EVANS	EVANS OFFICE SUPPLY 2550 PIEDMONT RD.NE. ATLANTA, GA. 30324	404-262-8888	YTD PURCH: YTD PAYMT: CURR. BAL:	$118,436.73 $99,000.00 $19,436.73	NO. : AMT. : DATE:	683 $10,000.00 06/01/80				
FICA	NATIONAL BANK OF GEORGIA FEDERAL DEPOSITORY 34 PEACHTREE ST. NW. ATLANTA, GA. 30313	404-586-8000	YTD PURCH: YTD PAYMT: CURR. BAL:	$11,000.00 $11,000.00 $0.00	NO. : AMT. : DATE:	748 $5,500.00 06/15/80				
FRTWAY	FREIGHTWAYS TRANSIT LINES 4280 FULTON IND. BLVD. SE ATLANTA, GA. 30336	404-691-3333	YTD PURCH: YTD PAYMT: CURR. BAL:	$496.59 $356.00 $140.59	NO. : AMT. : DATE:	657 $100.00 05/21/80				
GAINC	GEORGIA STATE REV. DEPT. INCOME TAX DIVISION 270 WASHINGTON ST. SW. ATLANTA, GA. 30303	404-656-4165	YTD PURCH: YTD PAYMT: CURR. BAL:	$32,250.73 $28,000.00 $4,250.73	NO. : AMT. : DATE:	777 $3,750.00 06/21/80				
GAPOWR	GEORGIA POWER COMPANY 96 ANNEX ATLANTA, GA. 30396	404-522-6060	YTD PURCH: YTD PAYMT: CURR. BAL:	$7,000.00 $7,000.00 $0.00	NO. : AMT. : DATE:	823 $1,000.00 07/10/80	DUE DAY : 10 DISC. DAY: 0	DISC.	51400	$1,000.00 $0.00 $0.00
GASALE	GEORGIA STATE REV. DEPT. SALES TAX DIVISION 270 WASHINGTON ST. SW. ATLANTA, GA. 30303	404-656-4071	YTD PURCH: YTD PAYMT: CURR. BAL:	$18,108.59 $16,000.00 $2,108.59	NO. : AMT. : DATE:	746 $6,500.00 06/15/80				
HARLEN	HARLEN INSURANCE AGENCY 2336 PEACHTREE RD. NE. SUITE 619 ATLANTA, GA. 30305	404-238-1212	YTD PURCH: YTD PAYMT: CURR. BAL:	$10,800.00 $9,600.00 $1,200.00	NO. : AMT. : DATE:	802 $1,200.00 06/31/80	DUE DAY : 31 DISC. DAY: 10	DISC.	52200	$1,200.00 $0.00 $24.00
IBM	INTERN. BUS. MACH. OFFICE PRODUCTS DIV. 148 CAIN ST. NE. ATLANTA, GA. 30303	404-659-3232	YTD PURCH: YTD PAYMT: CURR. BAL:	$1,080.00 $960.00 $120.00	NO. : AMT. : DATE:	778 $120.00 06/21/80	DUE DAY : 21 DISC. DAY: 0	DISC.	52100	$120.00 $0.00 $0.00
IRS	INTERNAL REVENUE SERVICE 4800 BUFORD HWY. CHAMBLEE, GA. 30341	404-522-0050	YTD PURCH: YTD PAYMT: CURR. BAL:	$34,000.00 $34,000.00 $0.00	NO. : AMT. : DATE:	747 $1,600.00 06/15/80				
JOHNDE	JOHNSON DELIVERY SERVICE 430 PHARR RD. NE. ATLANTA, GA. 30305	404-262-2555	YTD PURCH: YTD PAYMT: CURR. BAL:	$350.00 $350.00 $0.00	NO. : AMT. : DATE:	779 $50.00 06/21/80				
JOUR-C	ATLANTA JOURNAL-CONST. ADVERTISING DEPT. 72 MARIETTA ST. NW. ATLANTA, GA. 30313	404-577-5127	YTD PURCH: YTD PAYMT: CURR. BAL:	$1,100.00 $600.00 $500.00	NO. : AMT. : DATE:	542 $200.00 04/21/80				
KELLY	KELLY SUPPLY COMPANY 2055 LAWRENCEVILLE HWY. DECATUR, GA. 30033	404-634-1555	YTD PURCH: YTD PAYMT: CURR. BAL:	$97,264.77 $65,000.00 $32,264.77	NO. : AMT. : DATE:	801 $11,000.00 06/31/80				
M BANK	MERCHANTS BANK 1 PERIMETER WAY NE. DUNWOODY, GA. 30338	404-952-3535	YTD PURCH: YTD PAYMT: CURR. BAL:	$27,000.00 $24,000.00 $3,000.00	NO. : AMT. : DATE:	745 $3,000.00 06/15/78	DUE DAY : 15 DISC. DAY: 7	DISC.	25100 53200	$2,800.00 $200.00 $60.00
MARSH	MARSHALL, ALLEN & BOOSE 17 EXECUTIVE PARK 2670 N. DRUID HILLS RD. ATLANTA, GA. 30324	404-634-6666	YTD PURCH: YTD PAYMT: CURR. BAL:	$7,000.00 $7,000.00 $0.00	NO. : AMT. : DATE:	805 $1,000.00 07/01/80	DUE DAY : 1 DISC. DAY: 0	DISC.	53300	$1,000.00 $0.00 $0.00

Figure 9-22. Accounts payable report: vendor alphabetical list. (Courtesy of Retail Sciences, Inc., Peachtree Software Product.)

VENDOR ID	NAME / ADDRESS	PHONE	AMOUNTS		LAST CHECK		AUTO VOUCHER ENTRY	ACCOUNT	AMOUNT
NOSDA	NAT.OF.SUPPLY DLRS. AS. 725 S. RIVER ST. SUITE 714 ST. LOUIS, MO. 65555	314-298-2514	YTD PURCH: YTD PAYMT: CURR. BAL:	$675.00 $450.00 $75.00	NO. : AMT. : DATE:	749 $75.00 06/15/80	DUE DAY : 15 DISC. DAY: 0	52300 DISC.	$75.00 $0.00 $0.00
ROYAL	ROYAL IMPORTERS, LMTD. 347 AIRPORT IND. PARK COLLEGE PARK, GA. 30337	404-763-3333	YTD PURCH: YTD PAYMT: CURR. BAL:	$2,000.00 $1,100.00 $900.00	NO. : AMT. : DATE:	438 $200.00 03/01/80			
SDI	SOUTHERN DISTRIBUTORS INC 4350 BUFORD HWY. NE. CHAMBLEE, GA. 30341	(404) 633-5555	YTD PURCH: YTD PAYMT: CURR. BAL:	$105,129.17 $80,000.00 $25,129.17	NO. : AMT. : DATE:	818 $14,000.00 07/07/80			
SOBELL	SOUTHERN BELL TEL. & TEL. CENTRAL REMITTANCE CENTER 85 ANNEX	404-393-4511	YTD PURCH: YTD PAYMT: CURR. BAL:	$945.00 $840.00 $105.00	NO. : AMT. : DATE:	792 $105.00 06/25/80	DUE DAY : 25 DISC. DAY: 0	51300 DISC.	$105.00 $0.00 $0.00
WALLWH	WALLACE WHOLESALERS, INC. 3880 FULTON IND. BLVD. ATLANTA, GA. 30336	404-691-8888	YTD PURCH: YTD PAYMT: CURR. BAL:	$42,890.12 $32,000.00 $10,890.12	NO. : AMT. : DATE:	808 $5,800.00 07/01/80			
XEROX	XEROX CORPORATION 1801 PEACHTREE RD. NE. ATLANTA, GA. 30309	404-351-7920	YTD PURCH: YTD PAYMT: CURR. BAL:	$1,750.00 $1,750.00 $0.00	NO. : AMT. : DATE:	845 $250.00 07/12/80	DUE DAY : 12 DISC. DAY: 0	51200 DISC.	$250.00 $0.00 $0.00

Figure 9-22. (*Continued*)

TAYLOR OFFICE EQUIPMENT
ACCOUNTS PAYABLE
TRANSACTION REGISTER
07/15/80

TRANSACTION LIST

VENDOR	INVOICE NUMBER	INVOICE DATE	DEBIT DISTRIBUTION ACCT.	AMOUNT	CREDIT ENTERED VOUCHERS	DEBIT PAYMENTS	CREDIT DISCOUNTS TAKEN	CREDIT CASH
ALLEN	INV#00016	07/05/80	41101 42101	$4,000.00 $25.12	$4,025.12			
	INV#00022	07/10/80	41102 42102	$4,950.00 $58.76	$5,058.76			
	CREDIT ON ABOVE	07/10/80			-$50.00			
	INV#00034	07/11/80	41101 41102 42101 42102	$7,525.50 -$6,475.25 $189.11 $188.34	$14,378.20			
	INV#00056	07/14/80	41102 42102	$3,028.14 $548.45	$3,576.59			
ATLMAG			52100	$350.00	$350.00			
BANKAM		07/07/80	53300	$900.00	$900.00			
COX PR	AUTO VOUCHER		51100	$2,000.00	$2,000.00			
EVANS	0001258	06/16/80	41101	$10,000.00	$10,000.00			
	0001264	06/20/80	41102	$5,000.00	$5,000.00			
	0001287	06/31/80	41101 41102 42101 42102	$2,005.36 $2,005.36 $213.01 $213.00	$4,436.73			
			20100	-$111.00	-$111.00			
FRTWAY	WB#38795629	07/08/80	42101	$140.59	$140.59			
GAINC		07/15/80	21300	$4,250.73	$4,250.73			
GASALE		07/15/80	21400	$2,108.59	$2,108.59			
HARLEN	AUTO VOUCHER		52200	$1,200.00	$1,200.00			
IBM	AUTO VOUCHER		52100	$120.00	$120.00			
JOUR-C		05/21/80	52100	$100.00	$100.00			
		06/21/80	52100	$400.00	$400.00			
KELLY	AB 0076	07/01/80	41101 42101	$4,086.38 $927.57	$5,013.95			

Figure 9-23. Accounts payable report: vendor analysis report. (Courtesy of Retail Sciences, Inc., Peachtree Software Product.)

VENDOR	INVOICE NUMBER	INVOICE DATE	DEBIT DISTRIBUTION ACCT.	AMOUNT	CREDIT ENTERED VOUCHERS	DEBIT PAYMENTS	CREDIT DISCOUNTS TAKEN	CREDIT CASH
KELLY	AB 0088	07/03/80	41102	$4,000.00	$4,000.00			
	AB 0103	07/05/80	41101	$2,088.99	$2,088.99			
	AB 0203	07/07/80	41101	$3,095.95				
			41102	$3,095.95				
			42101	$951.72				
			42102	$951.71	$8,095.33			
	AB 0214	07/09/80	41102	$7,000.00	$7,000.00			
	AB 0346	07/13/80	41101	$3,000.00				
			41102	$3,000.00				
			42101	$33.25				
			42102	$33.25	$6,066.50			
			20100	-$178.00	-$178.00			
M BANK	AUTO VOUCHER		25100	$2,800.00				
			53200	$200.00	$3,000.00			
NOSDA	AUTO VOUCHER		52300	$75.00	$75.00			
ROYAL		04/01/80	41102	$900.00	$900.00			
SDI	B# 3384	07/02/80	41101	$14,000.00				
			42101	$793.58	$14,793.58			
	B# 3496	07/07/80	41102	$2,800.00				
			42102	$31.95	$2,831.95			
	B# 3738	07/14/80	41101	$3,522.25				
			41102	$3,386.58				
			42101	$355.55				
			42102	$239.26	$7,503.64			
SOBELL	AUTO VOUCHER		51300	$105.00	$105.00			
WALLWH		07/01/80	41101	$4,000.00	$4,000.00			
		07/12/80	41101	$3,333.67				
			41102	$3,333.66				
			42101	$111.40				
			42102	$111.39	$6,890.12			

Figure 9-23. (*Continued*)

TAYLOR OFFICE EQUIPMENT
ACCOUNTS PAYABLE
OPEN VOUCHERS
07/15/80

VENDOR ID	VOUCHER DATE	INVOICE NUMBER	INVOICE DATE	DUE AMOUNT	DUE DATE	DISCOUNT AMOUNT	DISCOUNT DATE	NET	PAY?
ALLEN	07/15/80	INV#00016	07/05/80	$4,025.12	08/05/80	$80.50	07/20/80	$3,944.62	NO
	07/15/80	INV#00022	07/10/80	$5,008.76	08/10/80	$100.18	07/25/80	$4,908.58	NO
	07/15/80	INV#00034	07/11/80	$14,378.20	08/11/80	$287.56	07/26/80	$14,090.64	NO
	07/15/80	INV#00056	07/14/80	$3,576.59	08/14/80	$71.53	07/29/80	$3,505.06	NO
				$26,988.67		$539.77		$26,448.90	
ATLMAG	07/15/80			$350.00	07/15/80			$350.00	YES
BANKAM	07/15/80		07/07/80	$900.00	07/31/80			$900.00	NO
COX PR	07/15/80	AUTO VOUCHER		$2,000.00	07/31/80	$40.00	07/21/80	$1,960.00	NO
EVANS	07/15/80	0001264	06/20/80	$5,000.00	07/20/80	$100.00	06/30/80	$4,900.00	NO
	07/15/80	0001287	06/31/80	$4,436.73	07/15/80	$88.73	07/10/80	$4,348.00	YES
	07/15/80	0001258		$0.00	07/02/80	-$200.00	07/02/80	$200.00	YES
	07/15/80			-$111.00	07/15/80			-$111.00	
				$9,325.73		-$11.27		$9,337.00	
FRTWAY	07/15/80	WB#38795629	07/08/80	$140.59	08/08/80			$140.59	NO
GAINC	07/15/80		07/15/80	$4,250.73	07/21/80			$4,250.73	NO
GASALE	07/15/80		07/15/80	$2,108.59	07/15/80			$2,108.59	YES

Figure 9-24. Accounts payable report: accounts payable voucher register. (Courtesy of Retail Sciences, Inc., Peachtree Software Product.)

VENDOR ID	VOUCHER DATE	INVOICE NUMBER	INVOICE DATE	DUE AMOUNT	DUE DATE	DISCOUNT AMOUNT	DISCOUNT DATE	NET	PAY?
HARLEN	07/15/80	AUTO VOUCHER		$1,200.00	07/31/80	$24.00	07/10/80	$1,176.00	NO
IBM	07/15/80	AUTO VOUCHER		$120.00	07/21/80			$120.00	NO
JOUR-C	07/15/80		05/21/80	$100.00	06/21/80			$100.00	YES
	07/15/80		06/21/80	$400.00	07/21/80			$400.00	NO
				$500.00		$0.00		$500.00	
KELLY	07/15/80	AB 0076	07/01/80	$5,013.95	08/01/80	$100.28	07/11/80	$4,913.67	NO
	07/15/80	AB 0088	07/03/80	$4,000.00	08/03/80	$80.00	07/13/80	$3,920.00	NO
	07/15/80	AB 0103	07/05/80	$2,088.99	08/05/80	$41.78	07/15/80	$2,047.21	YES
	07/15/80	AB 0203	07/07/80	$8,095.33	08/07/80	$161.91	07/17/80	$7,933.42	NO
	07/15/80	AB 0214	07/09/80	$7,000.00	08/09/80	$140.00	07/19/80	$6,860.00	NO
	07/15/80	AB 0346	07/13/80	$6,066.50	08/13/80	$121.33	07/23/80	$5,945.17	NO
	07/15/80			−$178.00	07/15/80			−$178.00	
				$32,086.77		$645.30		$31,441.47	
M BANK	07/15/80	AUTO VOUCHER		$3,000.00	07/15/80	$60.00	07/07/80	$2,940.00	YES

Figure 9-24. (*Continued*)

TAYLOR OFFICE EQUIPMENT
ACCOUNTS PAYABLE
CASH REQUIREMENTS
07/15/80

** DATA SORTED BY DUE DATE

PAY DATE	VENDOR	INVOICE NUMBER	INV. DATE	AMOUNT	DISCOUNT	NET	DAILY TOTAL	REQ. TO DATE
OPEN CR.	KELLY			−$178.00	$0.00	−$178.00		
	EVANS			−$111.00	$0.00	−$111.00	−$289.00	−$289.00
05/01/80	ROYAL		04/01/80	$900.00	$0.00	$900.00	$900.00	$611.00
06/21/80	JOUR-C		05/21/80	$100.00	$0.00	$100.00	$100.00	$711.00
07/02/80	EVANS	0001258		$0.00	−$200.00	$200.00	$200.00	$911.00
07/15/80	GASALE		07/15/80	$2,108.59	$0.00	$2,108.59		
	NOSDA	AUTO VOUCHER		$75.00	$0.00	$75.00		
	ATLMAG			$350.00	$0.00	$350.00		
	M BANK	AUTO VOUCHER		$3,000.00	$60.00	$2,940.00		
	EVANS	0001287	06/31/80	$4,436.73	$88.73	$4,348.00	$9,821.59	$10,732.59
07/20/80	EVANS	0001264	06/20/80	$5,000.00	$100.00	$4,900.00	$4,900.00	$15,632.59
07/21/80	IBM	AUTO VOUCHER		$120.00	$0.00	$120.00		
	JOUR-C		06/21/80	$400.00	$0.00	$400.00		
	GAINC		07/15/80	$4,250.73	$0.00	$4,250.73		
	WALLWH		07/01/80	$4,000.00	$80.00	$3,920.00	$8,690.73	$24,323.32
07/25/80	SOBELL	AUTO VOUCHER		$105.00	$0.00	$105.00	$105.00	$24,428.32
07/31/80	COX PR	AUTO VOUCHER		$2,000.00	$40.00	$1,960.00		
	HARLEN	AUTO VOUCHER		$1,200.00	$24.00	$1,176.00		
	BANKAM		07/07/80	$900.00	$0.00	$900.00	$4,036.00	$28,464.32
08/01/80	KELLY	AB 0076	07/01/80	$5,013.95	$100.28	$4,913.67	$4,913.67	$33,377.99
08/02/80	WALLWH		07/12/80	$6,890.12	$137.80	$6,752.32		
	SDI	B# 3384	07/02/80	$14,793.58	$295.87	$14,497.71	$21,250.03	$54,628.02
08/03/80	KELLY	AB 0088	07/03/80	$4,000.00	$80.00	$3,920.00	$3,920.00	$58,548.02
08/05/80	ALLEN	INV#00016	07/05/80	$4,025.12	$80.50	$3,944.62		
	KELLY	AB 0103	07/05/80	$2,088.99	$41.78	$2,047.21	$5,991.83	$64,539.85
08/07/80	KELLY	AB 0203	07/07/80	$8,095.33	$161.91	$7,933.42		
	SDI	B# 3496	07/07/80	$2,831.95	$56.64	$2,775.31	$10,708.73	$75,248.58
08/08/80	FRTWAY	WB#38795629	07/08/80	$140.59	$0.00	$140.59	$140.59	$75,389.17
08/09/80	KELLY	AB 0214	07/09/80	$7,000.00	$140.00	$6,860.00	$6,860.00	$82,249.17
08/10/80	ALLEN	INV#00022	07/10/80	$5,008.76	$100.18	$4,908.58	$4,908.58	$87,157.75
08/11/80	ALLEN	INV#00034	07/11/80	$14,378.20	$287.56	$14,090.64	$14,090.64	$101,248.39
08/13/80	KELLY	AB 0346	07/13/80	$6,066.50	$121.33	$5,945.17	$5,945.17	$107,193.56
08/14/80	SDI	B# 3738	07/14/80	$7,503.64	$150.07	$7,353.57		
	ALLEN	INV#00056	07/14/80	$3,576.59	$71.53	$3,505.06	$10,858.63	$118,052.19

Figure 9-25. Accounts payable report: cash requirement report. (Courtesy of Retail Sciences, Inc., Peachtree Software Product.)

AGEING DATE: 08/01/80

VENDOR	CURRENT	1 TO 30	31 TO 60	61 TO 90	OVER 90	CREDITS	TOTAL NET DUE
ALLEN	$26,988.67	$0.00	$0.00	$0.00	$0.00	$0.00	$26,988.67
ATLMAG	$0.00	$350.00	$0.00	$0.00	$0.00	$0.00	$350.00
BANKAM	$0.00	$900.00	$0.00	$0.00	$0.00	$0.00	$900.00
COX PR	$0.00	$2,000.00	$0.00	$0.00	$0.00	$0.00	$2,000.00
EVANS	$0.00	$9,436.73	$0.00	$0.00	$0.00	$111.00	$9,325.73
FRTWAY	$140.59	$0.00	$0.00	$0.00	$0.00	$0.00	$140.59
GAINC	$0.00	$4,250.73	$0.00	$0.00	$0.00	$0.00	$4,250.73
GASALE	$0.00	$2,108.59	$0.00	$0.00	$0.00	$0.00	$2,108.59
HARLEN	$0.00	$1,200.00	$0.00	$0.00	$0.00	$0.00	$1,200.00
IBM	$0.00	$120.00	$0.00	$0.00	$0.00	$0.00	$120.00
JOUR-C	$0.00	$400.00	$100.00	$0.00	$0.00	$0.00	$500.00
KELLY	$32,264.77	$0.00	$0.00	$0.00	$0.00	$178.00	$32,086.77
M BANK	$0.00	$3,000.00	$0.00	$0.00	$0.00	$0.00	$3,000.00
NOSDA	$0.00	$75.00	$0.00	$0.00	$0.00	$0.00	$75.00
ROYAL	$0.00	$0.00	$0.00	$0.00	$900.00	$0.00	$900.00
SDI	$25,129.17	$0.00	$0.00	$0.00	$0.00	$0.00	$25,129.17
SOBELL	$0.00	$105.00	$0.00	$0.00	$0.00	$0.00	$105.00
WALLWH	$6,890.12	$4,000.00	$0.00	$0.00	$0.00	$0.00	$10,890.12
TOTAL=	$91,413.32	$27,946.05	$100.00	$0.00	$900.00	$289.00	$120,070.37

TOTAL VENDORS LISTED = 18

Figure 9-26. Accounts payable report: aged payable report. (Courtesy of Retail Sciences, Inc., Peachtree Software Product.)

inventory control. If their guesses were wrong, sales were lost or capital was tied up.

The inventory of a wholesaler may contain many thousands of finished goods. A record must be kept in each item, and each record must be updated as items are sold or other items received from suppliers. About one-half to one-third of a small business firm's total assets may be invested in inventory. Even a small percentage reduction in the level of a company's inventory may release a sizable amount of capital. The development of optimum inventory control is potentially one of the most profitable areas of business.

The inventory of most manufacturing plants has to keep track of both raw materials and finished goods. If a company is to remain competitive, as the prices of raw materials change, a system should be capable of altering price policy accordingly on estimated cost, production cost, and final manufacturing cost. Flexibility and adaptability have been essential factors for the survival of small businesses, providing them with a competitive edge against larger businesses.

P R E - C H E C K   W R I T I N G   R E P O R T

FOR PAYMENT ON 02/27/80
TRX TYPES: R = REGULAR VOUCHER C = CREDIT VOUCHER
NOTE: DEFERRED ITEMS ARE NOT INCLUDED IN TOTALS. VENDORS WITH ZERO OR MINUS TOTALS ARE NOT INCLUDED IN TOTALS.

VENDOR #	NAME	TRX TYPE	VOUCHR #	INVOICE #	INVOICE DATE	DUE-DATE	DISCOUNT DATE	AMOUNT TO-BE-PAID	DISCOUNT TO-BE-TAKEN	NET-CASH REQUIRED
100000	COMMONPLACE OFFICE SUPPLIES	R	100001	COS10235	12/06/79	01/05/80	12/16/79	500.00	.00	500.00
		R	100002	COS13698	12/19/79	01/18/80	12/29/79	156.18	.00	DEFERRED
		R	100017	COS23555	01/19/80	02/18/80	01/29/80	294.86	.00	294.86
						VENDOR TOTALS:		794.86	.00	794.86
200000	MARINOS DISTRIBUTERS, INC.	R	100039	MDI34658	02/21/80	03/23/80	03/08/80	956.20	8.96	947.22
						VENDOR TOTALS:		956.20	8.98	947.22
300000	CALIFORNIA UTILITIES CO-OP	R	100041	CUO32564	02/15/80	02/25/80	02/15/80	119.50	.00	119.50
						VENDOR TOTALS:		119.50	.00	119.50
500000	FASTEST FREIGHT CO., INC.	R	100007	FFCI1345	12/10/79	12/17/79	12/10/79	15.23	.00	15.23
		R	100023	FFCI2012	01/24/80	01/31/80	01/24/80	14.47	.00	14.47
		R	100024	FFCI2803	01/24/80	01/31/80	01/24/80	35.28	.00	35.28
						VENDOR TOTALS:		64.98	.00	64.98
600000	HIGH-COURT MANUFACTURING CO.	R	100009	HCMC1492	12/05/79	01/19/80	12/15/79	958.49	.00	DEFERRED
		R	100027	HCMC2866	11/15/79	12/30/79	11/25/79	136.55	.00	136.55
						VENDOR TOTALS:		136.55	.00	136.55
700000	HEPPERMILL, STILLS, & STEIN	R	100047	HSS35652	02/15/80	03/17/80	03/02/80	81.83	.82	81.01
						VENDOR TOTALS:		81.83	.82	81.01
						GRAND TOTALS:		2,153.92	9.80	2,144.17

6 VENDORS TO BE PAID

Figure 9-27. Accounts payable report: pre-check writing report. (Courtesy of Mini-Computer Business Applications, Inc.)

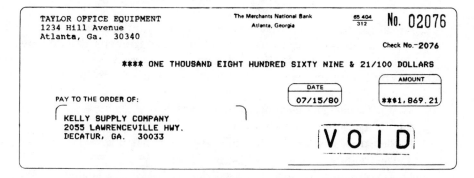

```
            TAYLOR OFFICE EQUIPMENT
            1234 Hill Avenue                          No. 02076
            Atlanta, Ga.   30340

KELLY SUPPLY COMPANY      INVOICE NUMBER    DATE    AMOUNT    DISCOUNT    NET AMT
2055 LAWRENCEVILLE HWY.     AB 0103         07/05   2088.99     41.78     2047.21
DECATUR, GA.   30033                               -178.00      0.00     -178.00
                                                                       ----------
         DATE                                         TOTAL =         $1869.21
       07/15/80

     CHECK NUMBER
        2076
```

NEGATIVE AMOUNTS ARE CREDITS APPLIED ON THIS PAYMENT

```
  TAYLOR OFFICE EQUIPMENT        The Merchants National Bank   65 404    No. 02076
  1234 Hill Avenue                     Atlanta, Georgia         312
  Atlanta, Ga.   30340
                                                          Check No.-2076

          **** ONE THOUSAND EIGHT HUNDRED SIXTY NINE & 21/100 DOLLARS

                                                  AMOUNT
                                          DATE
  PAY TO THE ORDER OF:                 07/15/80    ***$1,869.21

    KELLY SUPPLY COMPANY
    2055 LAWRENCEVILLE HWY.
    DECATUR, GA.   30033                    V O I D
```

Figure 9-28. Accounts payable report: check. (Courtesy of Retail Sciences, Inc., Peachtree Software Product.)

```
                            TAYLOR OFFICE EQUIPMENT
                                ACCOUNTS PAYABLE
                                 CHECK REGISTER
                                   07/15/80
```

VENDOR ID	VENDOR NAME	CHECK NUMBER	CHECK DATE	INVOICE NUMBER	DATE	AMOUNT	DISCOUNT	NET / TOTAL
ATLMAG	ATLANTA MAGAZINE	2072	07/15/80		07/15/80	$350.00	$0.00	$350.00
							TOTAL THIS CHECK =	$350.00
EVANS	EVANS OFFICE SUPPLY	2073	07/15/80	0001287	07/15/80	$4,436.73	$0.00	$4,436.73
				0001258	07/15/80	$0.00	-$200.00	$200.00
					07/15/80	-$111.00	$0.00	-$111.00
							TOTAL THIS CHECK =	$4,525.73
GASALE	GEORGIA STATE REV. DEPT.	2074	07/15/80		07/15/80	$2,108.59	$0.00	$2,108.59
							TOTAL THIS CHECK =	$2,108.59
JOUR-C	ATLANTA JOURNAL-CONST.	2075	07/15/80		07/15/80	$100.00	$0.00	$100.00
							TOTAL THIS CHECK =	$100.00
KELLY	KELLY SUPPLY COMPANY	2076	07/15/80	AB 0103	07/15/80	$2,088.99	$41.78	$2,047.21
					07/15/80	-$178.00	$0.00	-$178.00
							TOTAL THIS CHECK =	$1,869.21
M BANK	MERCHANTS BANK	2077	07/15/80	AUTO VOUCHER	07/15/80	$3,000.00	$0.00	$3,000.00
							TOTAL THIS CHECK =	$3,000.00

Figure 9-29. Accounts payable report: check register. (Courtesy of Retail Sciences, Inc., Peachtree Software Product.)

VENDOR ID	VENDOR NAME	CHECK NUMBER	CHECK DATE	NUMBER	INVOICE DATE	INVOICE AMOUNT	DISCOUNT	NET / TOTAL
NOSDA	NAT.OF.SUPPLY DLRS. AS.	2078	07/15/80	AUTO VOUCHER	07/15/80	$75.00	$0.00	$75.00
							TOTAL THIS CHECK =	$75.00
ROYAL	ROYAL IMPORTERS, LMTD.	2079	07/15/80		07/15/80	$900.00	$0.00	$900.00
							TOTAL THIS CHECK =	$900.00
WALLWH	WALLACE WHOLESALERS, INC.	2080	07/15/80		07/15/80	$4,000.00	$80.00	$3,920.00
							TOTAL THIS CHECK =	$3,920.00

NUMBER OF CHECKS WRITTEN: 9   TOTAL CHECKS WRITTEN = $16,848.53

Figure 9-29. (*Continued*)

Functions and Features

An automated inventory control system should balance the inventory level for the lowest total cost by helping management decide how much the inventory level should be increased or decreased. Among the possible variables built into an inventory control system are the following:

1. When should new quantities be reordered?
2. How much should be reordered?
3. Should the reorder point be raised, lowered, or left as is?
4. What is the predicted future demand for an item?
5. At what rate is a certain item being sold: per week? per month?

TAYLOR OFFICE EQUIPMENT
ACCOUNTS PAYABLE
TRANSACTION REGISTER
07/15/80

GENERAL LEDGER TRANSACTION REGISTER

ACCOUNT NUMBER	DATE	DESCRIPTION	SC	DEBIT	CREDIT
20100	07/15/80		A		$289.00
21300	07/15/80		A	$4,250.73	
21400	07/15/80		A	$2,108.59	
25100	07/15/80		A	$2,800.00	
41101	07/15/80		A	$60,658.10	
41102	07/15/80		A	$48,974.94	
42101	07/15/80		A	$3,740.90	
42102	07/15/80		A	$2,376.11	
51100	07/15/80		A	$2,000.00	
51300	07/15/80		A	$105.00	
52100	07/15/80		A	$970.00	
52200	07/15/80		A	$1,200.00	
52300	07/15/80		A	$75.00	
53200	07/15/80		A	$200.00	
53300	07/15/80		A	$900.00	
20100	07/15/80	ENTERED VOUCHERS	A		$130,070.37
20100	07/15/80	PAYMENTS	A		$0.00
10200	07/15/80	CASH	A		$0.00
20100	07/15/80	DISCOUNTS TAKEN	A		$0.00
		TOTAL		$130,359.37	$130,359.37

Figure 9-30. Accounts payable report: general ledger distribution report. (Courtesy of Retail Sciences, Inc., Peachtree Software Product.)

The automated inventory control system can be divided into two approaches: invoicing and order entry. The invoicing approach is sometimes referred to as postbilling and the order-entry approach is referred to as pre-billing. Most microcomputer systems support only the invoicing approach. Many small business computer and minicomputer systems can support the order-entry approach. The invoicing approach (postbilling) is a one-step billing process. The system will not accept any invoice information until after the order is filled. So the system generates an invoice only when an order is complete. This approach usually cannot maintain a backorder file in the system and cannot provide open-order capability.

On the other hand, the order entry (prebilling) approach can provide greater flexibility and capability in the billing process and maintenance of various files. Order entry and billing are two different steps in this approach. The system will accept order-entry information at any time. Open-order may be changed, deleted, added, and inquired of prior to billing. Backorder files are provided under this approach. Quantity shipped and quantity back-ordered can be adjusted prior to billing. Many inventory control systems using this approach can support selective billing and partial billing. The selective billing provides the ability to bill only selected orders. The partial billing provides the ability to bill only a portion of an individual account.

In general, an automated inventory control system should be examined for the following functions and features:

1. Inventory item maintenance should be able to add, change, and delete items from the inventory as needed.
2. The system should be able to check outstanding orders and backorders before deleting an item and provide a safeguard against losing valid information.
3. When entering invoices and orders, the system should provide the capability of overriding the price.
4. The system should be able to change invoices and orders as needed before invoicing or billing.

As the functions and features of inventory control systems become more sophisticated, it is becoming more common to see the inventory control system interfaced with the accounts receivable system. This feature allows the automatic transfer of information on invoices to customer statements subsequently generated by the accounts receivable system. Some inventory control systems can support bill-of-materials processing (BOMP) and materials requirement planning (MRP) in addition to raw materials and finished goods inventory control. Both BOMP and MRP are very useful in manufacturing complex products for jobs such as governmental projects. Only a limited number of current small computers can support BOMP and MRP, because both require an amount of storage that exceeds the capacity of most small computers.

Checklist for Inventory Control

1. Does the system support invoicing (postbilling)?   YES ____   NO ____

2. Does the system support order entry (prebilling)?   YES ____   NO ____

3. What is the maximum number of inventory items allowed in the system?   _____

4. Does the system support only finished goods inventory?   YES ____   NO ____

5. Does the system support raw material goods inventory in addition to finished goods inventory?   YES ____   NO ____

6. Can the system support bill-of-materials processing (BOMP)?   YES ____   NO ____

7. Can the system support materials requirements planning (MRP)?   YES ____   NO ____

8. Does the system automatically reorder items when supplies reach a low point?   YES ____   NO ____

9. Can the reorder point be easily raised or lowered when needed?   YES ____   NO ____

10. Does the system have the ability to override the item's price if necessary?   YES ____   NO ____

11. Does the system have multiple-price-level capability?   YES ____   NO ____

12. Does the system have the ability to credit returned items?   YES ____   NO ____

13. Does the system provide for adjustments to quantity backordered?   YES ____   NO ____

14. Does the system provide quantity adjustments prior to invoicing and billing?   YES ____   NO ____

15. Does the system provide backorder reporting?   YES ____   NO ____

16. Does the system provide full backorder retention and control?   YES ____   NO ____

17. Does the system provide selective billing capability, which can bill only selected orders?   YES ____   NO ____

18. Can the system provide partial billing?   YES ____   NO ____

19. Can the system forecast consumer buying trends?   YES ____   NO ____

20. Can the system determine at what rate a certain product is being sold?   YES ____   NO ____

21. Can the inventory control system be interfaced with the accounts receivable system?   YES ____   NO ____

22. Can the system automatically transfer the information on the invoices created by the inventory control system to the customer statement subsequently generated by the accounts receivable system?   YES ____   NO ____

Files for Inventory Control

There are primarily three files that may be associated with an inventory control system: the inventory master file, order-entry file, and the receipt transaction file (Fig. 9-31). If the system supports a full backorder retention and control, the backorder file should be included.

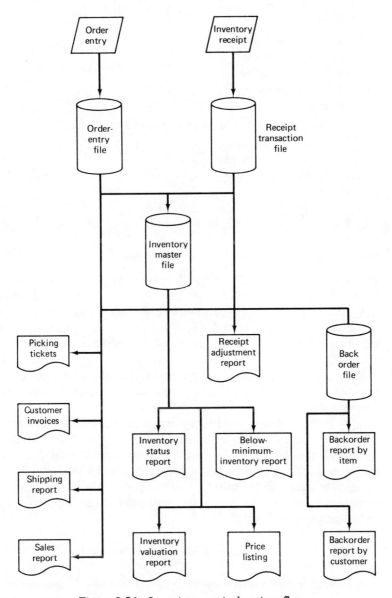

Figure 9-31. Inventory control system flow.

Reports and other output that may be provided by an inventory control system include:

1. Picking tickets
2. Customer invoices
3. Shipping report
4. Sales report
5. Inventory status report
6. Reorder point report
7. Inventory valuation report
8. Price listing
9. Receipts register and warehouse transfer audit trail
10. Backorder report
11. Open-order report by customer
12. Inventory activity report
13. Open invoices

Figures 9-32 to 9-44 show sample inventory control reports.

9-4.5 Payroll System

The main purpose of a payroll system is to prepare payroll checks and distribute labor costs to the proper accounts while accumulating the necessary information for government reporting. The amount of expenditures for labor costs and related payroll taxes has a significant effect on the net income of most businesses. It is not unusual for a business to expend about one-third of its sales revenue for labor and labor-related expenses. Therefore, it is important that the payroll segment of the accounting system provide safeguards to ensure that payments are made in accordance with management's plans and specific authorizations.

A computerized payroll system can provide assistance with the time-consuming task of preparing employees' paychecks. Various federal, state, and local laws require that employers accumulate certain data in their payroll records for each employee for each payroll period. Periodic reports of these data must be submitted to the appropriate governmental agencies and remittances made for amounts withheld from employees and for taxes levied on the employer.

Functions and Features

Payroll system software packages can provide assistance with the tasks of preparing employees' paychecks and the related forms and reports. This

PICK TICKETS BY WAREHOUSE

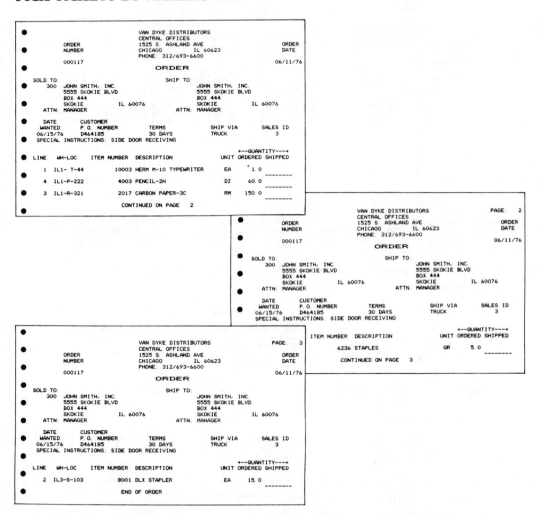

Figure 9-32. Inventory control report: picking tickets. (Courtesy of Nixdorf Computer Inc.)

VANDYKE DISTRIBUTORS
1525 SOUTH ASHLAND AVE.
CHICAGO, ILLINOIS 60623
PHONE
(312) 693-6600

INVOICE NO.		DATE
000111DI	INVOICE	06/11/76

SOLD TO:	JOHN SMITH, INC. 5555 SKOKIE BLVD BOX 444 SKOKIE IL 60076 MANAGER	SHIP TO:	JOHN SMITH, INC. 5555 SKOKIE BLVD BOX 444 SKOKIE IL 60076 MANAGER

WANT DATE	CUSTOMER P.O. NO.	TERMS	SHIP VIA	ORDER NO.	ORDER DATE	
06/15/76	D464185	30 DAYS	TRUCK	000117	06/11/76	

SPECIAL INSTRUCTIONS
SIDE DOOR RECEIVING

ITEM NUMBER	DESCRIPTION	UNIT	ORDERED	SHIPPED	BACK ORD	PRICE	DISCOUNT	EXTENSION
10003	HERM M-10 TYPEWRITER	EA	1.0	1.0	0.0	210.50		210.50
4003	PENCIL-2H	* DZ	60.0	60.0	0.0	1.22	7.32	65.88
2017	CARBON PAPER-3C	* RM	150.0	150.0	0.0	18.25	198.47	2539.03
6236	STAPLES	GR	5.0	5.0	0.0	198.56	22.34	970.46
8001	DLX STAPLER	EA	15.0	15.0	0.0	21.25	15.94	302.81

SALE TOTAL	DISCOUNT	NON-TAXABLE	TAXABLE	SALES TAX	MISC	FREIGHT	PAY THIS AMOUNT
4088.68	81.77	2604.91	1483.77	0.00	0.00	0.00	4006.91

Figure 9-33. Inventory control report: customer invoice. (Courtesy of Nixdorf Computer Inc.)

VAN DYKE DISTRIBUTORS
CENTRAL OFFICES

ORDER NUMBER

1525 S. ASHLAND AVE
CHICAGO   IL 60623
PHONE: 312/693-6600

ORDER DATE

000117

ORDER

06/11/76

SOLD TO:
300 JOHN SMITH, INC.
5555 SKOKIE BLVD
BOX 444
SKOKIE   IL 60076
ATTN: MANAGER

SHIP TO:
JOHN SMITH, INC.
5555 SKOKIE BLVD
BOX 444
SKOKIE   IL 60076
ATTN: MANAGER

DATE WANTED	CUSTOMER P.O. NUMBER	TERMS	SHIP VIA	SALES ID
06/15/76	D464185	30 DAYS	TRUCK	3

SPECIAL INSTRUCTIONS: SIDE DOOR RECEIVING

LINE	WH-LOC	ITEM NUMBER	DESCRIPTION	UNIT	QUANTITY ORDERED	SHIPPED
1	IL1- T-44	10003	HERM M-10 TYPEWRITER	EA	1.0	_____
4	IL1-P-222	4003	PENCIL-2H	DZ	60.0	_____
3	IL1-R-321	2017	CARBON PAPER-3C	RM	150.0	_____
5	IL2-S-101	6236	STAPLES	GR	5.0	_____
2	IL3-S-103	8001	DLX STAPLER	EA	15.0	_____

END OF ORDER

Figure 9-34. Inventory control report: shipping report. (Courtesy of Nixdorf Computer Inc.)

DATE: 06/11/76 VAN DYKE DISTRIBUTORS

CUSTOMER NUMBER NAME	LAST ORDER	PROFIT YTD SALES MTD	CURR YTD LAST YTD	JAN JUL	FEB AUG	MAR SEP	APR OCT	MAY NOV	JUN DEC
100 ESSEX ENTERPRISES	06/11/76	7.20 0.00	5813.66 11256.35	1495.88 300.44	85.33 833.55	955.65 245.00	1883.80 995.00	1003.00 933.56	35.00 100.03
200 LINCOLN PARK OFFICE MACH.	06/11/76	246.93 696.78	2812.98 8655.35	255.65 847.87	0.00 223.80	486.00 132.44	1865.68 120.00	120.25 155.45	30.00 122.54
300 JOHN SMITH, INC.	06/11/76	1047.35 4088.68	14460.35 26355.26	5268.20 1502.36	1277.26 422.32	2833.60 935.27	2300.50 3442.65	185.30 2563.37	31.16 166.65
400 NORTHWESTERN UNIVERSITY	06/11/76	65.99 0.00	1389.41 2856.39	54.88 44.42	144.85 24.65	266.30 143.80	145.50 38.88	78.90 120.23	688.65 98.88
500 CHICAGO AUTO PARTS INC.	05/25/76	339.85 1656.44	1693.23 3566.24	265.11 285.66	438.34 45.20	219.22 155.65	166.97 346.95	122.24 422.30	225.00 355.45
600 RATOC OFFICE FURNISHINGS	06/11/76	138.34 0.00	1032.62 365.29	135.20 0.00	0.00 0.00	0.00 45.90	25.66 122.56	32.64 0.00	829.00 16.56
700 MISSOURI DRUM & BRAKE INC	05/25/76	294.60 2188.72	8949.54 1235.36	1395.24 128.30	2955.60 468.33	1686.37 498.64	1355.50 855.60	1168.34 1486.79	130.19 2566.30
800 JOHNSON RETAIL STORES INC	06/11/76	0.59 0.00	113.43 635.80	0.00 0.00	21.10 0.00	53.26 156.39	44.32 76.38	0.00 26.60	-5.25 0.00
900 BECKER OFFICE FORMS	06/05/76	3.50 0.00	4150.26 7259.60	258.30 948.35	488.80 788.80	524.56 265.98	663.60 155.50	1576.50 125.50	-6.00 204.60
1000 NIXDORF COMPUTER INC.	06/07/76	0.00 0.00	756.31 1599.89	125.35 142.65	163.50 150.32	148.36 121.35	164.32 130.28	129.39 140.39	0.00 141.10
• • • FINAL TOTALS • • •		2136.17 8630.62	41171.79 63785.53	9253.81 4200.05	5574.78 2956.97	7173.32 2700.42	8615.85 6283.80	4416.56 5974.19	1957.75 3772.11

Figure 9-35. Inventory control report: customer sales history. (Courtesy of Nixdorf Computer Inc.)

DATE: 06/11/76 VAN DYKE DISTRIBUTORS

ITEM NUMBER	DESCRIPTION	UNIT	PROD CODE	BUYER CODE	WH LOC	COMMTD	BACK ORD	ON-HAND	ON-ORDER	AVAIL	REORDER POINT
1000	PAPER CLIPS	CS	01	1	IL1 R-321	25.0	3.0	5272.0	0.0	5244.0	85.0
					IL4 R-432	0.0	0.0	400.0	0.0	400.0	
					IL5 R-505	0.0	0.0	500.0	0.0	500.0	
					• TOTAL •	25.0	3.0	6172.0	0.0	6144.0	
2017	CARBON PAPER-3C	RM	02	01	IL1 R-321	1050.0	0.0	4100.0	0.0	3050.0	75.0
					IL2 R-289	0.0	0.0	100.0	200.0	100.0	
					IL3 L-19	0.0	0.0	300.0	0.0	300.0	
					• TOTAL •	1050.0	0.0	4500.0	200.0	3450.0	
3000	ADDING MACHINE	EA	1	1	IL1 R-321	2.0	0.0	247.0	0.0	245.0	50.0
					IL2 R-220	0.0	0.0	171.0	0.0	171.0	
					IN1 F-623	0.0	0.0	100.0	0.0	100.0	
					MI1 G-45	0.0	0.0	25.0	25.0	25.0	
					MO1 M-401	0.0	0.0	67.0	0.0	67.0	
					• TOTAL •	2.0	0.0	610.0	25.0	608.0	
3001	ADDING MACHINE	EA	03	01	IL1 L-321	9.0	0.0	26.0	0.0	17.0	20.0
					IL2 L-220	0.0	0.0	25.0	0.0	25.0	
					IN1 D-719	0.0	0.0	31.0	0.0	31.0	
					MI1 G-202	0.0	0.0	25.0	0.0	25.0	
					MO1 M-622	0.0	0.0	25.0	0.0	25.0	
					• TOTAL •	9.0	0.0	132.0	0.0	123.0	
4003	PENCIL-2H	DZ	04	01	IL1 P-222	45.0	0.0	268.0	0.0	223.0	50.0
					IL5 P-623	0.0	0.0	209.0	0.0	209.0	
					MI1 P-109	0.0	0.0	55.0	0.0	55.0	
					MO1 P-119	0.0	0.0	60.0	200.0	60.0	
					• TOTAL •	45.0	0.0	592.0	200.0	547.0	
5015	RING BINDERS	CS	05	02	IL5 B-114	82.0	0.0	67.0	0.0	-15.0	50.0
					IN1 R-113	0.0	5.0	18.0	0.0	13.0	
					MI1 R-88	0.0	0.0	15.0	0.0	15.0	
					• TOTAL •	82.0	5.0	100.0	0.0	13.0 • BELOW MIN •
6236	STAPLES	GR	01	03	IL2 S-101	0.0	0.0	24.0	0.0	24.0	10.0
					IL4 S-303	0.0	0.0	47.0	0.0	47.0	
					IN1 S-301	0.0	0.0	88.0	0.0	88.0	
					MI1 S-264	0.0	0.0	3.0	100.0	3.0	
					• TOTAL •	0.0	0.0	162.0	100.0	162.0	
7055	FILE CABINET	EA	01	02	IL2 C-707	0.0	6.0	6.0	0.0	0.0	10.0
					IN1 C-308	0.0	0.0	1.0	10.0	1.0	

Figure 9-36. Inventory control report: inventory status report. (Courtesy of Nixdorf Computer Inc.)

DATE: 06/11/76   VAN DYKE DISTRIBUTORS

ITEM NUMBER	DESCRIPTION	UNIT	BUYER CODE	ON B.O.	CMTD	ON-HAND	ON-ORDER	AVAIL	REORDER POINT	DATE OF LAST ORD	EOQ
5015	RING BINDERS	CS	02	80.0	19.0	100.0	0.0	1.0	50.0	02/25/76	25.0
9000	DELUXE 3 HOLE PUNCH	EA	19	0.0	0.0	0.0	0.0	0.0	100.0	03/15/76	30.0
10003	HERM M-10 TYPEWRITER	EA	02	0.0	9.0	44.0	10.0	35.0	50.0	05/15/76	10.0

TOTAL # OF ITEMS LISTED 3

Figure 9-37. Inventory control report: reorder point report. (Courtesy of Nixdorf Computer Inc.)

INVENTORY VALUATION REPORT

DATE 06/11/76   VAN DYKE DISTRIBUTORS

ITEM NUMBER	DESCRIPTION	UNIT	PROD CODE	WH LOC	QUANTITY ON-HAND	VALUE	MTD SALES	COST EXTENSION	COST
1000	PAPER CLIPS	CS	01	IL1 R-321	5272.0	24251.200	19.0	85.400	4.600
				IL4 R-432	400.0	1840.000			
				IL5 R-505	500.0	2300.000			
				* TOTAL *	6172.0	28391.200			
2017	CARBON PAPER-3C	RM	02	IL1 R-321	4100.0	49466.500	400.0	4826.000	12.065
				IL2 R-289	100.0	1206.500			
				IL3 L-19	300.0	3619.500			
				* TOTAL *	4500.0	54292.500			
3000	ADDING MACHINE	EA	1	IL1 R-321	247.0	25008.750	1.0	101.250	101.250
				IL2 R-220	171.0	17313.750			
				IN1 F-623	100.0	10125.000			
				MI1 G-45	25.0	2531.250			
				MO1 M-401	67.0	6783.750			
				* TOTAL *	610.0	61762.500			
3001	ADDING MACHINE	EA	03	IL1 L-321	26.0	1469.000	0.0	0.000	56.500
				IL2 L-220	25.0	1412.500			
				IN1 D-719	31.0	1751.500			
				MI1 G-202	25.0	1412.500			
				MO1 M-622	25.0	1412.500			
				* TOTAL *	132.0	7458.000			
4003	PENCIL-2H	DZ	04	IL1 P-222	268.0	97.820	60.0	21.900	0.365
				IL5 P-623	209.0	76.285			
				MI1 P-109	55.0	20.075			
				MO1 P-119	60.0	21.900			
				* TOTAL *	592.0	216.080			
5015	RING BINDERS	CS	05	IL5 B-114	67.0	1758.750	0.0	0.000	26.250
				IN1 R-113	18.0	472.500			
				MI1 R-88	15.0	393.750			
				* TOTAL *	100.0	2625.000			
6236	STAPLES	GR	01	IL2 S-101	24.0	3931.200	5.0	819.000	163.800
				IL4 S-303	47.0	7698.600			
				IN1 S-301	88.0	14414.400			
				MI1 S-264	3.0	491.400			
				* TOTAL *	162.0	26535.600			
7055	FILE CABINET	EA	01	IL2 C-707	6.0	189.600	10.0	316.000	31.600
				IN1 C-308	1.0	31.600			
				MI1 C-306	26.0	821.600			
				MO1 C-243	43.0	1358.800			
				* TOTAL *	76.0	2401.600			
8001	DLX STAPLER	EA	03	IL3 S-103	640.0	8006.400	15.0	187.650	12.510
				IL5 S-116	522.0	6530.220			
				* TOTAL *	1162.0	14536.620			
9000	DELUXE 3 HOLE PUNCH	EA	01	IL1 R-324	800.0	9880.000	0.0	244.000	12.350
				IL2 R-224	200.0	2470.000			
				* TOTAL *	1000.0	12350.000			
10003	HERM M-10 TYPEWRITER	EA	04	IL1 T-44	22.0	2740.100	3.0	373.650	124.550
				IN1 T-491	2.0	249.100			
				MI1 T-565	10.0	1245.500			
				MO1 T-36	14.0	1743.700			
				* TOTAL *	48.0	5978.400			
				* TOTAL VALUE *		216547.500			

Figure 9-38. Inventory control report: inventory valuation report. (Courtesy of Nixdorf Computer Inc.)

INVENTORY MASTER PRICE LISTING

DATE: 06/11/76   VAN DYKE DISTRIBUTORS

ITEM NUMBER	DESCRIPTION	UNIT	PROD CODE	PRICE 1	PRICE 2	PRICE 3
1000	PAPER CLIPS	CS	01	6.50	6.00	5.25
2017	CARBON PAPER-3C	RM	02	18.25	16.23	14.85
3000	ADDING MACHINE	EA	1	155.00	149.50	139.75
3001	ADDING MACHINE	EA	03	85.15	79.50	66.88
4003	PENCIL-2H	DZ	04	1.22	0.89	0.67
5015	RING BINDERS	CS	05	54.35	48.60	41.75
6236	STAPLES	GR	01	198.56	183.50	175.25
7055	FILE CABINET	EA	01	85.50	77.89	63.25
8001	DLX STAPLER	EA	03	21.25	18.75	16.75
9000	DELUXE 3 HOLE PUNCH	EA	01	22.50	18.05	16.20
10003	HERM M-10 TYPEWRITER	EA	04	210.50	200.00	185.88
10044	NOTE PAD	CS	02	22.50	18.50	17.25
100052	LINED PAPER	DZ	01	2.40	2.20	2.10

FROM: 1000
TO: 100052

TOTAL # OF ITEMS LISTED 13

Figure 9-39. Inventory control report: price listing. (Courtesy of Nixdorf Computer Inc.)

INVENTORY RECEIPTS REGISTER

DATE: 06/11/76

ITEM NUMBER	DESCRIPTION	UNIT	WH	LOC	OLD QUANTITY ON-HAND	OLD QUANTITY COMMITTED	QUANTITY AVAIL	RECEIVED	NEW QUANTITY ON-HAND	NEW QUANTITY AVAIL	NEW COST
2017	CARBON PAPER-3C	RM	IL2	R-289	100.0	0.0	100.0	75.0	175.0	175.0	12.175
			* TOTAL *		100.0	0.0	100.0	75.0	175.0	175.0	
4003	PENCIL-2H	DZ	MI1	P-109	55.0	0.0	55.0	50.0	105.0	105.0	0.368
			* TOTAL *		55.0	0.0	55.0	50.0	105.0	105.0	
10003	HERM M-10 TYPEWRITER	EA	IN1	T-491	7.0	0.0	7.0	3.0	10.0	10.0	124.750
			* TOTAL *		7.0	0.0	7.0	3.0	10.0	10.0	

TOTAL # OF ITEMS LISTED 3

WAREHOUSE TRANSFER AUDIT TRAIL

DATE: 06/11/76   VAN DYKE DISTRIBUTORS

ITEM NUMBER	DESCRIPTION	UNIT	TRANSFER QUANTITY	FROM WAREHOUSE CODE	FROM WAREHOUSE OLD QOH	FROM WAREHOUSE NEW QOH	TO WAREHOUSE CODE	TO WAREHOUSE OLD QOH	TO WAREHOUSE NEW QOH
6236	STAPLES	GR	25.0	IN1	88.0	63.0	MI1	3.0	28.0
2017	CARBON PAPER-3C	RM	175.0	IL1	3900.0	3725.0	IL2	175.0	350.0

TOTAL ITEMS LISTED 2

Figure 9-40. Inventory control report: receipts register and warehouse transfer audit trail. (Courtesy of Nixdorf Computer Inc.)

BACK ORDER REPORT

DATE: 06/11/76

VAN DYKE DISTRIBUTORS

ITEM NUMBER	DESCRIPTION	UNIT	QUANTITY ON ORD	QUANTITY ON BO	ORDER NUMBER	BO LVL	DATE ORDERED	DATE WANTED	CUSTOMER NUMBER NAME
5015	RING BINDERS	CS	0.0	5.0	000125	1	05/25/76	06/15/76	500 CHICAGO AUTO PARTS INC.
	** TOTAL **			5.0					
7055	FILE CABINET	EA	10.0	6.0	000118	1	06/11/76	06/11/76	200 LINCOLN PARK OFFICE MACH.
	** TOTAL **			6.0					

2 ITEM(S) LISTED

Figure 9-41. Inventory control report: backorder report. (Courtesy of Nixdorf Computer Inc.)

INVENTORY ACTIVITY REPORT

DATE: 06/11/76

VAN DYKE DISTRIBUTORS

ITEM NUMBER	DESCRIPTION	UNIT	QUANTITY MTD	THIS YTD LAST YTD	JAN JUL	FEB AUG	MAR SEP	APR OCT	MAY NOV	JUN DEC
1000	PAPER CLIPS	CS	19.0	231.0 / 242.0	25.0 / 33.0	56.0 / 2.0	91.0 / 64.0	44.0 / 37.0	15.0 / 58.0	29.0 / 19.0
2017	CARBON PAPER-3C	RM	400.0	218.0 / 203.0	26.0 / 23.0	41.0 / 49.0	19.0 / 46.0	22.0 / 68.0	102.0 / 86.0	208.0 / 103.0
3000	ADDING MACHINE	EA	1.0	33.0 / 28.0	3.0 / 22.0	5.0 / 19.0	8.0 / 14.0	2.0 / 31.0	15.0 / 7.0	1.0 / 26.0
3001	ADDING MACHINE	EA	3.0	23.0 / 19.0	3.0 / 12.0	5.0 / 18.0	1.0 / 5.0	8.0 / 9.0	6.0 / 1.0	3.0 / 11.0
4003	PENCIL-2H	DZ	60.0	101.0 / 108.0	12.0 / 9.0	22.0 / 56.0	18.0 / 41.0	23.0 / 19.0	26.0 / 8.0	37.0 / 51.0
5015	RING BINDERS	CS	0.0	814.0 / 708.0	225.0 / 124.0	289.0 / 254.0	125.0 / 25.0	52.0 / 148.0	123.0 / 345.0	457.0 / 111.0
6236	STAPLES	GR	5.0	2467.0 / 2331.0	1000.0 / 336.0	125.0 / 153.0	254.0 / 236.0	965.0 / 125.0	123.0 / 221.0	251.0 / 103.0
7055	FILE CABINET	EA	10.0	75.0 / 62.0	21.0 / 9.0	10.0 / 11.0	4.0 / 4.0	17.0 / 12.0	23.0 / 7.0	14.0 / 3.0
8001	DLX STAPLER	EA	15.0	60.0 / 47.0	10.0 / 1.0	6.0 / 7.0	12.0 / 15.0	9.0 / 18.0	23.0 / 12.0	2.0 / 9.0
9000	DELUXE 3 HOLE PUNCH	EA	0.0	453.0 / 407.0	100.0 / 25.0	56.0 / 29.0	29.0 / 198.0	125.0 / 123.0	143.0 / 100.0	19.0 / 67.0
10003	HERM M-10 TYPEWRITER	EA	3.0	53.0 / 48.0	10.0 / 9.0	5.0 / 4.0	25.0 / 15.0	1.0 / 1.0	12.0 / 42.0	2.0 / 10.0

TOTAL # OF ITEMS LISTED   11

Figure 9-42. Inventory control report: activity report. (Courtesy of Nixdorf Computer Inc.)

is done by calculating the gross pay, withheld taxes, other deductions, and net pay, and printing the payroll checks and reports. Virtually all payroll packages will perform at least these functions. Fine, but what criteria should be used in judging the merits of one payroll system versus another? Specifically, what constraints should be applied to all payroll systems to determine which one best satisfies the needs of the business? There are five general constraints that one should apply when attempting to determine whether or not a specific payroll package is "right."

1. The system must generate paychecks accurately and on time.
2. The system must be simple to administer because it is supposed to simplify, not complicate.

OPEN ORDER LISTING

DATE: 06/11/76   VAN DYKE DISTRIBUTORS

ORDER NUMBER	BO LVL	ORDER DATE	CUSTOMER NUMBER	NAME	ITEM NUMBER	N S	DESCRIPTION	UNIT	QUANTITY ORDERED	PRICE	DISC%	EXTENSION
000116	0	06/11/76	800	JOHNSON RETAIL STORES INC	4003		PENCIL-2H	DZ	25.0	1.22	10.00	27.45
					3000		ADDING MACHINE	EA	2.0	155.00	2.00	303.80
					5015		RING BINDERS	CS	80.0	48.60	14.00	3343.68
											*** TOTAL **	3674.93
000117	0	06/11/76	300	JOHN SMITH, INC.	10003		HERM M-10 TYPEWRITER	EA	1.0	210.50	0.00	210.50
					4003		PENCIL-2H	DZ	60.0	1.22	10.00	65.88
					2017		CARBON PAPER-3C	RM	150.0	18.25	7.25	2539.03
					6236		STAPLES	GR	5.0	198.56	2.25	970.46
					8001		DLX STAPLER	EA	15.0	21.25	5.00	302.81
											*** TOTAL **	4088.68
000118	0	06/11/76	200	LINCOLN PARK OFFICE MACH.	10003		HERM M-10 TYPEWRITER	EA	2.0	200.00	5.50	378.00
					7055		FILE CABINET	EA	12.0	63.25	16.00	637.56
											*** TOTAL **	1015.56
000119	0	06/11/76	100	ESSEX ENTERPRISES	10003		HERM M-10 TYPEWRITER	EA	4.0	210.50	5.50	795.69
					4003		PENCIL-2H	DZ	20.0	1.22	6.00	22.94
					1000		PAPER CLIPS	CS	25.0	6.50	0.00	162.50
					2017		CARBON PAPER-3C	RM	50.0	18.25	5.00	866.88
					9000		DELUXE 3 HOLE PUNCH	EA	1.0	22.50	0.00	22.50
					5015		RING BINDERS	CS	2.0	54.35	2.15	106.36
											*** TOTAL **	1976.87
000120	0	06/11/76	600	RATOC OFFICE FURNISHINGS	10003		HERM M-10 TYPEWRITER	EA	5.0	200.00	10.00	900.00
					3001		ADDING MACHINE	EA	9.0	79.50	6.00	672.57
					8001		DLX STAPLER	EA	25.0	18.75	10.00	421.88
					7055		FILE CABINET	EA	15.0	77.89	12.00	1028.15
											*** TOTAL **	3022.60
000125	0	05/25/76	500	CHICAGO AUTO PARTS INC.	2017		CARBON PAPER-3C	RM	100.0	16.23	7.25	1505.33
					7055		FILE CABINET	EA	2.0	77.89	3.00	151.11
					5015		RING BINDERS	CS	5.0	48.60	3.00	235.71
											*** TOTAL **	1892.15
000126	0	05/25/76	700	MISSOURI DRUM & BRAKE INC	2017		CARBON PAPER-3C	RM	150.0	14.85	7.25	2066.01
					7055		FILE CABINET	EA	2.0	63.25	3.00	122.71
											*** TOTAL **	2188.72
000127	0	06/05/76	900	BECKER OFFICE FORMS	2017		CARBON PAPER-3C	RM	1000.0	14.85	7.25	13773.38
											*** TOTAL **	13773.38

8 ORDERS LISTED.   26 DETAIL LINES.   3 DETAIL LINES / ORDER (AVERAGE).   *** FINAL TOTAL ** 31632.89

Figure 9-43. Inventory control report: open-order report by customer. (Courtesy of Nixdorf Computer Inc.)

INVENTORY ACTIVITY SUMMARY

DATE: 06/11/76   VAN DYKE DISTRIBUTORS

ITEM NUMBER	N S	DESCRIPTION	COMMITTED TODAY	COMMITTED TOTAL	ON HAND	BACK ORDERED	TOTAL AVAIL	ON ORDER
1000		PAPER CLIPS	25.0	26.0	6172.0	0.0	6146.0	0.0
2017		CARBON PAPER-3C	1450.0	2700.0	4900.0	0.0	2200.0	200.0
3000		ADDING MACHINE	2.0	2.0	610.0	0.0	608.0	25.0
3001		ADDING MACHINE	9.0	9.0	132.0	0.0	123.0	0.0
4003		PENCIL-2H	105.0	105.0	652.0	0.0	547.0	200.0
5015		RING BINDERS	87.0	24.0	100.0	75.0	1.0	0.0
6236		STAPLES	5.0	5.0	167.0	0.0	162.0	100.0
7055		FILE CABINET	31.0	24.0	86.0	8.0	54.0	10.0
8001		DLX STAPLER	40.0	40.0	1677.0	0.0	1637.0	0.0
9000		DELUXE 3 HOLE PUNCH	1.0	1.0	1000.0	0.0	999.0	0.0
10003		HERM M-10 TYPEWRITER	12.0	12.0	51.0	0.0	39.0	10.0

11 ITEM(S) LISTED

Figure 9-44. Inventory control report: inventory activity summary. (Courtesy of Nixdorf Computer Inc.)

283

3. The system should make all necessary calculations automatically or else it would be better to use a simple adding machine.

4. The system should produce, on request, any report that is needed to carry on regular business procedures.

5. The system should have sufficient internal audit trails and controls to make certain that the money is going to the proper places in the proper amounts.

A computerized payroll system can accumulate the necessary information for government reporting and print governmental reports such as W-2's, 940's and 941's.

In addition, hard-copy reports generated by the system may be useful in negotiations with labor unions, settling employee grievances, and determining vacations, sick leaves, and retirement pensions.

Checklist for a Payroll System

1. Can the system hold all information for the total number of employees that may work for you in a given year? YES _____ NO _____

2. Can the system handle hourly, salaried, and commission pay types? YES _____ NO _____

3. Can the system handle the various pay periods as needed? YES _____ NO _____
   (i.e., daily, weekly, biweekly, semimonthly, monthly, quarterly, and yearly)

4. Can the system handle the varying pay rates as needed? YES _____ NO _____
   (i.e., regular, overtime, special)

5. Does the system come with all the tax calculation routines that will be needed? YES _____ NO _____

6. Does the system provide tax tables? Are the tax tables updated by the user or is there a subscription service YES _____ NO _____
   that provides yearly updates? YES _____ NO _____

7. Does the system provide labor distribution? YES _____ NO _____

8. Does the system make provisions for special exceptions? YES _____ NO _____
   (i.e., floating employees, pay rate changes in midperiod)

9. Does the system have the capability to handle bonuses and other special pay types with or without taxes? YES _____ NO _____

10. Are manual check handling and check voiding provided? YES _____ NO _____

11. Are a sufficient number of deductions provided? YES _____ NO _____

12. Does the system provide for one-time deductions such as union initiation fees? YES _____ NO _____

13. Will the system print payroll checks? Is the check YES _____ NO _____
    format acceptable? Can the format be easily modified? YES _____ NO _____

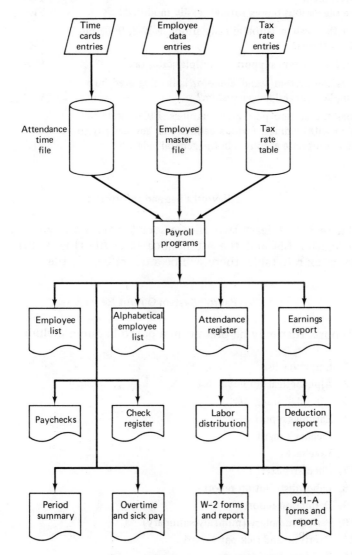

Figure 9-45. Payroll system flow.

Can check printing be restarted from any point in a run in the event of a forms jam?　　　　YES ____　　NO ____
　　　　YES ____　　NO ____

14. Does the system provide for reporting to all levels of government?　　　　YES ____　　NO ____
    Are the various report formats easily modified?　　　　YES ____　　NO ____

15. Can the system automatically produce W-2, 940, and 941-A forms?　　　　YES ____　　NO ____

16. Does the system support a multiple-states tax table?　　　　YES ____　　NO ____

17. Does the system stand alone or is it integrated into a complete general ledger system?　　　　YES ____　　NO ____

18. Does the system post gross earnings, FICA, state tax, other withholdings, various deductions, and net pay to the appropriate accounts in the general ledger?　　　　YES ____　　NO ____

Payroll Files and Information

There are at least two files associated with a payroll system: the employee master file and the attendance time file (Fig. 9-45). If the system handles a tax rate table, there will be a tax rate table file.

Payroll System Output Reports

Reports that may be present in a payroll system include:

1. Employee list
2. Alphabetical employee list
3. Attendance register
4. Earnings report
5. Precheck register
6. Paychecks
7. Check register
8. Labor distribution report
9. Deduction report
10. Period summary (monthly summary)
11. Overtime and sick pay report
12. W-2 forms and reports.
13. Employer's quarterly and annual federal tax return forms and reports
14. Employer's state and local tax return forms and reports.

Figures 9-46 to 9-57 show sample payroll reports.

```
                                    TAYLOR OFFICE EQUIPMENT
                                       PAYROLL SYSTEM
                                       EMPLOYEE LIST
                                         03/01/79

101/MPT  PRESTON T. MILLS              MARITAL ST.=M        DATE EMP. =05/01/74      STATUS=A
         24 MAIN STREET                FED.EXEMPT.=3        DATE TERM.=//0
         DECATUR, GA. 30343            ST. EXEMPT.=3        PAY PERIOD = S           PAY TYPE = S
         231-72-4343                   CITY=0              ST.=10                   PAY RATE =      $760.000
CURRENT: HOURS   OVERTIME   OTHER   DATE   CHECK NO.    DEDUCTIONS:    INSURANCE    MISC #1     MISC #2
          0        0          0     //0                                 $12.50      $1.50       $0.00

                            CURRENT      MONTH        QUARTER       YEAR
EARNINGS  -REGULAR     :     $0.00     $2,020.00     $2,020.00    $2,020.00
          -OVERTIME    :     $0.00       $0.00         $0.00        $0.00
          -OTHER HRS.  :     $0.00       $0.00         $0.00        $0.00
          -COMMISSIONS :     $0.00       $0.00         $0.00        $0.00
          -MISC.       :     $0.00       $0.00         $0.00        $0.00
DEDUCTIONS-FICA        :     $0.00      $122.21       $122.21      $122.21
          -FEDERAL     :     $0.00      $252.05       $252.05      $252.05
          -STATE       :     $0.00      $48.54        $48.54       $48.54
          -LOCAL       :     $0.00       $0.00         $0.00        $0.00
          -INSURANCE   :     $0.00      $37.50        $37.50       $37.50
          -MISC. #1    :     $0.00       $4.50         $4.50        $4.50
          -MISC. #2    :     $0.00       $0.00         $0.00        $0.00

101/SSC  SUSAN S. CARMELL              MARITAL ST.=S        DATE EMP. =06/12/76      STATUS=A
         EAST HENDERSON DRIVE          FED.EXEMPT.=1        DATE TERM.=//0
         TUCKER, GA. 30341             ST. EXEMPT.=1        PAY PERIOD = S           PAY TYPE = S
         230-94-5991                   CITY=0              ST.=10                   PAY RATE =      $350.000
CURRENT: HOURS   OVERTIME   OTHER   DATE   CHECK NO.    DEDUCTIONS:    INSURANCE    MISC #1     MISC #2
          0        0          0     //0                                 $4.00       $1.50       $0.00

                            CURRENT      MONTH        QUARTER       YEAR
EARNINGS  -REGULAR     :     $0.00     $1,050.00     $1,050.00    $1,050.00
          -OVERTIME    :     $0.00       $0.00         $0.00        $0.00
          -OTHER HRS.  :     $0.00       $0.00         $0.00        $0.00
          -COMMISSIONS :     $0.00       $0.00         $0.00        $0.00
          -MISC.       :     $0.00       $0.00         $0.00        $0.00
DEDUCTIONS-FICA        :     $0.00      $63.54        $63.54       $63.54
          -FEDERAL     :     $0.00     $129.24       $129.24      $129.24
          -STATE       :     $0.00      $29.49        $29.49       $29.49
          -LOCAL       :     $0.00       $0.00         $0.00        $0.00
          -INSURANCE   :     $0.00      $12.00        $12.00       $12.00
          -MISC. #1    :     $0.00       $4.50         $4.50        $4.50
          -MISC. #2    :     $0.00       $0.00         $0.00        $0.00
```

Figure 9-46. Payroll report: employee list. (Courtesy of Retail Sciences, Inc., Peach tree Software Product.)

```
                                 TAYLOR OFFICE EQUIPMENT
                                    PAYROLL SYSTEM
                                    END OF MONTH
                                      03/01/79

                                   MONTHLY SUMMARY


        TOTAL ACTIVE EMPLOYEES =  6            TOTAL INACTIVE EMPLOYEES =  1

        TOTAL CURRENT: REGULAR HOURS =   0
                       OVERTIME HOURS=   0
                       OTHER HOURS   =   0
                                        ----
                       TOTAL HOURS    =   0

                                 MONTH        QUARTER        YEAR
        EARNINGS   -REGULAR    :  $6,931.70    $6,931.70    $6,931.70
                   -OVERTIME   :    $172.97      $172.97      $172.97
                   -OTHER      :     $15.00       $15.00       $15.00
                   -COMMISSIONS:  $2,200.00    $2,200.00    $2,200.00
                   -MISC.      :      $0.00        $0.00        $0.00
        DEDUCTIONS -FICA       :    $566.16      $566.16      $566.16
                   -FEDERAL    :  $1,117.82    $1,117.82    $1,117.82
                   -STATE      :    $228.07      $228.07      $228.07
                   -LOCAL      :      $0.00        $0.00        $0.00
                   -INSURANCE  :    $194.00      $194.00      $194.00
                   -MISC. #1   :     $12.00       $12.00       $12.00
                   -MISC. #2   :     $30.00       $30.00       $30.00
```

Figure 9-47. Payroll report: monthly summary. (Courtesy of Retail Sciences, Inc., Peachtree Software Product.)

MINI-COMPUTER BUSINESS APPLICATIONS, INC.

ALPHABETICAL EMPLOYEE LIST

EMP NO	NAME	STREET	CITY	ST	ZIP	SOC-SEC-NO	EMP TYPE	PAY FREQ	TERM DATE
9999	Bartholomew, Anatoly R.	62 Craig St.	Chino Canyon	CA	92109	934-56-0781	N	M	
3000	Bitteroot, Merlin	63 Elmont Circle	Los Angeles	CA	90112	105-06-9907	S	S	
8000	Bond, Jennifer	456 Wheatstone Ave. # 102	San Pedro	CA	91004	917-67-3054	H	W	
7000	Clineworthy, Cy	3907 North First St.	Hallsmith	NJ	21333	400-85-1311	S	M	
2000	Colt, Harold L.	613 Northwest Crystal Place	Pasadena	CA	92145	523-60-7124	S	M	
1000	Gilbert, William R.	2568 Girard Ave.	No. Hollywood	CA	91225	302-56-8972	H	W	
6000	Mathews, Timothy C.	881 East Tinkerton Hwy.	Sconnasset	NY	25604	380-93-4504	H	W	05/15/80
9500	Pavloski, Donald K.	36555 Greenville, SW	Torrance	CA	92221	560-44-7877	H	B	
5000	Phillips, Charlene Alta	16 Crescent Ridge Rd., # B23	Inglewood	CA	92150	456-88-7911	S	S	
4000	Silverton, Andrea	5674 Beach Blvd. West	Hermosa Beach	CA	90034	107-53-9007	H	W	
9000	Zelterman, Linda	89 Old Harristown Rd.	Brooklyn	NY	25514	653-86-4785	S	M	

11 EMPLOYEES   0 DAILY   4 WKLY   1 BI-WKLY   2 SEMI-MONTHLY   4 MONTHLY   0 QUARTERLY   1 TERMINATED

Figure 9-48. Payroll report: Time register. (Courtesy of Mini-Computer Business Applications, Inc.)

MINI-COMPUTER BUSINESS APPLICATIONS, INC.

P A Y R O L L   T I M E   R E G I S T E R

FOR THE PAY PERIOD ENDING 06/27/80
EMPLOYEE TYPES: H = HOURLY   S = SALARY
PAY FREQUENCIES: H = HOURLY   S = SALARY
PAY FREQUENCIES: D = DAILY   W = WEEKLY   B = BI-WEEKLY   S = SEMI-MONTHLY   M = MONTHLY   Q = QUARTERLY
DISTRIBUTION TYPES: S = SALARY %   R = REGULAR HOURS   O = OVERTIME HOURS   X = SPECIAL HOURS

DEPT NO	EMP NO	NAME / SOC-SEC-NO	TYPE	WAGE-ACT	FREQ	SALARY SUPP-EARN	REGULAR OVRTIME	SPECIAL HOLIDAY	SICK VAC	DESC	TYPE	AMOUNT	VAC WKS	WKS WRK
100	1000	Gilbert, William R. 302-56-8972	H	5020-100	W	.00 / .00	36.00 / .00	.00 / .00	.00 / .00	XMASCLB	D	12.00	1	.90

DISTRIBUTION: TYPE ACCOUNT NO

TYPE	ACCOUNT NO		HRS-%	RATE	JOB-NO	DESC
R	5020-100	Wages & Salaries - PFC 100	17.00	4.500	100000	Turquoise Trail Enterprises
R	5020-100	Wages & Salaries - PFC 100	6.50	4.500	300000	King Systems
R	5020-100	Wages & Salaries - PFC 100	12.50	4.500	600000	Agressive Advertising, Inc.

3000	Bitteroot, Merlin 105-06-9907	S	5020-100	S	600.00 / .00	.00 / .00	.00 / .00	.00 / .00					2.17

DISTRIBUTION: TYPE ACCOUNT NO

TYPE	ACCOUNT NO		HRS-%	RATE	JOB-NO	DESC
S	5020-100	Wages & Salaries - PFC 100	46.00		200000	Beta-Trac, Inc. # 56-8992
S	5020-200	Wages & Salaries - PFC 200	54.00			

4000	Silverton, Andrea 107-53-9007	H	5020-100	W	.00 / .00	36.00 / .00	.00 / .00	.00 / 4.00	MEALS / TIPS / UNIFRMS	M / T / D	22.00 / 67.55 / 16.49		.90

DISTRIBUTION: TYPE ACCOUNT NO

TYPE	ACCOUNT NO		HRS-%	RATE	JOB-NO	DESC
R	5020-100	Wages & Salaries - PFC 100	36.00		400000	Happytime Plastic Products

5000	Phillips, Charlene Alta 456-88-7911	S	5020-100	S	.00 / .00	78.80 / 8.00	.00 / .00	8.00 / .00	BONUS	E	50.00		2.17

DISTRIBUTION: TYPE ACCOUNT NO

TYPE	ACCOUNT NO		HRS-%	RATE
R	5020-100	Wages & Salaries - PFC 100	3.500	

GRAND TOTALS: 262.80   13.00   16.00
                  27.50   .00   4.00

Figure 9-49. Payroll report: paychecks. (Courtesy of Mini Computer Business Applications, Inc.)

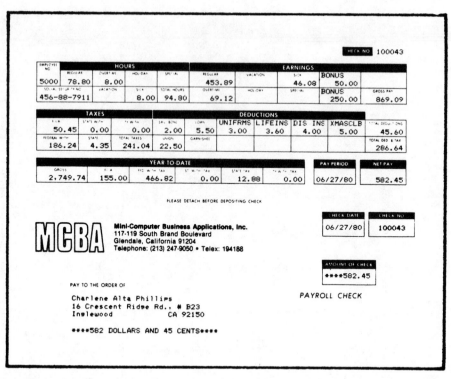

Figure 9-50. Payroll report: payroll check register. (Courtesy of Mini-Computer Business Applications, Inc.)

```
RUN DATE: 01-JUL-80                    MINI-COMPUTER BUSINESS APPLICATIONS, INC.

                                   P A Y R O L L   C H E C K   R E G I S T E R

FOR THE PAY PERIOD ENDING 06/27/80      CHECK TYPES:  R = REGULAR    V = VACATION

CHECK     CHECK     CHECK     CHECK    EMPL   NAME
  #       DATE      TYPE     AMOUNT     #


100039   06/27/80    R         91.16   1000   William R. Gilbert
100040   06/27/80    V        125.19   1000   William R. Gilbert
100041   06/27/80    R        681.29   3000   Merlin Bitteroot
100042   06/27/80    R         79.56   4000   Andrea Silverton
100043   06/27/80    R        582.45   5000   Charlene Alta Phillips
100044   06/27/80    R         50.26   8000   Jennifer Bond
100045   06/27/80    R        463.93   9500   Donald K. Pavloski
100046   06/27/80    R      1,325.54   7000   Cy Clineworthy
100047   06/27/80    R      1,356.56   9000   Linda Zelterman
100048   06/27/80    R      1,577.22   2000   Harold L. Colt


   10 CHECKS    TOTAL:    6,333.16
    9 REGULAR
    1 VACATION
```

Figure 9-51. Payroll report: deduction report. (Courtesy of Mini-Computer Business Applications, Inc.)

```
RUN DATE: 01-JUL-80                  MINI-COMPUTER BUSINESS APPLICATIONS, INC.

                          O V E R T I M E   A N D   S I C K   P A Y   R E P O R T

EMPLOYEE TYPES:  H = HOURLY      S = SALARY      N = NON-EMPLOYEE
```

DEPT #	EMPL #	NAME	EMP TYP	-----PERIOD-TO-DATE-----			---QUARTER-TO-DATE---			------YEAR-TO-DATE------		
				OVRTIM HRS	SICK HRS	SICK PAY	OVRTIM HRS	SICK HRS	SICK PAY	OVRTIM HRS	SICK HRS	SICK PAY
0100	1000	Gilbert, William R.	H	.00	.00	.00	8.00	.00	.00	8.00	.00	.00
	3000	Bitteroot, Merlin	S	8.00	4.00	27.65	30.00	4.00	27.65	30.00	4.00	27.65
	4000	Silverton, Andrea	H	.00	.00	.00	6.00	.00	.00	6.00	.00	.00
	5000	Phillips, Charlene Alta	S	22.00	8.00	46.08	22.00	8.00	46.08	22.00	8.00	46.08
	8000	Bond, Jennifer	H	4.00	.00	.00	8.00	.00	.00	8.00	.00	.00
	9500	Pavloski, Donald K.	H	.00	8.00	50.40	6.00	20.00	126.00	6.00	20.00	126.00
	9999	Bartholomew, Anatoly R.	N	.00	.00	.00	.00	.00	.00	.00	.00	.00
7 EMPLOYEES		DEPARTMENT TOTALS:		34.00	20.00	124.13	80.00	32.00	199.73	80.00	32.00	199.73
		DEPARTMENT AVERAGES:		4.86	2.86	17.73	11.43	4.57	28.53	11.43	4.57	28.53
0200	7000	Clineworthy, Cy	S	.00	.00	.00	.00	.00	.00	.00	.00	.00
	9000	Zelterman, Linda	S	.00	.00	.00	.00	.00	.00	.00	.00	.00
2 EMPLOYEES		DEPARTMENT TOTALS:		.00	.00	.00	.00	.00	.00	.00	.00	.00
		DEPARTMENT AVERAGES:		.00	.00	.00	.00	.00	.00	.00	.00	.00
0300	2000	Colt, Harold L.	S	15.50	.00	.00	15.50	.00	.00	15.50	.00	.00
	6000	Mathews, Timothy C.	H	.00	.00	.00	.00	.00	.00	.00	.00	.00
2 EMPLOYEES		DEPARTMENT TOTALS:		15.50	.00	.00	15.50	.00	.00	15.50	.00	.00
		DEPARTMENT AVERAGES:		7.75	.00	.00	7.75	.00	.00	7.75	.00	.00
11 EMPLOYEES TOTAL		COMPANY TOTALS:		49.50	20.00	124.13	95.50	32.00	199.73	95.50	32.00	199.73
		EMPLOYEE AVERAGES:		4.50	1.82	11.28	8.68	2.91	18.16	8.68	2.91	18.16

Figure 9-52. Payroll report: overtime and sick pay report. (Courtesy of Mini-Computer Business Applications, Inc.)

MINI-COMPUTER BUSINESS APPLICATIONS, INC.

D E D U C T I O N S   R E G I S T E R

DETAIL WITHIN DEPARTMENT

FOR DEPARTMENT: 100
FOR THE PAY PERIOD ENDING 06/27/80   CHECK TYPES: R = REGULAR   V = VACATION
FREQUENCIES USED ON THIS RUN: THIS PAY PERIOD: WBSMQ
VACATION CHECK 1: W   VACATION CHECK 2: NONE   VACATION CHECK 3: NONE   VACATION CHECK 4: NONE

EMPL #	NAME SOC-SEC-#	EMP-TYPE	CHK-TYP	SAV-BD UNION	LOAN GARNSH	D/E-1	D/E-2	D/E-3	D/E-4	D/E-5	D/E-6	TD/E-1	TD/E-2	TD/E-3	TOTAL DEDUCTIONS
1000	Gilbert, William R. 302-56-8972	H	R	10.00 9.00	5.00 .00							12.00 XMASCLB			36.00
1000	Gilbert, William R. 302-56-8972	H	V	10.00 .00	5.00 .00										15.00
3000	Bitterroot, Merlin 105-06-9907	S	R	11.00 .00	.00 .00	3.00 UNIFRMS					4.00 CRUNION				18.00
4000	Silverton, Andrea 107-53-9007	H	R	.00 1.58	.00 .00									16.49 UNIFRMS	18.07

MINI-COMPUTER BUSINESS APPLICATIONS, INC.

D E D U C T I O N S   R E G I S T E R

FOR DEPARTMENT: 100
FOR THE PAY PERIOD ENDING 06/27/80   CHECK TYPES: R = REGULAR   V = VACATION
FREQUENCIES USED ON THIS RUN: THIS PAY PERIOD: WBSMQ
VACATION CHECK 1: W   VACATION CHECK 2: NONE   VACATION CHECK 3: NONE   VACATION CHECK 4: NONE

7 CHECKS

TOTALS:		G/L ACCT-#	DESCRIPTION
SAVING BND	48.00	2140-100	Savings Bonds Liability
LOAN	70.75	2145-100	Loan Repayment
UNION	60.93	6650-100	Union Dues
LIFEINS	8.60	2180-100	Accruals
DIS INS	10.50	2180-100	Accruals
XMASCLB	22.00	2180-100	Accruals
VACCLUB	10.00	2180-100	Accruals
UNIFRMS	31.49	2180-100	Accruals
CRUNION	4.00	2180-100	Accruals
BREAKGE	13.28	6550-100	Breakage

RUN DATE: 01-JUL-80   MINI-COMPUTER BUSINESS APPLICATIONS, INC.

                               D E D U C T I O N S   R E G I S T E R

FOR DEPARTMENT: ALL
FOR THE PAY PERIOD ENDING 06/27/80   CHECK TYPES: R = REGULAR   V = VACATION
FREQUENCIES USED ON THIS RUN: THIS PAY PERIOD: WBSMQ
VACATION CHECK 1: W   VACATION CHECK 2: NONE   VACATION CHECK 3: NONE   VACATION CHECK 4: NONE

10 CHECKS   TOTALS: G/L ACCT-#   DESCRIPTION
                SAVING BND   56.50 2140-100   Savings Bonds Liability
                LOAN   79.95 2145-100   Loan Repayment
                UNION   60.93 6650-100   Union Dues
                LIFEINS   16.90 2180-100   Accruals
                DIS INS   12.50 2180-100   Accruals
                XMASCLB   30.20 2180-100   Accruals
                VACCLUB   12.80 2180-100   Accruals
                UNIFRMS   39.49 2180-100   Accruals
                CRUNION   28.00 2180-100   Accruals
                BREAKGE   13.28 6550-100   Breakage

Figure 9-53. Payroll report: deduction report. (Courtesy of Mini-Computer Business Applications, Inc.)

293

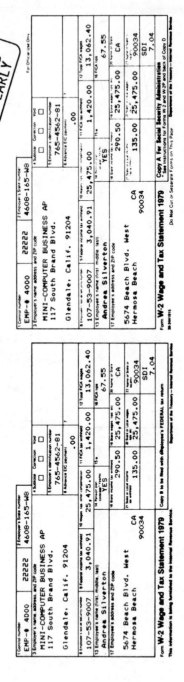

Figure 9-54. Payroll report: W-2 form and report. (Courtesy of Mini-Computer Business Applications, Inc.)

294

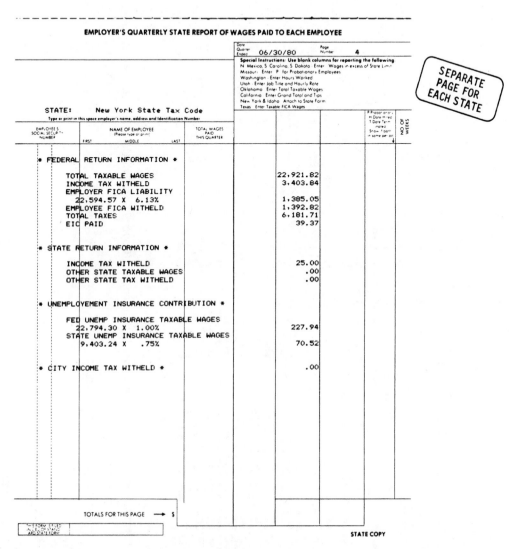

EMPLOYER'S QUARTERLY STATE REPORT OF WAGES PAID TO EACH EMPLOYEE

| Date Quarter Ended: | 06/30/80 | Page Number: | 4 |

Special Instructions: Use blank columns for reporting the following
N. Mexico, S. Carolina, S. Dakota - Enter Wages in excess of State Limit
Missouri - Enter P for Probationary Employees
Washington - Enter Hours Worked
Utah - Enter Job Title and Hourly Rate
Oklahoma - Enter Total Taxable Wages
California - Enter Grand Total and Tips
New York & Idaho - Attach to State Form
Texas - Enter Taxable FICA Wages

SEPARATE PAGE FOR EACH STATE

STATE: New York State Tax Code

Type or print in this space employer's name, address and Identification Number

| EMPLOYEE'S SOCIAL SECURITY NUMBER | NAME OF EMPLOYEE (Please type or print) FIRST MIDDLE LAST | TOTAL WAGES PAID THIS QUARTER | | | P Probationary H Date Hired T Date Terminated Show 1 here in same period | NO. OF WEEKS |

* FEDERAL RETURN INFORMATION *

    TOTAL TAXABLE WAGES   22,921.82
    INCOME TAX WITHELD   3,403.84
    EMPLOYER FICA LIABILITY
      22,594.57 X 6.13%   1,385.05
    EMPLOYEE FICA WITHELD   1,392.82
    TOTAL TAXES   6,181.71
    EIC PAID   39.37

* STATE RETURN INFORMATION *

    INCOME TAX WITHELD   25.00
    OTHER STATE TAXABLE WAGES   .00
    OTHER STATE TAX WITHELD   .00

* UNEMPLOYEMENT INSURANCE CONTRIBUTION *

    FED UNEMP INSURANCE TAXABLE WAGES
      22,794.30 X 1.00%   227.94
    STATE UNEMP INSURANCE TAXABLE WAGES
      9,403.24 X .75%   70.52

* CITY INCOME TAX WITHELD *   .00

TOTALS FOR THIS PAGE ⟶ $

THIS FORM FILED IN LIEU OF STATE AND STATE FORM

STATE COPY

Figure 9-55. Payroll report: Employer's Quarterly State Report. (Courtesy of Mini-Computer Business Applications, Inc.)

RUN DATE: 01-JUL-80

MINI-COMPUTER BUSINESS APPLICATIONS, INC.

P A Y R O L L   C H E C K   R E C O N C I L I A T I O N   R E P O R T

FOR CHECKING ACCOUNT: 1020-100 Checking Account - First Nat'l

CHECK NO	CHECK DATE	EMP NO	NAME	SOC-SEC-NO	UNPAID CHECK-AMOUNT	PAID CHECK AMOUNT	DATE RECONCILED
100010	05/16/80	4000	Silverton, Andrea	107-53-9007		131.95	06/01/80
100012	05/16/80	8000	Bond, Jennifer	917-67-3054		72.07	06/01/80
100013	05/16/80	9500	Pavloski, Donald K.	560-44-7877		392.10	06/01/80
100014	05/23/80	1000	Gilbert, William R.	302-56-8972		115.19	06/01/80
100038	06/20/80	8000	Bond, Jennifer	917-67-3054	65.55		
100039	06/27/80	1000	Gilbert, William R.	302-56-8972	91.16		
100040	06/27/80	1000	Gilbert, William R.	302-56-8972	125.19		
100041	06/27/80	3000	Bittercoot, Merlin	105-06-9907	681.29		
100042	06/27/80	4000	Silverton, Andrea	107-53-9007	79.56		
100043	06/27/80	5000	Phillips, Charlene Alta	456-88-7911	582.45		
100044	06/27/80	8000	Bond, Jennifer	917-67-3054	50.26		
100045	06/27/80	9500	Pavloski, Donald K.	560-44-7877	463.93		
100046	06/27/80	7000	Clineworthy, Cy	400-85-1311	1,325.54		
100047	06/27/80	9000	Zelterman, Linda	653-86-4785	1,356.56		
100048	06/27/80	2000	Colt, Harold L.	523-60-7124	1,577.22		
100049	07/01/80	9999	Bartholomew, Anatoly R.	934-56-0781	302.53		

TOTALS: 12,251.47   2,686.43

Figure 9-56. Payroll report: payroll check reconciliation report. (Courtesy of Mini-Computer Business Applications, Inc.)

RUN DATE: 01-JUL-80   MINI-COMPUTER BUSINESS APPLICATIONS, INC.

J O B   D I S T R I B U T I O N   R E P O R T

FOR THE PERIOD 05/01/80 TO 06/30/80

JOB #   DESCRIPTION

100000 Turquoise Trail Enterprises

ACCOUNT # DESCRIPTION: 5020-100 Wages & Salaries – PFC 100

AP PR	VOUCH# CHECK#	VENDOR EMPL-#	P.O.-# RATE	INVOICE# HOURS	INV-DATE CHK-DATE	AMOUNT DISTRIBUTED
PR	100001	1000		40.00	05/02/80	.00
PR	100001	1000		40.00-	05/02/80	.00
PR	100003	8000	4.500	40.00	05/02/80	180.00
PR	100004	1000	3.555	26.00	05/02/80	92.43
PR	100008	1000	6.300	35.00	05/02/80	220.50
PR	100014	1000	4.500	40.00	05/16/80	180.00
PR	100017	1000	4.500	40.00	05/23/80	180.00
PR	100019	4000	4.500	15.00	05/30/80	67.50
PR	100020	5000	3.500	36.00	05/30/80	126.00
PR	100022	9500		SALARY	05/30/80	250.00
PR	100028	4000	9.450	6.00	05/30/80	56.70
PR	100032	4000	3.500	21.00	06/06/80	73.50
PR	100036	1000	3.500	40.00	06/13/80	140.00
PR	100039	1000	4.500	40.00	06/20/80	180.00
PR	100043	5000	4.500	17.00	06/27/80	76.50
PR	100043	5000	8.640	8.00	06/27/80	69.12
PR	100045	9500	5.760	25.00	06/27/80	144.00
PR	100045	9500	6.300	47.00	06/27/80	296.10
PR	100045	9500	12.600	13.00	06/27/80	163.80

ACCOUNT TOTAL: 2,496.15

JOB TOTAL: 2,496.15

600000 Aggressive Advertising, Inc.

ACCOUNT # DESCRIPTION: 5020-100 Wages & Salaries – PFC 100

AP PR	VOUCH# CHECK#	VENDOR EMPL-#	P.O.-# RATE	INVOICE# HOURS	INV-DATE CHK-DATE	AMOUNT DISTRIBUTED
PR	100005	1000	4.500	20.00	05/09/80	90.00
PR	100012	8000	3.555	35.00	05/16/80	124.43
PR	100021	1000	6.750	8.00	05/30/80	54.00
PR	100030	8000	3.555	12.00	05/30/80	42.66
PR	100033	5000	4.500	40.00	06/13/80	180.00
PR	100039	5000		SALARY	06/13/80	175.00
PR	100039	1000	4.500	12.50	06/27/80	56.25
PR	100045	9500	6.300	19.00	06/27/80	119.70

ACCOUNT TOTAL: 842.04

JOB TOTAL: 842.04

GRAND TOTAL: 9,284.46

297

Figure 9-57. Payroll report: job distribution report. (Courtesy of Mini-Computer Business Applications, Inc.)

10

COMPUTER RENT, LEASE, OR PURCHASE SELECTION

10-1 BASIC CONCEPTS OF COMPUTER ACQUISITION EVALUATION METHODS

The present-value method permits a comparison of the options of renting, leasing, or purchasing a particular computer system. A cash flow in a future time period is rendered equivalent to a single expenditure of cash in the present time period. This technique enables us to quantify the timing differences of the cash payments for different financing methods. Therefore, we can compare the relative importance of not having to pay out a huge capital sum immediately and of having different repayment periods with different interest rates.

If the reader is already familiar with the present-value concept, economic life, salvage value, and various depreciation methods, it is possible to skip to Section 10-2. Otherwise, the reader must first understand the present-value and basic concepts thoroughly before he can apply the present-value method to computer acquisition and evaluation.

10-1.1 Present-Value Concept

Determining the true return on investment requires consideration of the present value of future savings. The underlying principle behind the present-value method of calculating the return on an investment is that money has a time value [2]. A dollar in hand has a greater value than a dollar that we will receive (or yield) one year from today and a still greater value than a dollar that we will receive (or yield) two years from today. Consequently, the savings that will accrue in the future cannot be compared directly with the investment that will be made in the present. The problem of timing can be defined by shifting the savings from the future to the present for the purpose of comparison. The shift is accomplished by using the present-value concept. Where present-value tables are available, mathematical computation of the present value is a simple matter. (See Appendix II, Tables A and B.) When such tables are not available, the present value of a saving of $100.00 to be received in three years at a rate of return of 6% can be determined by the formula. Thus, the present value of $100.00 at the end of three years is $84.00.

$$\text{present value} = \frac{\$100.00}{(1 + 0.06)^3}$$
$$= \$84.00$$

If a present-value table such as Table B is available, the present value of $1.00 at the end of the three years at a rate of 6% is found to be $0.8396. Thus, the present value of $100.00 at the end of three years is $83.96, which is the product of $100.00 times $0.8396. A generalized formula for the present value of $1.00 can be written

$$PV = \frac{F}{(1 + i)^n}$$

where PV = present value at time zero
$\quad\quad$ F = future amount
$\quad\quad$ i = interest rate
$\quad\quad$ n = number of periods before you get the future amount

Using this formula, we offer a further example to clarify the ambiguity of different values under different periods. A company is issuing a 3-year, non-interest-bearing note that promises to pay a lump sum of $10,000 exactly 3 years from now. The proceeds from this note will be invested in a small business computer. How much would you pay for this 3-year note if you desired a rate of return of 9%, compounded annually?
The situation for years 0, 1, 2, and 3 is depicted as follows:

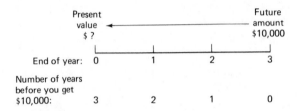

We will examine the chart, period by period. Assuming that you purchase the $10,000 note at the end of year 2 instead of immediately (year 0), how much would you be willing to pay? If you wish to earn 9% annually on every $1.00 invested, you would want to receive $1.09 in 1 year for every $1.00 you invest today. Therefore, at the end of year 2, you would be willing to pay ($1.00/$1.09)($10,000) for the right to receive $10,000 at the end of year 3. According to the formula for the present-value concept,

$$PV_2 = \frac{\$10,000}{(1 + 0.09)^1} = \$9,174$$

If you purchase the $10,000 note at the end of year 1, how much would you be willing to pay? At the end of year 1, you are willing to pay [$1.00/($1.09)^2] ($10,000) for the right to receive $10,000 at the end of year 3. According to the formula for the present-value concept:

$$PV_1 = \frac{\$10,000}{(1 + 0.09)^2} = \$8,417$$

Following is a summary of present values for each year end:

	Present value			Future amount
	$7,722 ←	←	←	$10,000
End of year:	0	1	2	3
Number of years before you get $10,000:	3	2	1	0
Present value at year end	3			$10,000
Present value at year end	2		$9,174	
Present value at year end	1	$8,417		
Present value at year end	$7,722 0			

10-1.2 Economic Life

Economic life is defined as the period of time over which a company can reasonably expect to accrue savings or benefits from a computer [2]. In other words, economic life is a synonym for equipment obsolescence. (See "Equipment Obsolescence" in Section 10-2.1.) Primarily, two concepts have a bearing on economic life: physical life and technological life. Physical life is the number of years that the computer will continue to perform the technical job for which it was procured. Technological life is the period of time that elapses before a new computer is developed which makes the present equipment obsolete. Physical life and technological life are relevant in an economic analysis only insofar as they assist in determining economic life [2].

Computers are designed with a physical life far in excess of the time necessary to recover a purchase investment. The physical life of main computers is more than 12 years. Therefore, economic life should not be a limiting factor as long as it would be estimated as less than the actual physical life of a main computer.

Computer-leasing companies have been able to take advantage of the long physical life of a computer in their leasing business. By basing their arrangements on an economic life of 10 years, instead of the 4 or 5 years commonly used by computer vendors, the leasing companies can offer much less costly contracts.

The economic life estimated can be critical to the lease/purchase decision, and the purchaser must be cautious not to lean too heavily on obsolescence as the primary rationale. A great deal of thought and analysis will probably be required to arrive at the estimated economic life of a computer system. A 1-year difference could change the decision from lease to purchase, or vice versa [2].

Most industrial users employ a standard 8 years as the maximum economic life for all electronic data-processing proposals. It is important, for purposes of comparison, that similar projects generally be assigned the same economic life, especially within the same company. However, the user should realize that assignment of the same economic life for different computer systems will affect the accuracy of the economic analysis. Again, the user should carefully analyze all aspects of the problem and alternative solutions before arriving at the estimated economic life of a computer system.

10-1.3 Salvage Value

Another important factor in deciding whether to purchase, lease, or rent is the salvage or residual value of the computer at the end of its economic life. The salvage value is the current market price of an asset being considered for replacement. It may also be defined as the value of a capital asset at the end of a specified period. One of the old stories of the computer industry was that computers would have no resale value, but this has proven not to be true. There is usually some firm that considers a used computer adequate for its needs, although new-generation computers may be on the market [2].

We remind the reader that the lessor owns the property at the expiration of the lease, although in a financial lease (full-payout lease) arrangement, the lesee usually has an option to purchase the computer. Superficially, it appears that when residual values are large, purchasing will be less expensive than leasing. However, even this obvious advantage of owning is subject to substantial qualification. The obsolescence factor may be so large that it is doubtful whether residual values will be of a great order of magnitude. If residual values appear favorable, competition among leasing companies themselves will force leasing rates down to the point where potential residual values are fully recognized in the leasing contract rates. Thus, the existence of residual values on a computer is not likely to result in substantially lower purchase costs.

It is difficult to generalize about the relationship between residual value and the comparative costs of leasing and purchasing computer systems. The results depend on the degree of optimism in the evaluations of future value and future-value changes to which the individual customer is exposed. The assignment of a residual (or market) value to the equipment at some future date is probably the most difficult estimate to make in financial analysis. If the residual value is too optimistic, losses are experienced at resale or trade-in time. On the other hand, assigning a zero dollar value as the residual value may be entirely unrealistic. Under such circumstances, it may be advisable to assign both the most pessimistic and the most optimistic values for residual value, with analysis under both conditions. Statistically, it may be possible to determine the most probable outcome under these circumstances.

Figure 10-1 shows the approximate yearly resale value of a computer. We will use this approximation of percentage of purchase price in estimating the salvage value of the computer for the purpose of our study. For example, on the graph, the resale value at year 6 is approximately 35% of the purchase price. Thus, with a purchase price of $40,000, we would estimate the resale value at $14,000. A specific computer salvage value varies depending on the computer manufacturer and model of the computer; therefore, the user should investigate the salvage value of his specific computer before making a decision on the financial arrangement.

10-1.4 Depreciation

Assigned values of depreciation can substantially affect the cash flow analysis for a purchased system. The buyer of any expensive capital equipment should be acquainted with the optimum depreciation schedules allowed by law. In addition, the future projected tax position of the corporation should be considered in order to calculate its after-tax cash flow.

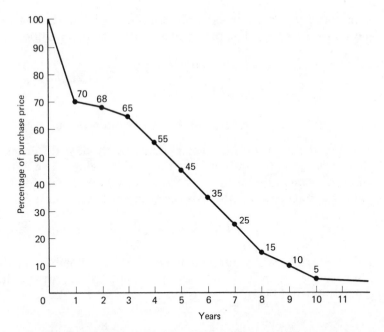

Figure 10-1. Resale value of computers. [Reprinted by permission of the publisher from *Financing for Growth: Internal Expansion and Merger Techniques*, by Donald H. Shuckett et al., © 1971 by American Management Associations, (p. 61).]

The three most commonly used ways to compute depreciation—the straight-line, sum-of-the-years'-digits, and double-declining-balance methods, are summarized briefly here.

We assume the following facts about the computer to demonstrate the various depreciation methods:

Cost of a computer	$40,000
Economic life	8 years
Salvage value at the end of 8 years*	$40,000 \times \dfrac{15\%}{100} = \$6,000$

Straight-Line Method

Using the straight-line method, the cost, less the salvage value, is generally deducted in equal amounts over the period of the equipment's estimated

*See Figure 10-1.

economic life. For our example computer system, costing $40,000, with an economic life of 8 years, the annual depreciation would be

$$\frac{\$40,000 - \$6,000}{8} = \$4,250$$

Sum-of-the-Years'-Digits Method

Using the sum-of-the-years'-digits method, a different fraction is applied each year to the cost less the salvage value. The denominator represents the cumulative total of the years of the economic life of the computer. Thus, for an economic life of 8 years, the denominator is 36:

$$8 + 7 + 6 + 5 + 4 + 3 + 2 + 1 = 36$$

The numerator is the number of years of life remaining at the beginning of the year for which the computation is made. Thus, for the first year, the depreciation would be

$$(\$40,000 - \$6,000) \times \frac{8}{36} = \$7,556$$

For the second year,

$$(\$40,000 - \$6,000) \times \frac{7}{36} = \$6,611$$

and so forth.

Double-Declining-Balance Method

Under the double-declining-balance method, the amount of depreciation taken each year is subtracted from the cost of the equipment before computing the next year's depreciation, so that the same depreciation rate applies to a smaller declining balance each year. Thus, a larger depreciation deduction is taken for the first year and a gradually smaller deduction is taken in each succeeding year. Under this method, the salvage value is not deducted from the cost of the equipment, but the computer system cannot be depreciated below its reasonable salvage value. Deducting at twice the rate used for the straight-line method, the depreciation for the first year would be

$$\frac{2(\$40,000 - 0)}{8} = \$10,000$$

TABLE 10-1
Three Methods of Depreciating a $40,000 Small Business Computer

Year	Straight-Line Method	Sum-of-the-Years'-Digits Method	Double-Declining-Balance Method
1	$11,250[a]	$13,778[a]	$16,000[a]
2	3,250	5,056	6,000
3	3,250	4,333	4,500
4	3,250	3,611	3,375
5	3,250	2,889	2,531
6	3,250	2,167	1,899
7	3,250	1,444	1,424
8	3,250	722	1,068
Total	$34,000	$34,000	$34,000

[a] Includes $8,000 depreciation for the first year at 20%.

for the second year,

$$\frac{2(\$40,000 - \$10,000)}{8} = \$7,500$$

for the third year,

$$\frac{2(\$40,000 - \$17,500)}{8} = \$5,625$$

and so forth.

The three methods are compared in Table 10-1. For a computer system costing $40,000, the additional first-year depreciation of 20% would be $8,000, with $32,000 remaining to be depreciated (using straight-line and sum-of-the-years'-digits methods) over the economic life of the equipment. The estimated salvage value is $6,000.

We see in Table 10-1 that the timing of the depreciation deduction in each of the three methods is significant. The double-declining-balance method provides the most depreciation and consequently has the largest tax effect in the earlier years of the computer's economic life. This results in the largest savings from a cash flow standpoint, since in the present-value concept a dollar this year is worth more than a dollar next year. Therefore, it is usually advantageous to use the double-declining-balance method.

10-2 RENTAL, LEASE, OR PURCHASE CONTRACT?

Once a firm decides to acquire a computer, it must determine which vendor's product offers the necessary capability for the least cost. Analyses of costs are typically made by comparing the rent, lease, and purchase alternatives.

How to acquire the computer system (i.e., whether to rent, lease, or purchase) may pose as difficult a problem as the initial decision to acquire it. Too often, the financial options are not completely understood and the most economical decision may be overlooked. By using the techniques of a present-value method, a discounted cash flow method, or a break-even method, the underlying concepts that lead to a rent, lease, or purchase decision may be revealed, thereby helping the manager to make the best decision in view of the company's situation.

However, before addressing detailed financial analyses, a summary of the typical rent, lease, and purchase contracts will clarify the options.

10-2.1 Rental Contract

The computer industry, spearheaded by IBM, started as a rental industry. It was not until January 1956, by virtue of the IBM Consent Decree, that IBM was required to sell its equipment. Despite the decree, however, IBM has always encouraged its users to rent their equipment [3]. Readers will discover in Chapter 11 that the rental contract, as compared to lease or purchase contracts, is the most advantageous for computer manufacturers.

Today, small business computer systems ranging in price between $10,000 and $50,000 are installed primarily by outright sale or full-payment lease. However, large computers or main-frame computers are for the most part still rented from their manufacturers. Rental contracts find a high level of usage in the computer industry because of the following factors: (1) low risk, (2) financial leverage, (3) equipment obsolescence, and (4) flexibility. Following is a discussion of each factor.

Low Risk

Under the rental agreement, the user is liable for a prepaid, fixed minimum payment. The agreement, however, can be terminated by a minimum of 90 days' written notice by either party. Under this agreement, the risk of ownership remains with the vendor. The user has no obligation for such expenses as insurance and maintenance; however, he is responsible for paying taxes that may be levied on the rental contract by the state or local government.

Risk is negligible under a rental agreement because the user does not need to raise a lump sum of capital for purchase or to keep the agreement more than a required period.

Financial Leverage

If the equipment is rented from the manufacturer, pressure can be applied more readily for services or other support. If the services are unsatisfactory, withholding payment is one way of obtaining service. An installment purchase, with monthly payments to the manufacturer, has a similar advantage. Not withstanding this, the manufacturer should provide comparable support regardless of acquisition method.

Equipment Obsolescence

Obsolescence has been the principal argument for equipment rental. Presumed flexibility of the rental method allows rapid replacement if technical obsolescence occurs. It should be noted, however, that rapid replacement may be highly undesirable and uneconomical if a large investment in systems planning has not been recovered. Two concepts have a primary bearing on obsolescence: physical obsolescence and technological obsolescence.

Physical Obsolescence. A machine should be replaced when it no longer performs efficiently. However, computers are designed with lives far in excess of the time necessary to recover a purchase investment. The following is a conservative estimation of physical obsolescence in computer equipment:

Main computer	12–16 years
Printers, card readers	8–10 years
Disks and drums	10–14 years
Terminals	10–14 years

Therefore, physical obsolescence should not be a factor if the break-even point for all types of equipment and combinations of acquisition methods is less than 8 years [3].

Technical Obsolescence. Technological life is the period of time that elapses before new equipment is developed which makes the present equipment obsolete. Some people argue that dramatic technical breakthroughs increase effectiveness from one generation to the next by several orders of magnitude. Thus, it is much safer to rent a computer than to purchase one. This sounds like a very logical and convincing statement. However, the manufacturers themselves must recover their investments in research and hardware and software development, an effort that requires revenue periods in excess of 5 years (in the past, about 7 years) for each new system [3]. Furthermore, the rate of technological advancement in the computer is mostly predictable. Speeds are bounded by the nanosecond speed of light. Therefore, it is unlikely that the purchase of a newly announced machine would result in significant technical obsolescence in the near future. Moreover, if the system continues to provide the service required, technical obsolescence should not affect the user.

Flexibility

Flexibility is probably the best argument for a rental contract. When the user has a continually varying mix of jobs that require different configurations of equipment, it is to his or her advantage to be able to move equipment rapidly in or out of the installation without penalty charges [4].

In summary, aside from cash availability, the principal cost elements of the rental contract are as follows:

1. Monthly rental payment.
2. Overtime payments for use in excess of a stated amount (extra-shift use, over and above the standard monthly base hours, represents an additional cost to the user).
3. Investment tax credit can be passed to the user. However, since investment tax credit is based on the write-off period for equipment by the manufacturer—usually 4 years—only $3\frac{1}{3}\%$ is allowed under current IRS regulations.
4. Taxes that may be levied on the rental contract by the state or local government.

10-2.2   Lease Contract

A lease is an agreement by a lessee to pay for the use of a real, tangible asset owned by the lessor. The lessee pays the lessor a fee for the use, rather than the purchase of an asset. The lease payment then substitutes for interest and principle payments on debt. Normally, the lessor, as owner, bears the cost of the lease, including interest and administrative costs.

In the computer industry, lease contracts are available through "third parties" or directly from the vendors. The so-called "third-party" lease is one in which a third-party company will purchase the equipment from the manufacturer and lease it to the user. The terms can be flexible and negotiable, depending on the risk to the lessor; thus the longer the duration of the lease, the more favorable the terms and conditions possible for the user [4].

For purposes of analysis, it is convenient to divide all leasing contracts into two broad categories: (1) financial (or full-payout) lease and, (2) operating (or non-full-payout) lease.

Financial (or Full-Payout) Lease

A financial (full-payout) lease is defined as a contract under which the lessee agrees to make a series of payments to the lessor which, in total, exceed the purchase price of the asset acquired. Typically, payments under a financial (full-payout) lease are spread over a period of time equal to the major portion of the useful life of the asset acquired. During the initial term of the lease, the contract is noncancellable by either party; that is, the lessee is irrevocably committed to continue leasing the asset.

The user (or lessee) essentially has the rights of purchase and assumes the risks normally assumed by the purchaser. However, the legal title is retained by the lessor. The lessee's payments are designed to recover for the lessor:

Total cost of the equipment

Cost of money required to purchase the equipment by the lessor

Administrative and clerical costs

Legal fees

The legal fee for arranging the transaction might be thought of either as the profit for the lessor or as the fee that might be paid an investment banker for acting as a third party in arranging financing.

Under the financial (full-payout) lease, the lessor still owns the equipment, although the lessee will normally have the option to purchase. The financial (full-payout) lease is generally used to obtain financial benefit for the lessee (i.e., lower payments over the useful life of the equipment as compared to a rental).

Operating (Non-Full-Payout) Lease

Operating (non-full-payout) leases are almost the same as manufacturers' rental contracts. The essential differences are the unlimited availability of the equipment for the lessee and the length of commitment.

The unlimited availability of the equipment is important in the financial analysis of the lease contract. There are no overtime-use payments associated with a lease contract, in contrast to a rental contract.

The terms of an operating (non-full-payout) lease contract generally start with a minimum commitment of 2 years and can go as high as 10 years. Monthly payments average 10 to 30% less than the manufacturer's rental price.

Leasing offers certain advantages: (1) a lump sum of capital is not needed, (2) income tax deductions, and, (3) a flexible contract, under which one can negotiate, among other variables, investment tax credit, maintenance, property tax and insurance, obsolescence of equipment, and depreciation and interest. We now discuss these advantages.

1. *A lump sum of capital is not needed.* The company need not spend a lump sum of money in the beginning. The financial responsibility is passed on to the lessor, and the lessee can preserve his or her borrowing capacity or equity structure for other uses. This may have a favorable influence on future financing costs, since the lease form of financing is not shown on the balance sheet and the ratios that are important to investors (debt/equity, earnings coverage, return on assets) may be positively affected.

Many companies have capital expenditures that require various time-consuming levels of authorization. Leasing may obviate the need for these approvals and thereby facilitate the acquisition of computer systems.

2. *Income tax deduction of lease.* One of the frequently claimed advantages for computer leasing is that a leasing contract permits the lessee to enjoy a more advantageous stream of income tax expense deductions than would be possible if he or she owned the computer and could only deduct depreciation and interest. In fact, it may be possible to achieve some advantage if the lease payments are scheduled in such a way that they are higher in the earlier years of the lease than the sum of depreciation and interest, and conversely, lower in the later years. When these conditions are present, the present value of the tax deductions received under the lease plan is greater than the present value of the tax deductions under ownership.

This same advantage may be achieved in another way under financial leases (or full-payout leases). The agreement may be drawn for a relatively short initial term, for example, 4 years. During this time, the lessor recovers the entire cost of the computer and the user (lessee) can deduct his payments to the lessor as expenses, whereas if the lessee were to purchase the computer, he would have to depreciate it over a longer period, perhaps 8 years.

To protect the public from abuses stemming from this tax loophole, the Internal Revenue Service adopted Revenue Ruling 55-540 in 1955. The effect of this ruling is to eliminate any tax advantage for leasing contracts which are, in all important respects, really purchase transactions. However, most leasing contracts today can be, and are, written in such a way that they will qualify for tax treatment as leases [1].

For a transaction to be acceptable as a "true lease," the IRS requires the lessor to assume a significant risk both during the lease term and in the period after its expiration. This general guideline translates into measurements of fluctuations in yearly rentals, the relationship of the amount of purchase or renewal options at the end of the basic lease term to the anticipated fair value of the asset at the time, and the difference between the lease term and the economic useful life of the asset [1]. According to IRS regulations, the ideal lease arrangement would include the following characteristics:

Lease payments would be approximately the same throughout the basic lease term.

Purchase options are not fixed amounts but are based on fair values at the end of the lease term.

The estimated fair market value of an asset at the end of the lease term is at least 10% of the asset's original cost.

The lease term is less than 80% of the asset's useful life.

It is difficult to predict how far one can deviate from this pattern. Therefore, one should exercise caution in executing an ambiguous lease. The following specific examples may clarify some of the ambiguity in the "true lease" acceptable by the IRS.

Example 1. A 6-year lease on an 8-year asset with a $1 purchase option and annual rentals of 30% in the second year and 10% in each of the remaining 4 years would be questionable, even if the contract were restructured so that the payments were mostly equal throughout the 6-year period. But this still would not necessarily meet the IRS classification of a "true lease." It would be better to treat the transaction as a purchase.

Example 2. A 4-year "lease" on an 8-year asset, with an option to purchase at 5% of original cost, would be an installment purchase. The same lease with an option to purchase at fair market value at the end of the lease term would be a true lease. The rentals under these two leases would be vastly different for the IRS.

3. *Flexible contract.* Generally speaking, lease contracts are the most flexible of all contracts available to a user (lessee) of a computer system. The user (lessee) can negotiate with the lessor for terms most beneficial to both parties. Some variables that affect the negotiations are now discussed. (These negotiations are somewhat unusual because each party is generally aware of the other's financial needs and requirements.)

The *investment tax credit* is a direct tax benefit for one of the parties. In certain cases, it could benefit one company more than another. If one of the companies has been operating in a loss period, it may not need the investment tax credit because its tax would not be as large as in other periods. Another case might occur when the user has already made massive investments. In such cases, by relinquishing the investment tax credit, the user may be able to negotiate a lower lease price.

One of the two parties (lessor or lessee) must pay for *maintenance*, and the cost is the same for either party. There may be local advantages for one party or the other to assume the maintenance obligation. For example, the user may already have a maintenance contract with the manufacturer for other computer equipment and could perhaps extend it to include the leased equipment. On the other hand, the lessor may have a national contract with a maintenance organization.

If *obsolescence* is one of the risks the lessor does not wish to bear, he may pass this on to the lessee. The lessee may be able to carry this risk at a lower cost because of his knowledge and experience in disposing of, or releasing, the computer system once the lease has expired. On the other hand, if the lessee does not want to carry this risk, the lessor would expect to adjust the lease payment upward to compensate for the risk of computer obsolescence.

Property tax and insurance is also a cost that one of the two parties must pay, and the cost is the same for either party. Therefore, it depends primarily on the user's selection of leasing arrangements: financial (full-payout) or operating (non-full-payout) lease. (See the discussions of these leases at the beginning of this section.)

10-2.3   Purchase Contract

Under a purchase contract, the purchaser bears all the risks of ownership, including maintenance, insurance, taxes, and computer obsolescence [4]. When a company decides that the purchase of a computer system is desirable, the company has a few alternative methods of financing and acquisition: purchase for cash, purchase on an installment plan (or some other method involving debt financing), or acquisition via a financial lease.

For the purposes of analysis, it is convenient to divide all purchase contracts into two broad categories: (1) purchase with funds on hand, and (2) purchase with borrowed funds.

Purchase with Funds on Hand

There are several important factors affecting this financial arrangement. Aside from cash availability, the principal cost elements of this purchase method are as follows:

Initial purchase cost
Cost of money on purchase price
Maintenance (except for a warranty period)
Insurance
Residual value
Full investment tax credit
Tax advantage of accelerated depreciation

Assigned values of depreciation can substantially affect the cash flow analysis for a purchased system. This will be clearly demonstrated in Section 10-3. The buyer of any computer system should be acquainted with the optimum depreciation schedules allowed by law. In addition, the future projected tax position of the company should be considered in order to estimate its after-tax cash flow accurately.

Purchase with Borrowed Funds

Another method of purchasing computer systems is to negotiate a loan from financing institutions. In this way, the company can benefit from trading on equity as well as avoid a capital outlay at the time of purchase. However, the net cash flows under this alternative may prove to be the same as for ownership, assuming that the company can borrow funds at the cost of capital.

The principal cost elements of this purchase method are almost the same as purchase with funds on hand (*except for interest* cost paid to the financing institution). The financing institution would probably be a computer manufacturer in the case of an installment purchase arrangement. Otherwise, bank loans would be the standard arrangement.

10-3 COMPUTER ACQUISITION AND EVALUATION WITH PRESENT-VALUE METHOD

Now that the advantages and disadvantages of rent, lease, and purchase alternatives are clear from Section 10-2, we will discuss computer financing methods. Under what circumstances should you lease a computer? Is it more beneficial for your company's cash position to buy a computer? Should you rent a computer in order to wait for a new computer to come on the market?

Before coming to a decision on any such questions, readers would be reminded of points that were raised in Chapters 1 and 4. One of these points is that the manager should investigate other capital investment which may give a better return on investment (ROI) than investing in a computer system. The same criteria should be used for selecting a computer as for any other piece of equipment.

Figure 10-2 shows the simplified steps of the financial decision of acquiring a computer. It gives only a general idea of what is involved concerning the typical situation and typical circumstances. Without some analytical methods, there is no clear-cut way to determine whether you should rent, lease, or purchase. An analytical approach that will give you a reasonable answer is the present-value method, also called the discounted cash flow method. The present-value method will consider all cash flows from the date of purchase through the expected life of the equipment. These cash flows will take into account your payments, depreciation, investment tax credits, maintenance costs, insurance and property taxes, and your company's tax rate.

The present-value method can be utilized to discount future cash flows back to the present day. As the present-value method is described in detail in Section 10-1.1, the theory is not discussed here.

To determine the present values of rent, lease, and purchase options, we need at least the following information:

1. Useful life of a computer
2. Purchasing value of a computer
3. Residual value (salvage value) of a computer
4. Discount rate (current cost of capital or rate of return)
5. Depreciation schedule
6. Investment tax credit
7. Maintenance cost
8. Rental payment cost
9. Lease payment cost

Figure 10-2. Simplified financial decision flowchart.

The useful life of a computer is the number of years that you expect to keep it. The IRS has established guidelines for computers which are classified under the heading of information systems. According to the IRS, the life of a computer is considered to be 6 years. In other words, it can be depreciated over a 6-year period. Of course, a longer period can be claimed, but then the cash benefits from the tax deduction are less. We can also depreciate software in a depreciation schedule, normally over a 5-year period. However, if the software is purchased as part of the total system, it must be depreciated over the same period that the hardware (a computer) is depreciated.

The residual or salvage value is the amount that you expect to sell the computer for at the end of its life. This is somewhat of a guess. Generally speaking, the residual value of a computer at the end of 6 years of life is 10 to 35% of the original purchase cost.

The discount rate is the current rate of return on investment or current cost of capital. If you are making an investment in a computer, you have the alternative of investing the same money in some other capital equipment. You should be sure that the rate of return from your business is the best you can get. If the company can make more money by investing in new manu-facturing equipment, you should not invest in a computer. The discount rate will vary depending on the company's ability to earn more from the money invested.

The IRS has established guidelines for reasonable amounts of deprecia-tion, and has approved three methods of depreciation: double-declining-balance, straight-line, and sum-of-the-years'-digits. Double-declining-balance and sum-of-the-years'-digits are called "accelerated" depreciations because you take a higher proportion of depreciation in the first few years than in the last few years. Straight-line is, of course, constant over the whole period of the life of the computer. Accelerated depreciation can be used only on a new computer. If you buy a used computer, you are limited to straight-line depreciation.

In selecting the method of depreciation, you should take into account whether you wish to conserve cash now and use it later, or whether it would be more beneficial to have a more even distribution of cash flow over the life of the computer. In the former case, you will want to take the maximum deduction now and would use an accelerated method. In the latter case, you would use the straight-line method.

Investment tax credit is another important factor to consider. This is a direct credit against taxes, currently 10% if the life of a computer is esti-mated as 7 years or longer. The investment tax credit percentage varies from year to year as determined by the federal government. The government raises the investment tax credit when it wants to stimulate investment and lowers it when they do not want investment. At present, if you were to owe the government $10,000 in taxes for the year and you bought a computer costing $10,000 during the year, you could deduct 10% of $10,000, or $1,000, from the $10,000 tax as an investment tax credit.

ABC Company Case

A fictitious company called ABC wishes to acquire a minicomputer. The management of ABC Company unanimously decides to computerize its operation. The manager of ABC Company is assigned the task of finding the best financial method of acquiring a minicomputer.

The manager collects the following pertinent information:

1. Useful life of a computer—6 years
2. Purchasing value of a computer—$30,000
3. Residual value of a computer—15% of purchasing cost
4. Discount rate (rate of return of ABC Company)—12%
5. Depreciation schedule—double declining balance
6. Investment tax credit—10$

7. Maintenance cost—$1,200/year
8. Rental payment cost—$8,400/year ($700/month)
9. Lease payment cost—$5,400/year ($450/month)

Which method is best for ABC Company? Is it the rental, lease, or purchase method?

The present-value method of analysis carried out here is presented for three possibilities: (1) manufacturer's rental option, (2) third-party lease option, and (3) purchase option with residual.

10-3.1 Manufacturer's Rental Option

Table 10-2 presents the analysis of the manufacturer's rental option and projects the cash flow for 6 years. The total monthly rental from Table 10-2 ($700/month) is multiplied by 12 to give a total yearly figure of $8,400. Tax savings for a year is 55% of the yearly rental, deductible as part of the corporate tax. This leaves an after-tax cash flow of $3,780 for each year (except for year 0).

The present-value cost for year 1 at 12% is calculated by multiplying the after-tax cost by the present-value factor of 0.89286 (see Table 10-3). In other words, the year 1 after-tax cash flow, $3,780, is multiplied by the present-value factor of 0.89286, giving the year 1 present-value cost, $3,375.

The figure for year 2 is obtained in the same manner as for year 1, by multiplying the after-tax cost for that year by the present-value factor of 0.79719 for year 2. The same process is repeated for the rest of the years. These present-value costs for each of the 6 years are summed to arrive at a total present-value cost, $15,541. This result, $15,541, is compared with the figures from Tables 10-4 and 10-5.

TABLE 10-2
Present-Value Cash Flow Analysis for Manufacturer's Rental Contract ($30,000 Minicomputer)

				Year			
	0	*1*	*2*	*3*	*4*	*5*	*6*
Rental payment ($700/month)		$8,400	$8,400	$8,400	$8,400	$8,400	$8,400
Tax savings (55%)		(4,620)	(4,620)	(4,620)	(4,620)	(4,620)	(4,620)
After-tax cash flow		3,780	3,780	3,780	3,780	3,780	3,780
Present-value cost at 12%	15,541[a]	3,375	3,013	2,691	2,402	2,145	1,915

[a]Present-value cost at 12% discount years 1–6 for rental
$$= 3,375 + 3,013 + 2,691 + 2,402 + 2,145 + 1,915$$
$$= \$15,541$$

TABLE 10-3
Present-Value Factors

				Year			
	0	1	2	3	4	5	6
Present-value factor at 12%		0.89286	0.79719	0.71178	0.63552	0.56743	0.50663

10-3.2 Third-Party Lease Option

Table 10-4 shows the analysis for third-party lease with full-payment (financial lease) option.

The lease payments are constant throughout the life of the lease in the financial (or full-payout) lease agreement. The monthly lease payment from Table 10-4 ($450/month) is multiplied by 12 to give a total yearly figure of $5,400. Maintenance cost per year is $1,200 (or 12 times the monthly rate, $100). Maintenance expenses in this case are constant over the 6 years. Considering the current rate of inflation, an increase in the maintenance cost could be added. It would be more realistic to include the estimated cost increase (5 to 10% per year). For the sake of simplicity, constant yearly maintenance costs are assumed in this analysis.

The total of the lease payment and maintenance cost is the pre-tax cash flow. Of this total figure, 55% is deductible as part of the corporate tax and is entered in Table 10-4 as "tax savings." The after-tax cash flow is the difference between the pretax cash flow and the tax savings.

The present-value costs are obtained by the same process used for the rental figures. The present-value cost for year 1 at 12% is calculated by multiplying the after-tax cost by the present-value factor of 0.89286 (see Table 10-3). The year 1 after-tax cash flow, $2,970, is multiplied by the present-value factor of 0.89286, giving the year 1 present-value cost, $2,652. The

TABLE 10-4
Present-Value Cash Flow Analysis for Third-Party Lease ($30,000 Minicomputer)

				Year			
	0	1	2	3	4	5	6
Lease payment ($450/month)		$5,400	$5,400	$5,400	$5,400	$5,400	$5,400
Maintenance ($100/month)		1,200	1,200	1,200	1,200	1,200	1,200
Pre-tax cash flow		6,600	6,600	6,600	6,600	6,600	6,600
Tax savings (55%)		(3,630)	(3,630)	(3,630)	(3,630)	(3,630)	(3,630)
After-tax cash flow		2,970	2,970	2,970	2,970	2,970	2,970
Present-value cost at 12%	12,211[a]	2,652	2,368	2,114	1,887	1,685	1,505

[a] Present-value cost at 12% discount rate years 1–6 for lease
= 2,652 + 2,368 + 2,114 + 1,887 + 1,685 + 1,505
= $12,211

317

same process is repeated for the rest of the years. The present-value costs for each of the 6 years are summed to arrive at a total present-value cost, $12,211.

10-3.3 Purchase Option

Table 10-5 shows the analysis of a purchase option. The calculations are somewhat different from rental and lease options. An initial cash outlay of the total purchase price of the computer system is made at the beginning.

Depreciation is calculated using the double-declining-balance method. Depreciation is assumed to take place at the end of each year. It should be noted that the depreciation is heavily weighted during the early years when using the double-declining-balance method.

The insurance and property tax are calculated by taking 1% of the value of the computer at the beginning of each year.

Maintenance cost per year is the same as a lease option, $1,200. The actual pretax cash flow is the sum of insurance and property tax and maintenance. The depreciation, although considered as an expense, is not an actual cash outflow. However, the tax savings is calculated as 55% of the sum of the actual pretax cash flow and depreciation. Therefore, the year 1 tax savings is 55% of $11,500, or $6,325. The after-tax cash flow (except in year 0) is calculated as the tax savings minus the pretax cash flow. The present value costs are generated from the after-tax figures in the same manner as for rental and lease options.

TABLE 10-5
Present-Value Cash Flow Analysis for Purchase with Residual Value ($30,000 Minicomputer)

	Year						
	0	*1*	*2*	*3*	*4*	*5*	*6*
Purchase payment	$30,000	—	—	—	—	—	—
Depreciation	—	$10,000	$6,667	$4,444	$2,963	$1,975	$1,317
Insurance	—	300	300	300	300	300	300
Maintenance	—	1,200	1,200	1,200	1,200	1,200	1,200
Pre-tax cash flow	30,000	1,500	1,500	1,500	1,500	1,500	1,500
Tax savings (55%)	—	(6,325)	(4,492)	(3,269)	(2,455)	(1,911)	(1,549)
Investment tax credit	(2,000)						
After-tax cash flow	28,000	(4,825)	(2,992)	(1,769)	(995)	(411)	(49)
Present-value cost at 12%	14,683[a]	(4,308)	(2,385)	(1,259)	(607)	(233)	(25)

[a] Present-value years 1–6 = (4,308) + (2,385) + (1,259) + (607) + (233) + (25)
$$= (8,817)$$
After-tax cash flow − present-value years 1–6 = 28,000 − 8817
$$= 19,183$$
19,183 − residual value (15%) = 19,183 − 4,500
Final present-value cost at 12% = $14,683

These present-value costs for each of the 6 years are summed to arrive at a total present value, $8,817. If the life cycle of a computer is estimated at 7 years or more, the investment tax credit is 10% or whatever percentage the government assigns for that year. In our example, the life cycle of a computer is estimated as 6 years. Therefore, in year 0 the investment tax credit is $2,000, which is $6\frac{2}{3}$% of the purchase price.

The residual value is the resale value of a computer at the end of its life cycle. The residual value is assigned to a computer on a "best estimate" basis at the end of the period. In ABC Company's case, it is estimated as 15% of the original computer cost, which is $4,500.

The final present-value cost is calculated as the sum of the total present values for year 1 to 6 ($8,817) and the residual value ($4,500) subtracted from the after-tax cash flow ($28,000). Thus, the final present-value figure for the purchase option is $14,683.

10-3.4 Conclusion for ABC Company

It is of no real surprise that the rental present-value cost ($15,541) is more than the purchase present-value cost ($14,683) and the lease present-value cost ($12,211). In the case of ABC Company, it is clear that the lease option is the best financial alternative. Lease contracts are available from manufacturers or third parties who purchase a computer from a manufacturer and lease it to the user. Terms from third parties are generally quite flexible and negotiable. For example, the user company can negotiate such terms as who should take the investment tax credit and/or who should pay the maintenance cost. After considering these alternatives, the manager of ABC Company should choose the third-party lease method for acquiring the minicomputer.

Figure 10-3 shows a break-even-point chart for renting, leasing, and purchasing, based on the discount rates. The present-value cost in dollars is the y axis on the graph. The manufacturer's rental cost is the highest line, which slopes down to the right as the discount rate increases. The lease-cost line and purchase-cost line are crossed at between 7 and 8% of the discount rate. Let's analyze these lines at each discount rate. If you consider your company's discount rate (the rate of return after taxes on assets) to be 6%, it would be better to purchase a computer. On the other hand, if you consider your company's discount rate to be 9%, it becomes better to lease a computer. The break-even point on this example is between 7 and 8% of the discount rate. As the discount rate increases, in other words, as the amount of money the company can generate from the business increases, it becomes more important to be able to lease a computer. Readers should not generalize the result of ABC company's case, however. Each company's situation must be analyzed separately. Your company's unique cash position, tax situation, and availability of credit will determine the decision.

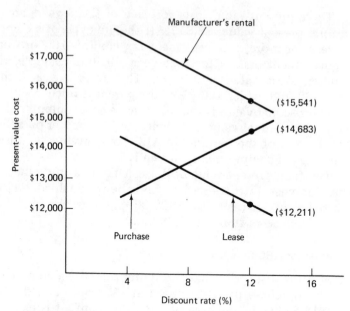

Figure 10-3. Break-even-point chart for ABC company.

The present-value cash flow analysis should be utilized as an important yardstick in determining the best financial method (rent, lease, or purchase) to use in acquiring a computer.

REFERENCES

[1] BRUCE J. KIRCHENBAUM, "Lease or Buy Decision without Tears: The Present Value Approach," *Financial Executive*, February 1972, p. 30.

[2] DONALD H. SHUCKETT, HARLAN J. BROWN, and EDWARD J. MOCK, "Financing for Growth," American Management Association, Inc., 1971.

[3] DICK H. BRANDON, "Computer Acquisition Method Analysis," *Datamation*, September 1972, pp. 76-79.

[4] TED SZATROWSKI, "Rent, Lease, or Buy," *Datamation*, February 1976, pp. 59-68.

11

HOW TO AVOID COMPUTER
CONTRACTING PITFALLS

11-1 DISPUTABLE AREAS AND QUESTIONS

The author has studied numerous computer purchase contracts, ranging from those of large manufacturers such as IBM to small vendors' contracts. The study revealed that there is a great deal of variation among standard computer purchase agreements. Some contract clauses are very unspecific in terms of quantity, method, date, and time. With this type, it is probable that legal disputes will occur if anything goes wrong. On the other hand, some contracts are "boilerplate"-type contracts, printed in very fine print on several pages. They are more specific, but are written in such a way that the average layman would have a difficult time understanding the clauses.

Most buyers cannot read through contracts without feeling frustration and a certain amount of desperation. A good contract should specify the rights and duties of the contracting parties in a clear and comprehensive manner, so that both parties clearly understand their rights and duties before signing the contract.

The following are sample areas and questions that the contracting parties should address and answer specifically in terms of their rights and duties, in order to protect themselves.

1. Hardware configuration

   a. What is the configuration of the system, including the CPU, printers, terminals, and disks?

   b. What are the model numbers, features, types, quantities, and prices?

2. Hardware expandability

   a. Will future equipment or next-higher-level equipment be compatible with the present system?

   b. Will application programs and operating systems be convertible to future equipment?

   c. What is the vendor's policy toward attaching other manufacturers' equipment?

3. Hardware performance

   a. What methods will be used in testing computer performance? Will individual program testing, job-stream testing, system testing with live data, and/or combination of the above be used?

   b. What is the MTBF (i.e., mean time between failures) of the system?

   c. What recourse is available if this system fails to meet the performance tests?

4. Hardware warranties

   a. Does the vendor warrant that each machine will be in good working order on the date of the delivery?

   b. Does the vendor warrant that the machine and all its parts will be newly manufactured?

   c. What is the warranty period? 6 months? 1 year?

   d. Does the warranty include labor and materials?

5. Software copyright

   a. If the vendor sells you someone else's program, what protection do you have against the real program owner?

   b. If the vendor supplies only the object deck program, which is in machine language form, how many copies can the buyer keep?

   c. If the computer breaks down, can the buyer take the object deck program to some other computer installation? That is, can the buyer run the programs elsewhere, thereby continuing his business using the backup system?

   d. Is the object deck (machine language program) compatible with the backup system? In other words, can you run the program on the backup computer?

6. Program modification

   a. If the buyer wishes to change sections of the program, does the vendor supply the source programs?

   b. If the buyer wishes a change or modification in the program, does the vendor supply this service? If so, what is the cost arrangement?

7. Software performance

a. What methods and test data will be used in testing the operating system and/ or application programs?

b. What recourse is available if the system programs and/or application programs fail to meet the tests?

c. After acceptance of the system, if the buyer finds errors in the system software and/or application programs, does the vendor correct them at no charge? If not, what will the cost be?

d. What will be done about time and money loss due to vendor-produced program errors?

8. Price and transportation

a. Who pays the transportation cost?

b. Who pays the transportation insurance?

c. Who pays taxes, fees, excise tax, duties, and/or other charges?

d. Who takes the risk of loss?

e. What is the actual acceptance date?

f. For what time period can either party postpone the acceptance date?

g. During what time period can the buyer cancel the order without penalty?

h. What recourse is available if the vendor is late in delivering the equipment?

9. Maintenance

a. How fast will the vendor respond to system malfunction?

b. How fast will the vendor respond to the program error?

c. How long is the MTTR (i.e., mean time to repair) of this vendor?

d. If the vendor goes bankrupt, who will be able to maintain the system?

11-2 TIMING OF THE CONTRACT

It is important to recognize that the timing of the contract negotiation is of significance. It does no good to negotiate a hardware maintenance contract after the hardware has been delivered, because the leverage the user has over the vendor is insignificant after delivery. The contract must be negotiated while sufficient leverage is available to ensure that fallback positions and alternatives can be exercised. In hardware contracting, therefore, the best time to negotiate a contract is just after the vendor has been selected through a competitive procurement procedure, so that there is, in fact, a standby alternative—another vendor.

In the selection process, it is desirable to ensure that more than one vendor submit proposals that satisfy the user's requirements. Even if it is decided in advance that a specific vendor has the best resources to satisfy the user's needs, it is still a good idea to obtain proposals from more than one vendor. This will provide the necessary negotiating leverage with the preselected vendor [1].

Prior to negotiation of the contract, a determination should be made as to whether the computer should be purchased, rented, or leased through a third party. The difference among these acquisition methods can be significant and can often affect the cost, as discussed in previous chapters. The various methods can result in different types of contracts between parties, so the determination must be made prior to the final negotiation.

11-3 CONTRACTS AND CLAUSES

What should and should not be included in the contract? What are the favorable or unfavorable clauses in the contract for the buyer? The vendor generally is in a much better position than the buyer, since the vendor is protected by large capital and corporate attorneys. Moreover, the contract is normally on the vendor's form, prepared by its attorneys to protect the vendor against the most obvious and most frequently occurring problems. The vendor-drawn contract also usually contains those boilerplate clauses traditionally put forth by vendors, such as warranty disclaimers, all tending to avoidance of any liability. It can be safely stated that the standard contract in the computer field is inadequate, especially from the buyer's point of view. As a result, the negotiation and development of a contract primarily benefits the buyer, and Section 11-4 is addressed to the buyer for that reason.

It is expected that sales by the small computer industry will soon exceed $5 billion. Of this amount, the majority of small computer sales and services will be obtained without the benefit of an *adequate contract*. It is highly possible that litigation and dissatisfaction in the field will increase according to the increase of small business computers' sales and the increase in complexity of computer use. Therefore, it is wise to have an adequate contract when acquiring a small business computer.

This chapter is not intended as a text on writing contracts; rather it provides legal analysis of standard commercial computer contract clauses. It will concentrate on standard contracts such as hardware purchase, software development or modification, leasing hardware and/or software, and maintenance contracts.

A number of texts deal effectively with the art of writing EDP contracts, including *Data Processing Contracts* by Brandon and Segelstein [2] and *Data Processing Contracts and the Law* by Bernacchi and Larsen [3].

The subject is so complicated and so intertwined that it is almost impossible to produce a text that covers the subject completely and adequately. Section 11-4 (reprinted by permission of *Data Management* magazine) takes an *initial step* in covering at least the basic components of a vendor–user relationship in computer purchase or leasing. The examples provided are designed to put forth useful ideas for consideration by vendors and buyers.

11-4   SYNTAX: LEGAL ANALYSIS OF STANDARD COMMERCIAL COMPUTER PURCHASE AND LEASE CONTRACTS*

Once the appropriate computer selection has been made and negotiations begin for obtaining the right to use the computer system, it is essential to analyze the factors and considerations of the commercial computer contract.

It is important to determine if the legal relationships within the language of this agreement are going to assure that the actual physical system installed at the customer's location will meet the criteria, procedures, and validation methods used in selecting the particular configuration.

Furthermore, the EDP user, before contracting for computer equipment, must decide whether he or she will purchase, rent, or lease the equipment, or perhaps simply contract for outside services. The user must first ascertain his or her basic needs for electronic data processing and then apply those needs to the characteristics that each of the three methods manifests.

Five major manufacturers of computer equipment and 25% of users submitted various copies of their standard contract forms for this study.[†]

The ultimate goal of this analysis of standard contract forms[‡] is to develop a general model, which will include all relevant provisions that should be considered during negotiations for the purchase of computer systems.

11-4.1   Methodology

In defining the contractual language of standard computer purchase agreements, a rather non-rigorous development was made of the following language characteristics: syntax, semantics, and pragmatics.[§]

---

[*]Phillip J. Scaletta, Jr., and Joseph L. Walsh, reprinted from *Data Management*, October 1972, pp. 12–20; November 1972, pp. 37–42. Copyright *Data Management* magazine, Data Processing Management Association. All rights reserved.

[†]The respondents were CDC, Honeywell, IBM, NCR, and UNIVAC.

[‡]The types of contracts supplied were purchase, lease, maintenance, education/training, systems engineering services, software agreements, etc.

[§]Jean E. Sammet [*Programming Languages: History and Fundamentals* (Englewood Cliffs, N.J., Prentice-Hall, Inc. 1969), pp. 51–57] defines the three language characteristics as follows: "By *syntax* we mean a rigorous statement of what sequences of characters are considered correct in the language and, ultimately what character sequences constitute a (syntactically) legal program. A single legal string can have a great many meanings; the collection of all these meanings for each legal string is called the *semantics* of the language. The pragmatics is the relationship of these strings and their meanings to the user."

The syntax analysis requires the use of three notational symbols.

1. When material is enclosed in braces { }, a choice may be made of one of the enclosed items.
2. Material enclosed in brackets [ ] represents an optional item which may be included or omitted.
3. Material preceded by an asterisk * represents an item which is not part of any standard contract language and is included for illustrative purposes only.

Consider the following definitions:

$$P = \text{provision (contractual statement)}$$

$$CT = \text{clause or term (CT is included in P)}$$

Some simple examples using these notational symbols are: (a) {P}, (b) [P], (c) *P.

Example (a) implies that the provision P is common to all standard purchase contracts (i.e., it appeared in each of the five manufacturers' standard contracts analyzed in this study). Example (b) implies that P is not included in all standard purchase contracts (i.e., it could have appeared in one to four of the analyzed contracts). Example (c) implies that P is not found in any of the analyzed contracts but is included for illustrative purposes.

Since a provision (P) is comprised of clauses and terms (CT's), there is variability among standard contracts in that identical provision (P's), at a concept level, may be comprised of different CT's. Such occurrences are exhibited by:

$$P = CT_1 \begin{Bmatrix} CT_2' \\ CT_2'' \\ CT_2''' \end{Bmatrix} CT_3 \begin{bmatrix} \begin{Bmatrix} CT_4' \\ CT_4'' \\ CT_4''' \end{Bmatrix} CT_5 \end{bmatrix}$$

The possible combinations of P are:

1→ 1. CT_1 CT_2' CT_3
    2. CT_1 CT_2' CT_3 CT_4' CT_5
    3. CT_1 CT_2' CT_3 CT_4'' CT_5
2→ 4. CT_1 CT_2' CT_3 CT_4''' CT_5
    5. CT_1 CT_2'' CT_3
    6. CT_1 CT_2'' CT_3 CT_4' CT_5
1→ 7. CT_1 CT_2'' CT_3 CT_4'' CT_5
    8. CT_1 CT_2'' CT_3 CT_4''' CT_5
    9. CT_1 CT_2''' CT_3

$1\rightarrow10.$ CT_1 $\text{CT}''_2{}'$ CT_3 CT'_4 CT_5
11. CT_1 $\text{CT}''_2{}'$ CT_3 CT''_4 CT_5
12. CT_1 $\text{CT}''_2{}'$ CT_3 $\text{CT}''_4{}'$ CT_5

if you allow the material within the bracket and braces to be assembled in these combinations. (Note: the symbol $2\rightarrow$ in the preceding exhibit implies that P, as defined by combination number 4, appeared in two separate standard purchase contracts.)

This is *not* the case in this study, in that all of the above combinations would not have appeared in the standard contracts. For example, it might very well be true that the only CT relationships that could have appeared in one or more of the standard contracts analyzed are combinations 1, 4, 7, and 10, and the others did not appear in any of the contracts analyzed.

The purpose of grouping the CT's into braces and/or brackets is to clearly identify variable items within the framework of the provision. An example using the above P definition is:

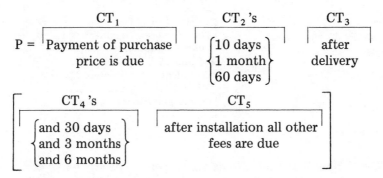

Then each of the following combinations would have appeared in a separate standard contract:

1. CT_1 "10 days" CT_3
7. CT_1 "1 month" CT_3 "and 3 months" CT_5
10. CT_1 "60 days" CT_3 "and 30 days" CT_5

and this combination would have appeared in two of the standard contracts.

4. CT_1 "10 days" CT_3 "and 6 months" CT_5

The semantic and pragmatic characteristics of the contract language are exhibited in the actual wording of the provisions (P) and identified in the narrative following each provision's structural analysis.

11-4.2   General Structure of Computer Purchase Agreements

There are basically twenty-five provisions (P) comprising a generalized standard computer purchase agreement (Table 11-1).

TABLE 11-1

Contract Provisions

P1	Scope of Agreement
P2	[Title]
P3	Price and Transportation
P4	[Price Protection Period]
P5	Risk of Loss
P6	Installation
P7	Taxes
P8	Terms
P9	Security Interest
P10	[Maintenance]
P11	[Training]
P12	[Supplies]
P13	[Additional Features, etc.]
P14	Patent Indemnity
P15	[Warranty]
P16	Limitation of Liability
P17	[Disputes]
P18	[Termination]
P19	[Time Limit on Legal Action]
P20	[Change in Equipment Location]
P21	Assignment of Agreement
P22	[Confidential Information]
P23	State Laws Governing Agreement
P24	[Invalid Provisions]
P25	[Meeting of the Minds]

The first nine provisions (P1–P9) specify what constitutes the agreement, when the computer becomes property of the customer, what costs the customer must bear, and what duties the customer is expected to perform during the initial procurement of the system.

The next four provisions (P10–P13) state which basic services and materials the vendor will provide.

The following group of three provisions (P14–P16) constitute the heart of the contract, listing the duties the vendor will or will not assume given system failures or inadequacies and patent infringement.

Provisions (P17–P19) involve disputes with the vendor over alleged defaults of the agreement and rights of termination. Provisions (P20–P24) specify general considerations which tie up loose ends for the vendor. The final provision (P25) states that the customer has read, understands, and is in complete agreement with everything written into the contracts.

Eleven of the provisions appeared in each of the five standard purchase contracts analyzed. The other fourteen provisions appeared in from one to four of the analyzed contracts (see Table 11-2 for the exact number of contracts in which each provision appeared).

TABLE 11-2
Number of Contracts in which Each Number Appeared

Number of Contracts	Provision (P) Number																								
	1	2	3	4	5	6	7	8	9	10	11	12	13	14	15	16	17	18	19	20	21	22	23	24	25
1											X		X			X					X				
2																		X	X	X				X	X
3			X							X		X													
4		X													X										
5	X	X			X	X	X	X							X		X				X		X		

There is a great deal of variance among standard computer purchase agreements, and as the analysis continues variances increase.

11-4.3 Analysis of Provisions

Each of the analyzed provisions has been detailed in such a manner as to highlight the variable material contained within the rights and duties expressed in the current standard computer purchase contracts. The narrative following each provision will give some interpretation of the provision, as well as suggesting other clauses or terms that should be considered while negotiating the provision. The provisions will be analyzed using the following format:

> P "X" TITLE—WHERE "X" is a digit (e.g., P1), TITLE identifies the provision
> P—where P is the syntax analyzed provision
> NARRATIVE—explanations and suggestions concerning P

Knowledge of the variable terms and the unspecified considerations of the standard commercial computer purchase contracts will yield the customer a strengthened position at the bargaining table when negotiating with any vendor.

Scope of Agreement (P1)

This agreement constitutes the complete and exclusive statement of the agreement between the parties. It supersedes all proposals, oral or written, and all other communication between the parties relating to the subject matter of this agreement.

This agreement may not be released, discharged, changed or modified except by an instrument in writing, executed on behalf of vendor and of the customer. [Any terms and conditions of any purchase order or other instruments issued by the customer in connection with this agreement, which are in addition to or inconsistent with the terms and conditions of this agreement, shall not be binding on the vendor and shall not apply to this agreement.]

> The term "this agreement" is used herein includes
>
> Any applicable Installment Payment Agreement, Supplement, or future written amendment made in accordance herewith
> *All previous memorandums on salesman's comments, communications, representations and modifications, agreements of any nature which relates to the subject matter herein, etc.

The customer, by accepting this provision as is, is limiting himself to those provisions specified in writing within the agreement. "While it is sometimes possible after lengthy and expensive litigation to prove that oral or written representations were made by the supplier and relied on by the user, and that these representations were really part of the contract, it's much cheaper to have a lawyer make sure that the representations are in the contract to start with" [5].

This provision reflects the "Parol Evidence" rule of law which says that no oral evidence may be admitted in court to contradict, alter or vary the terms of a signed written contract. This theory of law holds that you should not sign unless you have read and understand the document and that all of the provisions you negotiated for are in writing.

The vendor's agents often make many commitments, promises, representations, etc., to a prospective customer, which are understandably in good faith. However, when the customer enters into negotiations with the vendor, he should incorporate all relevant commitments, promises, representations, etc., into the language of the contractual agreement by direct reference. Thus, the user provides himself with protection against the effects of the "oversell and underachievement" phenomenon. Also, the customer should make provision for all future modifications to his system ordered in writing (i.e., P13) to be embodied into this written agreement.

Title (P2)

> Title to the equipment furnished under this agreement shall pass to the Customer
>
> On the date of shipment from Vendor, [or on the date of acceptance of the Agreement by Vendor, whichever is later]
> Upon Vendor's receipt of payment of the full purchase price balance

This simply states at what point in time the customer obtains title to the equipment. There is a considerable amount of variation in the terms of this provision. The actual location of the transfer is necessary in determining what state taxes may be applicable. This clause can also be important from an accounting standpoint, for depreciation purposes. Also, the customer may not want title to pass until after installation is complete and certain tests are run on the equipment.

Price and Transportation (P3)

The price shown herein is F.O.B.

{Vendor Plant, or point of shipping.}

Charges for all transportation, rigging and drayage [and cost of insurance] upon the equipment covered by this agreement are to be paid by the customer. Vendor shall deliver the equipment, in accordance with the delivery schedule, which is mutually agreed to by the customer and the vendor. [The method of shipment must be consistent with the nature of the machines and hazards of transportation.]

The provision states that transportation costs will be added to the purchase price. "It is customary for shipping charges to be borne by the prospective user; however, the costs of in-transit insurance, physical installation and final test of the hardware are absorbed by the manufacturer" [5].

It should be noted that there is no legal duty for the customer to pay shipping charges and this item is clearly negotiable. In the past, computer manufacturers succeeded in having the user accept their terms and conditions, much as we accept a standard insurance policy. That generation in the history of EDP contracts is past and users are now negotiating for what they want. Manufacturers are listening, reluctantly in many cases, but the user's voice will be heard and negotiation for terms is becoming a reality.

The provision also makes direct reference to a delivery schedule that is to be mutually agreed upon. It does not mention any recourse available to the customer if he fails to reach a mutual agreement with the vendor. Items that would be considered in reaching an agreement are: the actual date of delivery, whether either party could postpone delivery, penalty clauses for the failure of delivery caused by either party, etc.

If the customer is to assume the shipment costs, he should be allowed some privileges in determining the how, who, and when of delivery.

Price Protection Period (P4)

If Vendor's established purchase price for any equipment shall be lower

Upon date of shipment;
Upon date of installation or 45 days after plant shipments, whichever comes first,

than the purchase price for such equipment as specified in this agreement, the Customer shall have the benefit of such lower price.

The purchase price specified herein shall not be subject to any price increases established by Vendor.

$$\left\{ \begin{array}{l} \text{During the three months immediately prior to the date} \\ \text{of machine shipment—Within the eighteen month period} \\ \text{commencing on the date the agreement is accepted by} \\ \text{Vendor.} \end{array} \right\}$$

$$\left[\begin{array}{l} \text{In the event that equipment has not been delivered [or certified by} \\ \text{Vendor as ready for use] within stated period [and such delay is} \\ \text{caused or requested by the Customer], Vendor may, upon prior written} \\ \text{notice to the Customer, increase the purchase price balance to reflect} \\ \text{any such established price increase.} \end{array} \right]$$

Customer may terminate the agreement for such equipment in its entirety by furnishing written notice to Vendor within

$$\left\{ \begin{array}{l} \text{fifteen} \\ \text{thirty} \end{array} \right\}$$

days of notification of the price increase, otherwise the higher prices shall be effective.

If Vendor's established purchase price for any equipment shall be higher on a date not within the protection period as defined above, the price stated in the agreement shall be increased accordingly.

The provision specifies when the original purchase price may be increased, and the termination rights of the customer if such increases occur. It also states if the purchase price is lower before a specific occurrence the customer receives the lower price. The clause which states that the purchase price can be increased if not delivered or certified ready for use even if it is not the customer's fault is particularly disturbing. The customer should insist that this not be the case if he is not at fault. Again, the material within the braces and/or brackets exhibits the variability of common terms among the vendors' contracts.

Risk of Loss (P5)

Vendor and its insurers relieve the customer from risk of loss or damage to the vendor's equipment up to

$$\left\{ \begin{array}{l} \text{date of delivery} \\ \text{and including the date of installation} \end{array} \right\}$$

$$\left[\begin{array}{l} \text{, except for loss or damage caused by nuclear reaction, nuclear} \\ \text{radiation, or radioactive contamination [caused by the} \\ \text{customer]} \end{array} \right].$$

The risk of loss or damage shall be on the customer

$$\left\{ \begin{array}{l} \text{Upon the date of delivery} \\ \text{After the date of installation} \end{array} \right\}.$$

This provision indicates that the customer is not required to assume any risk of loss or damage up to a specific date. There are some rather unusual exceptions; if they occur the customer would be responsible even though they were not caused by the customer. This seems to be a rather hard item for the customer to accept, and in fact, he should not. There are some differences as to when the customer must assume the full risk, and naturally the customer should negotiate for that date which provides him with the greatest protection.

Installation (P6)

Appropriate installation site specifications will be furnished by the vendor to customer at least

$$\left\{ \begin{array}{l} \text{Thirty (30) days;} \\ \text{In a timely manner} \end{array} \right\} \text{prior to delivery date.}$$

The customer shall, at his expense, have the site prepared in accordance with the vendor's site specification

[{Fifteen (15) days; Thirty (30) days}] before the scheduled
$$\left\{ \begin{array}{l} \text{installation;} \\ \text{delivery} \end{array} \right\} \text{date.}$$

Equipment purchased under this agreement shall be installed and placed in good working order, and the vendor shall certify this fact to the customer.

All boxing, crating, and skidding used in the shipment of the equipment shall be the property of the

$$\left\{ \begin{array}{l} \text{Customer;} \\ \text{Vendor and shall be returnable at its option} \end{array} \right\}.$$

$$\left\{ \begin{array}{l} \text{The date on which the Vendor notifies Customer the equipment is installed, ready for use;} \\ \\ \text{The day (Monday through Friday) following that on which (i) Vendor determines that the equipment has been placed in good working order, or (ii) the equipment is delivered and the Customer fails to provide a suitable installation environment} \end{array} \right\}$$

shall be the installation Date of such equipment for all purposes of this Agreement.

> All charges for installation, including charges [for any necessary materials and] for any labor as may be necessary for placement and unpacking of equipment shall be at Customer's expense.

According to this provision the installation site preparation are the responsibility of the customer and must be prepared in accordance with vendor's site specifications. If the site is not prepared by the customer before the specified date, the vendor may not have to perform any of the tests required to place the equipment in good working order.

This provision states that the vendor shall certify to the customer when the system is in good working order but gives no actual time period. The customer should establish a definite acceptance date, which will be the day that the system is expected to have passed all acceptance tests. If the vendor should fail to meet this deadline, penalties would be imposed.

Acceptance tests should be specified and should include the diagnostic and engineering program tests used by the manufacturer's installation team.

It is important in any new system to test all components and their interaction as part of the overall system. A system should operate without serious equipment failure for a mutually agreed-upon period (usually 40 to 80 hours) before being considered for final acceptance tests.

The final acceptance test procedures should be explicit. Good acceptance procedures involve these factors:

1. The schedule for the acceptance test period should be clearly defined. This schedule should show how the time throughout the day should be allocated to period of operations, idleness, preventive maintenance, etc. The acceptance test period should last at least 30 days in order to obtain a good estimate of both the mean time between failures (MTBF) and mean time to repair (MTTR).

2. During each of the operating periods, the nature of the work which the computer is doing should be clearly defined. The work which the computer should do during the operations period might be divided into cycles. In each cycle the following should be performed:

   a. Process actual, but tested, data for key applications.

   b. Process special data designed to test all of the special features of the equipment and any program packages supplied. (Experience has shown that a selection of actual data will not begin to test all of the possible conditions, therefore, a special input is desirable. Conversely, a set of special data can never be developed to predict all the unusual conditions which occur in practice; therefore, a large section of actual data is also desirable.)

3. Use diagnostic routines which exercise all parts of the equipment, including peripheral units.

By repeating this cycle of tests throughout an operating period, a good test of the system can be obtained. Of course, each program should be designed to check its own operation so that any errors which the system makes are promptly reported. Any output should be checked against specified standard results. The minimum performance level required for acceptability during the test period must be agreed upon in advance. This agreement might include minimum mean time between failures, maximum mean repair time, maximum repair time, and minimum percentage operating time out of total on-time.

The acceptance test should assure the customer that the physical system being installed meets the criteria, procedures, and validation methods used in selecting the configuration.

The costs of the physical installation of the equipment are passed on to the customer in some standard contracts. Usually these costs are borne by the vendor (as cited earlier) and the customer should not be willing to accept such terms.

Taxes (P7)

Customer shall also pay all federal, state, county or other local taxes, however designated, levied or based upon the prices hereunder or on this Agreement or the equipment or its use, and any taxes or amounts in lieu thereof paid or payable by vendor with respect to the foregoing, exclusive of taxes based on net income. Any personal property taxes assessable on the equipment after

{Delivery [to carrier]; Installation and certification;
Ownership passes to customer}

shall be borne by the customer.

This provision passes all tax liabilities on to the customer. These additional costs should be included in the acquisition evaluation. The most favorable tax considerations should be negotiated by the customer with all tax credits passed on to the customer. Furthermore, a detailed list of all applicable taxes should be included in this provision, so the customer has a clear picture of all the additional costs incurred from tax sources.

Terms (P8)

Vendor shall issue an invoice covering the equipment as specified herein

$$\left[\begin{cases} \text{On date such equipment is shipped from Vendor's Factory;} \\ \text{Upon certification or delivery of the equipment by Vendor} \end{cases} \right]$$

Payment of such invoice shall be made in full

{Upon; Within ten (10) days after}

the date of installation.

[unless otherwise provided in an Installment Payment Agreement between Vendor and Customer]

net thirty (30) days; after date of

{[Certification or] delivery; Invoice}.

Failure to pay when due any amount due hereunder shall entitle vendor to collect a late charge for such delinquent payment or interest thereon as stated in the invoice.

Vendor shall issue invoices for such additional charges as may be applicable to this sale under transportation and taxes hereof each such invoice shall be due and payable thirty (30) days from the date of invoice.

This Agreement

Must be received by Vendor on or before the date of installation of equipment; Shall become effective upon the date accepted [and signed]

This provision specifies when the vendor will issue invoices for the amount due on the equipment and when full payment is expected. There is some variation as to when the invoices will be issued and when payment is due. The customer should try to retain the cash required to pay the purchase price within the firm for a long as possible, if the time value of money effect is to be exploited.

One clause states that for failure to pay any amount when due, the vendor is entitled to collect a late charge. It does not specify how this late charge is to be computed and it certainly should do so.

Security Interest (P9)

Vendor retains and reserves a security interest in each unit of the equipment sold hereunder until the full amount due (including the purchase price and other charges payable to Vendor) is paid to Vendor [unless otherwise provided in an Installation Payment Agreement]. A copy of this Agreement may be filed with appropriate state [and/or local] authorities at any time after a signature by the Customer as a financing statement in order to perfect Vendor's security interest. Such filing does not constitute acceptance of this Agreement by Vendor.

This provision specified that the vendor retains a security interest in the equipment sold under this agreement until all payables are received, enabling the vendor to maintain full rights toward the equipment if there is a failure of payment. This is one of the fairly standard provisions and varies in content and meaning only slightly among vendor's contracts.

Maintenance (P10)

The vendor, if requested, will provide the Customer with maintenance service, [and repair or replace parts,] for equipment purchased under this agreement on the basis of the Vendor's published prices and terms for its commercial customers then prevailing. Such service will be available to the customer for

So long as Vendor continues to generally provide it;
*"X" number of months and/or years; *The expected life of the equipment.

Usually, the maintenance requirements and procedures are defined in a separate agreement mutually arrived at by the customer and vendor. This provision states that maintenance service will be available to the customer, but gives no indication as to how long these services will be available. It seems reasonable that the customer be given some long-range figure on the availability of maintenance service other than the short-range period specified in a separate maintenance agreement. Although it should, this provision does not state the recourse open to the customer if a mutual agreement on maintenance service cannot be reached within a specified period of time.

Training (P11)

Vendor shall provide instruction in the operation of the equipment. No charge shall be made for such instructions.

Again, training requirements and procedures are usually mutually agreed upon by the customer and vendor in a separate schedule. The above provision is very limited and not very indicative of current vendor policies. "Almost all manufacturers now charge for some portion of their training and will probably be charging for more in the future" [7]. A list of all available training courses or programs offered to the customer should be incorporated in the above provision with the following information included:

1. Whether the course or program is free or whether there is a charge. (The actual costs should be specified.)
2. The type of personnel assigned to these training sessions.
3. Where the training courses or programs are to be located.

The customer should negotiate each of the above points.

The provision should include a statement of the recourse open to the customer if a mutual agreement about training cannot be reached within a specified time. The customer should also make provision for future training course and programs to be incorporated into the language of this provision.

Supplies (P12)

All supplies for use with the equipment are to be provided at Customer's expense and are to meet the specifications set forth by Vendor. Vendor agrees to sell to Customer for use with Customer's equipment at Vendor's published prices then prevailing for its commercial customers, such supplies (and separate parts) as it shall have available for sale and which may be suitable for use on, or in connection with the equipment.

The necessary supplies are usually specified in a separate agreement. Included in this provision should be:

1. A list of all available supplies and suggestions for which equipment they are suitable (the vendor should also indicate what other supplies, produced by other companies, are acceptable for use on this equipment).
2. A time period for which these supplies will be available to the customer (this would be a long range figure).

Additional Features, Configuration Changes, Model Conversions, Etc. (P13)

Vendor will, upon request, furnish to the Customer, at Vendor's established prices and terms prevailing at the time, any equipment attachments, features and engineering changes as Vendor shall have available for sale and which may be suitable for use on, or in connection with, the equipment. But Vendor makes no representation that such equipment, attachments, features or engineering changes which may be announced in the future, will be suitable for use on, or in connection with, these machines. By agreement between Vendor and Customer, changes in the configuration of the equipment described herein may be made prior to the date of shipment. Additional features and model conversions which are field installable may be ordered in writing by the Customer under this agreement, at any time after its acceptance by Vendor, for installation in the equipment subject to the then prevailing prices and terms and conditions.

For the effective and economic utilization of a computer installation, the availability of compatible equipment and features together with their marketing strategies on this compatibility-conversion issue. Yet some vendors state outright in their contracts that future equipment, attachments, features, etc., may not be suitable for use on, or in connection with, the equipment purchased in this agreement. Clearly the customer should require that a complete list of all the available equipment, attachments, features, etc., be incorporated in this provision. Another consideration, which might be incorporated, is to require the vendor to accept the responsibilities for converting over to a new type system or at least provide specific conversion aids (e.g., decompilers) which will significantly decrease these costs.

The complete generality of the statements made in this provision should be totally unacceptable to the prospective customer.

Patent Indemnity (P14)

Vendor shall defend any suit or proceeding brought against Customer so far as such suit is based on a claim that any unit of equipment sold hereunder (which reference shall include any part thereof), made to Vendor's designs and furnished hereunder constitutes an infringement of any patent of the United States, provided Vendor is notified promptly in writing of such suit and given full and complete authority, information and assistance (at Vendor's expense) for the defense of same. Vendor shall pay all damages and costs awarded therein against Customer, but Vendor shall not be responsible for any compromise made without its consent. If such equipment is, in such suit, held to constitute infringement and its use is enjoined. Vendor shall by its own election and at its own expense, either procure for Customer the right to continue using such equipment, modify it so that it becomes non-infringing, or remove such equipment, grant customer a credit less a reasonable depreciation and accept its return.

$$\left[\begin{array}{l}\text{The depreciation shall be an equal amount per year over the} \\ \text{life of the equipment as established by Vendor.}\end{array}\right]$$

The aforesaid provision is a modernized version of the Patent Indemnity clause that previously existed. For example, Control Data Corporation's patent infringement clause previously stated that if the user was sued because of CDC's patent infringement CDC would help the user, at the user's expense. Obviously, this one-sided provision was unacceptable once the purchaser realized that he was going to have to pay for the defense of a patent infringement caused by the vendor. This provision was later castigated from a public platform with some CDC people present, the form was soon changed. The provision now states that the vendor will take over the defense of any patent infringement suit based on vendor's equipment and that the vendor will pay any verdict for damage and court costs and any defense costs user may incur.

This provision also states that if the equipment constitutes an infringement, the vendor will try to arrange for the equipment to become non-

infringing, or simply remove the equipment and grant a credit less depreciation as determined by the vendor. Visualize the effect such equipment
removal would have on an information system that uses the equipment as its
main processing tool—utter chaos within the organization, not to mention
the fantastic monetary loss.

The customer should be held harmless in all ways, and a clause should
be inserted causing vendor to be liable for any consequential damages to
purchaser-user for any damage he may suffer due to down time, re-design of
his information system, or other loss due to the loss of user of the equipment. Hopefully, customer will attempt to modify this provision to protect
himself against potential loss which he may suffer due to a vendor's patent
infringement.

Warranty (P15)

Vendor warrants that at the date of original installation of the equipment,
all articles furnished herein will be free from defects in material and workmanship under normal use and service. Vendor's sole obligation under this
warranty shall be to repair or, at its option, replace free of charge any such
articles or parts thereof which, within

> {thirty days.; _____ months.; one year or three months depending
> upon the category.}

from the date of original installation, shall have been promptly reported by
Customer to Vendor as defective in material or workmanship, and is found by
Vendor's inspection at the site of installation to be defective in workmanship,
or material.

> Vendor warrants for a period (three months; one year) from date of
> original installation that the equipment listed herein will be free
> from defects in material and workmanship. Vendor's sole obligation
> in the event of breach of such warranty shall be repair or replace-
> ment of the defective unit at no charge to Customer, except for labor
> costs for repair or removal of the defective unit and installation
> of any replacement unit, and transportation charges for delivery of
> the replacement and return of the defective unit. Replacement parts
> shall become the property of Vendor.

> All items of equipment furnished under this agreement may not be newly
> manufactured. Items of equipment which are not newly manufactured
> have been thoroughly inspected, tested and checked for good service-
> ability and are warranted equivalent to new in performance. Newly
> manufactured equipment may contain some used parts which are warranted
> equivalent to new in performance when used in the equipment.

> Items which are of expendable nature both mechanical and electrical, such as ribbons, solid state components, capacitors, etc., are excluded from this warranty.

> This warranty shall not extend to any article that has been subjected to misuse, neglect, or accident or which shall have been altered or repaired (other than by Vendor) in such a manner as to affect adversely its performance stability of reliability.

> The terms of this warranty shall extend only to Customer as a original purchaser.

This provision warrants that the vendor will repair or replace, at its option, any articles furnished in the agreement for a specified period of time (which certain vendors often leave open for negotiation), free of all charge, providing the article is defective and the defect was promptly reported, and there has been no misuse, neglect, or accidental damage. There is often another warranty period in which the vendor will repair or replace certain items, but the customer will have to bear certain costs, namely labor and transportation.

The customer may also negotiate additional extended warranty periods and/or clauses, however, he may have to pay additional amounts for such protection as one would for insurance.

The Uniform Commercial Code, which has been enacted in nearly all states, imposes, by operation of law, an implied warranty of merchantability and an implied warranty of fitness for a particular purpose on goods sold by a vendor. Thus, the vendor may be required by law to repair or replace defective parts with or without specific words of warranty. These implied warranties imposed by operation of law, may, however, be limited or emasculated completely by contractual agreement of the parties. The customer should be wary of a clause usually found under "Limitation of Liability" to the effect that any other warranties (other than those listed in the warranty provision) implied or expressed are excluded from the contract. If the customer agrees to such a clause, he may be negating the law which was passed for consumer protection.

Replies to our survey produced several comments stating that one of the most important provisions of the contract from a negotiating standpoint was the "warranties" provision. One suggested that a list of the specific parts and labor covered under the warranty should be included in every contract.

In addition to the typical warranty provision, namely replacing or repairing defective parts, there should be some consideration given to the consequential damages that an EDP customer might suffer from equipment failure.

Most of the lawsuits brought by unsatisfied customers against vendor-suppliers of computers have involved breaches of warranties of fitness for purpose, performance, etc. Some of the more famous cases have been the *Ford Center Wholesale Grocers, Inc.* vs. *International Business Machine Corporation* in 1968 where the plaintiff won $53,200 for consequential damages resulting from a breach of warranty: the case of *Clements Auto Supply* vs. *The Service Bureau Corporation* (a subsidiary of IBM) in 1969, where the plaintiff won $480,000 in damages and of course the highly publicized Trans World Airlines case against Burroughs in 1971 in which the plaintiff asked for $70 million in damages.

The consequential damage warranty problem is extremely important in that machine failure in an EDP system can be much more costly to a company than machine failure of a drill press or some other typical industrial machine, thus the warranties should be negotiated accordingly.

For example, in a business where a considerable amount of the company's (the customer) transactions are handled via computer, a machine failure can result in very costly consequential damages. It seems reasonable, if the company knows the job flow through its computer system that consequential damages from equipment failure could be approximated and fit into a feasible distribution. Thus, it may be desirable during negotiations to have some estimates of the reliability of the particular configuration for which the company is negotiating (as established under P6, i.e., MTBF and MTTR). The manufacturer (vendor) is often the only one who can provide the user with the relevant performance figures of the equipment. Of interest would be the probabilistic distributions of the "time between failure" and the "time to repair."

With these distributions, and using a simple analytic technique (e.g., Monte Carlo Method), the company could obtain an expected consequential damage figure for a specified time period. Given the level of confidence if this figure, the company (customer) could negotiate for extended warranty on the manufacturer's part. These extensions would cover any skewed or excessive failure rates and/or time to repair. The extended warranty could take several forms.

The manufacturer would provide the company with something akin to high deductable insurance. The company would cover all losses up to the negotiated cash deduction (e.g., the expected consequential damage figure mentioned above).

Then the manufacturer would receive a cash penalty for the amount of loss which is in excess of the cash deduction figure. If the manufacturer is unwilling to negotiate the above, provisions could be made for a backup system that would be capable of processing all of the company's vital information. This form of warranty, while more acceptable to the company, would be difficult to negotiate.

This type of extended warranty will of course result in greater costs for the manufacturer, which no doubt will be passed on to the customer. This is still another point for negotiation, instead of an across-the-line increase on the equipment, the customer should be able to obtain a specified extended warranty for an agreed upon cost over and above the purchase price. This gives the customer who needs greater coverage the ability to purchase it, while being equitable to other customers.

One of the big drawbacks of purchasing a computer, as opposed to leasing, is that the vendor/customer relationship becomes far less intimate after the vendor receives his money. Negotiating this type of extended warranty is a reliable method of "tieing in" the vendor to the customer's operations.

For those who feel comforted in a leasing agreement (in that if the vendor does not respond, the customer just stops the monthly payments) should take a closer look at the termination provision in his contract. Take notice of how fast the vendor can repossess the equipment for failure of payment.

It may be of interest to know that this proposal for a warranty for consequential damages is not as esoteric as it may seem at first glance. Since IBM recently agreed to such a warranty provision, namely to accept unlimited liability for consequential damages when supplying General Services Administration (GSA) with systems. Obviously, GSA has more negotiating muscle than the normal customer, however, this is certainly a ripe area for further study and negotiation.

Limitation of Liability (P16)

The foregoing warranties are in lieu of all other warranties expressed or implied, including, but not limited to, the implied warranties of merchantability and fitness for a particular purpose.

In no event shall Vendor be liable for indirect, special or consequential damages of any nature arising out of the existence, furnishing, functioning or the Customer's use of any unit of equipment or any services provided herein. Vendor shall not be liable for any failure or delay in performance hereunder if such failure or delay is due, in whole or in part, to any cause beyond its control.

Vendor shall not be liable to Customer under any provision of this clause if any patent infringement or claim thereof is based upon the use of the equipment in connection with equipment, software or devices not delivered by Vendor, in a manner for which the equipment was not designed [in compliance with the design, plans or specifications furnished by or on behalf of the Customer as to the equipment, or the claimed infringement of any patent in which Customer or any subsidiary or affiliate of the Customer has a direct or indirect interest by license or otherwise.

> In no event shall Vendor be responsible for excessive wear or malfunction of the equipment caused by the use of the Customer of supplies not conforming to Vendor's specifications.

It is to be noted that the vendor commences this provision with the exculpatory clause which the customer has been warned to be wary of in the previous discussion of the warranty provision. Also, the vendor limits his liability under the Patent Indemnity provision and denies all liability for indirect special or consequential damages such as discussed under the previous provision.

It would appear this provision is rather autocratic as it now stands and should be subject to further explanation and negotiation in the best interests of both parties.

Disputes (P17)

> Should Customer terminate or cancel this Agreement and/or allege that Vendor is in default of this agreement, such issues shall be settled and determined by arbitration. If such allegation of default, whether denominated or based on breach of warranty, misrepresentation, or strict liability, is made as a defense in any suit, such suit shall be dismissed or stayed pending such arbitration. The arbitration shall be conducted under the then current rules of the American Arbitration Association, provided that the arbitrator shall be chosen from a panel of persons knowledgeable in electronic data processing. The decision and award of the arbitrator shall be final and binding and the award so rendered may be entered in any court having jurisdiction thereof. The arbitration shall be held and the award shall be deemed to be made, in the city wherein the Vendor branch office procuring this agreement is located.

One of the major conclusions of the ADAPSO's supplementary survey (dealing with contract analysis) was as follows: "In general, a very little satisfaction is obtained in taking a situation to court. If it is necessary to go to court, one should not be too optimistic about satisfactory settlement. Court action will usually be drawn out over a long period of time" [6].

Arbitration of disputes in business contracts is becoming more and more common since the queing time between filing a law suit in court and the time of final trial may be as long as five to seven years. Also, court litigation can be very costly in terms of lawyer fees and court costs. Arbitration is speedy since the parties can agree upon and select an arbitrator in a very few days, the case can be heard and the matter finally settled. Also, arbitration is comparatively inexpensive since there are no court costs or lawyer fees, the only necessary cost is the fee and expense of the arbitrator which are normally shared equally by the parties. The hearing is comparatively informal and can be held at a convenient place for both parties.

Termination (P18)

Vendor may, at its election, and without prejudice to any other right or remedy terminate this agreement and repossess the equipment upon the filing of a petition in bankruptcy by or against Customer [and the same be not dismissed within thirty days] or should Customer make an assignment for the benefit of creditors, or should a receiver be appointed or applied for by Customer.

Vendor may, at its election, treat this agreement as terminated by Customer and repossess the equipment in the event Customer cancels this agreement prior to delivery, or fails [upon ten days written notice,] to make payments due hereunder or fails to perform any other obligation to be performed by the Customer hereunder and unless it is determined that Customer had cause for termination.

Vendor shall be entitled to receive its damages. [Customer's obligation to pay all charges which shall have accrued shall sruvive any termination of this agreement of any portion thereof.]

Vendor may, at its election, terminate this agreement upon ten days prior written notice to the Customer, at any time following Vendor's acceptance hereof and prior to installation and certification of the equipment in the event of the failure of the Customer to make any cash deposit required or in the event of materially adverse changes in the Customer's credit during such interval as revealed by generally recognized credit reporting services.

Termination of this agreement or any other agreement with Customer for any of these reasons shall be sufficient justification for termination, at Vendor's option, of any or all other agreements between Vendor and Customer.

This provision lists under what conditions the vendor may terminate this agreement. It also states that the vendor may treat this agreement as terminated by the customer and repossess the equipment if the customer fails to make payments due or fails to perform any other obligation to be executed.

An optional clause states that if the vendor terminates this agreement with the customer, he then has the right to terminate any or all other agreements with the customer. Before agreeing to this clause, the customer should evaluate the consequences of termination of any or all other agreements with the vendor.

Time Limit on Legal Action (P19)

> No action, regardless of form, arising out of the transactions under this agreement, may be brought by either party more than {one (1); two (2)} years after the cause of action has accrued [except that an action for nonpayment may be brought within one year after the date of the last payment].

This provision is a simple mechanism which the vendor can use to limit the time period when the customer or vendor can file suit after the cause of action has occurred.

Each state has in their particular code of laws a Statute of Limitations limiting the time in which an aggrieved party to a contract may bring an action in court. Those statutes vary with regard to the time limitation, for example one state may have a six year limitation whereas another state may have a ten year limitation. This provision sets a definite time limit for filing a law suit regardless of where the contract was executed or in what state the parties reside. This is a good provision for both parties.

Change in Equipment Location (P20)

> Customer agrees to promptly inform vendor of any change in the equipment location during the warranty period; not to remove any equipment from the locations at which it is installed, except in emergency without prior written consent of Vendor, which consent shall not be reasonably withheld.

The customer is required merely to notify the vendor of any change in location or installation of the equipment. Moving and re-installing sensitive EDP equipment could cause damage to the equipment which could later be claimed as a defect under warranty. Vendor simply wants to be in a position to limit his warranty liability.

Assignment of Agreement (P21)

> This agreement is not assignable without permission from Vendor and any prohibited assignment shall be null and void.

This provision simply reflects the general rule of law with regard to assignment of contracts. The general rule is that where an assignment of a contract or agreement would materially change the duties of the obligor (vendor) or materially increase the obligor's risks then no valid assignment can be made without the permission of the obligor. Obviously, the assignment of this purchase contract to a financially irresponsible third party or a third party who would use the equipment in a manner adverse to the manner and purpose for which it was designed, could materially affect the duties and increase the risks of the obligor-vendor. Thus, the vendor is simply attempting to control any additional risks by limiting assignments to those situations which do not adversely affect the vendor.

Confidential Information (P22)

All drawings, diagrams, specifications, and other material furnished by Vendor relating to the use and service of the Equipment including the information contained therein, shall remain the property of Vendor and may not be reproduced or distributed in any way except with the written permission of Vendor. All information relative to the design details, operating characteristics and/or coding systems of Equipment supplied direct or indirectly by Vendor (except such information as may be established to be in the public domain or which is disclosed pursuant to judicial or governmental action) shall be received by the Customer in confidence and the Customer shall exercise reasonable care to hold such information in confidence.

This provision specifies that the customer shall keep all information provided by the vendor confidential, except such information as may be established to be in the public domain or which is disclosed pursuant to judicial or governmental action. To prevent any misunderstandings between the customer and vendor, a specific list of the information the vendor wants held in confidence should be included in this provision.

There should also be a general statement concerning information the customer wants to be kept confidential. This would provide that any of the vendor's personnel who would be exposed to such information would hold it in confidence for a specific period of time.

State Laws Governing Agreement (P23)

This Agreement shall be governed by the laws of the state

{where Vendor is located; *where Customer is located; *otherwise agreed upon}.

This provision related to the problem of conflict of laws. If the parties do not agree that the agreement shall be governed by the laws of a certain state, for example—where the vendor is located, where the customer is located or where the transaction is actually consummated, then in case of litigation the court will have to decide what state law applies to the particular contract, there are considerable differences in the various state laws. Thus, it is wise to agree and specify in the contract which state law applies, then in case of litigation both sides will at least be aware of the specific law that applies to the contract. Vendor's choice is usually the law of the state of their contracting office.

Invalid Provisions (P24)

> If any provision or provisions of this Agreement shall be held to be invalid, illegal or unenforceable in any respect under the law of any state, or of the United States of America, the validity, legality and enforceability of the remaining provisions shall not in any way be affected or impaired thereby.

This provision could insure the benefit of either party. As a general rule of law, if a court finds a part of a contract illegal, it may find the illegal part taints the entire contract and the whole contract will be declared void. This provision insures that even if one provision is found contrary to law that the balance of the contract will be enforced. Thus, neither party can escape the general obligation through a legalistic loophole.

Meeting of the Minds (P25)

> The Customer represents that he has read this agreement, understands it and agrees to all terms and conditions stated herein.

The provision states that the customer has read, understands and agrees to the right and duties expressed in this legal relationship.

This provision reflects a basic contract law principle, that is, in order for a contract to be enforceable there must be a meeting of the minds of the offeror and the offeree, the contract must be legal in nature, there must be consideration and the parties must have legal capacity to contract.

Meeting of the minds means mutual assent or mutual agreement to the terms as set out in the contract. The customer should use this provision as a reminder to check if all the oral promises made to him are, in fact, in their written document, does he really understand all the provisions and their implications to him. If not, now is the time to find out, not after the contract is signed and a law suit is pending. Your lawyer is a good man to have at your side at this state of the transaction rather than at your side defending you in the courtroom later.

Other Provisions

Other provisions which should be included in the current general structure shown previously in Table 11-1 are as follows:

P1.4 *Duration
P1.6 *Terminology
P13.5 *Available
       Application Software

While no syntax structure will be given, a few comments are appropriate.

The first provision (P1.4) would give a specified period during which every provision would exert its full effect. The actual period could be something like the effective life of the machine. The second provision (P1.6) would entail the exact and detailed definition of every technical or vague term in the agreement to help prevent future legal action resulting from a misunderstanding or misinterpretation of the various contractual terms. Provision (P13.5) would be a simple list of all the available application software, the cost for each package, and a specified period during which the customer could obtain these programs.

Each of these suggested provisions and the suggested clauses and terms to be added to or modified in the current standard provisions should be incorporated in the current standard computer purchase agreements by negotiations. While to some, negotiations may seem to be a futile effort, much information has been obtained to counter this belief. (This information was obtained in a supplementary request for data sent to two hundred firms who are users of computer equipment.)

REFERENCES

[1] D. H. BRANDON and S. SEGELSTEIN, *Data Processing Contracts* (New York: Van Nostrand Reinhold Company, 1976).

[2] Ibid.

[3] R. L. BERNACCHI and G. H. LARSEN, *Data Processing Contracts and the Law* (Boston: Little, Brown and Company, 1974).

[4] ROBERT PRATT BIGELOW, *Computers and the Law; An Introductory Handbook* (New York: Commerce Clearing House, 1966, p. 42).

[5] Auerback Special Report, p. 23:010.

[6] Ibid., p. 23:010.223.

[7] FREDERIC G. WITHINGTON, *The Use of Computers in Business Organizations* (Reading, Mass.: Addison-Wesley Publishing Company, 1966).

12

FURTHER ASSISTANCE FOR SMALL BUSINESSES

12-1 WHAT IS A SMALL BUSINESS?

What is a small business? What is classified as a small business? IBM or General Motors are obviously not small businesses. Also, although a computer hobby shop at the corner or a mom–pop store are obviously small businesses, the problem of determining what a small business is does not usually categorize the businesses that fall between these extremes. It is at the point where a small business becomes a big business that this determination becomes truly difficult. One could say that a small business is one that has 500 employees; but what about one that has 501 employees and $5,000,001 in sales? Is it still a small business? Does one more employee and one extra dollar really make a difference?

Actually, there are a number of definitions of small business. Fortunately, the federal government organized these definitions when Congress passed the Small Business Act in 1953, creating the Small Business Administration (SBA). The Federal Small Business Administration uses seven different definitions of a small business, based on types of federal aid. These definitions, which are related to loan eligibility, are representative and I believe will be useful to the reader.

The Small Business Administration defines a small business as follows:

"A small business is one that is independently owned and operated, not dominant in its field and meets employment or sales standards developed by the SBA agency." Most important, it must be under a certain maximum size, which varies according to the type of business: manufacturing, wholesaling, service, retail, construction, or agricultural. These standards are as follows:

1. *Manufacturing.* The number of employees may range up to 1,500, depending on the industry in which the applicant is primarily engaged. Therefore, the upper limit may be less.
2. *Wholesaling.* Yearly sales not over $9.5 to $22 million, depending on the type of industry.
3. *Services.* Annual receipts not exceeding $2 to $8 million, depending on the industry in which the applicant is primarily engaged.
4. *Retailing.* Annual sales or receipts not over $2 to $7.5 million, depending on the industry.
5. *Construction.* General construction: average annual receipts not exceeding $9.5 million for the three most recently completed fiscal years. Special trade construction: average annual receipts not exceeding $1 or $2 million for the three most recently completed fiscal years, depending on the industry.
6. *Agriculture.* Annual receipts not exceeding $275,000. They are the smallest so defined. Since 1976, small, independent farms have been included in the definition of small businesses [1].

There are certain other businesses that are excluded from the small business category. They are gambling establishments, newspapers, radio and television companies, nonprofit enterprises, speculators in property, those engaged in lending or in financial real property, and recreational or amusement facilities that do not contribute to the health or general well-being of the public.

Table 12-1 indicates the range of the maximum size allowable by the SBA. To determine whether or not a business qualifies as small, please refer

TABLE 12-1
Maximum Size Standard for Small Business by SBA for Loan Eligibility

Industry	Number of Employees	Values of Output, Sales, or Receipts
Manufacturing	500–1,500	
Wholesaling		$9.5–22 million
Servicing		$2.0–8 million
Retailing		$2.0–7.5 million
Constructing		
General		$9.5 million
Special trade		$1.0–2.0 million
Agriculture		$275,000

to the detailed *Code of Federal Regulations* [2] or inquire at one of the SBA offices listed in Table 12-2.

The SBA's definition of small business is very practical and precise in terms of dollars and cents. However, the disadvantage of using annual sales or receipts is that there is a need to consider the nature of a particular business and the state of the economy. What is a dollar worth today as opposed to its potential worth 10 years from now?

Recognizing that quantitative definitions pose their own problems, the Committee for Economic Development formulated the following definition

TABLE 12-2
SBA Field Office Addresses

Boston	Massachusetts 02114, 150 Causeway Street
Holyoke	Massachusetts 01040, 326 Appleton Street
Augusta	Maine 04330, Federal Building, U.S. Post Office, 40 Western Avenue
Concord	New Hampshire 03301, 55 Pleasant Street
Hartford	Connecticut 06103, Federal Office Building, 450 Maine Street
Montpelier	Vermont 05602, Federal Building, 2nd Floor. 87 State Street
Providence	Rhode Island 02903, 702 Smith Building, 57 Eddy Street
New York	New York 10007, 26 Federal Plaza, Room 3100
Hato Rey	Puerto Rico 00919, 255 Ponce De Leon Avenue
Newark	New Jersey 07102, 970 Broad Street. Room 1635
Syracuse	New York 13202, Hunter Plaza. Fayette & Salina Streets
Buffalo	New York 14202, 111 West Huron Street
Albany	New York 12207, 99 Washington Avenue
Rochester	New York 14604, 55 St. Paul Street
Philadelphia	Bala Cynwyd. Pennsylvania 19004, One Bala Cynwyd Plaza
Harrisburg	Pennsylvania 17108, 1500 North Second Street
Wilkes-Barre	Pennsylvania 18703, 34 South Main Street
Baltimore	Towson, Maryland 21204, 7800 York Road
Wilmington	Delaware 19801, 844 King Street
Clarksburg	West Virginia 26301, Lowndes Bank Building, 109 N. 3rd Street
Charleston	West Virginia 25301, Charleston National Plaza, Suite 628
Pittsburgh	Pennsylvania 15222, Federal Bldg., 1000 Liberty Avenue
Richmond	Virginia 23240, Federal Bldg., 400 N. 8th Street
Washington	D.C. 20417, 1030 15th Street, N.W., Room 250
Atlanta	Georgia 30309, 1401 Peachtree Street, N.E.
Biloxi	Mississippi 39530, 111 Fred Haise Bldg.
Birmingham	Alabama 35205, 908 South 20th Street
Charlotte	North Carolina 28202, Addison Bldg., 222 South Church Street
Columbia	South Carolina 29201, 1801 Assembly Street
Coral Gables	Florida 33134, 2222 Ponce de Leon Blvd.
Jackson	Mississippi 39205, Petroleum Bldg., Pascagoula and Amite Streets
Jacksonville	Florida 32202, Federal Office Bldg., 400 W. Bay Street
Louisville	Kentucky 40202, Federal Office Bldg., 600 Federal Place
Tampa	Florida 33607, Federal Building, 500 Zack Street
Nashville	Tennessee 37219, 404 James Roberston Parkway
Knoxville	Tennessee 37902, 502 South Gay Street
Memphis	Tennessee 38103, Federal Building, 167 North Main Street

TABLE 12-2 *(Continued)*

Chicago	Illinois 60604, Federal Office Bldg., 219 South Dearborn Street
Springfield	Illinois 62701, 502 East Monroe Street
Cleveland	Ohio 44199, 1240 E. 9th Street
Columbus	Ohio 43215, 34 North High Street
Cincinnati	Ohio 45202, Federal Building, 550 Main Street
Detroit	Michigan 48226, 1249 Washington Blvd.
Marquette	Michigan 49855, 201 McClellan Street
Indianapolis	Indiana 46204, 575 North Pennsylvania Street
Madison	Wisconsin 53703, 122 West Washington Avenue
Milwaukee	Wisconsin 53203, 735 West Wisconsin Avenue
Eau Claire	Wisconsin 54701, 500 South Barstow Street
Minneapolis	Minnesota 55402, 12 South Sixth Street
Dallas	Texas 75202, 1100 Commerce Street
Albuquerque	New Mexico 87110, 5000 Marble Avenue, N.E.
Houston	Texas 77002, 808 Travis Street
Little Rock	Arkansas 72201, 611 Gaines Street
Lubbock	Texas 79408, 1205 Texas Avenue
El Paso	Texas 79901, 109 North Oregon Street
Lower Rio Grande Valley	Harlingen, Texas 78550, 219 East Jackson Street
Corpus Christi	Texas 78408, 3105 Leopard Street
Marshall	Texas 75670, 505 East Travis Street
New Orleans	Louisianna 70113, 1001 Howard Avenue
Oklahoma City	Oklahoma 73118, 50 Penn Place
San Antonio	Texas 78205, 301 Broadway
Kansas City	Missouri 64106, 911 Walnut Street
Des Moines	Iowa 50309, New Federal Bldg., 210 Walnut Street
Omaha	Nebraska 68102, Federal Bldg., 215 North 17th Street
St. Louis	Missouri 63101, Federal Bldg., 210 North 12th Street
Wichita	Kansas 67202, 120 South Market Street
Denver	Colorado 80202, 721 19th Street, Room 426
Casper	Wyoming 82601, 100 East B Street
Fargo	North Dakota 58102, 653 2nd Avenue, North
Helena	Montana 59601, 613 Helena Avenue
Salt Lake City	Utah 84138, Federal Building, 125 South State Street
Sioux Falls	South Dakota 57102, National Bank Bldg., 8th and Main Avenue
San Francisco	California 94102, Federal Bldg., 450 Golden Gate Avenue
Fresno	California 93721, Federal Bldg., 1130 O Street
Honolulu	Hawaii 96813, 1149 Bethel Street
Agana	Guam 96910, Ada Plaza Center Building
Los Angeles	California 90014, 849 South Broadway
Las Vegas	Nevada 89121, 301 East Stewart
Phoenix	Arizona 85004, 112 North Central Avenue
San Diego	California 92101, 110 West C Street
Seattle	Washington 98104, 710 Second Avenue
Anchorage	Alaska 99501, 1016 West Sixth Avenue
Fairbanks	Alaska 99701, 501½ Second Avenue
Boise	Idaho 83701, 216 North 8th Street
Portland	Oregon 97205, 921 Southwest Washington Street
Spokane	Washington 99210, Courthouse Bldg., Room 651

of a small business [3]. According to their definition, a small business is one that shares two or more of the following characteristics:

1. Management is independent. Usually, the managers are the owners.
2. An individual, or a small group, supplies the capital and holds ownership.
3. The area of operations is mainly local. The owner(s) and workers live in the local community. Markets need not, however, be local.
4. In comparison to other organizations within the industry, the business is small. So what might seem large in one field would definitely be small in another.

The definition also outlines the common characteristics of all small businesses:

1. Original investment funds come from the owner or his or her relatives or friends.
2. Current operations are financed through bank or trade-supplied credit.
3. Growth derives mainly from reinvestment of earnings in the business.
4. Such a business has a restricted market and is seldom predominant either in its industry or in the business life of its home community.

This type of definition would seem useful. There are no restrictions on physical size or capacity. It is therefore unnecessary to adjust the definition constantly depending on the area of activity.

12-2 WHAT SERVICES CAN SMALL BUSINESS GET FROM THE GOVERNMENT, SBDC, UNIVERSITIES, AND OTHER INSTITUTIONS?

Essentially, small business has not institutionalized its skills of financial and market power as have the giant corporations. Small businesses exist because of their adaptability to the market and personalized skills. They share ownership, control, decisions, and returns of the business as little as possible, and they evolve—many of today's giant corporations were once small businesses. Today there are more than 13 million small businesses, accounting for approximately 75% of all retail and wholesale volume, 40% of manufacturing, 90% of services, and, in general, 95% of all business enterprises. These small businesses face various problems which the government (Small Business Administration), SBDC (Small Business Development Center), universities, and other institutions can help them solve.

The first SBDC was inaugurated at California State Polytechnic University, Pomona, in December 1976. Presently, the number of SBDCs are limited to nine in eight states. However, according to one SBA official, the number of SBDCs may eventually reach more than 200, located throughout the United States. The SBDC is unique in its ability to draw upon the resources of the university, the Small Business Administration, and business communities. It is designed to provide varied types of management assistance to the small business community. The SBDC offers confidential management counseling, prebusiness workshops, problem clinics, courses, and conferences. Balanced management skills are vital to the success of small business. About 90% of small businesses fail within 10 years and Dun & Bradstreet attributes over 90% of these failures to "management inexperience and incompetence." The SBDC offers the businessperson the opportunity to strengthen management skills, thereby improving the chance for success.

Major SBDC services and programs [4] are listed below:

Management counseling. Confidential discussions to identify specific management problems, suggest alternative techniques of modern management, and guide the establishment of an acceptable plan for corrective action.

Prebusiness workshops. One-day examination of the management factors necessary for the successful launching of a new business. A close look at the steps involved in careful planning before and upon entering the business world. Relevant topics are discussed by experts from both the university and business communities.

Problem clinics. Round-table discussions of specific management topics. An opportunity to participate, discuss, ask questions, and solve problems with a specialist and other business people.

Courses and conferences. Management subjects taught in depth by specialists in a series of classes or as a seminar. These may involve a series of ongoing classes or a one-day examination of a particular aspect of doing business.

The major supplier of small business services is the federal government in the form of the Small Business Administration (SBA). Although varied, these services fall into roughly four groups: management assistance, financial assistance, procurement and contract assistance, and technical assistance.

12-2.1 Management Assistance

A Small Business Administration study [5] describes the typical management problem:

The development of effective management is one of the most important problems of small business in most industries. Since the founder of a small firm is usually a technical man, he frequently does not have the required business background. His problem is aggravated by the fact that he cannot afford to retain the specialists in such fields as finance, marketing, or production that are possible in a large company. As the company grows, the talents of the original founder are diluted because his time is required for administrative duties.

Following are some of the organizations and programs that small business people may take advantage of to solve their management problems.

SBA Field Offices. Approximately 100 SBA field offices provide staff to confer individually with owners of small firms regarding specific management problems and to coordinate other consultation services available to small business. (See Table 12-2 for SBA field offices and addresses.)

The Small Business Institute. The Small Business Institute (SBI) is the Small Business Administration's newest management assistance agency. Extended personal counseling is provided at no charge to small businesspersons by the faculty, senior, and graduate students of nearly 400 of the nation's leading business schools.

Service Corps of Retired Executives. The Service Corps of Retired Executives (SCORE) is an organization of over 6,000 retired business executives—both men and women—who volunteer their services to help small business owners solve their problems. Assigned SCORE counselors visit the owners in their places of business. They analyze each business and its problems, offer solutions, and assist the owner through the critical period. This service is also provided at no cost.

Active Corps of Executives. The Active Corps of Executives (ACE) supplements SCORE's services. ACE ensures that management counseling is continually updated. Its members are active executives from all major industries, professional and trade associations, educational institutions, and many of the professions.

The Call Contracting Program. The Call Contracting (formerly 406) Program provides management and technical assistance to firms and individuals qualifying under Section 7(i)(j) of the Small Business Act, as amended in 1974. The professional consultants who provide this assistance must meet strict standards and are selected through competitive bidding or careful negotiation. Assistance is provided according to the specific needs of the individual recipient in categories ranging from junior and senior accounting to complex engineering and electronics. This service is also offered without charge.

International Trade. The SBA works closely with the Department of Commerce, Eximbank, Overseers Private Investment Corp., and other governmental and private agencies to provide small business with assistance and information on export opportunities.

Management Training. To meet local small business needs, SBA's management training program encompasses four types of training for present and prospective small business owners: courses, conferences, problem clinics, and pre-business workshops.

1. *Courses.* The SBA cosponsors management courses for current owners with colleges, universities, trade and professional associations, local business groups, and other organizations.

2. *Management conferences.* The SBA offers a number of conferences on a variety of subjects through professional associations, chambers of commerce, educational institutions, and other groups.

3. *Problem clinics.* The SBA offers short clinics for small businesspersons on specific common problems.

4. *Workshops for prospective small business owners.* These generally relate to personal and legal requirements, financing, organization and planning, records, and sources of business information. The program is maintained on a practical level with the participation and assistance of successful business owners. Efforts are generally directed to the characteristics and problems of a specific business.

Training Materials. The SBA makes available a variety of materials for its co-sponsored management training programs. Some are offered free of charge and a small fee is charged for others. Table 12-3 lists some of the free management assistance publications. If you would like to have a complete list of publications, ask your nearest SBA office.

12-2.2 Financial Assistance

The Small Business Administration study [6] indicates the following financial problems:

> As to financial problems, one area of concern should be the necessity of establishing adequate accounting procedures to permit accurate reporting of financial conditions to management. Small firms must have this information in order to know their costs and to prepare budgets and plans for the future. Without careful financial control, they are at a considerable disadvantage against large competitors.
>
> The rapid growth of small firms in the industry often leaves them in a position of requiring additional capital. Their funds become tied up in inventories and accounts receivable, and their profits are needed to pay taxes. While they would like to borrow to finance further growth, their limited collateral prevents them from doing so. Therefore, they must resort to equity capital. Raising the necessary funds can be a difficult problem, particularly if the company has not planned its growth carefully. Successful small firms find it highly desirable to have on the board of directors an experienced financial man who can evaluate the various methods of financing and suggest sources from which funds might be available.

With the need of small business for financial assistance in mind, let's look at the services available to small businesses, the majority of which are provided by the SBA offices. The SBA offers small businesses many services in the financial area, such as:

Small business loans
Economic injury disaster loans
Product disaster loans

TABLE 12-3
Free Management Assistance Publications[a,b]

Publication Number	Publication Title
32	How Trade Associations Help Small Business
46	How to Analyze Your Own Business
49	Know Your Patenting Procedures
80	Choosing the Legal Structure for Your Firm
82	Reducing the Risks in Product Development
85	Analyzing Your Cost of Marketing
92	Wishing Won't Get Profitable New Products
111	Steps in Incorporating a Business
161	Proving Fidelity Losses
162	Keeping Machines and Operators Productive
169	Designing Small Plants for Economy and Flexibility.
170	The ABC's of Borrowing
174	Is Your Cash Supply Adequate?
176	Financial Audits: A Tool for Better Management
177	Planning and Controlling Production for Efficiency
178	Effective Industrial Advertising for Small Plants
179	Breaking the Barriers to Small Business Planning
180	Guidelines for Building a New Plant
181	Numerical Control for the Smaller Manufacturer
182	Expanding Sales through Franchising
185	Matching the Applicant to the Job
186	Checklist for Developing a Training Program
187	Using Census Data in Small Plant Marketing
188	Developing a List of Prospects
189	Should You Make or Buy Components?
190	Measuring the Performance of Salesmen
191	Delegating Work and Responsibility
192	Profile Your Customers to Expand Industrial Sales
193	What Is the Best Selling Price?
194	Marketing Planning Guidelines
195	Setting Pay for Your Management Jobs
196	Tips on Selecting Salesmen
197	Pointers on Preparing an Employee Handbook
198	How to Find a Likely Successor
199	Expand Overseas Sales with Commerce Department Help
200	Is the Independent Sales Agent for You?
201	Locating or Relocating Your Business
203	Are Your Products and Channels Producing Sales?
204	Pointers on Negotiating DOD Contracts
205	Pointers on Using Temporary-Help Services
206	Keep Pointed toward Profit
207	Pointers on Scheduling Production
208	Problems in Managing a Family-Owned Business
209	Preventing Employee Pilferage
211	Termination of DOD Contracts for the Government's Convenience
212	The Equipment Replacement Decision
214	The Metric System and Small Business
215	How to Prepare for a Preaward Survey

TABLE 12-3 (*Continued*)

Publication Number	Publication Title
216	Finding a New Product for Your Company
217	Reducing Air Pollution in Industry
218	Business Plan for Small Manufacturers
219	Solid Waste Management in Industry
220	Basic Budgets for Profit Planning
221	Business Plan for Small Construction Firms
222	Business Life Insurance

[a]See Table 12-2 for the SBA field office addresses.

[b]These leaflets deal with functional problems in small manufacturing plants and concentrate on subjects of interest to administrative executives.

Displaced business loans

Economic opportunity loans for small business

Occupational safety and health loans

Physical disaster loans

Lease guarantees for small business

Surety bond guarantees

Coal mine health and safety loans

State and local development company loans

Minority vendors programs

Small business investment company program

These loans and programs are described in the following sections.

Small Business Loans

The small business loan program has three primary objectives:

1. To promote small businesses' contribution to economic growth and a healthy competitive environment.
2. To stimulate small business in designated deprived areas.
3. To promote minority entrepreneurship opportunities.

The program provides funds that may be used for construction, expansion, or conversion of facilities; for purchasing buildings, equipment, or materials; or for working capital.

Among the types of loans available, two are the direct and the immediate participatory loans. A direct loan is provided by the SBA if a small business cannot obtain one from a lending institution. An immediate loan is a mixture of money from the SBA and a lending institution. Small corporations can also obtain SBA pool loans for normal business operations. Furthermore, banks, in cooperation with the SBA, can make simplified loans to small businesses if their credit ratings are good, in the same way they give them to large corporations. The economic loan is another service that makes it possible for the disadvantaged man or woman to obtain a loan and management assistance from the SBA.

Handicapped assistance loans are still another category under which two different types of loans are made: one for nonprofit organizations dealing with handicapped people, and one for individual handicapped people who are starting or already own a small business.

The small business loan for health facilities also fits into this area. The Small Business Administration will provide financial assistance to privately owned hospitals and to convalescent and nursing homes for expansion, improvements, and general operations.

Economic Injury Disaster Loans

The objective is to assist business concerns suffering economic injury as a result of certain presidential, SBA, and Department of Agriculture disaster designations. Currently, this program provides direct loans for up to 30 years in amounts of up to $500,000.

Displaced Business Loans

The objective is to assist small businesses to continue in business, or purchase a business, if substantial economic injury has been suffered as a result of displacement by, or location in or near, a federally aided program such as urban renewal or highway construction. The program provides direct loans and guaranteed insured loans.

Economic Opportunity Loans for Small Business

The objective is to provide management assistance and loans up to $50,000, with maximum maturity of 15 years, to low-income or socially or economically disadvantaged persons for the operation of small businesses.

This program provides direct loans and guaranteed insured loans, advisory services, and counseling.

Occupational Safety and Health Loans

The objective is to assist small business concerns which are likely without this special assistance to suffer substantial economic injury caused by compliance with standards established by the Occupational Safety and

Health Act of 1970. This program provides direct loans and guaranteed insured loans.

Physical Disaster Loans

The objective is to provide loans for victims of physical disasters so that they can restore their business. The SBA provides disaster loans in case of storms, floods, earthquakes, or other catastrophes. They make loans to help individuals, business concerns, and nonprofit organizations to repair physical damage or overcome economic injury.

Lease Guarantees for Small Business

The objective is to enable small business concerns to obtain leases by guaranteeing rent payment under such leases. This program guarantees a maximum amount of $2,500,000, or $15,000 in any one month, whichever is less, of aggregate rental under one lease.

SBA also offers a lease guarantee program that will give small businesses a credit rating by issuing an insurance policy to the lessor, guaranteeing the rent for a small business.

Surety Bond Guarantee

The surety bond program offered by the SBA helps small contractors who cannot obtain a bond by themselves. The SBA guarantees up to 90% of a surety bond, and up to $500,000 on contracts for performance bonds.

Coal Mine Health and Safety Loans

The objective is to help small coal mine operators comply with federal health standards.

State and Local Development Company Loans

The purpose of this program is to provide loans to local development companies to enable them to provide long-term loans to small businesses located in their areas. Development companies are corporations chartered for the express purpose of promoting economic development within a particular area.

A local development company is an enterprise incorporated under the laws of the state where the project is to locate, formed for the purpose of furthering the economic development of its particular and specified community and environs, possessing authority to promote and assist the growth and development of small business concerns in the area covered by its operation. It must be primarily composed of and controlled by persons residing or doing business in the locality.

Proceeds of these loans may be used for plant construction, expansion, modernization, or conversion including purchase of land, buildings, *machinery, and equipment*, but not for working capital [7].

Minority Vendors Program

Objectives are:

To identify minority-owned businesses capable of supplying goods or services to major corporations.

To develop specialized programs or assistance to overcome minority-firm deficiencies as identified by major corporations.

To identify new business venture opportunities in which the minority business community can engage.

The SBA's minority enterprise program is directed toward minority-owned, -operated, and -managed businesses. Headquarters are in Washington, D.C., and field representatives are available in regional and district offices to aid and assist the minority businessperson. This assistance consists of advice on financial statements and business projections, preparation of loan applications, and related material.

Small Business Investment Company Program

Under the Small Business Investment Act, the SBA licenses, regulates, and helps to provide financing of privately and publicly owned small business investment companies, commonly termed SBICs. The objective is to improve and stimulate the national economy in general and the small business segment in particular by making long-term capital available to small businesses. It also funds minority small business investment companies (MSBIC). SBICs are directly interested in and have a direct financial stake in the growth and development of companies to which they provide loans. Thus, they almost always demand equity when they grant loans.

However, most successful small businessmen and businesswomen do not believe that the Small Business Investment Companies have proven to be a successful solution to the need for equity capital, because most of the provisions of the Small Business Investment Act appear to favor the SBICs more than the small businesses themselves. If the Small Business Administration is to continue to provide financial assistance to small firms, it must place more emphasis on the quality of the company's management and its prospects rather than on its available collateral.

12-2.3 Procurement and Contract Assistance

The Small Business Administration study [8] shows the following contract procurement problems for the small business:

> Marketing problems of small firms are connected with government contracts. When these companies are very small or when they are competing for contracts in new fields, they have difficulty in being recognized as a reputable supplier. Even after they have established a reputation, they have some disadvantage against large competitors because of their weaker bargaining position. Any single contract is relatively more important to them than it is to a large firm, so they cannot afford to bargain as much for better terms or for a higher fee.

Contract procurement and technical assistance revolves around selling to the federal government. The SBA offers a wide range of assistance to small businesses that want to obtain prime government contracts and related subcontracts. These include: (1) joint set-aside programs and (2) subcontract programs.

1. *Joint Set-aside Program.* Set-asides are made by the government for the purchase of property and services, including but not limited to, contracts for maintenance, repair, construction, research and development, and for the disposal of real and personal property, including timber, minerals, and strategic materials.
2. *Subcontract Programs.* Procurement and technical assistance is also available. The SBA arranges for the fulfillment of contracts by subcontracting to small business concerns for the manufacturing, supplying, or assembling of equipment, supplies, or parts.

The SBA also provides procurement assistance for minority business development. The objective is to ensure participation of businesses owned and controlled by disadvantaged persons in federal contracting and establishing small manufacturing service and construction concerns that will become independent and self-sustaining in a normal competitive environment.

12-2.4 Technical Assistance

Development of successful new products is another problem for small firms in industry. They must spend their research and development dollars wisely to develop profitable products. They obtain some assistance from government research and development contracts, but these must be carefully selected to develop skills and reputation in a chosen area of specialization.

The SBA obtains these government contracts for research and development (R&D) for small businesses. Furthermore, it provides technical assistance for product improvement and development and also apprises small businesses of the results of various R&D efforts conducted by major corporations or the government.

These services may be characterized as production and product assistance, and technology utilization and assistance.

Grants for small business research services is still another aid to the small business world. The SBA will grant money to a small business for the gathering of information relating to managing, financing, and operations.

Management and Technical Assistance for Disadvantaged Businesspersons

The objective is to provide management and technical assistance through public or private organizations to existing or potential businesspersons who are economically or socially disadvantaged or who are located in areas of high unemployment concentration. This assistance consists of project grants.

However, all these services will not help small businesspersons who do not know they are available. Thus, the SBA tries to maintain contact with local small business communities, informing them of their services and encouraging them to make use of same. One special section of the SBA, the Minority Small Business program (MSB), specializes in advertising the SBA's services to potential minority small businesspersons.

In conclusion, the SBA and its affiliates offer a wide range of services to owners and managers of small businesses who wish to take advantage of them.

12-3 SUCCESSFUL SMALL BUSINESSES

The Small Business Administration study [9] indicates that the common characteristics of the successful small businesses are the following:

1. *Good management.* Although most small firms in the industry have been started by people with technical backgrounds, those that are successful have also recognized the importance of the economic aspects of operating a business. The management of these companies also have strong capabilities in other fields such as finance, marketing, production, and personnel relations. They have been particularly adept at selecting and inspiring their employees, in order to obtain enthusiastic participation in the achievement of the company's objectives. Development of the company has not been left to chance, but has been carefully planned by the management.

Successful small companies do not feel that they have any disadvantage in competing with large firms, either for technical or production personnel.

They compensate for their inability to offer high starting salaries by other financial incentives, such as stock option plans for professional and management people, and profit-sharing plans for other employees. Many technical and management people prefer to work for small firms because of the greater opportunity to contribute significantly to the success and growth of the organization. Small companies have the additional advantage of close personal relationship between management and employees; as a result, most of them have had little or no labor problems.

2. *Unique product.* Products handled by successful small firms are very diverse. Although there are exceptions, the most common characteristic of the products are fairly small size, a relatively high degree of complexity, and a market which is limited or must be developed. In most cases they compete on the basis of quality or uniqueness, rather than on the basis of price. Successful small companies rarely compete in the field of consumer products or other mass-produced items.

Many successful small companies have chosen to specialize in selected areas. They have concentrated their efforts and have developed reputations in specialized fields.

3. *Growth.* One outstanding characteristic of nearly all the successful small companies is a strong compulsion to grow. Growth is essential not only to keep abreast of a rapidly growing industry, but also to maintain technical superiority. Another reason for growth is diversification, so that a small company is not so vulnerable to the loss of a single product line.

4. *Product Oriented Research and Development.* In order to develop technologically advanced proprietary products, the successful small companies spend considerable sums on research and development. They also conduct a large amount of research and development under government contracts. Their own efforts are concerned more with product development than with basic research, because they must have immediate and direct returns.

Small firms feel that they derive greatest benefit when they select carefully their government research and development contracts so that they develop skills and reputation in a field of specialization. They consider it unwise to conduct research indiscriminately in widely different areas. Internally sponsored research and development programs are also carefully selected to obtain maximum benefit from the products that result.

5. *Product Planning and Good Marketing.* Marketing has become a more important function in successful small firms than it was a decade ago, because of the increasing competition in the industries. These companies emphasize product planning to be sure that they are offering what the market demands.

REFERENCES

[1] Small Business Administration, *SBA Business Loans* (Washington, D.C.: SBA, 1977), pp. 1–3.

[2] Code of Federal Regulations, *Business Credit & Assistance* (Washington, D.C.: U.S. Government Printing Office, January 1977).

[3] H. N. Broom and J. G. Longnecker, *Small Business Management* (Cincinnati, Ohio: South Western Publishing Co., 1966).

[4] Small Business Administration, *SBA: What It Is; What It Does* (Washington, D.C.: SBA, 1980).

[5] Small Business Administration, *A Study of Small Businesses in the Electronics Industry* (Washington, D.C.: SBA, 1962), p. 117.

[6] Small Business Administration, *A Study of Small Businesses in the Electronics Industry* (Washington, D.C.: SBA, 1962), p. 118.

[7] The New York Times, *Guide to Federal Aid for Cities and Towns* (New York: New York Times, Inc. 1971), p. 161.

[8] Small Business Administration, *A Study of Small Businesses in the Electronics Industry* (Washington, D.C.: SBA, 1962), p. 122.

[9] Small Business Administration, *A Study of Small Businesses in the Electronics Industry* (Washington, D.C.: SBA, 1962), pp. 93–111.

APPENDIX I

COMPUTER
ACQUISITION CASES

CASE A

Pomona Water Works Supply Company*

Alternatives:
Interactive Time-Sharing System
In-House Computer System
Leasing Business Minicomputer

INTRODUCTION

Mr. K. R. Ishi, owner of the Pomona Water Works Supply Company, expressed the desire to develop a better business system for his company. He needed to determine if his company should implement a computerized system, and if so, whether he could afford it. To this end, he requested a computer consultant to perform a systems analysis of his company's information flow and business accounting system. The consultant felt there was a need

*The weighted-score method and T. H. Athey's System approach are used in this case [T. H. Athey, *A Systematic Systems Approach* (Englewood Cliffs, N.J.: Prentice-Hall, Inc., in press)].

to investigate the company's background and problems in detail, and began an extensive review of the company from its beginning.

Historical Background

The Pomona Water Works Supply Co. began business in 1955 as a sole proprietorship by Mr. K. R. Ishi's father. He operated the business from his garage after he retired from the ABC Water Company. The knowledge and contacts he had obtained while working at the water company helped him to start his own business. Three years later, in 1958, Mr. Ishi joined the Pomona Water Works Supply Co. and formed a partnership with his father.

Then, in 1973, Mr. Ishi bought his father out, and in turn his son, Taka Ishi, joined the business. In January 1974, the company was incorporated. Mr. Ishi purchased a plot of land and built a new warehouse. A class 1, licensed truck driver was hired. In that year, their gross sales were $150,000. In 1975, they hired an experienced salesman on a salary and commission basis. Sales increased to $750,000 for the year and business was rapidly picking up. In 1977, sales reached $900,000 and it became necessary to hire a warehouseman. On September 1, 1981, the company opened an office in a newly carpeted and air-conditioned building adjacent to the warehouse. Mr. Ishi rents these buildings to the corporation. The business performed extraordinarily well and sales reached $1.2 million.

The predicted sales for the next few years will range from $1.5 to $1.8 million. At the present time, Mr. Ishi is the sole stockholder of 50,000 shares.

Problem Statement

The Pomona Water Works Supply Co. has the volume of sales and inventory to warrant computer facilities. They house approximately 500 inventory items purchased from 70 vendors. Sales from 110 customer accounts have reached $1.2 million. All accounting and inventory procedures are performed manually. Records of past charges and prices are maintained in drawers or cabinet files for easy access because each customer has his own price structure. Mr. Ishi retains mentally much of the knowledge regarding the customer's pricing structures, sales techniques, and a necessary intuition for when inventory items need to be reordered. Because of the amount of paperwork that has to be done manually, many procedures are not performed on as timely or accurate a basis as they should be. Such procedures are: making entries into the general ledger, taking time to make up budgets, and issuing customer statements.

The information sheets in Figure A-1, outlining accounting and inventory procedures, and the flowcharts in Figure A-2 illustrate the Pomona Water Works Company's present system.

Order Entry/Invoicing

Number of sales orders/month	175
Average number of part lines/order	12
Do you have scheduled shipments?	Yes
Average number of expense (sales, tax, freight, etc.) and comment lines/order	2
Number of one-time "ship-to" (or drop-ship) customers	1 or 2
Average number of days a customer sales order is in the house	3-5 days av. 2-3 weeks big jobs
Do you have sales commissioning?	Yes
If yes, do you have "split" commissions (paying more than one salesperson for a sale)?	Yes
Number of invoices/month	400
Number of credit memos/month	5
Number of part lines/invoice	24
Number of salespeople	2

Payroll

Number of employees	7
Number of pay periods	Weekly, commission monthly

Accounts Payable

Number of vendors	70
Number of open invoices	None
Number of distributions to the general ledger/invoice	0
Number of distributions to jobs	0
Percentage of invoices offering discounts	2%
Number of checks written per month	115-120

Figure A-1. Accounting and inventory procedures for Pomona Water Works Company.

Accounts Receivable

Total number of customer accounts (bill-to and ship-to)	110
Number of open invoices	None
Number of cash receipts/month	100-120
Number of customer statements/month	5

General Ledger

Number of general ledger accounts (chart of accounts)	85
Do you have comparative financials?	No
Do you have budgeting?	No
If yes, how many accounts have budgets?	N/A
Number of general journal entries per month	15

Cost Planning and Control (Job Cost)

Number of jobs open	None

Inventory Control

Number of part numbers	Not used
Number of stocking locations	Not used
Number of items that you would like to track for 13 months sales or usage history	200
Number of material withdrawals receipts and issues/month	None

At the present time, the company does not have an inventory system but would like to set one up. The number of items on inventory at this time is 500.

Purchase Orders

Number of open purchase order line items	N/A
Number of purchase order line items entered/month	80-100 12 lines/order

Figure A-1. (*Continued*)

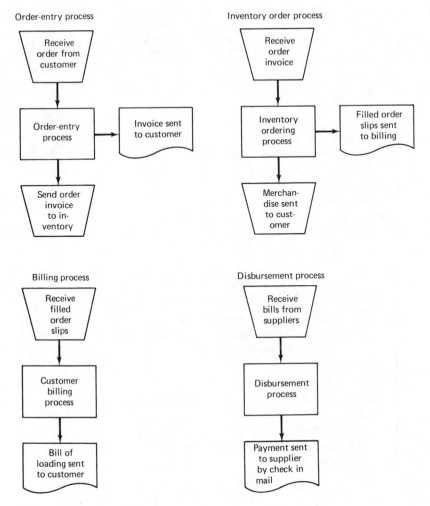

Figure A-2. Flowcharts for Pomona Water Works Company.

SYSTEM ANALYSIS

Return on Investment

Mr. Ishi would probably use current assets to finance computer facilities, and would require a minimum of 15 to 20% return on investment to protect the profits the firm is now making. The current year assets are noted in Figure A-3, and a statement of income is provided in Figure A-4. From these two statements, the current return on investment (ROI) can be calculated as follows:

$$\text{ROI} = \frac{\text{profit on sales}}{\text{total assets}} = \frac{\$56,098}{\$282,051} = 19.8\%$$

Assets

Current assets			
Cash		$ 16,297	
Accounts receivable	$256,357		
Less: doubtful accounts	42,830	213,527	
Merchandise inventory		46,823	$276,647
Fixed assets			
Equipment		12,655	
Less: accumulated depreciation		7,378	5,277
Other assets			
Organization costs: net			127
Total assets			$282,051

Liabilities and Stockholders' Equity

Current liabilities			
Accounts payable		$ 67,435	
Payroll and sales tax payable		25,405	
Federal income taxes payable		7,746	
Accrued expense payable		13,882	$114,468
Long-term liabilities			
Due to stockholders			55,000
Stockholders' equity			
Capital stock outstanding		50,000	
Retained earnings		62,583	112,583
Total liabilities and stockholders' equity			$282,051

Figure A-3

The projected assets are noted in Figure A-5, and a projected statement of income is provided in Figure A-6. Again, from these two statements the projected return on investment can be calculated as follows:

$$\text{ROI} = \frac{\text{profit on sales}}{\text{total assets}} = \frac{\$87,006}{\$401,661} = 21.6\%$$

Since the ROI reached 21.6%, it met the minimum requirement set by Mr. Ishi. The Pomona Water Works Company's financial position can support computer facilities.

Pomona Water Works Supply Co.
Statement of Income
for the Current Year Ended December 31

Sales		$1,182,794
Cost of goods sold		
Inventory beginning January 1, 1980	$ 57,855	
Purchases	970,388	
Freight in	390	
Total	$1,028,633	
Less: ending inventory December 31, 1980	45,211	983,422
Gross profit		199,372
Operating expenses		
Auto and truck expenses	$ 13,900	
Advertising	312	
Legal and accounting	1,844	
Depreciation	2,731	
Dues	30	
Interest	46	
Insurance	2,790	
Office expense	1,500	
Rent	3,680	
Repairs	657	
Salaries	38,950	
Contract labor	355	
Taxes	7,145	
Telephone	2,637	
Utilities	555	
Miscellaneous expenses	425	
Profit contribution	13,735	
Employee welfare	200	
Total		91,492
Net operating profit before tax		$ 107,880
Federal income tax		51,782
Net income		56,098

Figure A-4

Cost Savings

The operating cost savings summaries shown in Figures A-7 and A-8 are estimates of incorporating computer facilities at the Pomona Water Works Co. for the next 5 years. These estimates will be instrumental in figuring the break-even point (Figure A-9) where the company will begin to start making a greater profit over the costs of the company facilities.

```
Pomona Water Works Supply Co.
Projected Balance Sheet
December, Next Year

                          Assets

Current assets
  Cash                        $ 16,297
  Accounts receivable           333,264
  Merchandise inventory          46,823        $396,384

Fixed assets
  Equipment                     12,655
  Less: depreciation             7,378           5,277
            Total assets                       $401,661
```

Figure A-5

```
Pomona Water Works Supply Co.
Projected Income Statement
December 31, Next Year

Net sales                                      $1,587,000
  Cost of goods (30% increase)    $1,278,448
  Less:  tangible cost saving        -37,000
                                   $1,241,448    1,241,448
      Gross profit                            $  345,552

Operating expenses
  Salaries                            53,742
  Other expenses                     101,491
  Lease a computer                    21,000
                                   $ 176,233      176,233

Gross operating income                           169,319
  Interest on debt                                 2,000
  Net income before tax                          167,319
  Federal income tax                              80,313
  Net income                                      87,006
```

Figure A-6

Users of the System

Since Mr. Ishi is going to make the decision regarding computer facility selection, he should know the areas in which a computer could benefit his company. After studying the current system and employees, the computer consultant concluded that Mr. Ishi and the company employees would be able to utilize a computerized business system. For instance, Mr. Ishi and Taka

374

Operating Cost Summary (thousands of dollars)	Year				
	1	2	3	4	5
Salary	$ 2	—	—	—	—
Maintenance	20	22	25	27	30
Hardware	25	—	—	—	—
Programs	4	2	1	1	1
Totals	51	24	26	28	31
Cumulative totals	51	75	101	129	160

Figure A-7

Cost Savings Summary (thousands of dollars)	Year				
	1	2	3	4	5
Tangible cost savings	6	7	8	9	10
Elimination of redundant tasks	4	5	6	7	8
Accounts receivable reduction	5	7	9	11	13
Sales analysis	10	12	14	15	17
Totals	25	31	37	42	48
Cumulative totals	25	56	93	135	183
Intangible cost savings					
Improved customer service	4	5	6	7	8
Sales forecast improvements[a]	1380	1587	1825	2098	2413
Totals	1384	1592	1831	2105	2421
Cumulative totals	1384	2976	4807	6912	9333

[a] Sales are forecasted to increase approximately 15% each year.

Figure A-8

Ishi might use the system to obtain sales analysis and other management reports and information that can easily be made available by the use of a computer. This would assist them in making decisions as president and manager, respectively, of the Pomona Water Works Company. The salesman could access information about customer accounts and the various pricing structures. The warehouseman could use inventory information on the computer

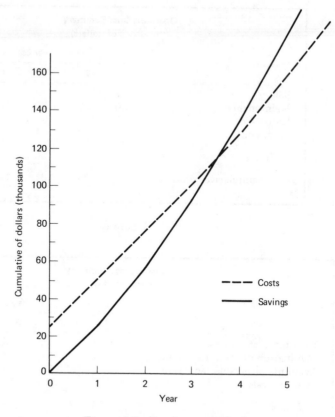

Figure A-9. Break-even analysis.

to strengthen, maintain, and access the inventory system and procedures. The system would be of great assistance to the secretary/bookkeeper in doing the bookkeeping, checking on customer accounts for the salesman, and with the ordering, purchasing, and scheduling of inventories and deliveries. The truck drivers could also use computer-generated reports to determine the items to be delivered and count of items to be picked up at different vendor locations for replenishing of stock. Each driver would also receive a delivery route scheduled by the computer to save both fuel and time for efficiency.

Constraints

The constraints Mr. Ishi established to make an alternative solution feasible are:

1. All operating and equipment costs and supplies must be less than $21,000 per year.
2. The system must be cost-saving and provide profits in the near future.

376

3. There must be no increase in personnel, and the system must be designed for the quality of employees now working at the company.
4. The system should be easy to learn and operate.
5. All information and records must be easy to maintain and access.
6. All programs must be packaged so as not to require hiring a programmer.
7. The programs must include accounting, inventory, and sales analysis applications.
8. The physical size of the hardware must be no larger than a medium-size office desk.
9. The system must be quiet and not require a separate air-conditioned room.
10. If an in-house computer is chosen, the purchase or rental price must not exceed $25,000. If leased, it must be with an option to buy.

These are the constraints that he established in discussion. In addition, there are external constraints that he would probably encounter in utilizing a computerized system. These external constraints include:

1. There must be sufficient records and reports of sales, purchases, business expenses, and depreciation of equipment in the event of an IRS audit.
2. There must be sufficient reports regarding the amount of sales tax charged to customers for the State Board of Equalization.
3. In conformity with the federal government's Privacy Act, the information contained within the memory and storage of the computer, and any records printed out about the employees or customer accounts, must be protected by appropriate security procedures (to keep information out of the hands of unauthorized personnel and other outside parties).

Criteria

There are numerous criteria to consider in analyzing the different computer facilities available for a small business. These factors of comparison, and how they relate to one another, are only preliminary measures which will provide a better understanding as to which alternative will be best suited for the company.

Hardware configurations will describe the computer components that each system incorporates. The components vary according to the design of the system and also depend on whether a system is designed for in-house or time-sharing use. Comparable alternatives will include at least one terminal in the office and, preferably, another in the warehouse. The printer must be capable of printing forms and sales analysis reports. The central processing unit must meet specifications to handle the 500 inventory items and the accounting and inventory procedural programs.

Hardware specifications can vary slightly and still meet the needs of the company. The word size, memory size, and mass storage capacity will be considered. The system must be equipped to handle an increase or an upgrade of compatible equipment. The specifications will be what each basic system has to offer, and for comparison purposes those specifications that would make each system more on the same comparable level.

The software will be evaluated on the provision of a utility program to aid in maintaining and running the system, the number of languages the system can utilize, and the availability of package programs for accounting, inventory, and sales analysis. A system with more software applications will be considered more efficient and valuable. The capability of the present staff to handle all procedures is a major objective. Therefore, the system chosen should provide software that is easy to learn and use.

Customer education is offered by computer firms or time-sharing services to the small business that is about to engage in computer facilities, and is of major importance for the continuance of a profitable business. The quality of the education should be evaluated accurately from the observer's point of view before classes or training are taken. This can be done by considering how many days of training will be provided, the course content, and the cost to the customer. The prospective customer can then determine whether the customer education is sufficient and valuable enough for all the costs concerned.

Reliability and availability are two factors that should not be neglected in the selection of computer facilities. An in-house computer system should be as close to 100% reliable as possible, whereas the reliability of a time-sharing service's computer would be beyond the direct control of the Pomona Water Works Supply Co. A time-sharing company should take all measures to ensure a highly reliable service. The availability of an in-house system varies from that offered by a time-sharing service. In either case, hopefully, the computer will be available whenever it is to be accessed, or within a reasonably short time thereafter.

Computer facilities maintenance is also a major concern. If a system does not operate properly, the user will be tempted to feel that present methods were more reliable and more likely to get the job done. The computer firm's maintenance service methods should be evaluated. This could be accomplished by checking their past records and determining how often their systems needed repair. The monthly maintenance costs are important in regard to the overall cost structure established in the constraints. Usually, if a time-sharing service is installed, a large part of the maintenance concerns are beyond direct control; however, equipment on the premises will need upkeep and a quality time-sharing service should incorporate adequate maintenance service to provide the best computer service possible.

The initial cost of the computer facilities most attracts the company's attention and is a very important factor. The initial cost will include the basic price of the computer system, if purchased, the first outlay for a monthly leasing fee, or the minimum payment for the time-sharing service. The lower the cost, the more desirable the system.

The monthly operating cost will consist of any monthly charge incurred from the operation or use of a computer system. The cost will include monthly maintenance charges; software packages monthly rental, if any; supplies such as forms or paper on which the output data will be printed; the total sum of weekly wages of any computer-dedicated personnel; and miscellaneous charges incurred by incorporating computer facilities.

Physical characteristics will be based on approval of the components used in the office. If the computer is in-house, Mr. Ishi stated that (1) the total size could not be much larger than a medium-size office desk; (2) the components should require an environment other than a temperature-controlled office room with an air-filter system; and (3) the system must be relatively quiet the major part of the day; for example, a printer may increase the noise level of the office but would not be used 8 hours daily.

The criterion of physical characteristics is the least important because esthetics is largely subjective and a small business computer would usually not be excessive in size. Also, because of modern technology, computer systems and all their components have generally been designed to operate in the normal business environment so as not to require any extra or special facilities. This permits more small businesses to utilize computer facilities with the least amount of extra cost or difficulty and still obtain the capabilities of some larger computers.

Finally, one should determine if security measures are special features included in the system (hardware as well as software) or consist of a special safe or a locking system in the office and warehouse.

These criteria should provide some idea as to how a weighted-score analysis can be used to choose the right alternative for a company. After some investigation of feasible alternatives, three possible alternative solutions have been identified for Mr. Ishi's company.

ALTERNATIVES

The first alternative is an interactive time-sharing system offered by Rapid Time-Sharing Co. It is a remote computing service located in the general vicinity of Pomona Water Works Supply Co., which would reduce communication-line costs. Data terminals could be located in both the general office for managerial and clerical use and in the warehouse for inventory purposes. The computer supplying the terminals is powerful enough to support 500 inventory items, accounting reports, sales analysis information, and inventory data.

The system suggested by the Rapid Time-Sharing representative for Mr. Ishi's firm is the Rapid 123, their computer-based business system for the distribution industry. The system offers (1) inventory management, (2) credit management—the ordering and paying habits of each customer, and (3) customer services—verifying credit and inventory and controlling pending orders, backorders, and stockouts. It also provides profit-generating features, such as measuring current-month and year-to-date sales. As their brochure states, the Rapid 123 handles inventory, accounts receivable, sales, purchasing, and order entry/invoicing operations more efficiently to help make better decisions, run a more orderly business, and achieve greater profits.

Since the estimated monthly charges do not exceed $1,600, the service's annual costs will not exceed the $21,000 established as a constraint. Instructional use will accompany implementation of the system. Application programs for accounting, sales analysis, and inventory procedures will be included, and the remote computing service center has proven to be a reputable firm.

The second alternative is a small business minicomputer that would be purchased as an in-house system. This is the NTC 499, which will provide one keyboard console terminal for the general office; a printer that will be able to handle specialized forms at 120 characters per second (cps); the central processing unit (CPU) will have 64K bytes of memory and the capability of handling 500 inventory items, accounting, sales analysis, and inventory procedure programs to produce the proper information and reports in the aforementioned areas. Training will be provided to facilitate easier implementation. The physical appearance of the system will be sufficiently attractive and small to place in the office. The purchase price of the system is less than the stipulated $25,000 and maintenance costs will be low ($2,400 annually). The total cost is $24,600.

The third feasible alternative would be the ADVAC BC/8 business minicomputer leased with the option to buy. This would allow Mr. Ishi to verify that the equipment is suitable for his purposes. This system will be much the same as any other small business computer. However, with the lease, it is possible that different hardware components could be tested until the proper system is designed for the Pomona Water Works Supply Co.

The BC/8 system offers many packages. The one selected for comparison includes a CPU with 128K bytes of memory, shared direct memory access (DMA) controller, one work station with keyboard, dual diskette drives (1-megabyte diskette), plus a 20-megabyte cartridge disk, a bidirectional 200-cps printer, and an additional cathode ray tube (CRT) work station for the warehouse area.

The maintenance costs of $338 monthly ($4,056 yearly) will be added on to the lease price, and excellent application programs are available. The physical components of this system will be sufficiently attractive and small to place in the office. Training will be provided. The lease will cost approximately $7,200 per year, and the initial charge for software will be $1,000. Thus, the first year's cost will be $12,256, substantially less than the maximum of $25,000.

WEIGHTED-SCORE ANALYSIS

The weighted-score analysis technique applies relative weights to each criterion, which then becomes the multiplier for each system's distinct criteria ratings given to make the analysis decision.

A measuring device called a performance chart is established by proceeding through a series of steps as follows. First, each criterion is assigned a relative value, as demonstrated in Table A-1. Each criterion is then assigned a specific value derived from this ranking. Subsequently, each alternative system is measured against the criteria and assigned a numerical score. Alternative systems are then compared according to their cumulated values. The weighted-score chart set up for this study is shown in Table A-2. Scoring standards for each system parameter are 0 to 10, with 10 being the maximum score obtainable for each criterion.

Discussion of Scores

The ADVAC BC/8 proves to be the best alternative, as it received the highest total score on the weighted score.

Hardware was one of the important criteria. On this criterion, the BC/8 received the highest rating of the three systems. The system consists of a central processing unit that combines a control processor, which is an Intel 8086; a 16-bit microprocessor; and a macroprocessor comprised of four microprocessor chips. The packaged system will include a CPU with 128K bytes of memory, shared direct memory access controller, work station with keyboard, dual diskette drives (1-megabyte diskette), one 20 megabyte cartridge disk, and a 200-cps bidirectional character printer. These peripherals and the CPU adequately satisfy the Pomona Water Works and Supply Company's needs.

Software is a very important criterion, and the BC/8 offers BASIC, FORTRAN, COBOL, RPG, and DBMS. In an effort to keep with target markets, ADVAC has introduced an accounting management system, a wholesale application management system, and a general business applications system, which covers all the application areas Mr. Ishi's firm needs.

This system is available on a lease with an option to buy. The initial cost of the lease would be $8,200 plus $338 monthly maintenance fees. The terms of the lease would be a 5-year extended term plan. A lease-to-sale conversion is encouraged, with the following purchase option credit plan:

> 80% of the monthly lease charges will be credited toward the purchase price if the purchase occurs within the first 6 months of the lease.
>
> 60% of the monthly lease charges will be credited toward the purchase price if the purchase occurs after the first 6 months of the lease.
>
> The maximum purchase option credit can never exceed 45% of the purchase price. (This point is usually reached after 30 months of leasing.)

	0	1	2	3
Criterion		Marginal		Below Average
Hardware (minimum CPU, number of terminals, printers, type of disk)		CPU (32K), 1 terminal, 30 cps printer, floppy		CPU (48K), 1 terminal (1 option), 45 cps or 120 cps printer, floppy or cartridge
Specifications (word, memory, disk size, upgrade)		4-bit, 32K, 1M no		8-bit, 48K, 5M yes, up to 10M
Software (languages, application programs)		BASIC, general accounting		BASIC, FORTRAN, general accounting, sales analysis
Initial costs		$25,000		$23,000
Customer education		1 day seminar		3 days instruction
Reliability and availability		80% reliable, 1–2 hr/day		95% reliable, 50% of time
Maintenance		1 week service, $20/hr fee		2 days service, $20/hr fee
Monthly operating costs		$1,750		$1,500
Physical characteristics		Larger than 2 large office desks, temperature control		Size of 2 large office desks, temperature control
Security		None		Software (password)

Criterion	Weight	NTC 499	ADVAC BC/8	Rapid
Hardware	5	5(25)	7(35)	5(25)
Specifications	5	5(25)	5(25)	5(25)
Software	5	4(20)	5(25)	4(20)
Initial cost	5	1(5)	7(35)	3(15)
Customer education	3	6(18)	6(18)	10(30)
Reliability and availability	3	10(30)	7(21)	7(21)
Maintenance	3	10(30)	6(18)	10(30)
Monthly operating costs	3	10(30)	8(24)	1(3)
Physical characters	1	7(7)	6(6)	6(6)
Total Scores		190	207	175

Average	Above Average	Outstanding
CPU (64K), 2 terminals, 45 cps and 120 cps printers, Winchester or cartridge	CPU (128K), 4 terminals, 45 cps and 300 Lpm printers, Winchester and cartridge	CPU (256K), 8 terminals, 300 and 600 Lpm printers, disk pack
8-bit, 64K, 10M yes, up to 20M	16-bit, 128K, 20M yes, up to 80M	16-bit, 256K, 50M yes, up to 300M
BASIC, FORTRAN, COBOL, report generator, general accounting, inventory, sales analysis	BASIC, FORTRAN, COBOL, RPG, DBMS, general accounting, most applications	BASIC, FORTRAN, COBOL, RPG, PASCAL, DBMS, report generator, general accounting, all applications
$17,000	$14,000	$11,000
7 days instruction	12 days instruction	18 days instruction
95% reliable, 80% of time	95% reliable, 95% of time	99.9% reliable, 99.9% of time
1 day service, $17/hr fee	8 hour service, $12/hr fee	5 hour service, $10/hr fee
$1,250	$1,000	$850
Size of one large office desk	Size of medium–large office desk	Size of regular office desk
Software (password) hardware (key)	Software (password, account number) hardware (key) lock	Software (password, account number) hardware (key, other code) alarm system, lock

ADVAC provides quite an extensive educational training period and seminars. Reliability and availability are both estimated to be 95%. Maintenance service covers both preventive and remedial maintenance from 8:00 a.m. to 3:00 p.m. 5 days a week, with monthly maintenance schedules starting the day of the sale or lease.

The physical characteristics fit within the constraints, as the system is housed in a "stand-alone desk-style unit." The system is designed for an office atmosphere in looks and in noise level. As for security, the office itself has an alarm system and bolted doors, but a safe should be purchased to lock away the diskettes. The system has password security in order to get into the application programs.

As can be seen, the BC/8 meets the company's constraints and the reports generated will meet the external constraints.

CONCLUSION

In proceeding through the weighted-score method of comparing criteria and facts with feasible alternatives, the ADVAC BC/8 is seen to be the best of the alternative systems in this case.

With the installation and implementation of the ADVAC BC/8, the Pomona Water Works Supply Co. will benefit from computer facilities.

CASE B

The Dalton Finance Business Office*

Alternatives:
Enhanced Manual System
Time-Sharing System
In-House Computer

INTRODUCTION

Problem Statement

The home office of Dalton Finance Company in Los Angeles, California, is responsible for all accounting functions of the business in the Los Angeles area and also provides banking services for three car dealers. Their manual accounting system was the subject of a previous efficiency study.

Lately, Jim Talbert, the business manager, has recognized that this system cannot handle the paperwork and the president, Ralph Goodwin, has observed delays in the receipt of financial reports from the business office.

Findings

A preliminary investigation has revealed that the office staff is working at full capacity and that the system is backlogged in several areas. Compared to other businesses, the office handles an excessive amount of paperwork for its work volume. This is due to the complexity of serving three independent car dealers with a single accounting system. Moreover, state and federal regulations require many checking and posting procedures, thus limiting potential improvements of the manual system.

Implementation of changes recommended in the previous system study has further increased the work load. The old and revised systems are operating simultaneously for data verification and this duplication adds to the backlog.

*This case was originally written by Roger Manfield. The weighted-score method and T. H. Athey's System Approach are used in the case [T. H. Athey, *A Systematic Systems Approach* (Englewood Cliffs, N.J.; Prentice-Hall, Inc., in press)].

Moreover, Mr. Talbert wishes to expand services with minimum additional cost. Because of expansion plans and the need to reduce paperwork, a computer system has always been a distinct possibility. Since the Dalton branch office in San Francisco is currently in the process of computerization with a TR400 accounting computer, Mr. Talbert requested that the study address the possibility of adding a computer to the Los Angeles office.

Dalton is a very small organization with only four clerks and one supervisor in addition to Mr. Talbert. None of the office personnel has had any contact with computerized systems.

Considerations

Mr. Talbert directed the consultant to identify possible solutions to the problems in the system and to present feasible alternatives to him, including the recommendation of a "best" solution. If acceptable, Dalton will implement this recommendation.

Given such a broad range of action, the consultant will assist Dalton's management in defining the criteria, constraints, and value weightings.

CONSTRAINTS AND CRITERIA

Constraints

Legal/Regulatory. Record-keeping functions are subject to state and federal regulations. These limit both the number of possible adjustments to the manual system and possible approaches to computerization. Those most relevant to machine options specify that current records must be retained on the premises, thus eliminating the use of a remote batch service bureau.

Turnabout Time. Accurate reports should be available quickly and be updated as frequently as necessary. Balance reports for ledgers and for trust accounts must have sufficiently current information to keep the manager up to date. Financial reports must be timely enough to allow short-term investments of available funds for interest income.

Cost. The management is uncertain about this area. Rough estimates project initial cost at less than $30,000 and amortized cost over 5 years as less than or equal to hiring another office worker at approximately $10,000 per year. As nothing more definite is available, the solution should seek to minimize costs.

Personnel and Skills. The new system must not displace any office workers and will have to make maximum use of existing office skills. Specialized retraining should be kept to a minimum.

Space Used. The office is already crowded. Any new unit must be desk-size or smaller.

Work Capacity. The system must be able to handle the present workload of 250 accounting transactions per day and to store existing files.

Growth Capability. The new system must afford the capability of at least 100% expansion.

Criteria

Cost. The new system will be judged on minimal additional cost.

Capacity. The new system will be judged on how much processing capability it affords. Obviously, an enhanced manual system can meet present capacity, whereas a computer system offers extended capabilities. The San Francisco office's TR400 system (16K core, 1-megabyte mass storage—preferably random access, 60-cps printer) will be used as a minimum specification for machine capacity.

Expandability. The new system will be judged on its capability for handling up to a 100% increase in workload.

Personnel Training. The system will be judged on ease of personnel training and minimization, availability, and cost of specialized training.

Outside Help. Systems will be judged on the need for additional outside help. Outside help may be used as an inexpensive supplement to regular personnel, as in the case of a part-time worker supplementing a manual system.

Backup. The new system will be judged on the availability of an effective backup system in the event of primary system failure. In a manual system, files are handled physically; however, the sheer volume of paper can be a very negative factor. In a machine-oriented system, records are retained on a magnetic medium that is easy to access through the machine. But if the machine fails, two questions arise: (1) is a compatible machine available in the interim, and (2) are there backup records and an audit trail of transactions? The efficiency of servicing and machine maintenance are also important.

ALTERNATIVES

Enhanced Manual System

The simplest and least radical way to improve the existing system would be to streamline the manual system within the bounds set by the legal constraints. This could be accomplished for the current volume of work by improving procedures and decreasing business hours. Additional office workers could handle an increased volume of work.

Examples of improving procedures follow: add a photocopy machine inside the office rather than continue to use the copier in another part of the building; revise the obsolete insurance report form to include the most current information; use more multipart forms when multiple copies are required; reduce the amount of duplicate record keeping, such as the present system of recording transactions on both ledger cards and in ledger books.

Decreasing business hours (during which the customer windows are open) frees time for batch operations at the beginning and end of each day. This is a common procedure in commercial banks.

Implementing such improvements would eliminate the backlog and possibly increase the maximum business volume by about 5 to 10%. However, the management desires additional expansion, and hiring more personnel would be the only way to further expand the manual system.

Because of the office's limited space, only one additional employee, whose salary would cost about $10,000 per year, could be accommodated. This new employee could increase throughput by 20%. In addition to improvements afforded by streamlined procedures, potential throughput for a six-person office would increase 20 to 30% above the present figure.

In conclusion, the enhanced manual system is simple but has limited expansion potential. However, improved procedures must be implemented, if only as an interim measure, regardless of final system selection.

Timesharing

Time-sharing is one of the viable computerization alternatives available to the Dalton company. This involves renting space on a remote computer accessed through a terminal installed in the office. The desk-size terminal would be the only equipment in the office and the time-sharing company would be responsible for all other equipment maintenance, operation, and so on. Time-sharing conforms to the regulation requiring availability of current records through terminal access to files. Furthermore, a time-sharing company offers a wide range of services, on a pay-as-you-go basis.

Time-sharing firms normally customize their program packages to the user. However, Dalton's legal restrictions would require extensive customization, which would be very expensive at the current rate of $30 per hour.

Package pricing is highly variable and most companies were unwilling to provide an estimate without their own systems study. However, Rapid Time-sharing Service Company was willing to provide a representative estimate, which included the following information.

As with most time-share companies, Rapid's prices comprise both fixed and variable costs. Fixed costs total $647 per month or $7,764 per year and include:

1. $472 per month for a reserved I/O port
2. $105 per month for a DECwriter terminal (essentially a second-generation Teletype)

3. $30 per month for a leased telephone line to the computer
4. $40 per month for a modem to translate the machine's language over the telephone

Variable costs include:

1. File storage at 4.8 cents per month per 512-byte block (the present 500K files would cost $48 per month)
2. Programming time at $30 per hour (application packages average 40 hours of programming approximating $1,200 per application)
3. Processing time at 0.36 cents per kilocore-second (total for Dalton totally unknown)

Time-sharing has almost unlimited capacity, but expansion is limited by how much the company is willing to pay in variable costs, particularly since expansion must be paid for as it occurs.

No information was available on the personnel training involved, but probably the only training required would be for a terminal operator, because all the expert personnel are at the other end of the time-share line.

Backup, security, and support are all the time-sharing service's responsibility. This would relieve Dalton of the need to provide these auxiliaries and would eliminate the need for maintaining their own expert personnel. It also means that Dalton would have no control over the computer itself. This could be a problem, but time-sharing firms are concerned with providing good-quality service to their customers.

As in any computerized system, time-sharing, if selected, will not be immediately functional. Judging from the San Francisco branch in-house system, a one-year changeover will probably be needed for time-sharing as well, during which subsystem after subsystem is transferred from manual to machine processing.

In-House Minicomputer

The final alternative is to buy or lease an in-house minicomputer for the office's exclusive use. As with time-sharing, this minicomputer would handle the normal accounting functions and generate the major routine financial reports.

The system at San Francisco provides a useful basis on which to estimate the system requirements because the two business offices are roughly comparable in size and operating budget. What about similarity of business operations? The San Francisco system is a TR 400 Accounting Computer (a programmable electronic accounting machine) with 16K of core and 1 megabyte of tape cassette mass storage. The programming language is BASIC, and the purchase price was $19,000 with $1,600 per year of maintenance expense. Currently, the machine is used 6 hours a day, for a 25% utilization rate. Payroll is the only subsystem presently on the machine; the others are to be added over a 1-year changeover schedule.

A proposed machine for the Los Angeles office should be comparable in cost, but should provide more mass storage (preferably random access) and larger core. It should also feature one of the standard programming languages, for example, BASIC or (preferably) COBOL.

Investigation of several computers resulted in the elimination of all but one because of price or capacity factors. The best machine is the Computer Data CD1500.

The CD1500 is a desk-size minicomputer that uses BASIC and offers 32K of core and 2 megabytes random-access mass storage on two diskette drives. It is available on a purchase-only basis for $21,000 plus $1,600 per year for maintenance. Application software is a flat $1,500 per program, and operator training is $150 per person. The 1500 is a new series machine, developed less than a year ago as an extension of the 1400 series; purchase orders are currently on a 6-month waiting list.

The CD1500 has enough capacity for more than 100% expansion of the present work load without additional hardware. Computer Data maintenance support and training are considered to be very fine, and BASIC programming provides the option of additional outside programming assistance should it prove necessary. The Los Angeles Dalton office would have complete control of the use and availability of the machine in an in-house system, but they would also be responsible for backup, security, and upkeep. Aside from actual Computer Data support, Dalton would be totally responsible for system efficiency.

As in time-sharing, a one-year changeover schedule would be required.

WEIGHTED-SCORE ANALYSIS

In this section the alternatives will be analyzed and rated by the weighted-score method. In this method each criterion is first assigned a weight corresponding to its importance. Then, alternatives are measured on a scale of 1 to 10 as to how well they meet each criterion, and each specific rating is multiplied by the corresponding criterion weight. Finally, all the products for each alternative are added to obtain total scores. The highest total becomes the best choice in this analysis technique.

Criteria and Weights

Cost. This will be the total monetary cost of the system over 5 years without the factor of inflation. There will be an inverse relationship between an alternative's cost and its rating. As this is one of the important considerations, it is weighted at 10.

Capacity. All the systems under consideration can meet the present capacity; therefore, this criterion is irrelevant and will be eliminated from the analysis.

Expandability. This will be the maximum amount of throughput each alternative system can handle, rated in increments of 10% above the present load. Since expansion is a prime target of management, it is also weighted at 10.

Personnel Training. This is a rather subjective estimate of ease of system use and the amount and difficulty of training, if required. Because of its non-repetitive nature and the subjectivity of the judging, it is weighted at 3.

Outside Help. The less outside help is required, the better for the company. However, because of the general availability of outside help if required, this criterion is not significant and is thus weighted at 1.

Backup. This applies to the computerized systems only. It measures how likely a system is to crash and, in such an event, how easily data processing can be maintained. This involves reliability estimates, maintenance reputation, and duplication of records. Since it is important to Dalton, it is weighted at 10.

Rating of Alternatives

The enhanced manual alternative is broken up into two alternatives: the null system with the existing five people in the office, and an expanded system with six people in the office.

Present Manual (Null) System. This assumes that the office hires no additional personnel. Additional cost is zero; therefore, the system receives the maximum rating of 10 for this criterion. System expandability, as mentioned in the preceding section, is, at most, 10% over present volume; therefore, it receives the minimum rating of 1. Required retraining sufficient to accommodate the revisions and of a type familiar to the office staff, is minimal, earning a high rating of 8. Outside help in general office skills is easily available and earns the maximum rating of 10. System backup would consist of the use of temporary personnel. Therefore, it is rated at 5.

Enhanced Manual (Expanded)System. This is identical to the enhanced manual (null) system, except that an additional worker will be hired to accommodate expansion. Cost per year is largely salary, approximately $10,000, for a total of $50,000 for a 5-year period. As the second largest 5-year system cost, this criterion is rated at 3. System expandability is 20% over the null system or 30% over present volume, which translates into a rating of 5. Personnel training, involving hiring and training a new person, is slightly more difficult than for the null system, and earns a rating of 6. Outside help becomes less practical as the office becomes overcrowded, so it is rated as 7. As in the null system, backup consists of using temporary personnel; therefore, it is rated as 5.

Time-sharing. This assumes that the office contracts with the Rapid Time-sharing Service. Variable costs, excluding processing, are calculated for the present volume. Fixed costs total $647 per month or $38,832 for 5 years; file storage is $48 per month at the present volume, totaling $2,880 for 5 years. Programming costs were estimated for four applications and total $4,800. The total for the above is $46,500. Processing costs and additional software would raise costs beyond $50,000. As the most expensive option, the system cost criterion is rated at 1. System expandability is almost un-limited, so a 10 rating is given. One should remember, however, that expansion would increase variable costs. The amount of personnel training required is unknown, but it is reputed not to be difficult; therefore, it is rated at an average value of 5. Outside help would be impractical, earning this criterion a minimal 1 rating. Backup is controlled by the time sharer, but is fairly good; thus, a rating of 7 is given.

In-House CD1500. This assumes the system configuration as described. Startup costs total $27,300, including $21,000 for hardware, $6,000 for four applications software packages, and $300 for training two operators from the existing office staff. The maintenance contract costs $1,600 per year—$8,000 over 5 years—and consumables are estimated at $500 per year —$2,500 for 5 years. The total system cost for 5 years is thus $37,800, falling between the null and the other two systems, and results in an average criterion rating of 5. System expandability is over 100% without adding any equipment, thus earning a 10 rating. Considerable personnel training is required, but is included in the purchase price; therefore, a rating of 7 is given. Outside help may be used in maintaining software; however, the level of quality under such an arrangement may not be high. For this reason, this criterion is given the average value, 5. Computer Data Maintenance enjoys a superlative reputation, but Dalton will be responsible for system backup. The combination of Computer Data Maintenance and Dalton's inexperience with computer backup results in a system backup criterion rating of 5.

Weighted-Score Chart

The results of the weighted-score analysis are shown in Table B-1. The column of numbers under each alternative is the raw reading and the weighted rating score. At the bottom of the chart, the weighted ratings scores have been totaled for comparison.

Weighted-Score Chart

Criterion	Weight	Present Manual (Null) System		Enhanced Manual (Expanded) System		Time-sharing		CD1500	
		Rating	Score	Rating	Score	Rating	Score	Rating	Score
5-year cost	10 X	10 =	100	3	30	1	10	5	50
Expandability	10 X	1 =	10	5	50	10	100	10	100
Personnel	3 X	8 =	24	6	18	5	15	7	21
Outside help	1 X	10 =	10	7	7	1	1	5	5
Backup	10 X	5 =	50	5	50	7	70	5	50
Total Scores			194		155		196		226

The in-house CD1500 minicomputer proves to be the best alternative as it received the highest total weighted score. The results of this comparison are best stated as follows: if no expansion of service is projected, the attractive option is the present manual null system using existing personnel. However, since expansion is planned by Mr. Talbert, the in-house DC1500 system is the best alternative.

EDP ECONOMIC BENEFIT ANALYSIS

As demonstrated in the preceding section, the weighted-score method is a workable approach. A cost/benefit approach provides a complementary analysis; combining the two presents a balanced picture of the relative merits of each alternative system.

In this section the operating costs of each system over 5 years are calculated (cost) and apportioned over the expansion potential of the system. The result will indicate the cost of the present volume of work in an expanded system—an indicator of the cost of expansion.

Savings

The management wishes to expand the office's work volume to a point where the operation of the office covers all costs. Therefore, the major benefit of a new system is its expansion potential over the existing system. The expansion potentials of the alternative system are tabulated below.

System	Potential (%)
Present manual system	0–10
Enhanced manual system	20–30
Rapid Time-sharing	100+
CD1500	100+

Obviously, the two computerized alternatives have the greatest potential benefit. However, these benefits will cost money, as explained next.

Costs

The monetary costs for each alternative system for 5 years are used in this analysis. These estimates are tabulated and itemized in Table B-2. In the table, the following assumptions were made:

1. Since the present manual (null) system has insignificant expansion potential and additional cost, it was deleted.
2. The additional worker in the enhanced manual system was assumed to cost $10,000 per year.
3. Processing time on the time-sharing system was assumed to be 1 kilocore-hour per day.
4. All continuing costs were adjusted for a 5% annual price inflation.

Figure B-1 shows that the CD1500 is greater in initial cost but less expensive over the long term than either of the other two alternatives.

Cost/Saving Ratio

This ratio demonstrates the additional cost of the present volume of work when the alternative system is running at its maximum capacity, or double present throughput, whichever is less. This is a more accurate index of comparative costs after planned expansion.

TABLE B-2
Alternative Systems' Itemized Costs over a 5-Year Period

	Year					
	0	1	2	3	4	5-year Total
Enhanced manual with additional worker	$10,000	$10,500	$11,025	$11,576	$12,155	$55,256
Rapid Time-sharing						
Fixed costs	7,764	8,152	8,560	8,988	9,437	42,901
Software (4)	4,800					4,800
File storage	576	605	635	667	700	3,183
Subtotal	13,140	8,757	9,195	9,655	10,137	50,884
Processing (estimated)	3,381	3,550	3,728	3,914	4,110	
Total	16,521	12,307	12,923	13,569	14,247	69,567
CD1500						
Hardware	22,500					
Software (4)	6,000					
Operator training (2)	300					
Maintenance	1,600	1,680	1,764	1,852	1,945	
Consumables	500	525	551	579	608	
Total	30,900	2,205	2,315	2,431	2,553	40,404

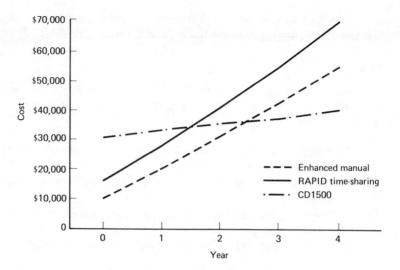

Figure B-1. Cumulative costs of alternative systems

The equation for this ratio analysis is:

$$\text{additional cost of present throughput} = \frac{\text{5-year cumulative cost}}{1 + \text{expansion potential}}$$

The ratios for the three alternative systems are as follows:
Enhanced manual (six-person office):

$$\text{additional cost} = \frac{\$55,256}{1 + 0.3} = \$42,505$$

Rapid Time-sharing:

$$\text{additional cost} = \frac{\$69,567}{1 + 1} = \$34,784$$

CD1500:

$$\text{additional cost} = \frac{\$38,904}{1 + 1} = \$19,452$$

With total costs thus adjusted to proportional revenue, the CD1500 in-house system becomes even more attractive. Of the three alternatives for expansion, the CD1500 is consistently shown as the lowest-priced for the capacity.

CONCLUSION

In conclusion, the revised version of the current manual system is considered to be the most cost-effective solution under the present circumstances. However, in the event of future expansion, the study indicates that the Computer Data CD1500 minicomputer would be the best alternative.

Since Mr. Talbert subsequently determined that expansion was necessary, the consultant recommends the CD1500 minicomputer system to replace the manual system. The implementation process will require 12 months to revise.

Dalton should begin immediately to implement the recommended revisions to the existing manual system. During the 12 months of conversion period, the revised manual system will be able to handle operations. The office will begin to implement a 1-year changeover schedule, during which the accounting subsystems will be transferred gradually from manual processing to computer processing, using a detailed computer system changeover plan. This 1-year implementation period will include testing, debugging, and integration of the subsystems into the complete system. Under this schedule, the computer will be fully operational and expansion can begin at the start of the next year.

CASE C

Ko's Best Architecture Associates*

Alternatives:
  Manual System
  Microcomputer System

BACKGROUND

Ko's associates designs and builds shopping centers and apartment complexes for industrial institutions and real estate companies. Annual sales are approximately $1 million. The firm has six employees and no previous use of computer-oriented data processing.

DATA-PROCESSING PROBLEM

The firm employs four architects, one licensed electrical engineer, and one secretary. Only the owner, Ko, does the costing on each proposal. Each proposal is composed of a listing of all items that would be installed in a particular building. Each item is defined by item number, name, size, descrip-

---

*Based on an actual computer business consulting case. Names and figures are modified or changed.

395

tion, and price. The average proposal takes 1 week to estimate and 3 days to type.

Ko would like to produce high-quality proposals faster (Figure C-1). The bottleneck is the time it takes to estimate each item. In addition, changes to any proposal require time-consuming re-costing. The situation would be significantly improved if a computer could be used to store an up-to-date listing of each item, including description, price, and other information. A service bureau would not provide the flexibility of immediate response and update that would be required for a workable system. A time-sharing system could provide these services but would be too expensive.

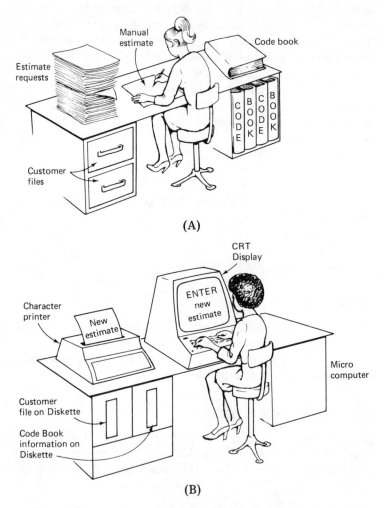

Figure C-1. (A) Manual costing for each proposal. (B) Microcomputer system with word-processing capability.

SOLUTIONS

A microcomputer system was employed for this operation. The system is composed of a 64K-byte microcomputer with 628,000 bytes of single-sided, double-density floppy disk, one cathode ray tube (CRT), and one hard-copy 180-cps output serial printer.

The system enables Ko to develop and print out a complete proposal in approximately 1 to 2 hours, thereby greatly increasing the time he has available to handle (more) proposals. Also, the average time to type the proposal for all building materials was reduced from 3 days to approximately 2 hours.

COST

Microcomputer system	$10,000
CPU (64K)	
Serial printer	
Display terminal (CRT)	
Dual-drive floppy disk	
Software development and consulting	$15,000

Additional features provided by the system at no extra hardware cost include:

Cost versus sales price displays

Ability to develop sample proposals

Word-processing capability

This system will enable the business to double its growth with no additional operational personnel required. Profits on sales are approximately 20%. An increase of $1 million in sales means an increase of approximately $200,000 of operational profit in 1 year. This will pay for the total cost of the system by a factor of 8:1.

CASE D

Wolf and Sons Hardware Distributing Company*

Alternatives:
Billing Machine
Service Bureau
Small Business Computer System

BACKGROUND

Wolf and Sons Hardware Distributing Company specializes in sales of construction equipment. Annual sales are approximately $3 million. The com-

*Based on actual computer business consulting cases. Names and figures are modified or changed.

pany has a total of 15 salespeople. There are over 7,000 items available in various sizes and types of inventory. Fifteen years ago, the company installed four key-driven billing machines. Each machine prepares 60 invoices per day. Output is punched paper tape, which is processed by a service bureau to provide very elaborate and comprehensive sales reports. These reports constitute the basis for controlling all elements of the sales department effort, including salaries and commissions for the sales personnel.

Accounts receivable are posted in a separate department. Inventory control is supported at the bin level by an old Kardex system, which is posted with several days lag time.

DATA-PROCESSING PROBLEMS

Invoice volume is growing to the point where additional personnel and equipment will soon be needed to support their existing method of invoicing. Additional sales data on a daily and weekly basis is required and cannot be obtained economically from the service bureau. In addition, the service bureau is raising its price to customers. The company wishes to solve its inventory control problem, only part of which is its posting method, the other part being its warehousing method. Furthermore, it wants to go to a prebilling method. Credit approval is also slow.

SOLUTIONS

The company installed a 64K-byte small business computer, a 10 million-byte cartridge disk, two cathode ray terminals (CRTs), and one serial printer.

1. This system reduced the billing department to two billers (operators) while providing for additional capacity, enabling the company to transfer these two experienced persons to the inventory control department.
2. Invoices were automatically credit checked at the time of the billing.
3. The sales reporting system was completely redesigned to provide spontaneous information to management.
4. This system does not require a data-processing manager and programmers.
5. Only the controller and her billing clerks operate and produce all the data from this operation.

Inventory control is planned but will not be implemented until warehouse problems are solved.

COST

Hardware	$30,000
Software and consulting	$30,000

To provide simplicity of operation in a complex internal process, extensive system design work as well as hardware/software selection was provided to the company.

The system saved the company $1,000 per month directly in service-bureau costs. This system, which can also handle its inventory control process and still has added capacity for normal growth, will pay for itself in $2\frac{1}{2}$ years.

CASE E

A Division of a Major Aerospace Corporation (Distributed Network)*

Alternatives:
On-Line Communication to the Central Data-Processing Facility at Main Office
Stand-Alone Minicomputer

BACKGROUND

The Nuclear Engineering Department has access to a number of large-scale computers at the central data-processing facility (Figure E-1A). All data-processing support comes from this facility, as they have none of their own.

DATA-PROCESSING PROBLEM

The department is required to develop a nuclear plant in-service inspection system. It will be designed to provide meaningful flaw detection information, in an expeditious manner, on various welds and base metal within a plant. The system would employ ultrasonic transducers mounted on a mechanism termed a Skate. The Skate, in turn, would be mounted on and move along a track with two degrees of positioning freedom. Movements of the Skate would be controlled by a computer so that the transducers may be positioned at all accessible locations necessary to provide a complete ultrasonic inspection of all welds in the primary coolant system of a plant.

The central data-processing facility provides its on-line service on a low-priority basis to drive the transducers. This approach, however, would be too expensive insofar as software development is concerned and would take too long to complete.

SOLUTIONS

A 64K-byte minicomputer was employed (Figure E-1B). The system included a dual-drive floppy disk (628K bytes of storage), one Teletype (TTY), two cassettes, and one display terminal.

*Based on an actual computer business consulting case. Names and figures are modified or changed.

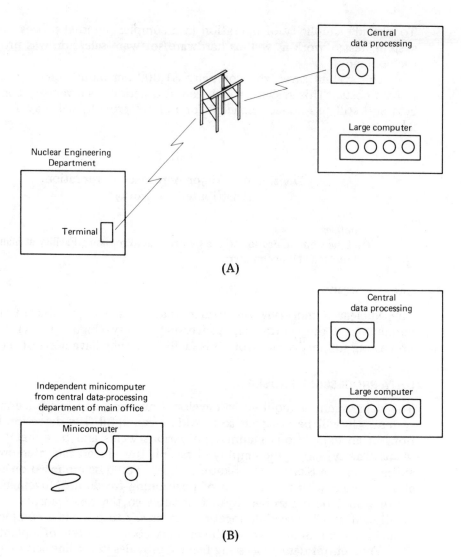

Figure E-1. (A) Current setup. (B) New setup.

The minicomputer controls the motion of the Skate, data acquisition, analysis, and output.

The minicomputer afforded the users complete independence of operation. Moreover, the software and hardware system was in operation sooner than that proposed by the central data processing facility could have been. (The system was operational in 5 months.)

Because of the flexibility and independence of the system, the department (utilizing programmers solely during the developmental phase of this activity) was able to meet all schedules and design criteria.

COST

Hardware	$30,000
Software and consulting	$33,000

This system represents a significant portion of the nuclear plant in-service inspection system. Costs saved using this method over that of alternative approaches will pay for the system in 2 years.

CASE F

West Coast Music Distributing Company*

Alternatives:
    Main-Frame Computer
    Large Service Bureau
    Minicomputer and Service Bureau

BACKGROUND

West Coast Music Distributing Company carries 5,000 items which come from 18 record manufacturers. The management has very progressive and aggressive sales plans. The annual sales are $20 million and growing rapidly. The company has two warehouses and seven retail stores throughout southern California.

The company previously installed an IBM 370. This system had the typical general computer profile. It required a data-processing manager, programmer, and operators. To justify its existence, it had to be used for a great many applications. It failed because the data-processing manager was an empire builder and not really proficient in solving complicated data-processing problems.

The company then chose to use a large service bureau. This solved many of the problems and actually gave the company better control over processing, but the volume being processed created a problem because of the method used to input (card punching), and was further complicated by the lack of sufficient controls. In addition, the service bureau costs were rising disproportionately to the value received.

DATA-PROCESSING PROBLEM

The company is looking for some way to automate dependably, as they are very dependent on data processing to run their business. They investigated various on-line approaches and found that costs were far out of line. In addition, they would suffer loss of control.

*Based on actual computer business consulting cases. Names and figures are modified or changed.

SOLUTION

The company installed a 128K-byte minicomputer (in-house) with 11 cathode ray terminals (CRT), 40 million bytes of disk, two serial printers, and one magnetic-tape device.

Nine of the CRTs are interactive and used for order entry. The others are used for straight data entry.

1. The entire input was streamlined and handled more efficiently.
2. Orders and invoices are now printed on-site.
3. The minicomputer provided a daily magnetic tape of all transactions for processing on a large computer at a service bureau. All file updating, report printing, and data manipulation are done at the service bureau.
4. The West Coast Music Distributing Company owns all programs. It is therefore able to shop for other service bureaus in case processing costs increase too sharply or quality of service decreases.
5. The service bureau was responsible for programming both machines and to produce reports for management.
6. There is no data-processing manager, programmer, or operators at the client's site (where the minicomputer is). Order takers and accounting clerks operate the system.
7. This total system provides order entry, order control, billing, accounts receivable, sales analysis (complicated and lengthy), accounts payable, and inventory control.

The system now provides more applications at lower cost and can expand both in terms of volume and additional applications. It supports the order taker right at the order-entry desk, and management has better control than ever before.

COST AND SAVINGS

Hardware	$65,000
Total software	62,500
Service bureau cost	2,500 per month

This entire operation, which handles more applications than before with fewer persons, actually costs less to run on a monthly basis than any of the prior systems.

The current daily operation, if supported via a commercial on-line system, would cost approximately $10,000 per month. The difference in cost alone pays for the system in 13 months.

Additional functions are currently being added, with no increase in hardware costs.

APPENDIX II

TABLES*

*Tables A & B in this appendix are reproduced with permission of the authors from S. Winton Korn and Thomas Boyd, *Accounting for Management Planning and Decision Making*, John Wiley & Sons, Inc., New York, New York, 1969.

$$P_s = A \left[\frac{1 - (1 + r)^{-n}}{r} \right]$$

Periods (n)	1%	1½%	2%	2½%	3%	3½%	4%	4½%	5%	6%	7%
1	0.9901	0.9852	0.9804	0.9756	0.9709	0.9662	0.9615	0.9615	0.9524	0.9434	0.9346
2	1.9704	1.9559	1.9416	1.9274	1.9135	1.8997	1.8861	1.8727	1.8594	1.8334	1.8080
3	2.9410	2.9122	2.8839	2.8560	2.8286	2.8016	2.7751	2.7490	2.7232	2.6730	2.6243
4	3.9020	3.8544	3.8077	3.7620	3.7171	3.6731	3.6299	3.5875	3.5460	3.4651	3.3872
5	4.8534	4.7826	4.7135	4.6458	4.5797	4.5151	4.4518	4.3900	4.3295	4.2124	4.1002
6	5.7955	5.6972	5.6014	5.5081	5.4172	5.3286	5.2421	5.1579	5.0757	4.9173	4.7665
7	6.7282	6.5982	6.4720	6.3494	6.2303	6.1145	6.0021	5.8927	5.7864	5.5824	5.3893
8	7.6517	7.4895	7.3255	7.1701	7.0179	6.8740	6.7327	6.5959	6.4632	6.2098	5.9713
9	8.5660	8.3605	8.1622	7.9709	7.7861	7.6077	7.4353	7.2688	7.1078	6.8017	6.5152
10	9.4713	9.2222	8.9826	8.7521	8.5302	8.3166	8.1109	7.9127	7.7217	7.3601	7.0236
11	10.3676	10.0711	9.7868	9.5142	9.2526	9.0016	8.7605	8.5289	8.3064	7.8869	7.4987
12	11.2551	10.9075	10.5753	10.2578	9.9540	9.6633	9.3851	9.1186	8.8633	8.3838	7.9427
13	12.1337	11.7315	11.3484	10.9832	10.6350	10.3027	9.9856	9.6829	9.3936	8.8527	8.3577
14	13.0037	12.5434	12.1062	11.6909	11.2961	10.9205	10.5631	10.2228	9.8986	9.2950	8.7455
15	13.8651	13.3432	12.8493	12.3814	11.9379	11.5174	11.1184	10.7395	10.3797	9.7122	9.1079
16	14.7179	14.1313	13.5777	13.0550	12.5611	12.0941	11.6523	11.2340	10.8378	10.1059	9.4466
17	15.5623	14.9076	14.2919	13.7122	13.1661	12.6513	12.1657	11.7072	11.2741	10.4773	9.7632
18	16.3983	15.6726	14.9920	14.3534	13.7535	13.1897	12.6593	12.1600	11.6896	10.8276	10.0591
19	17.2260	16.4262	15.6785	14.9789	14.3238	13.7098	13.1339	12.5933	12.0853	11.1581	10.3356
20	18.0456	17.1686	16.3514	15.5892	14.8775	14.2124	13.5903	13.0079	12.4622	11.4699	10.5940
21	18.8570	17.9001	17.0112	16.1845	15.4150	14.6980	14.0292	13.4047	12.8212	11.7640	10.8355
22	19.6604	18.6208	17.6580	16.7654	15.9369	15.1671	14.4511	13.7844	13.1630	12.0416	11.0612
23	20.4558	19.3309	18.2922	17.3321	16.4436	15.6204	14.8568	14.1478	13.4886	12.3034	11.2722
24	21.2434	20.0304	18.9139	17.8850	16.9355	16.0584	15.2470	14.4955	13.7986	12.5504	11.4693
25	22.0232	20.7196	19.5235	18.4244	17.4131	16.4815	15.6221	14.8282	14.0939	12.7834	11.6536
26	22.7952	21.3986	20.1210	18.9506	17.8768	16.8904	15.9828	15.1466	14.3752	13.0032	11.8258
27	23.5596	22.0676	20.7069	19.4640	18.3270	17.2854	16.3296	15.4513	14.6430	13.2105	11.9867
28	24.3164	22.7267	21.2813	19.9649	18.7641	17.6670	16.6631	15.7429	14.8981	13.4062	12.1371
29	25.0658	23.3761	21.8444	20.4535	19.1885	18.0358	16.9837	16.0219	15.1411	13.5907	12.2777
30	25.8077	24.0158	22.3965	20.9303	19.6004	18.3920	17.2920	16.2889	15.3725	13.7648	12.4090
40	32.8347	29.9158	27.3555	25.1028	23.1148	21.3551	19.7928	18.4016	17.1591	15.0463	13.3317
50	39.1961	34.9997	31.4236	28.3623	25.7298	23.4556	21.4822	19.7620	18.2559	15.7619	13.8007

8%	10%	12%	14%	16%	18%	20%	22%	24%	25%	26%	28%	30%	40%	50%
0.9259	0.9191	0.893	0.877	0.862	0.847	0.833	0.820	0.806	0.800	0.794	0.781	0.769	0.714	0.667
1.7833	1.7355	1.690	1.647	1.605	1.566	1.528	1.492	1.457	1.440	1.424	1.392	1.361	1.224	1.111
2.5771	2.4869	2.402	2.322	2.246	2.174	2.106	2.042	1.981	1.952	1.923	1.868	1.816	1.589	1.407
3.3121	3.1699	3.037	2.914	2.798	2.690	2.589	2.494	2.404	2.362	2.320	2.241	2.166	1.849	1.605
3.9927	3.7908	3.605	3.433	3.274	3.127	2.991	2.864	2.745	2.689	2.635	2.532	2.436	2.035	1.737
4.6229	4.3553	4.111	3.889	3.685	3.498	3.326	3.167	3.020	2.951	2.885	2.759	2.643	2.168	1.824
5.2064	4.8684	4.564	4.288	4.039	3,812	3.605	3.416	3.242	3.161	3.083	2.937	2.802	2.263	1.883
5.7466	5.3349	4.968	4.639	4.344	4.078	3.837	3.619	3.421	3.329	3.241	3.076	2.925	2.331	1.922
6.2469	5.7590	5.328	4.946	4.607	4.303	4.031	3.786	3.566	3.463	3.366	3.184	3.019	2.379	1.948
6.7101	6.1446	5.650	5.216	4.833	4.494	4.192	3.923	3.682	3.571	3.465	3.269	3.092	2.414	1.965
7.1390	6.4951	5.988	5.453	5.029	4.656	4.327	4.035	3.776	3.656	3.544	3.335	3.147	2.438	1.977
7.5361	6.8137	6.194	5.660	5.197	4.793	4.439	4.127	3.851	3.725	3.606	3.387	3.190	2.456	1.985
7.9038	7.1034	6.424	5.842	5.342	4.910	4.533	4.203	3.912	3.780	3.656	3.427	3.223	2.468	1.990
8.2442	7.3667	6.628	6.002	5.468	5.008	4.611	4.265	3.962	3.824	3.695	3.459	3.249	2.477	1.993
8.5595	7.6061	6.811	6.142	5.575	5.092	4.675	4.315	4.001	3.859	3.726	3.483	3.268	2.484	1.995
8.8514	7.8237	6.974	6.265	5.669	5.162	4.730	4.357	4.033	3.887	3.751	3.503	3.283	2.489	1.997
9.1216	8.0216	7.120	6.373	5.749	5.222	4.775	4.391	4.059	3.910	3.771	3.518	3.295	2.492	1.998
9.3719	8.2014	7.250	6.467	5.818	5.273	4.812	4.419	4.080	3.928	3.786	3.529	3.304	2.494	1.999
9.6036	8.3649	7.366	6.550	5.877	5.316	4.844	4.442	4.097	3.942	3.799	3.539	3.311	2.496	1.999
9.8181	8.5136	7.469	6.623	5.929	5.353	4.870	4.460	4.110	3.954	3.808	3.546	3.316	2.497	1.999
10.0168	8.6487	7.562	6.687	5.973	5.384	4.891	4.476	4.121	3.963	3.816	3.551	3.320	2.498	2.000
10.2007	8.7715	7.645	6.743	6.011	5.410	4.909	4.488	4.130	3.970	3.822	3.556	3.323	2.498	2.000
10.3711	8.8832	7.718	6.792	6.044	5.432	4.925	4.499	4.137	3.976	3.827	3.559	3.325	2.499	2.000
10.5288	8.9847	7.784	6.835	6.073	5.451	4.937	4.507	4.143	3.981	3.831	3.562	3.327	2.499	2.000
10.6748	9.0770	7.843	6.873	6.097	5.467	4.948	4.514	4.147	3.985	3.834	3.564	3.329	2.499	2.000
10.8100	9.1609	7.896	6.906	6.118	5.480	4.956	4.520	4.151	3.988	3.837	3.566	3.330	2.500	2.000
10.9352	9.2372	7.943	6.935	6.136	5.492	4.964	4.524	4.154	3.990	3.839	3.567	3.331	2.500	2.000
11.0511	9.3066	7.984	6.961	6.152	5.502	4.970	4.528	4.157	3.992	3.840	3.568	3.331	2.500	2.000
11.1584	9.3696	8.022	6.983	6.166	5.510	4.975	4.531	4.159	3.994	3.841	3.569	3.332	2.500	2.000
11.2578	9.4269	8.055	7.003	6.177	5.517	4.979	4.534	4.160	3.995	3.842	3.569	3.332	2.500	2.000
11.9246	9.7791	8.244	7.105	6.234	5.548	4.997	4.544	4.166	3.999	3,846	3.571	3.333	2.500	2.000
12.2335	9.9148	8.304	7.133	6.246	5.554	4.999	4.545	4.167	4.000	3.846	3.571	3.333	2.500	2.000

[a]To convert this table to values of an annuity in advance, take one less period and add 1.0000.

TABLE B
Present Value of $1.00
$$P = F_n(1 + r)^{-n}$$

Periods (n)	1%	1½%	2%	2½%	3%	3½%	4%	4½%	5%	6%	7%	8%
1	.9901	.9852	.9804	.9756	.9709	.9662	.9615	.9569	.9524	.9434	.9346	.9259
2	.9803	.9707	.9612	.9518	.9426	.9335	.9246	.9157	.9070	.8900	.8734	.8573
3	.9706	.9563	.9423	.9286	.9151	.9019	.8890	.8763	.8638	.8396	.8163	.7938
4	.9610	.9422	.9238	.9060	.8885	.8714	.8548	.8386	.8227	.7921	.7629	.7350
5	.9515	.9283	.9057	.8839	.8626	.8420	.8219	.8025	.7835	.7473	.7130	.6806
6	.9420	.9145	.8880	.8623	.8375	.8135	.7903	.7679	.7462	.7050	.6663	.6302
7	.9327	.9010	.8706	.8413	.8131	.7860	.7599	.7348	.7107	.6651	.6227	.5835
8	.9235	.8877	.8535	.8207	.7894	.7594	.7307	.7032	.6768	.6274	.5820	.5403
9	.9143	.8746	.8368	.8007	.7664	.7337	.7026	.6729	.6446	.5919	.5439	.5002
10	.9053	.8617	.8203	.7812	.7441	.7089	.6756	.6439	.6139	.5584	.5083	.4632
11	.8963	.8489	.8043	.7621	.7224	.6849	.6496	.6162	.5847	.5268	.4751	.4289
12	.8874	.8364	.7885	.7436	.7014	.6618	.6246	.5897	.5568	.4970	.4440	.3971
13	.8787	.8240	.7730	.7254	.6810	.6394	.6006	.5643	.5303	.4688	.4150	.3677
14	.8700	.8118	.7579	.7077	.6611	.6178	.5775	.5400	.5051	.4423	.3878	.3405
15	.8613	.7999	.7430	.6905	.6419	.5969	.5553	.5167	.4810	.4173	.3624	.3153
16	.8528	.7880	.7284	.6736	.6232	.5767	.5339	.4945	.4581	.3936	.3387	.2919
17	.8444	.7764	.7142	.6572	.6050	.5572	.5134	.4732	.4363	.3714	.3166	.2703
18	.8360	.7649	.7002	.6412	.5874	.5384	.4936	.4528	.4155	.3503	.2959	.2502
19	.8277	.7536	.6864	.6255	.5703	.5202	.4746	.4333	.3957	.3305	.2765	.2317
20	.8195	.7425	.6730	.6103	.5537	.5026	.4564	.4146	.3769	.3118	.2584	.2145
21	.8114	.7315	.6598	.5954	.5375	.4856	.4388	.3968	.3589	.2942	.2415	.1987
22	.8034	.7207	.6468	.5809	.5219	.4692	.4220	.3797	.3418	.2775	.2257	.1839
23	.7954	.7100	.6342	.5667	.5067	.4533	.4057	.3634	.3256	.2618	.2109	.1703
24	.7876	.6995	.6217	.5529	.4919	.4380	.3901	.3477	.3101	.2470	.1971	.1577
25	.7798	.6892	.6095	.5394	.4776	.4231	.3751	.3327	.2953	.2330	.1842	.1460
26	.7720	.6790	.5976	.5262	.4637	.4088	.3607	.3184	.2812	.2198	.1722	.1352
27	.7644	.6690	.5859	.5134	.4502	.3950	.3468	.3047	.2678	.2074	.1609	.1252
28	.7568	.6591	.5744	.5009	.4371	.3817	.3335	.2916	.2551	.1956	.1504	.1159
29	.7493	.6494	.5631	.4887	.4243	.3687	.3207	.2790	.2429	.1846	.1406	.1073
30	.7419	.6398	.5521	.4767	.4120	.3563	.3083	.2670	.2314	.1741	.1314	.0994
40	.6717	.5513	.4529	.3724	.3066	.2526	.2083	.1719	.1420	.0972	.0668	.0460
50	.6080	.4750	.3715	.2909	.2281	.1791	.1407	.1107	.0872	.0543	.0339	.0213

10%	12%	14%	16%	18%	20%	22%	24%	25%	26%	28%	30%	40%	50%
.9091	0.893	0.877	0.862	0.847	0.833	0.820	0.806	0.800	0.794	0.781	0.769	0.714	0.667
.8264	0.797	0.769	0.743	0.718	0.694	0.672	0.650	0.640	0.630	0.610	0.592	0.510	0.444
.7513	0.712	0.675	0.641	0.609	0.579	0.551	0.524	0.512	0.500	0.477	0.455	0.364	0.296
.6830	0.636	0.592	0.552	0.516	0.482	0.451	0.423	0.410	0.397	0.373	0.350	0.260	0.198
.6209	0.567	0.519	0.476	0.437	0.402	0.370	0.341	0.328	0.315	0.291	0.269	0.186	0.132
.5645	0.507	0.456	0.410	0.370	0.335	0.303	0.275	0.262	0.250	0.227	0.207	0.133	0.088
.5132	0.452	0.400	0.354	0.314	0.279	0.249	0.222	0.210	0.198	0.178	0.159	0.095	0.059
.4665	0.404	0.351	0.305	0.266	0.233	0.204	0.179	0.168	0.157	0.139	0.123	0.068	0.039
.4241	0.361	0.308	0.263	0.225	0.194	0.167	0.144	0.134	0.125	0.108	0.094	0.048	0.026
.3855	0.322	0.270	0.227	0.191	0.162	0.137	0.116	0.107	0.099	0.085	0.073	0.035	0.017
.3505	0.287	0.237	0.195	0.162	0.135	0.112	0.094	0.086	0.079	0.066	0.056	0.025	0.012
.3186	0.257	0.208	0.168	0.137	0.112	0.092	0.076	0.069	0.062	0.052	0.043	0.018	0.008
.2897	0.229	0.182	0.145	0.116	0.093	0.075	0.061	0.055	0.050	0.040	0.033	0.013	0.005
.2633	0.205	0.160	0.125	0.099	0.078	0.062	0.049	0.044	0.039	0.032	0.025	0.009	0.003
.2394	0.183	0.140	0.108	0.084	0.065	0.051	0.040	0.035	0.031	0.025	0.020	0.006	0.002
.2176	0.163	0.123	0.093	0.071	0.054	0.042	0.032	0.028	0.025	0.019	0.015	0.005	0.002
.1978	0.146	0.108	0.080	0.060	0.045	0.034	0.026	0.023	0.020	0.015	0.012	0.003	0.001
.1799	0.130	0.095	0.069	0.051	0.038	0.028	0.021	0.018	0.016	0.012	0.009	0.002	0.001
.1635	0.116	0.083	0.060	0.043	0.031	0.023	0.017	0.014	0.012	0.009	0.007	0.002	
.1486	0.104	0.073	0.051	0.037	0.026	0.019	0.014	0.012	0.010	0.007	0.005	0.001	
.1351	0.093	0.064	0.044	0.031	0.022	0.015	0.011	0.009	0.008	0.006	0.004	0.001	
.1228	0.083	0.056	0.038	0.026	0.018	0.013	0.009	0.007	0.006	0.004	0.003	0.001	
.1117	0.074	0.049	0.033	0.022	0.015	0.010	0.007	0.006	0.005	0.003	0.002		
.1015	0.066	0.043	0.028	0.019	0.013	0.008	0.006	0.005	0.004	0.003	0.002		
.0923	0.059	0.038	0.024	0.016	0.010	0.007	0.005	0.004	0.003	0.002	0.001		
.0839	0.053	0.033	0.021	0.014	0.009	0.006	0.004	0.003	0.002	0.002	0.001		
.0763	0.047	0.029	0.018	0.011	0.007	0.005	0.003	0.002	0.002	0.001	0.001		
.0693	0.042	0.026	0.016	0.010	0.006	0.004	0.002	0.002	0.002	0.001	0.001		
.0630	0.037	0.022	0.014	0.008	0.005	0.003	0.002	0.002	0.001	0.001	0.001		
.0573	0.033	0.020	0.012	0.007	0.004	0.003	0.002	0.001	0.001	0.001			
.0221	0.011	0.005	0.003	0.001	0.001								
.0085	0.003	0.001	0.001										

TABLE C
Small Business Computer System Vendors[a]

If more detailed information on computers and vendors is needed, Datapro reports and/or Auerbach reports are recommended.

Manufacturer	System Model	Word Length (bits)	Memory Capacity (bytes)	Type	Capacity (bytes)	Type	Speed
		CPU		Disk		Printer	
Advanced Information Design	2000-40	16	256K	Floppy	Std. (4) 4.8M	Serial	165 cps
				Cartridge	Opt. (4) 40M	Line	200–1200 lpm
				Pack	Opt. (4) 200M		
	2000-80	16	256K	Floppy	Opt. (4) 4.8M	Serial	165 cps
				Cartridge	Opt. (4) 128M	Line	200–1200 lpm
				Pack	Std. (4) 1200M		
	3000-60	16	256K	Floppy	Opt. (4) 4.8M	Serial	165 cps
				Cartridge	Std. (4) 40M	Line	200–1200 lpm
				Pack	Opt. (4) 200M		
	4000-80	32	2048K	Floppy	Opt. (4) 4.8M	Serial	165 cps
				Cartridge	Opt. (4) 128M	Line	200–1200 lpm
				Pack	Std. (4) 1200M		
	5000-80	16	256K	Floppy	Opt. (4) 4.8M	Serial	165 cps
				Cartridge	Opt. (4) 128M	Line	200–1200 lpm
				Pack	Std. (4) 1200M		
	6000-80	32	2048K	Floppy	Opt. (4) 4.8M	Serial	165 cps
				Cartridge	Opt. (4) 128M	Line	200–1200 lpm
				Pack	Std. (4) 1200M		
Alpha Micro-systems	AM1010	16	64–320K	Floppy	Std. 2.4M	Serial	55–180 cps
	AM1030	16	64–1024K	Cartridge	Std. 10M–360M	Line	300–900 lpm
	AM1050	16	64–1024K	Pack	Std. 90M 25–2400 M	Line	300–900 lpm

[a]Readers are advised to check the most recent information available from vendors, especially price ranges and application software. Readers are also advised to check response time when multiple terminals are employed in the system. Partitions represent maximum numbers for multiprogramming. I/O ports represent the maximum number of Input/Output ports.

Number of Terminals, Partitions, Lines, or I/O Ports	Software Language	Software Applications Software	Price Range	Telephone	Address
40	COBOL, RPG, FORTRAN, BASIC, Assembler, DBMS	General accounting, word processing	$15,800	(408) 744-0900	1240 Elko Drive, Sunnyvale, CA 94022
40	COBOL, RPG, FORTRAN, BASIC, Assembler, DBMS	General accounting, word processing	$37,800		
40	COBOL, RPG, FORTRAN, BASIC, Assembler, DBMS	General accounting, word processing	$22,800		
multiple users	COBOL, RPG, FORTRAN, BASIC, Assembler, DBMS	General accounting, word processing	$75,000		
80	COBOL, RPG, FORTRAN, BASIC, Assembler, DBMS	General accounting, word processing	$42,800		
multiple users	COBOL, RPG, FORTRAN, BASIC, Assembler, DBMS	General accounting, word processing	$125,000		
1–8	BASIC, PASCAL, LISP, Multitask, multi-user operating system	General purpose applications	$12,000 up	(714) 957-1404	17881 Sky Park North Irvine, CA 92714
1–24		Business data processing	$21,000 up		
1–24		Word processing	$26,500 up		

409

TABLE C (*Continued*)

Manufacturer	System Model	CPU		Disk		Printer	
		Word Length (*bits*)	Memory Capacity (*bytes*)	Type	Capacity (*bytes*)	Type	Speed
Apple Computer Inc.	Apple II	8	64K	Floppy Cartridge	143–858K 10–20M	Serial Line	60 cps 150 lpm
	Apple III	8	128K	Floppy Cartridge	143–572K 10–20M	Serial Line	60 cps 150 lpm
Applied Data Communications	Event-1000 2000 3000 (Intel 8080A base)	8-bit byte	65K	Floppy	2 std. 8 max. Opt. (4) 10M	Serial Line	1200 cps to 1400 lpm
Applied Data Processing Resource	100 (Nova 3 base)	16	256K	Pack	Std. 320M	Serial Line	165, 330 cps 300–600 lpm
Applied Digital Communications	102 (Micro Nova base)	16	64K	Floppy Cartridge	2 Std. 6 max. Opt. 10M	Serial Line	Std. 120 cps Optional
	103 (Inter-data 5/16 base)	16	64K	Floppy	2 Std.	Serial Line	Std. 120 cps Opt. 600 lpm
	202 (DG Nova 3)	16	256K	Floppy Cartridge	Optional 10M	Serial Line	Std. 120 cps Opt. to 600 lpm
	400 (PoP8)	12	32K	Floppy Cartridge Pack Fixed-head	Opt. (4) 1M Optional Optional Optional	Serial Line	Std. 120 cps Opt. to 600 lpm
	401 (Inter-data 8/16 E)	16	256K	Floppy Cartridge	Optional Std. 10M	Serial Line	Std. 120 cps Opt. 600 lpm
Applied Systems Corp.	ACS-80 (Intel 8080/85)	8, 16	64K	Floppy Cartridge Pack	Opt. 300K/ 500K Optional Optional	Serial Line	Opt. to 30 cps Opt. 100/ 300 lpm
J. Baker & Asso-ciates Distribution	11/03 (PDP-11/ 03)	16	56K	Floppy Cartridge	Opt. 1024K Std. 4.8M	Serial Line	Std. 180 cps Std. 230, 300 lpm

Number of Terminals, Partitions, Lines, or I/O Ports	Software		Price Range	Telephone	Address
	Language	Applications Software			
1 1	BASIC, COBOL, PASCAL	Personal home computer Education Small business applications	$995 with 4K RAM and 8K ROM (without Floppy and printer) $4,700 without printer	(408) 966-1010	10260 Bandley Dr. Cupertino, CA 95014
1-8 (partitions)	BASIC, DBMS	General purpose	$10,300	(714) 547-6954	1509 East McFadden, Santa Ana, CA 92705
1-16	BASIC, Assembler Extended BASIC DBMS	General accounting	$39,300	(203) 787-4107	33 Bernhard Road, North Haven, CT 06473
9-18 (I/O ports)	COBOL, FORTRAN, BASIC, Assembler	General accounting, manufacturing	$23,750	(609) 234-3666	214 West Main Street, Moorestown, NJ 08507
1-256 (I/O ports)	COBOL, FORTRAN, BASIC, Assembler	General accounting, job costing	$22,645		
12 (I/O ports)	COBOL, FORTRAN, BASIC, Assembler, ALGOL	General accounting, restaurant	$31,500		
NA	COBOL, FORTRAN, BASIC, Assembler, ALGOL	General accounting	$12,500		
4-256 (I/O ports)	COBOL, FORTRAN, BASIC, Assembler, TOTAL (DBMS)	General accounting	$49,230		
NA	COBOL, FORTRAN, BASIC, Assembler, PL/1	General accounting	$1,000 (basic system)	(313) 779-8700	26401 Harper Avenue, St. Clair Shores, MI 48081
1-3 (no. of communication lines)	FORTRAN, BASIC, Assembler, DIBOL (COBOL)	General accounting, manufacturing distribution	$34,995	(312) 677-9760	5135 West Golf Road, Skokie, IL 60076

TABLE C   (*Continued*)

| Manufacturer | System Model | CPU | | Disk | | Printer | |
		Word Length (bits)	Memory Capacity (bytes)	Type	Capacity (bytes)	Type	Speed
	System (PDP-11/ 34)	16	128K	Floppy Cartridge	Opt. 512K Std. 14M	Serial Line	Opt. 30 cps Opt. 230, 300 lpm
	System 2 (PDP-11/ 70)	16	4M	Floppy Cartridge Pack	Opt. 512K Std. 88M Opt. 176M	Serial Line	Opt. 30 cps Opt. 300, 900 lpm
Basic Four Corporation	200	8	40K– 64K	Cartridge	Std. 10M 20M	Serial	Std. 120 cps
	410	8	40– 128K	Cartridge	Std. 10M 40M	Serial Line	Std. 160 cps Opt. 150– 600 lpm
	610	8	64K– 192K	Pack	Std. 35M 300M	Serial Line	Std. 160 cps Opt. 150– 600 lpm
	730	8	96K– 256K	Pack	Std. 150M 300M	Serial Line	Opt. 160 cps Std. 300 lpm
Binary Data Systems	UCOM 1 (Nova 3/D base)	16	256K	Floppy Cartridge Pack	Optional Std. 40M Opt. 800M	Serial Line	Opt. 165 cps Std. 200– 1500 lpm
	UCOM II (Eclipse S/130 base)	16	256K	Floppy Cartridge Pack Fixed-head	Optional Std. 40M Opt. 800M Optional	Serial Line	Opt. 165 cps Std. 200– 1500 lpm
	UCOM III (Eclipse C/330)	16	512K	Floppy Cartridge Pack	Optional Std. 40M Opt. 800M	Serial Line	Opt. 165 cps Std. 200– 1500 lpm
BTI	5000/30	16	64K	Cartridge Pack	Std. 30M Opt. 120M	Line	Opt. 300– 900 lpm
	5000/60	16	64K	Cartridge Pack	Std. 60M Opt. 240M	Line	Opt. 300– 900 lpm

Number of Terminals, Partitions, Lines, or I/O Ports	Software		Price Range	Telephone	Address
	Language	Applications Software			
3–32 (I/O ports)	COBOL, RFG, FORTRAN, BASIC, Assembler, DIBOL (COBOL) DBMS	General accounting, manufacturing	$45,000		
3–64 (I/O ports)	COBOL, RFG, FORTRAN, BASIC, Assembler, DIBOL (COBOL) DBMS	General accounting, manufacturing	$100,000+		
2	BASIC	General accounting, medical, insurance, property management	$29,000	(714) 731-5100	14101 Myford Street Road, Tustin, CA 92680
8	BASIC	General accounting, medical, insurance, property management	$36,900		
16	BASIC	General accounting, medical, insurance, property management	$51,400		
32	BASIC	General accounting, medical, insurance, property management	$110,000		
64 (partitions)	COBOL, FORTRAN, BASIC, Assembler, DBMS	General accounting, wholesale, real estate, medical	$45,000	(516) 822-1585	88 Sunnyside Boulevard, Plainview, NY 18803
64 (partitions)	COBOL, FORTRAN, BASIC, Assembler, DBMS	General accounting, wholesale, real estate, medical	$150,000		
64 (partitions)	COBOL, FORTRAN, BASIC, Assembler, DBMS	General accounting,	$175,000		
8–32	BASIC, Assembler, DBMS	General accounting, manufacturing, education	$38,950	(408) 733-1122	650 North Mary Avenue, Sunnyvale, CA 94086
8–32	BASIC, Assembler, DBMS	General accounting, manufacturing, education	$42,950		

TABLE C *(Continued)*

Manufacturer	System Model	CPU		Disk		Printer	
		Word Length (bits)	Memory Capacity (bytes)	Type	Capacity (bytes)	Type	Speed
	8000	32	8M	Cartridge	Std. 32M	Line	Opt. 300–900 lpm
				Pack	Opt. 66, 126M, 8,000M		
Burroughs	B 80	8	60K/124K	Floppy	Opt. 6M	Serial	Std. 60, 180 cps
				Cartridge	Opt. 27.6M	Line	Opt. 160, 250 lpm
				Fixed-head	Opt. 37.6M		
	B 730/ B 720	64	80K	Floppy	Opt. 243K	Serial	Std. 60 cps
				Cartridge	Opt. 36.8M	Line	Opt. 85–400 lpm
	B 801	64	80K	Floppy	Opt. 486K	Serial	Std. 120 cps
				Cartridge	Opt. 36.8M	Line	Opt. 85–400 lpm
	B 810/ B 820	64	131K	Floppy	Opt. 2M	Serial	Opt. 120 cps
				Cartridge	Opt. 368M	Line	Opt. 85–750 lpm
				Pack	Opt. 521M		
	B 1815	16	131–262K	Floppy	Opt. 486K	Line	Opt. 85–1500 lpm
				Cartridge	Opt. 74.4M		
				Pack	Opt. 697.6M		
	B 1855	16	524–1048K	Floppy	Opt. 486K	Line	Opt. 85–1500 lpm
				Cartridge	Opt. 74.4M		
				Pack	Opt. 697.6M		
	B 1865	16	1M	Floppy	Opt. 486K	Line	Opt. 85–1500 lpm
				Cartridge	Opt. 74.4K		
				Pack	Opt. 697.6K		
	B 1885	16	512K–1048K	Floppy	Opt. 486K	Line	Opt. 85–1500 lpm
				Cartridge	Opt. 74.4K		
				Pack	Opt. 697.6M		
Business Controls Corporation	System 80/8	12	256K	Floppy	Opt. 670K	Serial	Opt. 180 cps
				Cartridge	Std. 40M	Line	Opt. 250–600 lpm
	80/11	16	204K	Floppy	Opt. 2048 K	Serial	Std. 180 cps
				Cartridge	Std. 40M	Line	Opt. 250–1200 lpm
				Pack	Opt. 1400M		

Number of Terminals, Partitions, Lines, or I/O Ports	Software		Price Range	Telephone	Address
	Language	Applications Software			
8–512	COBOL, RPG, FORTRAN, BASIC, Assembler, PASCAL, DBMS	General accounting, manufacturing, education	$86,850		
up to 3 programs	COBOL, RPG, DSC, MPL, NDL	General accounting	$18,510	(313) 972-7000	Burroughs Place, Detroit, MI 48232
4 (Data entry stations)	COBOL, RPG, AEL	General accounting	$30,400		
4 (number of communication lines)	COBOL, RPG, AEL, MPL, NDL	General accounting	$32,400		
4 (number of communication lines)	COBOL, RPG, AEL, MPL, NDL	General accounting	$37,400		
16	COBOL, RPG, FORTRAN, BASIC, NDL, UPL, AEL, DBMS	General accounting	$60,000		
16	COBOL, RPG, FORTRAN, BASIC, NDL, UPL, AEL, DBMS	General accounting	$91,928		
16	COBOL, RPG, FORTRAN, BASIC, NDL, UPL, AEL, DBMS	General accounting	$140,090		
1–16	COBOL, RPG, FORTRAN, BASIC, NDL, UPL, AEL, DBMS	General accounting	$148,320		
15 (partitions)	FORTRAN, BASIC, Assembler, DIBOL	Retail, wholesale, manufacturing	$29,990	(201) 791-7661	507 Boulevard, Elmwood Park, NJ 07407
2–63 (partitions)	COBOL, RPG, FORTRAN, BASIC, Assembler, DIBOL, DEC form DBMS-II	General accounting	$40,000		

TABLE C *(Continued)*

Manufacturer	System Model	CPU		Disk		Printer	
		Word Length (bits)	Memory Capacity (bytes)	Type	Capacity (bytes)	Type	Speed
Cado Systems Corporation (Benchmark Data System)	20 (CAT)	8	32K	Floppy	620K–4.8M	Serial	55–150 cps
	20/22	8	32–48K	Floppy	620K–4.8M	Serial	55–150 cps
				Cartridge (Winchester)	13.2–26.4 M	Line	300 lpm
	20/24	8	32–48K	Floppy Cartridge (Winchester)	620K–4.8M 13.2–26.4M	Serial Line	55–150 cps 300 lpm
	20/28	8	64–96K	Floppy Cartridge (Winchester)	620K–4.8M 13.2–105.6 M	Serial Line	55–150 cps 300 lpm
CDA, Inc.	100A (Nova 1200)	16	32K	Floppy	Std. 0.6M	Serial	Std. 30 cps
	400A (Nova 1200)	16	32K	Floppy	Std. 1.8M	Serial	Std. 30 cps
	500B (Nova 1200)	16	128K	Floppy	Std. 2.4M	Serial	Std. 120 cps
	500C (Nova 1200)	16	128K	Floppy	Std. 2.4M	Serial	Std. 120 cps
Century Computer Corporation	Century 300	8	60K	Floppy Cartridge Pack	Opt. 376K Std. 20M Opt. 100M	Serial Line	Std. 165 cps Opt. 300–600 lpm
	Century 400	16	250K	Floppy Cartridge Pack	Opt. 384K Std. 20M Opt. 80M–150M	Serial Line	Opt. 165 cps Std. 300–600 lpm
	Century 700	8, 16	96–512K	Floppy Cartridge Pack	Opt. 376K Std. 20M Opt. 80M–420M	Line	300 lpm
	Century 900	8, 16	64K 1M	Floppy Cartridge Pack	Opt. 376K Opt. 40M Opt. 600M	Line	600 lpm

Number of Terminals, Partitions, Lines, or I/O Ports	Software		Price Range	Telephone	Address
	Language	Applications Software			
1	BASIC (CADOL), Assembler, DBMS	General accounting, retail, wholesale, medical, property management, word processing	$13,995–$16,995	(213) 320-9660	2730 Monterey Street, Torrance, CA 90503
1-2	BASIC (CADOL), Assembler, DBMS	General accounting, retail, wholesale, medical, property management, word processing	$15,810–$21,820		
1-4	BASIC (CADOL), Assembler, DBMS	General accounting, retail, wholesale, medical, property management, word processing	$18,310–$25,320		
1-8	BASIC (CADOL), Assembler, DBMS	General accounting, retail, wholesale, medical, property management, word processing	$22,310–$32,310		
1	Assembler	General accounting, auto parts distribution a speciality	$19,800	(201) 944-2500	470 Commercial Avenue, Palisades Park, NJ 07650
1	Assembler	General accounting, auto parts distribution a speciality	$23,000		
1	Assembler	General accounting, auto parts distribution a speciality	$33,000		
1	Assembler	General accounting, auto parts distribution a speciality	$55,000		
6	BASIC, Assembler, CPL, DBMS	General accounting	$20,000	(425) 798-8000	1601 North Main Street, Walnut Creek, CA 94596
12	BASIC, Assembler, CPL	General accounting	$36,000		
20	BASIC, Assembler, CPL, MOD, FORTRAN	General accounting, distribution, finance	$35,000		
32	BASIC, Assembler, CPL, DBMS	General accounting, Finance, hotel inventory	$42,000		

TABLE C *(Continued)*

| Manufacturer | System Model | CPU | | Disk | | Printer | |
		Word Length (bits)	Memory Capacity (bytes)	Type	Capacity (bytes)	Type	Speed
	Century 1000	8, 16, 24	64K 1M	Floppy Cartridge Pack	Opt. 376K Opt. 40M Opt. 900M	— — —	— — —
Cincinnati Milacron	George (Series 40)	16	64K	Floppy	Std. 2.52M	Serial Line	Std. 60 cps Opt. 60–600 lpm
	George B (Series 60)	16	64K	Floppy Cartridge	Opt. 1.26M Std. 40M	Serial Line	Opt. 60 cps Std. 60–600 lpm
	George C (Series 70)	16	64K	Floppy Cartridge	Opt. 1.26M Std. 40M	Serial Line	Opt. 60 cps Std. 60–600 lpm
	George D (Series 80)	16	256K	Floppy Cartridge	Opt. 1.26M Std. 40M	Serial Line	Opt. 60 cps Std. 60–600 lpm
Commodore International Ltd.	Pet 2001	8	32K	Floppy	Opt. 300K	Serial	Opt. 45–150 cps
	CBM 8032	8	32K	Floppy	Opt. 300K–1M	Serial	Opt. 45–150 cps
Compal Computer System	Compal 8100	8	56K	Floppy	630K–2.4M	Serial	55–150 cps Optional
	Compal 8200	8	56–112K	Floppy Fixed-head (Winchester)	630K–2.4M Opt. 30M	Serial Line	55–150 cps Optional
Complete Computer Systems	10	16 + 1	256K	Floppy Cartridge	Opt. 1.2M Opt. 10M	Serial Line	Opt. 60 cps Opt. 300–600 lpm
	11	16 + 1	256K	Floppy Cartridge	Opt. 1.2M Std. 10M	Serial Line	Std. 120 cps Opt. 300–600 lpm
	12	16 + 1	256K	Floppy Cartridge	Opt. 1.2M Std. 10M	Serial Line	Std. 180 cps Opt. 300–600 lpm
	14	16 + 1	256K	Floppy Cartridge	Opt. 1.2M Std. 10M	Serial Line	Std. 180 cps Opt. 300–600 lpm

Number of Terminals, Partitions, Lines, or I/O Ports	Software		Price Range	Telephone	Address
	Language	Applications Software			
20	BASIC, Assembler, CPL, ALGOL, DBMS	General accounting, hotel, medicine, credit union	$50,000		
4 (communication lines)	RPG, Assembler	General accounting	$16,100	(513) 949-1200	Electronic Systems Division, Mason/Marrow Road, Lebanon, OH 45036
9 (communication lines)	RPG, Assembler	General accounting	$30,200		
9 (communication lines)	RPG, Assembler	General accounting	$30,300		
32 (communication lines)	RPG, Assembler Sys. Prog. Lang.	General accounting	$45,900		
1	BASIC, Visicalc	Personal and professional applications	$1,295 without disk and printer	(415) 326-4000	901 California Ave. Palo Alto, CA 94394
1	BASIC, Visicalc	Small business applications	$1,795 without disk and printer		
1	BASIC, COBOL, FORTRAN, PASCAL	General accounting, Distribution, reatial, legal, manufacturing	$11,500 up	(213) 992-4425	6300 Variel Avenue, Suite E, Woodland Hills, CA 91367
1	BASIC, COBOL, FORTRAN, PASCAL	General accounting, distribution, reatial, legal, manufacturing	$12,500 up		
1-16	FORTRAN, BASIC Assembler, "CREATE" DBMS	General accounting, property management	$30,940	(215) 441-4200	159 Gibraltar Road, Prudential Business Campus, Horsham, PA 19044
1-16	FORTRAN, BASIC Assembler, "CREATE" DBMS	General accounting, property management, inventory control	$33,605		
1-16	FORTRAN, BASIC, Assembler, "CREATE" DBMS	General accounting, property management, municipal budget acctg.	$33,825		
1-16	FORTRAN, BASIC, Assembler, "CREATE" DBMS	General accounting, property management, mail order prospect control	$45,275		

TABLE C *(Continued)*

Manufacturer	System Model	CPU Word Length (bits)	Memory Capacity (bytes)	Disk Type	Capacity (bytes)	Printer Type	Speed
	26	16 + 1	256K	Floppy	Opt. 1.2M	Serial	Std. 60–80 cps
				Cartridge	Std. 40M	Line	Std. 300 lpm
Compucorp	625	48	65K	Floppy	Std. 630K	Serial	Std. 80 cps
				Cartridge	Optional	Line	Optional
	625 Mk. II	64	256K	Floppy	Std. 630K	Serial	Standard
				Cartridge	Opt. 12M	Line	Optional
Compudata Systems	(DEC 500 Series)	16 + 2	512K	Floppy	Opt. 310K	Serial	Std. 180 cps
				Cartridge	Std. 5M	Line	Opt. 300 lpm
				Pack	Opt. 14, 88, 176 MB		
				Fixed-head	Opt. 512M		
	(IBM Series/1)	16	128K	Floppy	Opt. 2.5M	Serial	Opt. 120 cps
				Cartridge	Opt. 13M	Line	Opt. 155 lpm
	(DEC 300 series)	16 + 2	256K	Floppy	Opt. 310K	Serial	Std. 180 cps
				Cartridge	Std. 2.5/ 5M	Line	Opt. 300 lpm
				Pack	Opt. 14M		
Computer Automation	SyFA	16	304K	Cartridge	Std. 40M	Serial	Opt. 100, 165 cps
				Pack	Opt. 640M	Line	Opt. 300, 600 lpm
	Naked mini LSI-2	16	512K	Floppy	243–972K	Serial	30–180 cps
				Cartridge	4.92– 19.68M		
	Naked mini 4	16	32–128K	Floppy	243–972K		
				Cartridge	5–1200M	Line	600 lpm
Computer Covenant	CPBS 1	16	56K	Floppy	Opt. 512K	Serial	Std. 30 cps, 180 cps
				Cartridge	Opt. 10M	Line	Opt. 300 lpm
	CPBS 2	16	248K	Floppy	Opt. 512K	Serial	Std. 30, 180 cps
				Cartridge	Std. 10M	Line	Opt. 300– 1200 lpm
				Pack	Opt. 1408 M		
	CPBS 3	16	2048K	Floppy	Opt. 512K	Serial	Std. 30, 180 cps
				Cartridge	Opt. 10M	Line	Opt. 300– 1200 lpm
				Pack	Std. 1408 M		

Number of Terminals, Partitions, Lines, or I/O Ports	Software		Price Range	Telephone	Address
	Language	Applications Software			
1–16	FORTRAN, BASIC, Assembler, "CREATE" DBMS	General accounting, property management, job costing	$77,495		
1–8	BASIC, Assembler	General accounting, auto finance	$7,000	(213) 820-2503	1901 South Bundy Drive, Los Angeles, CA 90025
1–8	Extended BASIC Assembler	General accounting, auto bonds, auto finance	$7,000 (desk top)		
1–64 (I/O ports)	COBOL, RPG, FORTRAN, BASIC, DIBOL, DBMS	General accounting, manufacturing, distribution, retail	$60,000	(203) 226-4791	772 Post Road East (East State Street), Westport, CN 06880
4–56 (I/O ports)	COBOL, FORTRAN, Assembler	General accounting, manufacturing, distribution	$26,000		
1–8 (I/O ports)	FORTRAN, DIBOL	General accounting, manufacturing, distribution	$17,000		
32	FORTRAN, BASIC, SYBOL	Distributed processing	$45,000	(714) 833-8830	18651 Von Karman Avenue, Irvine, CA 92664
16	FORTRAN, BASIC, SYBOL		$11,500 up		
32	BASIC, FORTRAN		$11,500– $27,000		
4 (partitions)	FORTRAN, BASIC, Assembler, DIBOL-11, RMS-11	General accounting, manufacturing, distribution, wholesale	$24,000	(203) 667-6563	749 Farmington Avenue Farmington, CN 06032
16 (partitions)	COBOL, RPG, FORTRAN, BASIC, Assembler, DIBOL-11, RMS-11	General accounting, manufacturing, distribution, wholesale	$42,000		
60 (partitions)	COBOL, RPG, FORTRAN, BASIC, Assembler, DIBOL-11, RMS-11	General accounting, manufacturing, distribution, wholesale	$100,000		

TABLE C (*Continued*)

Manufacturer	System Model	CPU		Disk		Printer	
		Word Length (bits)	Memory Capacity (bytes)	Type	Capacity (bytes)	Type	Speed
Computer Hardware Inc.	2130	16	128K–4M	Cartridge Pack	Opt. 2M Std. 1200M	Serial Line	Opt. 60 cps Opt. 600 lpm
	3230	16	128K–4M	Cartridge Pack	Opt. 2M Opt. 80M	Serial Line	Opt. 60 cps Opt. 600 lpm
	4210	16	64K	Floppy Cartridge	Std. 1.0M Opt. 3M	Serial	Opt. 30, 180 cps
Computer Horizons	CHC Distribution System	16	248K	Pack	Std. 88M	Serial Line	Std. 180 cps Opt. 1200 lpm
Computer Interactions	Compro II	12	64K	Floppy Cartridge Pack	Opt. 256K Std. 256M Opt. 90M	Serial Line	Opt. 165, 300 cps Std. 300 lpm
Control Data	Cyber 18-10	16	64K	Floppy Cartridge	Opt. 560K Opt. 35.2M	Serial Line	180 cps Opt. 300–600 lpm
	Cyber 18-20	16	256K	Floppy Pack	Opt. 560K Opt. 400M	Line	Opt. 300–900 lpm
Constar Business Computing Co.	CORSTAR 310 (DEC 310)	12	64K (6-bit)	Floppy Cartridge	Std. 1.2M Opt. 1.28M	Serial Line	Std. 180 cps Opt. 300 lpm
	CORSTAR 350 (DEC 350)	16	256K	Floppy Cartridge Pack	Std. 1.2M Std. 19.2M Opt. 160M	Serial Line	Std. 180 cps Opt. 300 lpm
	CORSTAR 534 (DEC 534)	16	248K	Cartridge Pack	Std. 19.2M Opt. 704M	Serial Line	Opt. 180 cps Std. 300 lpm
	CORSTAR 570 (DEC 570)	16	1024K	Cartridge Pack	Std. 19.2M Std. 1408M	Serial Line	Opt. 180 cps Std. 300 lpm

Number of Terminals, Partitions, Lines, or I/O Ports	Software Language	Applications Software	Price Range	Telephone	Address
32 (partitions)	COBOL, RPG, FORTRAN, BASIC, Assembler, ALGOL, SNOBOL	General accounting, manufacturing, distribution, wholesale	Consult factory	(916) 929-2020	4111 North Freeway Boulevard, Sacramento, CA 95834
32 (partitions)	COBOL, RPG, FORTRAN, BASIC, Assembler, ALGOL, SNOBOL	General accounting, manufacturing, distribution, wholesale	Consult factory		
8 (partitions)	FORTRAN, Assembler	General accounting, manufacturing, distribution, wholesale	Consult factory		
32 (partitions)	COBOL, FORTRAN	General accounting, inventory, order processing	$150,000–$200,000	(212) 371-9600	375 Sylvan Avenue, Englewood Cliffs, NJ 07632
4 (partitions)	BASIC, FORTRAN	General accounting, pharm., medical	$50,000	(516) 365-9833	P.O. Box 1354, Roslyn Heights, New York, NY 11577
1	Assembler		$27,840	(616) 853-4656	P.O. Box 0, Minneapolis, MI 55440
16 (partitions)	FORTRAN, BASIC, MACRO, Assembler	Manufacturing, distribution	$29,940		
1	DIBOL	General accounting, manufacturing	$13,000–$23,000	(914) 428-5550	One Aqueduct Road, White Plains, NY 10606
4 (partitions)	DIBOL	General accounting, manufacturing, distribution	$36,000–$65,000		
32 (partitions)	COBOL, RPG II FORTRAN, BASIC PLUS II	General accounting, advertising agency, financial	$75,000–$125,000		
63 (partitions)	COBOL, RPG II FORTRAN, BASIC PLUS II	General accounting, advertising agency, financial publishing	$135,000–$250,000		

TABLE C   (*Continued*)

| Manufacturer | System Model | CPU | | Disk | | Printer | |
		Word Length (bits)	Memory Capacity (bytes)	Type	Capacity (bytes)	Type	Speed
Cromemco	System Three	8	32–64K	Floppy (up to 4)	256K	Serial (dot matrix or formed character)	55–180 cps
	Z-2H	8	64K	Hard disk (Winchester)	11–22M	Serial	55–180 cps
	Z-2D	8	64K	Floppy	92–184K	Serial	55–180 cps
Data Communications Corp.	TPS	16	256K	Floppy Cartridge Pack	Opt. 500K Std. 10M Opt. 92M	Serial Line	Std. 165 cps Opt. 300–1200 lpm
	DPS	16	256K	Floppy Cartridge Pack	Opt. 500K Std. 10M Opt. 92M	Serial Line	Std. 165 cps Opt. 300 lpm
	DCS	16	32K	Floppy Cartridge Pack	Opt. 500K Std. 100M Opt. 92M	Serial Line	Std. 165 cps Opt. 300–1200 lpm
	RTS	16	32K	Floppy Cartridge Pack	Opt. 500K Std. 10M Opt. 92M	Serial Line	Std. 165 cps Opt. 300–1200 lpm
Data General	CS/20	16	64K	Floppy	Std. 630K 1.3M	Serial Line	Opt. 60 cps, 180 cps Opt. 240, 300 lpm
	CS/40 Mod. 1	16	64K	Floppy Cartridge	Std. 315K Std. 10M	Serial Line	Std. 60, 180 cps Std. 300 lpm
	CS/40 Mod. C3	16	64K	Floppy Cartridge	Std. 315K Std. 10M–80M	Serial Line	Std. 60, 180 cps Std. 300 lpm
	CS/40 Mod. C4	16	64K	Floppy Cartridge Pack	Opt. 315K Std. 10M Std. 50M–760M	Serial Line	Std. 60 cps Opt. 300 lpm

Number of Terminals, Partitions, Lines, or I/O Ports	Software		Price Range	Telephone	Address
	Language	Applications Software			
1–7	BASIC, COBOL, FORTRAN, Multi-user BASIC, DBMS	Business data processing, manufacturing, property management, word processing	$5,990 with 8 inch disk printer	(415) 964-7499	2400 Charleston Road, Mountain View, CA 94043
1–7	BASIC, COBOL, FORTRAN, Multi-user BASIC, DBMS	Business data processing, manufacturing, property management, word processing	$9,995 with hard disk, printer		
1–7	BASIC, COBOL, FORTRAN, Multi-user BASIC, DBMS	Business data processing, manufacturing, property management, word processing	$2,890 with 5 inch disk		
39	COBOL, FORTRAN IV, V, BASIC, ALGOL, Assembler	General accounting, mortgage banking, general marketing	$85,000	(901) 345-3544	Minicomputer Division, 3000 Directors Row, Memphis, TN 38131
64	COBOL, FORTRAN IV, V BASIC, ALGOL, Assembler, RPG II DBMS (INFOS)	General accounting, mortgage banking, general marketing, mortgages	On request only		
39	COBOL, FORTRAN IV, V BASIC, ALGOL, Assembler, RPG II DBMS (INFOS)	General accounting, mortgage banking, general marketing, mortgage, broadcasting	$50,000		
39	COBOL, RPG FORTRAN IV, V, BASIC, Assembler	General accounting, broadcasting, service bureaus	$25,000		
1–1	COBOL, Interactive COBOL	Industries	$10,945	(617) 366-8911	Route 9, Southboro, MA 01581
1–1	COBOL, Interactive COBOL	Industries	$32,915		
1–4	COBOL, Interactive COBOL	Industries	$34,105		
1–4	COBOL, Interactive COBOL	Wholesale, distributing, health care	$56,340		

TABLE C (*Continued*)

Manufacturer	System Model	CPU		Disk		Printer	
		Word Length (*bits*)	Memory Capacity (*bytes*)	Type	Capacity (*bytes*)	Type	Speed
	CS/40 Mod. C6	16	192K	Floppy	Std. 315K	Serial	Std. 60, 180 cps
				Cartridge Pack	Opt. 10M Std. 50M–760M	Line	Std. 300 lpm
	CS/60 Mod. C3	16	64K	Floppy Cartridge	Opt. 315K Std. 20M–40M	Serial Line	Std. 180 cps Std. 300 lpm
	CS/60 Mod. C5	16	128K–256K	Floppy Cartridge	Opt. 315K Std. 20M–80M	Serial Line	Std. 180 cps Std. 300 lpm
	CS/60 Mod. C6	16	128K–512K	Floppy Cartridge Pack	Opt. 315K Opt. 10–30M Std. 50M–760M	Serial Line	Std. 180 cps Std. 300 lpm
Datapoint	2200	8	16K	Floppy Cartridge Pack	Opt. 1M Opt. 9.6M Opt. 50M	Serial Line	Opt. 120 lpm Opt. 300, 600 lpm
	3600	8	120K	N.A.	N.A.	Line	300–900 lpm
	5500	8	48K	Floppy Cartridge Pack	Opt. 1M Opt. 160M Opt. 200M	Serial Line	Opt. 120 lpm Opt. 300, 600 lpm
	6600	8	120K (user)	Floppy Cartridge Pack	Opt. 1M Opt. 160M Opt. 200M	Serial Line	Opt. 60/ 120 cps Opt. 300, 600 lpm
	8800	16	256–1024K	Pack	Std. 200M 1012M	Serial Line	80, 120 cps 300–600 lpm
	Diskette 1100	8	16K	Floppy	Std. 1M	Serial Line	Opt. 120 lpm Opt. 300–500 lpm
	1150	8	24K (user)	Floppy	Std. 1M	Line Serial	Opt. 300, 600 lpm Opt. 80/ 120 cps

426

Number of Terminals, Partitions, Lines, or I/O Ports	Software		Price Range	Telephone	Address
	Language	Applications Software			
1–9	COBOL, Interactive COBOL	Wholesale, distributing, health care	$63,640		
1–9	COBOL, Interactive COBOL	Distributed data processing, industries	$40,890		
1–9	COBOL, Interactive COBOL	Distributed data processing, industries	$50,290		
1–17	COBOL, Interactive COBOL	Distributed data processing, industries	$70,490		
4	RPG, BASIC, Assembler, DATABUS, SCRIBE	General accounting, banking, insurance	Price on request	(512) 690-7000	9725 Datapoint Drive, San Antonio, TX 78284
4	RPG, BASIC, Assembler, DATABUS, SCRIBE	General accounting, banking, insurance	Price on request		
16	RPG, BASIC, Assembler, DATABUS, SCRIBE, COBOL	General accounting, banking, insurance, government	$26,271		
24	RPG, BASIC, Assembler, DATABUS, SCRIBE, COBOL, DATASHARE	General accounting, banking, insurance, government	$31,685		
24	RPG, BASIC, Assembler, DATABUS, SCRIBE, COBOL, DATASHARE	General accounting, banking, insurance, government	$42,500		
1	RPG, BASIC, Assembler, DATABUS, SCRIBE, COBOL, DATASHARE	General accounting, banking, insurance	$12,880		
4	RPG, BASIC, Assembler, DATABUS, SCRIBE, COBOL, DATASHARE	General accounting, banking, insurance, government, public accounting	$14,480		

427

TABLE C   (*Continued*)

Manufacturer	System Model	CPU		Disk		Printer	
		Word Length (*bits*)	Memory Capacity (*bytes*)	Type	Capacity (*bytes*)	Type	Speed
	1170	8	48K (user)	Floppy	Std. 1M	Serial Line	Opt. 80/ 120 cps Opt. 300, 600 lpm
	1800	8	128K	Floppy Fixed-head	2M–4M 10–40M	Serial Line	160 cps 300– 900 lpm
Decision Data Computer Corp.	System/4	8	64K	Floppy Cartridge	Std. 2M Opt. 40M	Serial Line	Std. 120 cps Opt. 300/ 600 lpm
Digital Computer Control Synergist	1500	16	64K	Cartridge	Opt. 10M	Serial Line	Std. 30 cps Opt. 125 lpm
	1550	16	64K	Cartridge	Opt. 10M	Serial Line	Std. 30 cps Opt. 125 lpm
	2500	16	64K	Cartridge Pack	Std. 10M Opt. 96– 190M	Serial Line	Std. 275 cps Opt. 300, 600 lpm
	3700	16	256K	Cartridge Pack	Std. 10M Opt. 96– 190M	Serial Line	Opt. 30, 60, 180 cps Opt. 300, 600 lpm
Digital Equipment Corp. Datasystem	Datasystem 308 (VT 78 base)	12	32K (6-bit)	Floppy	Std. 670K	Serial Line	Opt. 45, 180 cps Opt. 300 lpm
	310 (PDP) 8/A base)	12	64K (6-bit)	Floppy Cartridge	Std. 670K Std. 12.8M	Serial Line	Opt. 30, 165 cps Opt. 300 lpm
	322 (LSI-II base)	16	56K	Floppy Cartridge	Std. 1M Opt. 19.2M	Serial Line	Opt. 30, 180 cps Opt. 240, 300 lpm
	324 (LSI-II base)	16	56K	Floppy Cartridge	Std. 7.2M Opt. 19.2M	Serial Line	Opt. 30, 180 cps Opt. 240, 300 lpm
	354 (PDP 11/34 base)	16	248K	Floppy Cartridge	Opt. 512K Std. 19.2M	Serial Line	Opt. 30, 180 cps Opt. 240, 300 lpm

Number of Terminals, Partitions, Lines, or I/O Ports	Software		Price Range	Telephone	Address
	Language	Applications Software			
4	RPG, BASIC, Assembler, DATABUS, SCRIBE, COBOL, DATASHARE	General accounting, banking, insurance, government, public accounting	$15,980		
9	RPG, BASIC, Assembler, DATABUS, SCRIBE, COBOL, DATASHARE	General accounting, banking, insurance, government, public accounting	$10,975 up		
2 (partitions)	RPG	General accounting, fuel oil	$22,000	(215) 674-3300	100 Witmer Road, Horsham, PA 19044
1–3 (I/O ports)	BASIC	General accounting	$8,000	(201) 575-9100	12 Industrial Road, Fairfield, NJ 07006
1–3 (I/O ports)	BASIC	General accounting, wholesale, distributer	$13,500		
1–9 (I/O ports)	BASIC, Assembler	General accounting, manufacturer, wholesale, distributor	$27,000		
1–17 (I/O ports)	BASIC, Assembler	General accounting, manufacturer, wholesale, distributor	$40,000		
1	DIBOL (COBOL)	Business accounting, small business accounting	$12,600	(617) 897-5111	Parker Street, PK 3-2, Maynard, MA 01754
1	DIBOL (COBOL)	Business accounting, small business accounting	$14,095		
4 (communication lines)	DIBOL (COBOL)	Business accounting, small business accounting	$19,315		
4 (communication lines)	DIBOL (COBOL)	Business accounting, small business accounting	$32,615		
8 (communication lines)	DIBOL (COBOL)	Business accounting, small business accounting	$37,950		

TABLE C (*Continued*)

| Manufacturer | System Model | CPU | | Disk | | Printer | |
		Word Length (*bits*)	Memory Capacity (*bytes*)	Type	Capacity (*bytes*)	Type	Speed
	357 (PDP 11/34 base)	16	248K	Floppy	Opt. 512K	Serial	Opt. 30, 180 cps
				Cartridge	Std. 112M	Line	Opt. 240, 300 lpm
	530 (PDP 11/34 base)	16	256K	Floppy	Opt. 512K	Serial	Std. 30, 180 cps
				Cartridge	Opt. 112M	Line	Opt. 240–1200 lpm
				Pack	Std. 1,408M		
	570 (PDP 11/70 base)	16	3M	Floppy	Opt. 512K	Serial	Std. 30, 180 cps
				Cartridge	Opt. 112M	Line	Opt. 240–1200 lpm
				Pack	Opt. 1,408M		
Digital Scientific Corporation	1130	16 (+2 parity)	128K	Cartridge	Opt. 512M	Line	Opt. 300, 600 lpm
				Pack	Opt. 160M		
	5010	16 (+2 parity)	128K	Cartridge	Opt. 1.24M	Serial	Opt. 180 cps
				Pack	Opt. 20M	Line	Opt. 300, 600 lpm
	5020	16 (+2 parity)	256K	Cartridge	Opt. 1.24M	Serial	Opt. 180 cps
				Pack	Opt. 20M	Line	Opt. 300, 600 lpm
Digital Systems	Galaxy/5 Model 130	8–20	1M	Pack	Std. 80M–1200M	Line	Std. 300–900 lpm
	Galaxy/5 Model 150	8–20	1M	Pack	Std. 80M–1200M	Line	Std. 300–900 lpm
	Galaxy 3	8–20	96–128K	Cartridge Pack	Std. 32M Opt. 80M–160M	Serial Line	Optional 300–900 lpm
Dimis, Inc.	Total 100	16	128K–4M	Floppy Cartridge	Optional Optional	Serial Line	Optional Std. 300 lpm
				Pack	Std. 80M, 800M 9200M		
Display Data Corporation	In Sight	8	128K	Cartridge	Std. 80M	Serial Line	Std. 120 cps Opt. 150–1100 lpm

Number of Lines, or I/O Ports	Software		Price Range	Telephone	Address
	Language	Applications Software			
8 (communication lines)	DIBOL (COBOL)	Business accounting, small business accounting	$51,170		
32 communication lines)	COBOL, RPG, FORTRAN, BASIC, Assembler, APL, DIBOL, Real Time, Interactive time sharing	Business accounting, data processing	$77,430		
63 (communication lines)	COBOL, RPG, FORTRAN, BASIC, Assembler, APL, DIBOL, Real Time, Interactive time sharing	Business accounting, data processing	$126,280		
4 (I/O ports)	COBOL, RPG, FORTRAN, Assembler	General accounting, civil engineering, education	$60,000	(714) 453-6050	11455 Sorrento Valley Road, San Diego, CA 92121
4-21 (I/O ports)	COBOL, RPG, FORTRAN, Assembler	General accounting, civil engineering, education	$18,000		
8-21 (I/O ports)	FORTRAN, Assembler	General accounting	$24,500		
1-150	RPG, FORTRAN, BASIC, COBOL, Assembler, LMP, FMP	General accounting, most industries	$34,700 (CPU only)	(301) 845-4141	P.O. Box 396, Walkersville, MD 21793
1-150	RPG, FORTRAN, BASIC, COBOL, Assembler, LMP, FMP	General accounting, most industries	$82,875 up		
1-15	RPG, FORTRAN, BASIC, COBOL, Assembler, LMP, FMP	General accounting, most industries	$49,500 up		
1-28	COBOL, FORTRAN, BASIC Assembler	General accounting, distribution	$110,000 up	(201) 671-1011	1060 Highway 35, Middletown, NJ 07748
1-32	Assembler	General accounting, auto dealers, contractors	$29,700 up	(301) 667-9211	Executive Plaza, Hunt Valley, MD 21031

TABLE C (*Continued*)

Manufacturer	System Model	CPU		Disk		Printer	
		Word Length (bits)	Memory Capacity (bytes)	Type	Capacity (bytes)	Type	Speed
Distribution Management Systems	DMS-1000-8	12	32K	Cartridge	Std. 6.4–25.6M	Serial / Line	Std. 180 cps / Opt. 300 lpm
	DMS-1000-11	16	248–2048K	Floppy / Cartridge	Opt. 256K / Opt. 28M Std. 1200M	Serial / Line	Std. 180 cps / Opt. 60–1200 lpm
Durango	F85	8	32–65K	Floppy / Pack	473–1890 K / 10–20M	Serial	165 cps
FINDEX	FINDEX	8	128–500 K (bubble memory)	Floppy built in	Std. 200–400K Opt. 2M	Serial built in	40–80 cps
Four-Phase Systems, Inc.	System IV/40	24	24K–96K	Floppy Cartridge	Opt. 354K Std. 10M	Serial / Line	Opt. 55 cps / Opt. 120–1000 lpm
	System IV/50	24	96K	Floppy Cartridge Pack	Std. 354K Std. 10M Opt. 270M	Serial / Line	Opt. 55 cps / Opt. 120–1000 lpm
	System IV/50	24	240K	Cartridge Fixed-head	2.5–13M 2.5–67M	Serial / Line	55 cps 120–1000 lpm
	System IV/70	24	96K	Floppy Cartridge Pack	Opt. 354K Std. 10M Opt. 270M	Serial / Line	Opt. 55 cps / Opt. 120–1000 cps
General Automation	GA 16/110	16	32–128K	Cartridge Pack	10–80M 80–2400M	Serial / Line	30–165 cps 300, 600 lpm
	GA 16/220	16	32–128K	Floppy Cartridge Pack	500K–2M 10–80M 80M, 300M 640–2400M	Serial / Line	30–165 cps 300, 600 lpm
	GA 16/230	16	128K	Floppy Cartridge Pack	500K–2M 10–80M 80M, 300M 640–2400M	Serial / Line	300–165 cps 300, 600 lpm

Number of Terminals, Partitions, Lines, or I/O Ports	Software		Price Range	Telephone	Address
	Language	Applications Software			
10 (partitions)	Assembler, DEAL, ORACLE	General accounting, distribution, warehouse control	$54,000	(617) 275-2000	11 Deangelo Drive, Bedford, MA 01730
30 (partitions)	Assembler, DEAL, ORACLE, COBOL, BASIC, FORTRAN	General accounting, distribution, warehouse control	$65,000		
1-4	BASIC, Real time, Multiprogramming	Small business accounting packages (turnkey)	$12,983	(408) 996-1001	10101 Bubb Road, Cupertino, CA 95014
1	BASIC, COBOL, FORTRAN, PL/1	Small business accounting, medical, scientific, engineering	$6,980– $13,480	(213) 775-1162	20775 S. Western Ave., Torrance, CA 90501
16	Assembler	Manufacturing, insurance, education	$30,315	(408) 255-0900	19333 Vallco Parkway, Cupertino, CA 95014
24	COBOL, Assembler	Manufacturing, insurance, education	$69,330		
16	COBOL, Assembler	Manufacturing, insurance, education	$64,615 up		
32	COBOL, RPG, Assembler	Manufacturing, insurance, education	$68,055		
1-16	BASIC, FORTRAN, Commercial FORTRAN, COBOL	Manufacturing, automatic equipment control, process control	$3,275 (CPU) $16,225– $43,875 for basic system with disk, printer, and terminal	(714) 778-4800	1055 South East St., Anaheim, CA 92805
1-16	BASIC, FORTRAN, Commercial FORTRAN, COBOL	Manufacturing, automatic equipment control, process control	$3,600 (CPU) $11,225– $61,825		
1-16	BASIC, FORTRAN, Commercial FORTRAN, COBOL	Manufacturing, automatic equipment control, process control	$7,325 (CPU) $14,950– $65,550		

433

TABLE C (*Continued*)

Manufacturer	System Model	CPU		Disk		Printer	
		Word Length (bits)	Memory Capacity (bytes)	Type	Capacity (bytes)	Type	Speed
	GA 16/240 (Instacode 20)	16	128– 512K	Floppy Cartridge	500K–2M 10–80M	Serial Line	30–165 cps 300, 600 lpm
				Pack	80M, 300M 640– 2400M		
	GA 16/440	16	64K–2M	Floppy Cartridge	500K–2M 10–80M	Serial Line	30–165 cps 300, 600 lpm
				Pack	80M, 300M 640– 2400M		
	GA 16/460	16	64K–2M	Floppy Cartridge	500K–2M 10–80M	Serial Line	30–165 cps 300, 600 lpm
				Pack	80M, 300M 640– 2400M		
	GA 16/470 (Instacode 55)	16	128K	Floppy Cartridge	500K–2M 10–80M	Serial Line	30–165 cps 300, 600 lpm
				Pack	80M, 300M 640– 2400M		
	GA 16/480	16	256K– 2M	Floppy Cartridge	500K–2M 10–80M	Serial Line	30–165 cps 300, 600 lpm
				Pack	80M, 300M 640– 2400M		
General Information Systems	ABLE-322	16	56K	Floppy	Std. 1024K	Serial	Std. (2) 180 cps
				Cartridge	Std. 20M	Line	Opt. to 1200 lpm
	ABLE-322F	16	56K	Floppy	Std. 1024K	Serial	Std. (2) 180 cps
				Cartridge	Std. 20M	Line	Opt. to 1200 lpm
	GIS-325	16	6M	Floppy	Opt. 1024K	Serial	Std. 180 cps
				Cartridge	Std. 10M	Line	Opt. 1200 lpm
				Pack	Opt. 20M		
	ABLE-350	16	256K	Cartridge	Std. 29M	Serial	Std. 180 cps
				Pack	Opt. 160M	Line	Opt. 1200 lpm
General Robotics	CD/X3S	16	32K	Floppy	Opt. 3.75M	Serial	Opt. 60– 180 cps
				Cartridge	Std. 20M	Line	Std. 300 lpm

Number of Terminals, Partitions, Lines, or I/O Ports	Software		Price Range	Telephone	Address
	Language	Applications Software			
1–16	BASIC, FORTRAN, Commercial FORTRAN, COBOL	Manufacturing, automatic equipment control, process control	$9,000 (CPU) $16,625– $67,550		
1–64	BASIC, FORTRAN, Commercial FORTRAN, COBOL	Manufacturing, automatic equipment control, process control	$12,000 (CPU) $19,625– $70,225		
1–64	BASIC, FORTRAN, Commercial FORTRAN, COBOL	Manufacturing, automatic equipment control, process control	$15,000 (CPU) $22,625– $73,225		
1–64	BASIC, FORTRAN, Commercial FORTRAN, COBOL	Manufacturing, automatic equipment control, process control	$16,000 (CPU) $23,625– $74,225		
1–64	BASIC, FORTRAN, Commercial FORTRAN, COBOL	Manufacturing, automatic equipment control, process control	$20,500 (CPU) $28,125– $78,725		
16 (partitions)	COBOL, RPG, FORTRAN, BASIC, Assembler, DIBOL	General accounting, CPA, medical, legal	$24,000	(714) 834-0220	P.O. Box 17388, Irvine, CA 92713
16 (partitions)	COBOL, RPG, FORTRAN, BASIC, Assembler, DIBOL	General accounting, CPA, medical, legal	$31,000		
4 (partitions)	FORTRAN, Assembler, DIBOL	General accounting, CPA, medical, legal	$24,000		
24 (partitions)	COBOL, RPG, FORTRAN, BASIC, Assembler	General accounting, CPA, medical, legal	$48,000		
8 (no. of communication lines)	COBOL, FORTRAN, BASIC, Assembler, APL, PASCAL, ALGOL	General accounting	$24,000	(414) 673-6800	57 West Main Street, Hartford, WI 53027

TABLE C   (*Continued*)

Manufacturer	System Model	CPU		Disk		Printer	
		Word Length (*bits*)	Memory Capacity (*bytes*)	Type	Capacity (*bytes*)	Type	Speed
	FD/X3S	16	32K	Floppy	Opt. 3.75M	Serial	Opt. 60–180 cps
				Cartridge	Opt. 20M	Line	Std. 300 lpm
	MVT/X3	16	32K	Floppy	Opt. 3.75M	Serial	Opt. 60 cps
				Cartridge	Opt. 20M		
GRI Computer Corp.	System 99	16	64K	Cartridge	Std. 6M	Serial	Opt. 100/165 cps
						Line	Opt. 250/600 lpm
	System 99 E	16	2048K	Cartridge	Std. 20M	Serial	Opt. 100/165 cps
						Line	Opt. 250/600 lpm
Harris Computer Systems	S110	24	96K–768K	Floppy	Opt. 310K	Serial	Opt. 30 cps
				Cartridge	Std. 10.8M	Line	Opt. 900 lpm
				Pack	Opt. 1200M		
	S120	24	192–768K	Floppy	Opt. 310K	Serial	Opt. 30 cps
				Cartridge	Std. 10.8M		
				Pack	Opt. 1200M	Line	Std. 300 lpm
	S130	24	288–768K	Floppy	Opt. 310K	Serial	Opt. 30 cps
				Cartridge	Std. 40M	Line	Std. 300 lpm
				Pack	Opt. 1200M		
	Harris 550	24	960–3072K	Floppy	310K		
				Cartridge	10.8M	Line	300–900 lpm
				Pack	40–300M		
Hewlett-Packard Data Systems Division	1000 Model 20	16	64K–2048K	Floppy	Opt. 1M	Serial	30, 180 cps
						Line	200–1250 lpm

436

Number of Terminals, Partitions, Lines, or I/O Ports	Software		Price Range	Telephone	Address
	Language	Applications Software			
8 (no. of communi-cation lines)	COBOL, FORTRAN, BASIC, Assembler, APL, PASCAL, ALGOL	General accounting	$17,000		
18 (no. of communi-cation lines)	COBOL, FORTRAN, BASIC, Assembler, APL, PASCAL, ALGOL	General accounting	$12,000		
4 (parti-tions)	RPG (INTER-ACTIVE), BASIC, Assembler	General account-ing, retail dis-tribution, con-struction, banking	$33,333	(617) 969-0800	320 Needham Street, Newton, MA 02164
9–80 (I/O ports)	RPG (INTER-ACTIVE), BASIC, Assembler	General account-ing, retail dis-tribution, con-struction, banking	$43,300		
256 (parti-tions)	COBOL, FORTRAN, Assembler, RPG, BASIC, SNOBOL, FORGO, DBMS	Multiuse, time-sharing	$85,000	(305) 974-1700	1200 Gateway Drive, Fort Lauderdale, FL 33309
256 (parti-tions)	COBOL, FORTRAN, Assembler, RPG, BASIC, SNOBOL, FORGO, DBMS	Multiuse, time-sharing	$125,000		
256 (parti-tions)	COBOL, FORTRAN, Assembler, RPG BASIC, SNOBOL, FORGO	Multiuse, time-sharing	$155,000		
	COBOL, FORTRAN, Assembler, RPG, BASIC, SNOBOL, FORGO	Multiuse, time-sharing	$255,000		
4	FORTRAN, BASIC, Assembler, ALGOL	General account-ing, manufac-turing	$22,000	(408) 257-7000	11000 Wolfe Road, Cupertino, CA 95014

TABLE C *(Continued)*

| Manufacturer | System Model | CPU | | Disk | | Printer | |
		Word Length (bits)	Memory Capacity (bytes)	Type	Capacity (bytes)	Type	Speed
	1000 Model 30	16	64K–2048K	Floppy	Opt. 2M	Serial	Opt. 30–180 cps
				Cartridge	Std. 160M	Line	Std. 200–1250 lpm
				Pack	Opt. 400M		
	1000 Model 45	16	128K–2048K	Floppy	Opt. 2M	Serial	Opt. 30–180 cps
				Cartridge	160M	Line	200–1250 lpm
				Pack	Opt. 400M		
Hewlett-Packard General Systems Division	3000 Series 30	16	256–1024K	Floppy Cartridge Pack	Std. 1.18M Std. 8–20M Opt. 50–150M	Serial Line	180 cps 400 lpm
	3000 Series 44	16	1M–4M	Floppy	Opt. 1.2M	Serial	Opt. 180 cps
				Fixed disk	Opt. 50M–1920M	Line	Opt. 400 lpm
	3000 Series III	16	256K–2048K	Pack	50M–960M	Serial Line	Opt. 180 cps 300–1250 lpm
Hewlett-Packard Desk-Top Computer Division	9825/9831	8	7K/8K–32K/33K	Opt. floppy	468K–15M	Serial Opt. line	30 cps–180 cps 250 lpm
	System 45	16	63K	Opt. floppy Pack	500K–24M 15M–6400M	Opt. serial Line	30–100 cps 480 lpm
	250	16	128–192K	Floppy Cartridge	3.6M 40M	Opt. Serial	30, 180 cps
Honeywell	Level 6 Model 23	16	32–128K	Floppy	512K–2M	Serial	Opt. 30–160 cps
				Cartridge	26–80M	Line	Opt. 240–900 lpm
	Level 6 Model 33	16	32–128K	Floppy	512K–2M	Serial	Opt. 30–160 cps
				Cartridge	10M–80M	Line	Opt. 240–900 lpm
				Pack	67M–256M		
	Level 6 Model 43	16	32–2048K	Floppy	512K–2M	Serial	Opt. 30–160 cps
				Cartridge	10M–80M	Line	Opt. 240–900 lpm
				Pack	67–256M		

Number of Terminals, Partitions, Lines, or I/O Ports	Software		Price Range	Telephone	Address
	Language	Applications Software			
4	FORTRAN, BASIC, Assembler, ALGOL	Manufacturing	$31,500		
4	FORTRAN, BASIC, Assembler, ALGOL	Manufacturing	$46,500		
32	COBOL, FORTRAN, Assembler, RPG, BASIC, APL	Manufacturing, education	$49,750	(408) 249-7020	5303 Stevens Creek Road, Santa Clara, CA 95050
96	COBOL, FORTRAN, Assembler, RPG, BASIC, APL	Manufacturing	$109,445		
1-64	COBOL, FORTRAN, Assembler, RPG, BASIC, APL	Manufacturing	$105,000		
1	BASIC, HPL	General accounting, real estate, medicine, engineering	$5900/$7200	(303) 226-3800	P.O. Box 1550, Fort Collins, CO 80522
1	BASIC	General accounting, text proc., inventory control, linear programming	$11,500 up		
6	BASIC	General accounting, manufacturing	$19,000 up	(303) 226-3800	P.O. Box 1550, Fort Collins, CO 80522
1-16	FORTRAN, Macro Assembler, COBOL, RPG	General accounting, hospital, manufacturing, inventory, education	$5,500	(617) 667-3111	300 Concord Road, Billerica, MA 08121
160	COBOL, FORTRAN, Assembler, RPG Macropreprocessor	Office automation, manufacturing	$7,275		
160	COBOL, FORTRAN, Assembler, RPG, Macropreprocessor	Office automation, manufacturing	$10,325		

TABLE C   (*Continued*)

Manufacturer	System Model	CPU		Disk		Printer	
		Word Length (bits)	Memory Capacity (bytes)	Type	Capacity (bytes)	Type	Speed
	Level 6 Model 47	16	32– 2048K	Floppy	512K–2M	Serial	Opt. 30– 160 cps
				Cartridge	10–80M	Line	Opt. 240– 900 lpm
				Pack	67–256M		
	Level 6 Model 53	16	32– 2048K	Floppy	512K–2M	Serial	Opt. 30– 160 cps
				Cartridge	10–80M	Line	Opt. 240– 900 lpm
				Pack	67–256M		
	Level 6 Model 57	16	32– 2048K	Floppy	512K–2M	Serial	Opt. 30– 160 cps
				Cartridge	10–80M	Line	Opt. 240– 900 lpm
				Pack	67–256M		
	Series 60 Level 62	8	48K– 224K	Floppy	Opt. 512K	Serial	30 cps console
				Cartridge	Opt. 46.4M	Opt. line	100– 1600 lpm
				Pack	Opt. 480M		
IBM	System/3	8	256K– 512K	Cartridge Pack	Opt. 9.9M Opt. 506M	Opt. serial Opt. line	80 cps 100– 1100 lpm
	System/32	8	16K– 32K	Floppy	303K 13.75M	Line Opt. serial	50–150 lpm 40, 80 cps
	System/34	8	32K– 128K	Floppy	1.2M	Opt. line	160, 300 lpm
				Cartridge	Std. 8.6M 128M	Opt. serial	40–120 cps
	System/38	8	512– 1536K	Floppy	Std. 240K– 24M	Serial	Opt. 40– 120 cps
				Fixed-head	Std. 129M– 387M	Line	Std. 300, 600 lpm
	Series I	16	16K– 128K	Floppy	492– 606K	Serial	120 cps
				Cartridge	9.3– 258M	Line	155– 414 lpm
	5100	8	16K– 64K	None	None	Opt. serial	80 cps
	5110	8	16K– 64K	Floppy	4.8M	Opt. serial	80, 120 cps
	5120	8	16K– 64K	Floppy	1.2M–4.8M	Serial	80, 120 cps
Infotecs, Inc.	Control Center II	12	64– 1024K	Floppy Cartridge	1.9–15.2M 34–808M	Serial Line	55–340 cps 300–600 lpm

Number of Terminals, Partitions, Lines, or I/O Ports	Software Language	Applications Software	Price Range	Telephone	Address
152	COBOL, FORTRAN, Assembler, RPG, Macropreprocessor	Office automation, manufacturing	$22,275		
152	COBOL, FORTRAN, Assembler, RPG, Macropreprocessor	Office automation, manufacturing	$22,175		
144	COBOL, FORTRAN, Assembler, RPG, Macropreprocessor	Office automation, manufacturing	$46,975		
744	COBOL, FORTRAN, BASIC, RPG	General accounting, distribution, manufacturing	$36,879		
3 (partitions)	COBOL, FORTRAN, BASIC, RPG11	General accounting, distribution, medicine, manufacturing, education	$22,430	(404) 256-7000	P.O. Box 2150, Atlanta, GA 30301
1	Macro assembler, RPG11	General accounting, distribution, medicine, manufacturing, word processing	$33,560		
8 local stations, 64 remote stations	COBOL, FORTRAN, BASIC, RPG11	General accounting, medicine, distribution, manufacturing	$34,700		
40	RPG	General accounting, industrial	$121,480		
1-12	FORTRAN, COBOL, PL/1	Process control engineering	$4,360 CPU only		
1	BASIC, APL	Finance analysis, statistics	$6,285	(404) 256-7000	P.O. Box 2150 Atlanta, GA 30301
1	BASIC, APL	Finance analysis, statistics	$8,475		
1	BASIC, APL	Finance analysis, statistics	$9,990		
16	HIBOL	General accounting, fuel oil, route distribution	$6,995	(603) 608-6750	One Perimeter Road, Manchester, NH 03103

TABLE C (*Continued*)

Manufacturer	System Model	CPU		Disk		Printer	
		Word Length (bits)	Memory Capacity (bytes)	Type	Capacity (bytes)	Type	Speed
International Computers, Ltd.	1501/40	8	16K	Fixed-head	2.5M	Opt. serial	165, 330 cps
						Opt. line	100–400 lpm
	1503/43	8	16K–32K	Cartridge	10M	Opt. serial	165/330 cps
				Fixed-head	10M	Opt. line	100–400 lpm
	2904	24	32–96K	Cartridge	9.8–270M	Line	150–1500 lpm
				Pack			
Jacquard Systems	J50 video-computer	16	32K–128K	Floppy	(2) 250K	Opt. line	To 1100 lpm
	J100 video-computer	16	32K–128K	Floppy	(2) 250K	Opt. line	To 1100 lpm
				Cartridge	(4) 80M	Opt. serial	30–160 cps
				Disk Pack	(4) 80M		
	J500 video-computer	16	32K–128K	Floppy	(2) 250K	Opt. line	To 1100 lpm
				Disk Pack	(4) 48M	Opt. serial	30–166 cps
Katcard Systems	KSL System 340	18	128K–2048K	Cartridge	10M	Line	600 lpm
				Pack	300M	Serial	165 cps
Keydata	Unity Series (DG base)	16	64K–256K	Pack	320M	Std. serial	165 cps
						Opt. line	70–1100 lpm
Litton/Sweda International	Litton 1600 Series (Nova 1220 base)	16	64K	Cartridge	40M	Serial	165 cps
Lockeed	System III	16	32K–256K	Opt. floppy	1M		
				Cartridge	40M	Serial	180 cps
				Opt. pack	600M	Opt. line	300, 600 lpm
Logical Machine Corp.	ADAM	16	32K–64K	Opt. floppy	250K		
				Cartridge	10.6M	Serial	165 cps
						Opt. line	200 lpm
	TINA	16	48K	Floppy	5M	Serial	110 cps

Number of Terminals, Partitions, Lines, or I/O Ports	Software		Price Range	Telephone	Address
	Language	Applications Software			
Daisey chain 63 (I/O ports)	COBOL, BASIC, Assembler, BTL, CDE, ADE	General accounting, government, inventory control, banking, POS	$13,600	(201) 246-3400	Turnpike Plaza, 197 Highway 18, East Brunswick, NJ 08816
Daisey chain 63 (I/O ports)	COBOL, BASIC, Assembler, BTL, CDE, ADE	General accounting, government, inventory control, banking, POS	$18,000		
	COBOL, RPG, FORTRAN, ALGOL	Multitasking, total DBMS	$35,000		
1	Assembler, BASIC	General accounting, distribution, processing, business, medicine, word processing	$11,500	(201) 575-8100	1639 11th Street Santa Monica, CA 90404
100 (partitions)	Assembler, BASIC	General accounting, distribution, processing, business, medicine, word processing	$14,900		
3 (I/O ports)	BASIC, Assembler	General accounting, distribution, processing, business, medicine, word processing	$9,200		
32 (I/O ports)	COBOL, FORTRAN, Assembler, RPG, BASIC COMFORT	General accounting, word processing, manufacturing, payroll	$38,000	(613) 731-8432	376 Churchill Avenue, Ottawa, Ontario, Canada KIZ5C3
24 (I/O ports)	Assembler, RPG	General accounting, plumbing, industrial supply, heating and air conditioning	$48,000	(617) 237-6930	20 William Street, Wellesley, MA 02181
8 (communication lines)	BASIC	General accounting, wholesale distribution, client accounting	$40,140	(201) 575-8100	34 Maple Avenue, Pine Brook, NJ 07058
8 (communication lines)	FORTRAN, RPG, Assembler	General accounting, insurance, medicine, banking	$29,950	(201) 757-1600	U.S. Highway 22, Plainfield, NJ 07061
5 (I/O ports)	NATURAL ENGLISH	General accounting, all industrial packages	$34,995	(408) 744-1290	1294 Hammerwood Avenue, Sunnyvale, CA 94086
7 (I/O ports)	NATURAL ENGLISH	General accounting, all industrial packages	$14,995		

TABLE C   (*Continued*)

Manufacturer	System Model	CPU		Disk		Printer	
		Word Length (*bits*)	Memory Capacity (*bytes*)	Type	Capacity (*bytes*)	Type	Speed
Microdata	Reality	16	16K– 128K	Cartridge Pack	40M 600M	Serial Line	165 cps 300–600 lpm
	Reality II	16	16K– 32K	Cartridge	10M	Serial Line	165 cps 300 lpm
	Royale	16	16K– 128K	Cartridge Pack	40M 600M	Serial Line	165 cps 300–600 lpm
Mini-computer Systems	MICOS	16	64K	Cartridge	9.8M	Serial Opt. line	60 cps 300 lpm
	MICOS11	16	65K– 256K	Opt. car- tridge Pack	9.8M 80M	Serial Opt. line	165 cps 300, 600 lpm
Minuteman Com- puter Corp.	1774	16	16K– 32K	Cartridge Opt. Pack	80M 1280M	Serial Opt. line	165 cps 300–900 lpm
	1775	16	16K– 192K	Cartridge Opt. Pack	80M 1280M	Serial Std. line	165 cps 300–900 lpm
	1776	16	32K– 192K	Cartridge Opt. Pack	80M 1280M	Serial Line	165 cps 300–900 lpm
Mitsubishi	8018	8	48–96K	Floppy Cartridge	243K–1M 500K–2M 10M–40M	Serial Line	120–200 cps 110 lpm
	8028	16	256– 512K	Floppy Cartridge Pack up to 8 drives	1.2–2.4M 10M–80M 50M–400M	Serial Line	200 cps 300–600 lpm

Number of Terminals, Partitions, Lines, or I/O Ports	Software		Price Range	Telephone	Address
	Language	Applications Software			
34 (I/O ports)	BASIC, ENGLISH, Assembler, RPG	General accounting, time-sharing, engineering, education	$40,300	(714) 540-6730	Red Hill Avenue, Irvine, CA 92705
34 (I/O ports)	BASIC, ENGLISH, Assembler, RPG	General accounting, time-sharing, engineering, education	$31,500	(714) 540-6730	Red Hill Avenue, Irvine, CA 92705
34 (I/O ports)	BASIC, ENGLISH, Assembler, RPG	General accounting, time-sharing, engineering, education	$35,995		
2 (partitions)	EXTENDED BASIC	General accounting, government, education, fuel, apparel, etc.	$28,750	(914) 592-8812	525 Executive Boulevard, Elmsford, NY 10523
16 (partitions)	EXTENDED BASIC	General accounting, government, education, fuel, apparel, etc.	$49,900		
2 (I/O ports)	COBOL, FORTRAN, Assembler, BASIC	General accounting, distribution, manufacturing, liquor wholesales	$24,340	(617) 890-4070	230 Second Avenue, Waltham, MA 02154
14 (I/O ports)	COBOL, FORTRAN, Assembler, BASIC	General accounting, distribution, manufacturing, liquor wholesales	$25,340		
14 (I/O ports)	COBOL, FORTRAN, Assembler, BASIC	General accounting, distribution, manufacturing, liquor wholesales	$26,840		
5	BASIC	Small business applications, general accounting packages, job costing, property management, sales accounting, word processing	$14,950– $17,550	(213) 979-6055	2200 W. Artesia Blvd., Compton, CA 90220
32	BASIC, COBOL, FORTRAN, RPG, DBMS	Small business applications, general accounting packages, job costing, property management, sales accounting, word processing	$19,900– $49,500		

445

TABLE C   (*Continued*)

Manufacturer	System Model	CPU		Disk		Printer	
		Word Length (bits)	Memory Capacity (bytes)	Type	Capacity (bytes)	Type	Speed
Mylee Digital Sciences	System 3000	16	88K– 152K	Floppy Cartridge Pack	Optional 12.5M Optional	Serial Opt. line	165 cps 300 lpm
NCR	Century 75	8	16K– 64K	Pack	9.98M	Line	200–450 lpm
	Century 101	8	16K– 128K	Cartridge Opt. Pack	19.6M 380M	Line	300–3500 lpm
	Century 151	8	32K– 131K	Cartridge Opt. Pack	19.6M 380M	Serial Opt. line	60 cps 300–3500 lpm
	499	16	12K– 32K	Opt. car- tridge	9.8M	Serial	75–130 cps
	8130	16	48K– 64K	Floppy	500K–4M	Serial Line	130 cps Opt. 200 lpm
	8150	16	48K– 64K	Floppy Opt. Pack	500K 40M	Serial Opt. line	130 cps 200 lpm
	8230	16	64K– 96K	Pack Opt. floppy	40M 250K	Opt. serial Opt. line	50 lpm 126– 600 lpm
	8250	16	48K– 128K	Pack Opt. floppy	80M 250K	Opt. serial Opt. line	50 lpm 125–600 lpm
NEC Information System, Inc.	Astra 205	16	128– 256K	Floppy	1.2–4.8M	Serial	55–120 cps
	210	16	128– 256K	Floppy	1.2–4.8M	Serial	55–120 cps

Number of Terminals, Partitions, Lines, or I/O Ports	Software		Price Range	Telephone	Address
	Language	Applications Software			
12 (partitions)	ACE	General accounting, distribution	$42,850	(314) 567-3420	155 Weldon Parkway, Maryland Heights, MD 63043
1-2 (I/O ports)	COBOL, FORTRAN, Assembler, BASIC, NEAT/3, RPG11	General accounting, all business applications	$56,850	(513) 449-2000	Main and K Streets, Dayton, OH 45409
9 (partitions)	COBOL, NEAT/3, FORTRAN IV, Assembler, BASIC, RPG11	General accounting, all business applications	$69,520		
9 (partitions)	COBOL, NEAT/3, FORTRAN IV, Assembler, BASIC, RPG LL	General accounting, all business applications	$120,325		
2	NEAT/AM	General accounting, all business accounting	$17,900		
1	COBOL, BASIC	General accounting, wholesale distribution, medicine, education, manufacturing	$14,065		
4	COBOL, BASIC	General accounting, wholesale distribution, medicine, education	$22,960		
5 (communication lines)	COBOL, Assembler	General accounting, wholesale distribution, medicine, education	$34,250		
24 (communication lines)	COBOL, Assembler	General accounting, wholesale distribution, medicine, education	$36,250		
1	BASIC, COBOL, Macro-Assembler, Interactive data, Management, Utility	General accounting, packages, order entry processing, inventory control, text processing	$11,000–$14,000 for basic system	(213) 515-0106	19401 South Vermont Ave., Suite D100, Torrence, CA 90502
1-4	BASIC, COBOL, Macro-Assembler, Interactive data management, Utility	General accounting, packages, order entry processing, inventory control, text processing	$13,000–$16,000		

TABLE C *(Continued)*

Manufacturer	System Model	CPU		Disk		Printer	
		Word Length (bits)	Memory Capacity (bytes)	Type	Capacity (bytes)	Type	Speed
	230	16	128–256K	Pack	20–80M	Line	300, 600 lpm
	250	16	512K	Pack	20–160M	Line	300, 600 lpm
	270	16	512K	Pack	20–320M	Line	300, 600 lpm
Nixdorf	8870	16	64K–128K	Cartridge	40M	Serial Opt. line	165 cps 300 lpm
Northrop Data Systems	BDS Series 500	Variable 8-32	16K–64K	Cartridge	10M	Line Opt. serial	150 lpm 30–120 cps
	BDS Series 1000	Variable 8-32	24K–64K	Cartridge	10M	Line Opt. serial	300 lpm 30–120 cps
	BDS Series 2000	Variable 8-32	32K–64K	Cartridge Opt. Pack	20M 80M	Line Opt. serial	300 lpm 30–120 cps
Ohio Scientific	C2-8p challenger II	8	48K	Floppy	Optional	Serial	Optional
Olivetti	A5 Model 10	64	0.5K–4K (user)	None	—	Serial	16 cps
	BCS 2025	8	64K	Floppy	2M–4M	Serial	60–200 cps
	BCS 2030	8	64K	Floppy Cartridge	Std. 2M–4M Opt. 20M	Serial	60–200 cps

Number of Terminals, Partitions, Lines, or I/O Ports	Software		Price Range	Telephone	Address
	Language	Applications Software			
1–4	BASIC, COBOL, Macro-Assembler, Interactive data management, Utility	General accounting, packages, order entry processing, inventory control, text processing	$23,000–$27,000		
16	BASIC, COBOL, Macro-Assembler, Interactive data management, Utility	General accounting, packages, order entry processing, inventory control, text processing	$27,000-up		
32	BASIC, COBOL, Macro-Assembler, Interactive data management, Utility	General accounting, packages, order entry processing, inventory control, text processing	$30,000-up		
32	BASIC	General accounting, distribution, medicine, garment, mortg. closing	$33,500	(617) 273-0480	168 Middlesex Turnpike Burlington, MA 01803
2	BASIC, Assembler	General accounting, medicine, furniture manufacturing	$29,500	(213) 637-1533	19000 South Vermont Avenue, Torrance, CA 90502
4 (communication lines)	BASIC, Assembler	General accounting, medicine, furniture manufacturing	$45,526		
8 (communication lines)	BASIC, Assembler	General accounting, medicine, furniture manufacturing	$63,089		
1	BASIC	Home computing, games, education	$825.00 up	(216) 562-3101	1333 S. Chillicothe Road, Aurora, Ohio 44202
1	Assembler, APLO	General accounting, credit union, education, distribution	$4,900	(212) 371-5500	500 Park Avenue, New York, NY 10022
1	BASIC	General accounting, credit union, education, distribution	$12,950		
1	BASIC	General accounting, credit union, education, distribution	$14,950		

TABLE C *(Continued)*

| Manufacturer | System Model | CPU | | Disk | | Printer | |
		Word Length (bits)	Memory Capacity (bytes)	Type	Capacity (bytes)	Type	Speed
	A7 (7074 CPU)	8	16K–48K (user)	Floppy Opt. cartridge Opt. hard disk	512K 20M 160M	Serial Opt. line	40 cps 300–600 lpm
	BCS 3030	8	40K–56K (user)	Floppy Opt. cartridge	1024K 20M	Opt. serial Opt. line	90–175 cps 300–600 lpm
	P 6060	—	16K–48K (user)	Floppy Opt. cartridge	1024K 20M	Opt. serial Line	80–175 cps Optional
Pertec Computer	MITS/ Altair 8800B	8	64K	Floppy	1.2M	Serial	Optional
	PCC 2000	8	64K	Floppy	1.2M	Serial	Optional
Phillips	P310	8	16K	Opt. floppy	1.024M	Serial Opt. line	50 cps 70 lpm
	P320	8	16K	Opt. floppy	1.024M	Serial Opt. line	50 cps 70 lpm
	P330	8	24K–32K	Opt. cartridge	9.2M	Serial Opt. line	40 cps 400 lpm
	P430	Variable	32K–128K	Cartridge	40M	Opt. serial Opt. line	100 cps 400 lpm
Prime	300	16	64K–512K	Opt. floppy Opt. cartridge Opt. Pack	2.4M 96M 2400M	Opt. serial Opt. line	140 cps 1220 lpm
	350	16	64K–512K	Opt. floppy Opt. cartridge Opt. Pack	1.2M 96M 2400M	Opt. serial Opt. line	140 cps 1220 lpm

Number of Terminals, Partitions, Lines, or I/O Ports	Software		Price Range	Telephone	Address
	Language	Applications Software			
2 (partitions)	RPG, PL/1, Assembler	General accounting, wholesale distribution, contractors	$13,125		
2 (partitions)	Assembler, RPG	General accounting, wholesale distribution, Utilities	$9,950		
N.A.	BASIC	General accounting, printers, job cost, financial	$6,600		
256 (I/O channels)	BASIC, COBOL-80, FORTRAN-80, CP/M, Multi-terminal executive	process control	$1,395 up	(213) 822-9222	12910 Culver Blvd., P.O. Box 92300, Los Angeles, CA 90066
256 (I/O channels	BASIC, COBOL-80, FORTRAN-80, CP/M, Multi-terminal executive	Business applications			
1	Assembler	General accounting, medicine, utilities, insurance, banking	$10,915	(516) 921-9310	175 Froelich Farm Boulevard, Woodbury, NY 11797
1	Assembler	General accounting, medicine, utilities, insurance, banking	$15,665		
1	Assembler	General accounting, insurance, banking, utilities	$21,000		
9 (partitions)	COBOL, BASIC, Assembler, RPG	General accounting, various industrial applications	$27,500		
31	COBOL, FORTRAN, Assembler, RPG, BASIC, FORMS	Graphics, statistics, general accounting for local government	$75,000	(617) 237-6990	40 Walnut Street, Wellesley, MA 02181
31	COBOL, FORTRAN, Assembler, RPG, BASIC, FORMS	Graphics, statistics, general accounting for local government	$100,000		

TABLE C (*Continued*)

Manufacturer	System Model	CPU Word Length (bits)	CPU Memory Capacity (bytes)	Disk Type	Disk Capacity (bytes)	Printer Type	Printer Speed
	400	16	128K–8M	Opt. floppy Opt. cartridge Opt. Pack	2.4M 96M 2400M	Opt. serial Opt. line	140 cps 1220 lpm
	500	16	256K–8M	Opt. floppy Opt. cartridge Opt. Pack	2.4M 96M 2400M	Opt. serial Opt. line	140 cps 1220 lpm
Programmed Control Corp.	Prophet 21 Model 1 (TI 960B)	16	32K–126K	Cartridge	5M	Serial Opt. line	30 cps 250 lpm
	Prophet 21 Model 2 (TI 990/10)	16	32K–2048K	Cartridge	100M	Opt. serial Opt. line	165 cps 250 lpm
Q1 Corporation	Q1/LMC	8	8K–64K	Floppy Opt. cartridge	250K 24M	Serial Opt. line	42–200 cps 300 lpm
	Q1/LITE	8	16K–64K (6K is ROM)	Floppy Opt. Pack Opt. bubble memory	500K 54M	Serial Opt. line	45–200 cps 300 lpm
	Mark 11	8	16K–64K (6K is ROM)	Floppy Opt. Pack Opt. bubble memory	300K 54M	Serial Opt. line	45–200 cps 300 lpm
Qantel	210	8	48K–64K	Floppy	to 5.2M	Opt. serial Opt. line	45–120 cps 300 lpm
	900, 950	8	32K–64K	Opt. floppy Cartridge	2.6M 6–36M	Serial Opt. line	120 cps 300–600 lpm
	1400	8	40K–128K	Cartridge Pack	12–48M 25–600M	Line Serial	300–600 lpm 120 cps
	1400-2	8	48K–128K	Pack Opt. floppy Opt. cartridge	25–600M 2.6M 12–48M	Line Opt. serial	300–600 lpm 120 cps

Number of Terminals, Partitions, Lines, or I/O Ports	Software Language	Software Applications Software	Price Range	Telephone	Address
63	COBOL, FORTRAN, Assembler, RPG, BASIC, FORMS	Graphics, statistics, general accounting for local government	$125,000		
63	COBOL, FORTRAN, Assembler, RPG, BASIC, FORMS	Graphics, statistics, general accounting for local government	$175,000		
22 (partitions)	PROPHET 21	General accounting, industrial distribution, wholesalers	$42,500	(609) 466-2900	2 East Broad Street, Hopewell, NJ 02525
128 (partitions)	PROPHET 21	General accounting, industrial distribution, wholesalers	$59,000		
1–64	Assembler, PL/1	General accounting, credit union, word processing	$17,950	(516) 543-7800	6 Dubon Court, Farmingdale, NY 11735
1–64	Assembler, PL/1	General accounting, general business, banks, credit unions, word processing	$21,000		
1–64	Assembler, PL/1	General accounting, general business, banks, credit unions, word processing	$7,625		
6	QICBASIC, Assembler	General accounting, medical clinics, CPA, wholesale distribution	$11,950	(415) 783-3410	3525 Breakwater Avenue, Hayward, CA 94545
1–16	QICBASIC, Assembler	General accounting, medical clinics, CPA, wholesale distribution	$27,900		
1–64	QICBASIC, Assembler	General accounting, medical clinics, CPA, wholesale distribution	$43,900		
1–64	QICBASIC, Assembler	General accounting, medical clinics, CPA, wholesale distribution	$64,900		

TABLE C (*Continued*)

| Manufacturer | System Model | CPU | | Disk | | Printer | |
		Word Length (*bits*)	Memory Capacity (*bytes*)	Type	Capacity (*bytes*)	Type	Speed
Quodata	E-500 (PDP-8/A base)	12	64K– 256K	Cartridge Floppy	64M Optional	Opt. serial Opt. line	180 cps 300–900 lpm
	E-600 (PDP-11/74 base)	16	32K– 256K	Cartridge Floppy Pack	— 500K 20–88M	Opt. serial Opt. line	180 cps 300–900 lpm
	E-700 (PDP-11/34 base)	16	128K– 248K	Pack Opt. floppy	20M 500K	Opt. serial Opt. line	180 cps 300–900 lpm
	E-940 (PDP-11/ 70 base)	16 or 32	256K– 2 mil- lion	Pack Opt. floppy	88M 500K	Opt. serial Opt. line	180 cps 300–900 lpm
	QDP/78 (PDP-8/A base)	12	32K (6 bit)	Floppy Cartridge	500K Optional	Serial Opt. line	180 cps 300–900 lpm
Randal Data Systems	Link-100	16	32K– 64K	Floppy	2.5M	Opt. serial Opt. line	30, 55, or 180 cps 300 lpm
	Link-200	16	32K– 64K	Cartridge	10M	Opt. serial Opt. line	30, 55, or 180 cps 300 lpm
	Link-500	16	64K– 128K	Floppy Pack	1.2M 200M	Serial Opt. line	180 cps 300 lpm
Radio Shack, A Division of Tandy Corp.	TRS 80	8	4–48K	Floppy	98–392K	Serial	60 cps
	TRS 80 II	8	32–64K	Floppy	416K–2M	Serial	120 cps
	TRS 80 III	8	16–32K	Floppy	178–670K	Serial	60 cps
Raytheon	PTS/1200 Mark 1	16	48K– 128K	Cartridge	300M	Opt. serial Opt. line	15–165 cps 600 lpm
	PTS/1200 Mark 11	16	48K– 128K	Cartridge	300M	Opt. serial Opt. line	15–165 cps 600 lpm

Number of Terminals, Partitions, Lines, or I/O Ports	Software Language	Applications Software	Price Range	Telephone	Address
32 (partitions)	COBOL (subset), FORTRAN, BASIC, Assembler, DIBOL	General industry	$33,000	(203) 728-6777	196 Trumbull Street, Hartford, CN 06103
32 (partitions)	COBOL, FORTRAN, Assembler, RPG, BASIC, FOCAL	General accounting, municipal government, education	$45,000		
63 (partitions)	COBOL, FORTRAN, Assembler, RPG, BASIC, PASCAL, APL, DIBOL	General accounting, government, education	$65,000		
63 (partitions)	COBOL, FORTRAN, Assembler, RPG, BASIC, PASCAL, APL, DIBOL	General accounting, government, education	$142,000		
4 (partitions)	COBOL, FORTRAN, Assembler, BASIC, QBDL	General accounting, general industry	$9,990		
1-2	BASIC, Assembler	General accounting, lumber industry, dental management	$12,750	(213) 320-8550	365 Maple Avenue, Torrance, CA 90503
16 (partitions)	BASIC	General accounting, lumber industry, dental management	$24,506		
16 (partitions)	BASIC, Assembler	General accounting, medicine, distribution	$45,900		
1	BASIC, SCRIPSIT	Personal computer and games	$500–$3000	(817) 390-3592	One Tandy Center, Fort Worth, TX 76102
1	BASIC, COBOL, FORTRAN	Small business applications, general accounting	$3,900 with floppy and without printer		
1	BASIC, COBOL, FORTRAN	Personal and professional applications	$3,625 with 2 floppys and a printer		
20 (partitions)	MACROL	Transport, insurance, finance	$23,120	(617) 762-6700	1415 Boston-Providence Turnpike, Norwood, MA 02062
20 (partitions)	MACROL	Transport, insurance, finance	$37,055		

TABLE C (*Continued*)

| Manufacturer | System Model | CPU | | Disk | | Printer | |
		Word Length (bits)	Memory Capacity (bytes)	Type	Capacity (bytes)	Type	Speed
Span Management Systems	(IBM Series 1 base)	16	16K–256K	Opt. floppy Opt. pack	606K 13.9M	Opt. serial Opt. line	120 cps 414 lpm
Sperry Univac	BC/7-600	8	48K–64K	Floppy	6M	Serial Opt. line	200 cps 125 lpm
	BC/7-700	8	48K–64K	Opt. floppy Opt. cartridge	4M 40M	Serial Opt. line	200 cps 125–600 lpm
	BC/7-800	8	128K	Opt. floppy Opt. cartridge	4M 40M	Serial Opt. line	200 cps 125–600 lpm
STC Systems	Ultimacc 2010	16	32K–64K	Cartridge Floppy	10–40M Optional	Serial Opt. line	165 cps 300–600 lpm
	Ultimacc 3010	16	32K–256K	Cartridge Floppy	10M–40M Optional	Opt. line	300–900 lpm
	Ultimacc 3080	16	32K–256K	Pack Floppy	80M–320M Optional	Opt. line	300–900 lpm
	Ultimacc 3300	16	32K–256K	Pack Floppy	300M–1200M Optional	Opt. line	300–900 lpm
Sycor	404	8	48K	Floppy	512K	Opt. serial	To 180 cps
	405	8	48K–64K	Floppy	2M	Opt. serial Opt. line	To 180 cps 300, 600 lpm
	410	8	40K–64K	Cartridge Opt. floppy	To 5M 256K	Serial Opt. line	To 180 cps 300 lpm
	440	8	24K–64K	Cartridge Opt. floppy	To 5M 256K	Opt. serial Opt. line	To 180 cps 300 lpm
	445	8	64K–256K	Opt. floppy Opt. Pack	256K 4–70M	Opt. serial	To 180 cps

Number of Terminals, Partitions, Lines, or I/O Ports	Software		Price Range	Telephone	Address
	Language	Applications Software			
8–256 (I/O ports)	Assembler, PASCAL	General accounting, many industrial packages	$35,000	(401) 438-2200	1 Catamore Boulevard, East Providence, RI 02914
1–2	RPG, ESCORT	General accounting, distribution, manufacturing	$21,795	(215) 542-4011	P.O. Box 500 Bluebell, PA 19424
1–4	RPG, ESCORT	General accounting, distribution, manufacturing	$31,200		
1–6	RPG, ESCORT	General accounting, distribution, manufacturing	$35,475		
8 (partitions)	COBOL, BASIC, Assembler, ENGLISH 210	General accounting, banking, manufacturing, distribution, government	$51,000	(201) 843-0560	B-210 Route 4, Paramus, NJ 07652
50 (partitions)	COBOL, BASIC, Assembler, ENGLISH 210	General accounting, banking, distribution, government, manufacturing	$62,000		
50 (partitions)	COBOL, BASIC, Assembler, ENGLISH 210	General accounting, banking, distribution, government, manufacturing	$75,000		
50 (partitions)	COBOL, BASIC, Assembler, ENGLISH 210	General accounting, banking, distribution, government, manufacturing	$87,000		
2 (partitions)	COBOL, BASIC, TAL 2000	General accounting, distribution, manufacturing, medicine	$6,250	(313) 995-8527	100 Phoenix Drive, Ann Arbor, MI 48104
3 (partitions)	COBOL, BASIC, TAL 2000	General accounting, distribution, manufacturing, medicine	$13,750		
6 (I/O ports)	COBOL, BASIC, TAL-2	General accounting, used in many industries	$25,230		
24 (I/O ports)	COBOL, BASIC, TAL-2	General accounting, used in many industries	$25,670		
16 (partitions)	COBOL, BASIC, TAL 11, TAL 2000	General accounting, distribution, manufacturing, medicine	—		

TABLE C (*Continued*)

Manufacturer	System Model	CPU		Disk		Printer	
		Word Length (bits)	Memory Capacity (bytes)	Type	Capacity (bytes)	Type	Speed
Systems Approach Ltd.	CS 20	16	64K	Floppy	(4) 1200K	Serial Opt. line	240 cps 300 lpm
	CS 40	16	64K– 192K	Floppy Opt. cartridge Opt. Pack	(2) 600K (4) 40M (4) 760M	Serial Opt. line	240 cps 300 lpm
	CS 60	16	64K– 256K	Floppy Opt. cartridge Opt. Pack	(2) 600K (4) 80M (4) 850M	Serial Opt. line	240 cps 300 lpm
Tal-Star	TDMS systems	16	128K– 256K	Pack Opt. floppy	300M 10M	Serial Line	10 cps 240 lpm
Tandem	T16/240-1	16	96K– 480K	Opt. Cartridge Opt. Pack	10M 160M	Opt. serial Opt. line	30 cps 120–1500 lpm
	T16/212-1	16	192K– 448K	Opt. cartridge Opt. pack	10M 160M	Opt. serial Opt. line	30 cps 120– 1500 lpm
	T16/244-1	16	192K– 512K	Opt. cartridge Opt. Pack	10M 160M	Opt. serial Opt. line	30 cps 120– 1500 lpm
Terak	8510	16	56K	Floppy	To 1024K	Opt. serial Opt. line	100 cps 300 lpm
	8510A	16	56K	Floppy	To 1024K	Opt. serial Opt. line	100 cps 300 lpm
Texas Instruments	TM 990/4	16	1–32K	Floppy	242–968K	Serial Line	30–150 cps 300–600 lpm
	TM 990/10	16	8–1024K	Floppy Cartridge	242–968K 3–200M	Serial Line	30–150 cps 300–600 lpm
	DS990 Model 1	16	64K	Floppy	Std. 1.15M 4.6M	N.A.	

Number of Terminals, Partitions, Lines, or I/O Ports	Software		Price Range	Telephone	Address
	Language	Applications Software			
1	COBOL	General accounting, medicine, distribution, service organization, manufacturing	$16,000	(613) 741-9500	1257 Alzoma Road Ottawa, Canada
4 (communication lines)	COBOL	General accounting, medicine, distribution, service organization, manufacturing	$41,000		
4 (communication lines)	COBOL	General accounting, medicine, distribution, service organization, manufacturing	$53,000		
15 (communication lines)	COBOL, FORTRAN, Assembler, RPG	General accounting, graphic arts, newspapers	$73,600	(609) 799-1111	P.O. Box T-100, Princeton Junction, NJ 08550
256 (partitions)	COBOL, FORTRAN, TAL	Transaction processing, banking, distribution	$59,750	(408) 996-6000	19333 Vallco Parkway, Cupertino, CA 95014
256 (partitions)	COBOL, FORTRAN, TAL	Transaction processing, banking, distribution	$92,800		
256 (partitions)	COBOL, FORTRAN, TAL	Transaction processing, banking, distribution	$87,100		
4 (communication lines)	FORTRAN, BASIC, Assembler, APL	General accounting, small business, education	$6,615	(602) 991-1580	14405 North Scottsdale Road, Suite 100, Scottsdale, AZ 85260
4 (communication lines)	FORTRAN, BASIC, Assembler, APL, PASCAL	Education, graphics	$7,850		
1	BASIC, FORTRAN, PASCAL	Personal computer, professional	$1,525 without disk and printer	(512) 258-7111	P.O. Box 2909, Austin, TX 78769
1	BASIC, FORTRAN, COBOL, PASCAL, RPG Multi-tasking	Small business applications	$3,450 without disk and printer		
1	BASIC, FORTRAN, COBOL, PASCAL	Personal computer, professional	$9,450		

TABLE C (*Continued*)

Manufacturer	System Model	CPU		Disk		Printer	
		Word Length (*bits*)	Memory Capacity (*bytes*)	Type	Capacity (*bytes*)	Type	Speed
	DS990 Model 2	16	64K	Floppy	Std. 2.3M 4.6M	Serial	150 cps
				Cartridge	Opt. 2–20M	Line	300, 600 lpm
				Pack	Opt. 2–400M		
	DS990 Model 4	16	128– 2048K	Floppy Cartridge	Opt. 1–4M Std. 10M	Serial Line	150 cps 300, 600 lpm
				Pack	Opt. 50M– 200M		
	DS990 Model 20	16	256– 2048K	Floppy Cartridge	Opt. 1–4M Opt. 50M	Serial Line	150 cps 300, 600 lpm
Wang	PCS-11	8	8K–32K	Opt. floppy	89K–176K	Opt. serial Opt. line	200 cps 600 lpm
	2200 LVP	8	32– 128K	Std. floppy Cartridge	1M–2M 8M–160M	Line	Opt. 200– 600 lpm
	2200T	8	16K– 32K	Opt. floppy Opt. cartridge	786K 20M	Opt. serial Opt. line	200 cps 600 lpm
	2200VP	8	16K– 64K	Opt. floppy Opt. cartridge	786K 20M	Opt. serial Opt. line	200 cps 600 lpm
	2200MVP	8	16K– 64K	Floppy Opt. cartridge	786K 20M	Opt. serial Opt. line	200 cps 600 lpm
	VS system	32	128– 512K	Floppy Cartridge Pack	318K 45M 72M	Serial Opt. line	120 cps 600 lpm
	VS 100	32	256– 512K	Floppy Cartridge Pack	318K 45M 72M	Line Opt. serial	To 600 lpm 120 cps

Number of Terminals, Partitions, Lines, or I/O Ports	Software		Price Range	Telephone	Address
	Language	Applications Software			
2	BASIC, FORTRAN, COBOL, PASCAL	Personal computer, professional	$12,995		
1–39	BASIC, FORTRAN, COBOL, PASCAL, RPG, TIFORM, DBMS 990	Business applications, industrial applications	$26,500		
1–39	BASIC, FORTRAN, COBOL, PASCAL, RPG, TIFORM, DBMS 990	Business applications, industrial applications	$75,750		
1	BASIC	General accounting, banking, insurance, distribution, manufacturing	$6,200 up	(617) 851-4111	836 North Street, Tewksbury, MA 08176
4	BASIC	General accounting, banking, insurance, distribution, manufacturing	$8,000		
1	BASIC	General accounting, banking, insurance, distribution, manufacturing	$5,000		
4	BASIC	General accounting, banking, insurance, distribution, manufacturing, medicine	$8,000		
8	BASIC	General accounting, banking, insurance, distribution, manufacturing	$9,000		
32	COBOL, BASIC, Assembler, RPG, PROCEDURE	General accounting	$22,000 up		
32	COBOL, BASIC, Assembler, RPG, PROCEDURE	General accounting	$22,000 up		

461

TABLE C *(Continued)*

| Manufacturer | System Model | CPU | | Disk | | Printer | |
		Word Length (bits)	Memory Capacity (bytes)	Type	Capacity (bytes)	Type	Speed
Warrex Computer Corporation	Centurion I	8	32K–64K	Floppy	616K	Serial	300 cps
	Centurion I-A	8	32K–60K	Floppy	616K	Opt. line	125–600 lpm
	Centurion IIA	8	32K–60K	Floppy	616K	Opt. line	125–600 lpm
				Opt. cartridge	10.4M–41.6M	Serial	Opt. 175 cps
	Centurion IIB	8	32K–60K	Cartridge	10.4M–41.6M	Serial	175 cps
	Centurion III	8	32K–60K	Cartridge	10.4M–41.6M	Line	125–600 lpm
	Centurion VI	8	32K–252K	Cartridge	10.4M–77.6M	Line	125–600 lpm
Xerox	Diablo 3000	8	32–64K	Floppy	Std. 2.5M–5M	Serial	Std. 40–200 cps
	Diablo 3200	8	32–64K	Floppy	Std. 5M–20M	Serial	Std. 40–200 cps
				Cartridge	Opt. 20M		
	Xerox 510	8	32–64K	Floppy	Std. 1.25M–2.5M	Serial	Std. 35–200 cps

Number of Terminals, Partitions, Lines, or I/O Ports	Software Language	Applications Software	Price Range	Telephone	Address
4–12 (I/O ports)	Assembler, CPL 1	General accounting, route accounting, inventory control	$14,900	(214) 233-8400	12505 North Central Expressway, Dallas, TX 75243
4–12 (I/O ports)	Assembler, CPL 1	General accounting, route accounting, inventory control	$20,000		
4–12 (I/O ports)	Assembler, CPL 1	General accounting, route accounting, inventory control	$30,000		
4–12 (I/O ports)	Assembler, CPL 1	General accounting, oil and gas accounting, medicine, banking, distribution	$36,000		
4–12 (I/O ports)	Assembler, CPL 1	General accounting, oil and gas accounting, medicine, banking, distribution	$40,000		
4–64 (I/O ports)	Assembler, CPL 1, CPL 11	General accounting, oil and gas accounting, medicine, banking, distribution	—		
1	DACL, Assembler	General accounting, word processing, office information system	$15,950 (Shasta General Systems price)	(408) 733-2300	4400 Oakmead Parkway, Sunnyvale, CA 94086
1–9	DACL, Assembler	General accounting, word processing, office information system	$27,750 (Shasta General Systems price)		
1–4	DACL, Assembler	General accounting, word processing, office information system	$11,995– $13,800		

INDEX